Environmental Histories o

This anthology surveys the ecological impacts of the First World War. Editors Richard P. Tucker, Tait Keller, J. R. McNeill, and Martin Schmid bring together a list of experienced authors who explore the global interactions of states, armies, civilians, and the environment during the war. They show how the First World War ushered in enormous environmental changes, including the devastation of rural and urban environments, the consumption of strategic natural resources such as metals and petroleum, the impact of war on urban industry, and the disruption of agricultural landscapes leading to widespread famine. Taking a global perspective, *Environmental Histories of the First World War* presents the ecological consequences of the vast destructive power of the new weaponry and the close collaboration between militaries and civilian governments taking place during this time, showing how this war set trends for the rest of the century.

Richard P. Tucker is Adjunct Professor in the School of Environment and Sustainability at the University of Michigan. He is the author of *Insatiable Appetite: The United States and the Environmental Degradation of the Tropical World* (2000) and of numerous publications on the environmental history of warfare.

Tait Keller is Associate Professor of History and former Director of the Environmental Studies and Sciences Program at Rhodes College. His publications include *Apostles of the Alps* and articles in journals such as *Annales* and *Environmental History*. He is a fellow with the American Council of Learned Societies and the Woodrow Wilson International Center for Scholars.

J. R. McNeill is Professor of History and University Professor at Georgetown University and the author of prize-winning books such as *Mosquito Empires* and *Something New under the Sun*. He is a member of the American Academy of Arts and Sciences, and served as President of the American Society for Environmental History (2011–2013) and of the American Historical Association (2019).

Martin Schmid is Associate Professor of Environmental History and Deputy Director (2016–2017) at the Institute of Social Ecology of University of Natural Resources and Life Sciences, Vienna. He is a founding member of the Center for Environmental History (ZUG) and served as its director in 2010–2011. He was a 2011 Fellow of the Rachel Carson Center for Environment and Society in Munich.

Environmental Histories of the First World War

Edited by

RICHARD P. TUCKER

University of Michigan, Ann Arbor

TAIT KELLER

Rhodes College, Memphis

J. R. MCNEILL

Georgetown University, Washington, DC

MARTIN SCHMID

University of Natural Resources and Life Sciences, Vienna

CAMBRIDGE
UNIVERSITY PRESS

CAMBRIDGE
UNIVERSITY PRESS

University Printing House, Cambridge CB2 8BS, United Kingdom

One Liberty Plaza, 20th Floor, New York, NY 10006, USA

477 Williamstown Road, Port Melbourne, VIC 3207, Australia

314–321, 3rd Floor, Plot 3, Splendor Forum, Jasola District Centre, New Delhi – 110025, India

79 Anson Road, #06–04/06, Singapore 079906

Cambridge University Press is part of the University of Cambridge.

It furthers the University's mission by disseminating knowledge in the pursuit of education, learning, and research at the highest international levels of excellence.

www.cambridge.org
Information on this title: www.cambridge.org/9781108429160
DOI: 10.1017/9781108554237

© Cambridge University Press 2018

First published 2018

Printed in the United States of America by Sheridan Books, Inc.

A catalogue record for this publication is available from the British Library.

Library of Congress Cataloging-in-Publication Data
NAMES: Tucker, Richard P., editor of compilation. | Keller, Tait, editor of compilation. | McNeill, John Robert, editor of compilation. | Schmid, Martin, 1974– editor of compilation.
TITLE: Environmental histories of the First World War / edited by Richard P. Tucker, University of Michigan, Ann Arbor, Tait Keller, Rhodes College, Memphis, J. R. McNeill, Georgetown University, Washington DC, Martin Schmid, Alpen-Adria University, Vienna.
DESCRIPTION: Cambridge ; New York, NY : Cambridge University Press, [2018] | Includes index.
IDENTIFIERS: LCCN 2018007006 | ISBN 9781108429160
SUBJECTS: LCSH: World War, 1914–1918 – Environmental aspects. | World War, 1914–1918 – Influence. | World War, 1914–1918 – Food supply. | Famine – History – 20th century. | Nature – Effect of human beings on.
CLASSIFICATION: LCC D523 .E68 2018 | DDC 940.3/1–dc23
LC record available at https://lccn.loc.gov/2018007006

ISBN 978-1-108-42916-0 Hardback
ISBN 978-1-108-45319-6 Paperback

Contents

Figures

Tables

Contributors

Raf De Bont is Assistant Professor in the Department of History at Maastricht University. He is the author of *Stations in the Field: A History of Place-Based Animal Research*.

Gerard J. Fitzgerald is a visiting scholar in the Department of History and Art History at George Mason University.

Zachary J. Foster received his PhD from the Department of Near Eastern Studies at Princeton University. He is a product manager at Academia.edu.

Jack Patrick Hayes is Associate Professor of History and Asian Studies at Kwantlen Polytechnic University and a research associate of the Center for Chinese Research at the University of British Columbia. He is the author of *A Change in Worlds on the Sino-Tibetan Borderlands*.

Ingo Heidbrink is Professor of History at Old Dominion University. His books include the two-volume *A History of the North Atlantic Fisheries*.

Tait Keller is Associate Professor of History at Rhodes College. He is the author of *Apostles of the Alps: Mountaineering, Nature, and Nationhood in Germany and Austria*.

Ernst Langthaler is Professor of Social and Economic History at Johannes Kepler University Linz. His books include *Schlachtfelder: Ländliches Wirtschaften in der nationalsozialistischen Agrargesellschaft 1938–1945* and *Agro-Food Studies*.

Roy MacLeod is Emeritus Professor of History at the University of Sydney. His books include *Archibald Liversidge, FRS: Imperial Science under the Southern Cross*.

J. R. McNeill is Professor of History at Georgetown University. His books include *Mosquito Empires* and *The Great Acceleration*, cowritten with Peter Engelke.

Graham Auman Pitts is Postdoctoral Fellow in International Studies at North Carolina State University.

Martin Schmid is Associate Professor of Environmental History at University of Natural Resources and Life Sciences, Vienna. His books include *Long-Term Socio-Ecological Research: Studies in Society: Nature Interactions across Spatial and Temporal Scales*.

Steven Serels is an associate research fellow at the Zentrum Moderner Orient in Berlin. He is the author of *Starvation and the State: Famine, Slavery and Power in Sudan 1883–1956*.

Thaddeus Sunseri is Professor of History at Colorado State University. He is the author of *Vilimani: Labor Migration and Rural Change in Early Colonial Tanzania, 1884–1915* and *Wielding the Ax: Scientific Forestry and Social Conflict in Tanzania, c. 1820–2000*.

Dan Tamïr is Adjunct Lecturer in the Department of Politics and Government at the Ben Gurion University of the Negev and a Researcher in the Department of Evolutionary Biology and Environmental Studies at the University of Zurich.

Richard P. Tucker is Adjunct Professor of History at the University of Michigan. His books include *Insatiable Appetite: The United States and the Environmental Degradation of the Tropical World* and *The Long Shadows: A Global Environmental History of the Second World War*, coedited with Simo Laakkonen and Timo Vuorisalo.

Frank Uekötter is Reader in Environmental Humanities at the University of Birmingham. His books include *The Green and the Brown: A History of Conservation in Nazi Germany* and *The Greenest Nation? A New History of German Environmentalism*.

Alice Weinreb is Associate Professor of History at Loyola University Chicago. She is the author of *Modern Hungers: Food and Power in Twentieth Century Germany*.

Anna-Katharina Wöbse is an environmental historian and researcher at the Justus-Liebig University, Giessen.

Acknowledgments

Many conversations among many scholars went into the design, development, and delivery of this project. It was clear that contributors who were laboring in the same or similar vineyards would benefit immeasurably from working together to shape their research and writing. Generous funding from the Rachel Carson Center for Environment and Society in Munich made a workshop possible. We are grateful to its codirectors, Christof Mauch and Helmuth Trischler, for their support.

The workshop was held in August 2014 at the Mortara Center for International Studies, Georgetown University, Washington, DC. We are grateful to Moira Todd and the entire staff of the Center for their efficient organization. Mira Achter of the Institute of Social Ecology in Vienna diligently helped to prepare the book manuscript.

Finally, we enthusiastically recognize our editor at Cambridge University Press, Deborah Gershenowitz, and her associate Kristina Deusch, who have supported and expedited our work immeasurably.

Mobilizing Nature for the First World War

An Introduction

Tait Keller

When future poet laureate of the United Kingdom John Edward Masefield called his 1917 account of the Somme Offensive *The Old Front Line*, he did so without irony. Thinking that the German army's withdrawal to its defensive position along the Hindenburg Line, some six miles away, marked a permanent British advance after the bloodiest battle on the Western Front, Masefield envisaged a landscape recovered from war:

> All wars end; even this war will some day end, and the ruins will be rebuilt and the field full of death will grow food, and all this frontier of trouble will be forgotten. When the trenches are filled in, and the plough has gone over them, the ground will not long keep the look of war. One summer with its flowers will cover most of the ruin that man can make, and then these places, from which the driving back of the enemy began, will be hard indeed to trace, even with maps. ... In a few years' time, when this war is a romance in memory, the soldier looking for his battlefield will find his marks gone. Centre Way, Peel Trench, Munster Alley, and these other paths to glory will be deep under the corn, and gleaners will sing at Dead Mule Corner.[1]

His title misplaced hope – the spring 1918 German offensives pushed deep past the British lines – but much of what he wrote proved prophetic. Whether through human efforts or nature's work, these battlefields were largely and relatively quickly assimilated back into the countryside. The French government established agencies straightaway to restore the land to agrarian uses even before the fighting had stopped. With the desire for a familiar prewar environment most communes resumed traditional

---

[1] John Masefield, *The Old Front Line* (New York: MacMillan, 1917), 9.

farming practices after the armistice.[2] Soon dense vegetation and productive farmland covered large swaths of the Western Front. Veterans' groups touring their former posts did indeed find the blossoming terrain unrecognizable from their memories of blasted trenches. The land's swift revitalization surprised Corinna Haven Smith, an American humanitarian worker in France who visited the once war-torn regions in 1920. While driving on the Menin Road to Ypres, a track that war artist Paul Nash had memorialized with his surreal paintings of twisted landscapes, Smith remarked: "Is this the same plain? It does not seem possible. ... Men are working in the fields. ... Grass has grown over the shell holes and sheep and goats are grazing among abandoned tanks. ... Only the trees have kept their record of suffering." The flourishing scenery led her to conclude that "[n]ature seem[s] always to make an effort to cover the scars of battle as soon as possible."[3] So covered are some scars still today that authorities have designated those districts with high concentrations of buried, unexploded shells as "red zones," places too dangerous for cultivation, tourism, or human habitation. These restricted areas effectively serve as armed nature reserves. Weapons that once wrecked the land now guard it against development. Yet despite the drama of battle and the profusion of deadly relics, human relationships with the natural world have changed little along the former killing fields, just as Masefield predicted.

Ecological succession and eager farmers may have mostly obscured the old front lines in France and Belgium, but the war left lasting traces on the environment elsewhere around the world. Mobilizing natural resources for the production of destruction brought the war home to lands far from the fighting. The dominance of the Western Front in public exhibits, popular memory, and school textbooks notwithstanding, the First World War was a global conflict that touched a variety of biomes, from the Atlantic Ocean, to the Tyrolean Alps, the Carpathian Mountains, the Mesopotamian desert, the African savanna, the coasts of China's Shandong Peninsula, and the beaches of the Solomon Islands. The Allies, anchored by the Triple Entente of Great Britain, France, and Russia, and later joined by Italy and the United States, faced the Central Powers led by Germany, with Austria-Hungary, Bulgaria, and the

---

[2] Hugh Clout, *After the Ruins: Restoring the Countryside of Northern France after the Great War* (Exeter: University of Exeter Press, 1996), 241–272.

[3] Corinna Haven Smith, *Rising above the Ruins in France: An Account of the Progress Made since the Armistice in the Devastated Regions in Re-Establishing Industrial Activities and Normal Life of the People* (New York: GP Putnam's Sons, 1920), 73–74, 141.

Ottoman Empire in tow. More than 30 countries eventually joined the conflict (most on the side of the Entente) in which some 65 million troops fought.

Combat varied. Major offensives involving masses of men and minuscule gains took place on the Western Front, where soldiers huddled in trenches that stretched from the English Channel to the Swiss border. Stalemate defined the war there with rare exceptions. Sweeping movement characterized the Eastern Front. Big German, Austro-Hungarian, and Russian armies ranged over hundreds of miles from the Baltic Sea down to the Black Sea, though despite stunning advances and tactical innovation neither side could achieve total victory. Winston Churchill later wrote, "[i]n the west, the armies were too big for the land; in the east, the land was too big for the armies."[4] First Lord of the Admiralty during the war, Churchill had championed the failed Dardanelles campaign and the doomed landings at Gallipoli. The Italian Front, known in some circles as the Alpine Front, witnessed war at high altitudes. Small patrols scrambled up the mountains, trying to capture the peaks and command the natural fortresses. German colonial troops engaged in guerilla warfare in East Africa, as did Arab forces fighting the Ottoman army in the Middle East.

Precise casualty figures for the war are impossible to know, but the consensus among historians is that between 8 to 9 million soldiers died and another 21 million were wounded. Considering starvation and violence on the home front, civilian deaths are even more difficult to calculate with numbers spanning from 7 to 10 million. Factor in the 1918 influenza pandemic and that range jumps to anywhere from 50 to 100 million. Whatever the gruesome arithmetic, the war ranks among the deadliest conflicts in human history. Eminent diplomat George Kennan famously called the war "the seminal catastrophe" of the twentieth century.[5]

While the war's vast historiography centers on the "seminal catastrophe" for the main European belligerents, recent scholarship has

[4] Winston Churchill, *The Unknown War: The Eastern Front* (New York: Scribner's Sons, 1931), 76. Cited in Timothy Dowling, *Eastern Front*, https://encyclopedia.1914–1918-online.net/pdf/1914–1918-Online-eastern_front-2014–10-08.pdf (accessed July 24, 2017).

[5] Among the best general histories of the war are Michael Neiberg, *Fight the Great War: A Global History* (Cambridge, MA: Harvard University Press, 2005); and Hew Strachan, *The First World War* (New York: Penguin, 2003). The most accessible English-language reference work on the war is *1914–18 Online. International Encyclopedia of the First World War* (https://encyclopedia.1914–1918-online.net/home.html) (accessed August 23, 2017), a website that offers hundreds of open-access scholarly articles and extensive bibliographies.

increasingly examined the conflict's peripheries in Africa, Asia, Latin America, and the Middle East.[6] This "global turn" has widened the scope of the war to include non-European battlefields, home fronts, and experiences, and the lives of otherwise overlooked noncombatants. New studies still engage in old debates. Familiar questions about origins, continuities, and legacies loom large. What remains absent, however, is an environmental history of the war. General surveys and recent encyclopedias of the war say little about the natural world.[7] They largely overlook the conflict's ecological disruptions and long-term environmental transformations. A growing number of environmental historians has taken an interest in war.[8] But few have focused on the Great War.[9]

---

[6] Examples include Mustafa Aksakal, *The Ottoman Road to War in 1914: The Ottoman Empire and the First World War* (New York: Cambridge University Press, 2010); Frederick Dickinson, *War and National Reinvention: Japan in the Great War, 1914–1919* (Cambridge, MA: Harvard University Press, 1999); Stefan Rinke, *Latin America and the First World War*, translated by Christopher Reid (New York: Cambridge University Press, 2017); Hew Strachan, *The First World War in Africa* (Oxford: Oxford University Press, 2004); and Guoqi Xu, *China and the Great War: China's Pursuit of a New National Identity and Internationalization* (New York: Cambridge University Press, 2005).

[7] John Horne, ed., *A Companion to World War I* (West Sussex: Wiley-Blackwell, 2010); Gerhard Hirschfeld, ed., *Brill's Encyclopedia of the First World War* (Boston, MA: Brill, 2012); and Jay Winter, ed., *The Cambridge History of the First World War* (New York: Cambridge University Press, 2016).

[8] For excellent introductions to studies on war and the environment, see Richard P. Tucker and Edmund Russell, eds., *Natural Enemy, Natural Ally: Toward an Environmental History of War* (Corvallis: Oregon State University Press, 2004); Charles E. Closmann, ed., *War and the Environment: Military Destruction in the Modern Age* (College Station: Texas A&M University Press, 2009); and Chris Pearson, Peter Coates, and Tim Cole, eds., *Militarized Landscapes: From Gettysburg to Salisbury Plain* (London: Continuum, 2010). See also Edmund Russell's pioneering book, *War and Nature: Fighting Humans and Insects with Chemicals from World War I to Silent Spring* (New York: Cambridge University Press, 2001).

[9] Dorothee Brantz, Environments of Death: Trench Warfare on the Western Front, 1914–1918. In Charles E. Closmann, ed., *War and the Environment: Military Destruction in the Modern Age* (College Station: Texas A&M University Press, 2009), 68–91; and Joseph P. Hupy, The Long-Term Effects of Explosive Munitions on the WWI Battlefield Surface of Verdun, France. *Scottish Geographical Journal* 122(3) (2006), 167–184. See relevant chapters in Marco Armiero, *A Rugged Nation: Mountains and the Making of Modern Italy* (Cambridge: White Horse Press, 2011); Tait Keller, *Apostles of the Alps: Mountaineering and Nation-Building in Germany and Austria, 1860–1939* (Chapel Hill: University of North Carolina Press, 2016); and Chris Pearson, *Mobilizing Nature: The Environmental History of War and Militarization in Modern France* (Manchester: Manchester University Press, 2012). Three books in particular include some environmental angles in their analyses: Christoph Nübel, *Durchhalten und Überleben an der Westfront: Raum und Körper im Ersten Weltkrieg* (Paderborn: Ferdinand Schöningh, 2014); Avner Offer, *The First World War: An Agrarian Interpretation* (New York:

Rather than merely filling a hole in First World War historiography or recycling old tropes about the conflict, this collection offers a means to radically rethink the war's history and meaning. Together the essays expand the duration, complexity, geography, and legacy of the conflict. Since environmental transformations and global resource extraction relevant to the war began before the start of hostilities and continued after the armistice, the authors extend the traditional time frame of the conflict. Several of the essays show that within the broader context of industrialization during the modern era, the First World War continued and intensified trends from the nineteenth century, not upsetting or subverting them. From an environmental standpoint, war lands were not so different from industrial wastelands. Pollution from factories did as much to damage the natural world as the shells they produced. Along these lines, perhaps the trenches in France were not so very different from the miles upon miles of furrows across the American prairies. As with the industrial and agricultural aspects, the environmental dimension blurs the distinction between military zones and civilian sectors, resulting in the increased vulnerability of entire populations, especially impoverished and marginalized ones in Africa and the Middle East.

Recent works on the First World War have emphasized the conflict's imperial contours and colonial subjects, giving voice to subaltern and oppressed groups.[10] A number of the authors in this collection show that such social and structural inequalities are inseparable from the war's ecological legacies. As a great industrial war, World War I marks a phase in the long transition from an agrarian era (based on biomass energy) to an industrial era (based increasingly on fossil fuels) that fundamentally defined geopolitics in the twentieth century. Industrial states became ever more efficient in managing raw materials and taking control of strategic resources in other parts of the globe. Major changes in the political map dictated in the peace

---

Oxford University Press, 1991); and William Storey, *The First World War: A Concise Global History* (Lanham, MD: Rowman and Littlefield, 2009).

[10] See Sanstanu Das, ed., *Race, Empire and First World War Writing* (New York: Cambridge University Press, 2011); Richard Fogarty and Andrew Tait Jarboe, eds., *Empires in World War I: Shifting Frontiers and Imperial Dynamics in a Global Conflict* (London: I. B. Tauris, 2014); John Howard Morrow, *The Great War: An Imperial History* (New York: Routledge, 2005); Heather Streets-Salter, *World War One in Southeast Asia: Colonialism and Anticolonialism in an Era of Global Conflict* (New York: Cambridge University Press, 2017); and Timothy Winegard, *Indigenous People of the British Dominions and the First World War* (New York: Cambridge University Press, 2012).

treaties helped determine subsequent competition for access to critical commodities. The thread of colonialism and resource extraction runs through several of the essays and ties together the environmental histories of war and empires.[11] Mobilizing natural resources reinforced the asymmetrical power relationships between Europe and its dominions. The environmental legacies of the war and the dynamics of imperialism in the twentieth century are inextricably bound together.

Taking the natural world into consideration also adds a critical, heretofore missing, facet to "Total War" scholarship, and in doing so links the First World War to other armed conflicts that both military and environmental historians have studied, most notably the American Civil War and the Second World War. Historians have employed the term "Total War" to analyze the limits of mobilization and unrestricted warfare, albeit with little attention paid to the natural world.[12] Several recent books on the American Civil War, however, incorporate the environmental dimension as a central component of the Total War framework. Environmental historians have shown that the fundamental connections between fighting forces and the natural world were a crucial feature of that war. Each side depended on a system of extraction, production, and supply – a military ecology – to function and fight. The US Civil War was an ecological struggle between two societies as much as it was an economic one. Unlike Rebel soldiers, who had to rely on the land around them for sustenance, Union forces drew on resources from distant systems of

---

[11] For more on the environmental history of empires, see William Beinart and Lotte Hughes, *Environment and Empire* (New York: Oxford University Press, 2007); Alfred Crosby, *Ecological Imperialism: The Biological Expansion of Europe, 900–1900*, 2nd edn. (New York: Cambridge University Press, 2004); Diana Davis, *Resurrecting the Granary of Rome: Environmental History and French Colonial Expansion in North Africa* (Athens: Ohio University Press, 2007); Richard Grove, *Green Imperialism: Colonial Expansion, Tropical Island Edens and the Origins of Environmentalism, 1600–1860* (New York: Cambridge University Press, 1996); John McNeill, *Mosquito Empires: Ecology and War in the Greater Caribbean, 1620–1914* (New York: Cambridge University Press, 2010); and Corey Ross, *Ecology and Power in the Age of Empire: Europe and the Transformation of the Tropical World* (New York: Oxford University Press, 2017).

[12] The series of books edited by Roger Chickering and Stig Förster comprises the best scholarly works on the idea of Total War: *Great War, Total War: Combat and Mobilization on the Western Front* (New York: Cambridge University Press, 2000); and *A World at Total War: Global Conflict and the Politics of Destruction, 1937–1945* (New York: Cambridge University Press, 2010). See also Manfred Boemeke and Roger Chickering, eds., *Anticipating Total War: The German and American Experience, 1871–1914* (New York: Cambridge University Press, 2006).

mass production.[13] That capacity to project power sustained troops across the globe during the Second World War. Analyzing the environmental history of the First World War illustrates just how much greater the scale of the Second World War was, particularly in Asia. Nevertheless, similar ecological needs shaped the contours of the conflict and the connections between armies and the natural world remained just as strong.[14] Soldiers still required sustenance to fight and belligerent countries needed strategic resources, raw materials, and animals to pursue their military objectives. For the supreme commands in the 1940s, the First World War offered a cautionary tale of environmental constraints on global industrial warfare.

Food is one such example. All belligerents faced the dilemmas of feeding troops and civilians, along with countless draft animals conscripted for the war. As Alice Weinreb shows, by 1914, food had become a core commodity in a global network that linked continents and hemispheres in mutually dependent relationships. Most nations exported and imported vast quantities of foodstuffs, fodder, or fertilizer. Germans in 1913 imported about 25% of their food, including eggs, dairy products, vegetable oils, fish, and meat. Great Britain produced only 35% of the calories its citizens consumed. Imports supplied more than 40% of British

---

[13] Mark Fiege, Gettysburg and the Organic Nature of the American Civil War. In Richard P. Tucker and Edmund Russell, eds., *Natural Enemy, Natural Ally: Toward an Environmental History of War* (Corvallis: Oregon State University Press), 93–109. For recent environmental history on the American Civil War, see Andrew McIlwaine Bell, *Mosquito Soldiers: Yellow Fever, Malaria, and the Course of the American Civil War* (Baton Rouge: Louisiana State University Press, 2010); Lisa Brady, *War upon the Land: Military Strategy and the Transformation of Southern Landscapes during the American Civil War* (Athens: University of Georgia Press, 2012); Brian Allen Drake, ed., *The Blue, the Gray, and the Green: Toward an Environmental History of the Civil War* (Athens: University of Georgia Press, 2015); Jim Downs, *Sick from Freedom: African-American Illness and Suffering during the Civil War and Reconstruction* (New York: Oxford University Press, 2012); Kathryn Shively Meier, *Nature's Civil War: Common Soldiers and the Environment in 1862 Virginia* (Chapel Hill: University of North Carolina Press, 2013); Megan Kate Nelson, *Ruin Nation: Destruction and the American Civil War* (Athens: University of Georgia Press, 2012); and Matthew M. Stith, *Extreme Civil War: Guerrilla Warfare, Environment, and Race on the Western Trans-Mississippi Frontier during the Civil War* (Baton Rouge: Louisiana State University Press, 2016).

[14] For more on the environmental history of the Second World War, see Simo Laakkonen, Richard P. Tucker, and Timo Vuorisalo, eds., *The Long Shadows: An Environmental History of the Second World War* (Corvallis: Oregon State University Press, 2017); Micah Muscolino, *The Ecology of War in China: Henan Province, the Yellow River, and Beyond, 1938–1950* (New York: Cambridge University Press, 2016); and William M. Tsutsui, Landscapes in the Dark Valley: Toward an Environmental History of Wartime Japan. *Environmental History* 8(2) (2003), 294–311.

domestic meat consumption and 80% of that trade came from Argentina and Uruguay. The Russian Empire ranked as the largest producer and exporter of wheat, the mainstay carbohydrate for most Europeans. Much of the fodder consumed by European farm animals likewise came from Russia, Argentina, and the United States. Weinreb explains that this food system shaped the war, just as the war transformed the global food economy. Regulating civilian food distribution and consumption became as crucial to the war effort as training soldiers or munitions production.

Among the Central Powers, the outbreak of hostilities warped global food networks in ways that threatened people's basic level of existence. When the Ottomans declared war, they stopped Russian grain supplies from reaching Western Europe. The Entente, however, turned to the Americas to prevent starvation while blockading its enemies' food shipments. More vulnerable to the vicissitudes of agricultural markets and poor domestic harvests, the Central Powers eventually faced famine. Ernst Langthaler examines the plight of the Austro-Hungarian Empire as it tried to sustain its citizens and soldiers. Before 1914, the Dual Monarchy was largely self-sufficient in basic foodstuffs. But the war created a food crisis that further and fatally destabilized the Empire. Russian occupation of rich farmland, the decrease in labor and capital, and adverse climatic conditions crippled agricultural production. State-induced market controls that provided little motivation for farmers to maximize grain production and inefficient institutional frameworks between the Austrian and Hungarian authorities worsened the situation. Langthaler concludes that with its inability to adequately mobilize food, the Austro-Hungarian monarchy began to collapse long before its legal dissolution in 1918.

Belligerent states needed proteins as well as carbohydrates for their militaries, but mobilizing animals both as a food source and as muscle power presented a host of challenges. In 1914, armies still relied heavily on horses as transport and draft animals. So too did farmers. For government officials, requisitioning horses from the hinterland could be politically and economically damaging. Horses were not the only species that played a notable role in the conflict. Pigs provided meat to soldiers and civilians, as well as manure to farmers. In a move of exceptional bureaucratic blundering, German officials, however, worried about hogs competing with humans for grain, slaughtered more than 9 million animals in the great "pig massacre" of 1915. Germans enjoyed a momentary bounty of pork, but grain shortages continued, now exacerbated by the massive reduction of fertilizer producers.[15] Mules, camels, and dogs, among others, also contributed to the war effort, yet little scholarly research exists on animals in the war.[16] Touched on only tangentially in this collection, the emerging field of animal studies offers exciting new avenues to analyze the mobilization of natural resources and how the war affected species besides humans.

Wartime mobilization demands drove rapid transformations in the arms manufacturing sector, as well as in mining, oil drilling, fishing, and logging. Gerard Fitzgerald analyzes the bonds among government, industry, and academe in the United States that helped to produce chemical weapons. He defines the Edgewood Arsenal facility as a militarized industrial workspace, where the manufacture of mustard gas poisoned workers in factories as it did soldiers in the fields. Environmental and public health issues, however, were largely neglected in light of the wartime national emergency. Roy MacLeod sheds light on the omnipresent but largely overlooked war over minerals as a neglected branch of environmental history. The war created new scientific and industrial organizations whose use of natural products created the tortured landscapes of Europe while transforming relationships between the civilian and military jurisdictions back home. MacLeod shows that most munitions depended upon minerals. Of the 80 known chemical elements in 1914, 30 were required in modern warfare. In many cases, the absence of small quantities of key elements could render factories useless and all but guarantee defeat. After the war, the uneven geographical distribution of key minerals played a central role in political settlements. MacLeod concludes that the conflict gave rise to a new global politics of strategic minerals, as well as a new discipline of mineral economics, and brought new forms of expertise to the care and conservation of valuable resources.

---

[15] Roger Chickering, *Imperial Germany and the Great War, 1914–1918*, 3rd edn. (New York: Cambridge University Press, 2014), 42–43. For more on the economic role that pigs have played, see Sam White, From Globalized Pig Breeds to Capitalist Pigs: A Study in Animal Cultures and Evolutionary History. *Environmental History* 16(1) (2011), 94–120.

[16] Several popular publications tell stories of horses and dogs in times of war. For an excellent scholarly analysis of the transatlantic horse trade, see Gene Tempest, *The Long Face of War: Horses and the Nature of Warfare in the French and British Armies on the Western Front* (PhD dissertation, Yale University, 2013). See also Alexander Morrison, Camels and Colonial Armies: The Logistics of Warfare in Central Asia in the Early 19th Century. *Journal of Economic and Social History of the Orient* 57 (2014), 443–485; and Andrekos Varnava, The Vagaries and Value of the Army Transport Mule in the British Army during the First World War. *Historical Research* 90 (2017), 423–446.

Perhaps no other natural resource became more valuable than oil. At first, in 1914, coal was the principal source of industrial energy. The progression of the war, however, accentuated the importance of petroleum. Dan Tamir argues that the First World War was a decisive moment in the appearance of petroleum in the global arena. Oil became indispensable. It propelled military innovation – tanks, airplanes, and submarines – and provided basic ingredients for TNT. In terms of quantity, oil did not play a central role in the war. But qualitatively it fueled the internal combustion engine that replaced the horse, freed more men from their work in the coal mines and the boiler rooms of ships, and enabled rapid movements for extended periods of time on land and at sea. Petroleum's emergence as the principal power source during the war provided the Entente with an energy advantage. Germany was a leading coal producer, but eventually its shortage of oil nearly immobilized both military machines and farming equipment. The Ottomans lacked the infrastructure to tap into their crude holdings. Russia had been extracting oil around the Caspian Sea for decades, but its rail system proved insufficient and the distances too vast to meet its allies' demands.[17] Instead, Mexico and the United States supplied more than 80% of the world's petroleum and played a crucial role in the conflict's outcome. Some ten days after the armistice, the British government hosted a dinner with the Inter-Allied Petroleum Conference. The former viceroy of India, Persia expert for the Foreign Office, and chairman of the dinner Lord Curzon famously declared, "The Allied cause had floated to victory upon a wave of oil." The director of France's Comité Général du Pétrole, Senator Bérenger, was even more adamant, albeit overly optimistic: "Oil – the blood of the earth was the blood of victory. . . . Germany had boasted too much of its superiority in iron and coal, but it had not taken sufficient account of our superiority in oil. . . . As oil had been the blood of war, so it would be the blood of the peace."[18]

Oil provided the means to modernize civilian fleets as well as military forces. Ingo Heidbrink offers a new perspective on the maritime environmental history of the North Sea. Previous accounts frame the First World War as beneficial to fish stocks since naval warfare and the conscription of

---

[17] For the specific problems of oil supply in Austria but also of other Central Powers, refer to Alison F. Frank, *Oil Empire: Visions of Prosperity in Austrian Galicia* (Cambridge, MA: Harvard University Press, 2005), 173–204.

[18] Cited in Daniel Yergin, *The Prize: The Epic Quest for Oil, Money, and Power* (New York: Free Press, 2008), 167.

steam trawlers reduced overfishing. Heidbrink challenges these histories with a longer view of North Sea fishing. Although fishing came to a near halt in autumn 1914, developments after 1918 led to massive overfishing. Fishing companies lost large numbers of their fleets with the outbreak of hostilities, but after the armistice they could purchase heavily discounted high-end ships from the navy and convert them into trawlers. With better technology the average catch per trawler exceeded prewar levels. Improved fishing fleets increased the total catch capacity, threatening fish stock levels in the North Sea.

Trees also faced overharvesting. Armies relied on lumber in countless ways. Timber beams kept trenches from collapsing. Wood planks saved soldiers from wallowing or drowning in mud. Trees provided the basic building material for wharves where soldiers disembarked, warehouses for munitions, barracks, railroad ties, telephone poles, and key airplane parts. Pit timber for coal mines, fuel wood, and pulp for paper supplies also aided the combatants' war efforts. As a result, deforestation accelerated among the belligerents, but in an uneven fashion. Ottoman forces leveled cedar forests in Lebanon. The British cut down nearly half of their productive forests, more than 450,000 acres, during the war. Desperate requests from London, along with major capital investment, expanded logging operations in western Canada, despite German submarines. The Panama Canal, opened in 1914, lowered import costs from Pacific ports. Soon British Columbia became Canada's leading timber exporter.[19] German and French timber stands fared better. German forces chopped down trees in occupied territories, exacting 5 million cubic meters of wood from Lithuania, nearly 5% of the Białowieża Forest. Most of France's forests lay well behind the front lines. With manpower diverted to the army, logging rates in those forested zones soon fell below prewar levels. Only after the arrival of American forestry divisions, the Tenth Engineering and the Twentieth Engineering Corps, did the forests in western France sustain heavy cutting. In the United States, American logging companies responded to rising lumber prices by expanding mechanized clear cutting operations. Lumber

[19] A. Joshua West, Forests and National Security: British and American Forestry Policy in the Wake of World War I. *Environmental History* 8 (2003), 270–293; and Richard P. Tucker, The World Wars and the Globalization of Timber Cutting. In Richard P. Tucker and Edmund Russell, eds., *Natural Enemy, Natural Ally: Toward an Environmental History of War* (Corvallis: Oregon State University Press, 2004), 110–141. For a broader discussion of forestry and warfare, see Andrée Corvol and Jean-Paul Amat, eds., *Forêt et guerre* (Paris: L'Harmattan, 1994); see also John McNeill, Woods and Warfare in World History. *Environmental History* 9(3) (2004), 388–410.

companies cared little for investing in reforestation programs or practicing selective cutting. But army generals saw similarities between the barren lands on the Western Front and the worst cutover areas back home and called for better forest management. Knowing that lumber held economic value, but realizing also that trees were critical to national security, several governments initiated conservation schemes to sustain timber stands.

Such geostrategic thinking and the desire to command more natural resources played into Japan's imperial expansion during the First World War. Jack Hayes examines the environmental footprint of military actions, as well as political and economic trends in East Asia, with a focus on the Japanese empire. Broadly speaking, the conflict sparked mostly indirect transformations of East Asia's physical environment and ecosystems as combat only reached a few limited locations and the European colonial powers could not exploit the region due to the vast distances involved. But as Hayes explains, the war afforded a strategic opening in East Asia for the Japanese. Expansion along the Asia Pacific rim entailed extracting the region's raw materials at new levels, along with lengthened reach of corporate and government-business systems. The war's environmental legacy in East Asia evolved into a political ecology of targeted and invasive natural resource exploitation in Japan's imperial ascent.

Imperial networks turned the War in the Middle East and Africa into cataclysm. Graham Pitts and Zachary Foster discuss famine in the Levant. Pitts explores the international dimension of the catastrophe. The war made the famine and created a landscape of enormous violence in Lebanon, which suffered more deaths per capita than any belligerent nation. Where food was contraband, starvation resulted as an "externality" of the war. Locusts did not help. They devoured ten to fifteen percent of the wheat and barley fields and eighty percent of fruits and vegetables. Incorporation into the global capitalist market in the nineteenth century had offered protections against famine, but Foster finds that the undoing of those safety nets during the war helps explain the magnitude of starvation. Dependence on the global system became a liability when the locusts hit. Steven Serels highlights how the war further destabilized food systems of the African Red Sea coasts. Structural weaknesses in the global food market left those populations vulnerable. On account of poor harvests and a currency crisis, many African communities struggled to purchase sufficient sustenance. His contribution also emphasizes that environmental and economic troubles continued after the armistice. Droughts and inflation crippled recovery in the region even when the guns fell silent. In sub-Saharan Africa, imperial exploitation transformed landscape cover, upset disease ecologies, and changed the colonial powers' perceptions of Africa's importance as a resource supplier. Thaddeus Sunseri emphasizes how population disruptions and livestock loss had significant repercussions on the environment. All colonial territories were expected to provide military labor, and forced recruitment upset local economies severely with long-term consequences for the spread of disease. Guerrilla war prevented animal controls, such as quarantine, culling infected cattle, and the strategic application of vaccines that had kept diseases in check. Rinderpest, along with tick and tsetse vectors of other diseases, now spread rapidly along military routes. Humans also suffered a panoply of disease, including bubonic plague, dysentery, sleeping sickness, smallpox, and malaria. Sunseri concludes that the war continued the overall African population decline that had begun in the 1880s.

The 1918 influenza pandemic had the greatest impact on population decline in Africa and around the world. The war environment spread ancient diseases; it also created conditions for the spread of more virulent ones. The movement of millions created the perfect conduit for the influenza H1N1 virus. Although long overlooked by historians of the First World War, the pandemic of 1918–1919 and the war are inseparable. Even so, influenza's appearance and mutation in 1918 were seemingly coincidental. Virologists cannot prove that wartime conditions produced the causative virus. Neither can scientists show that the war turned a rather mild H1N1 virus into a pathogen of unprecedented lethality.[20] However, densely packed humans – in trenches, barracks, transport ships, troop depots, factories, mine shafts, and the like – did serve as ideal transporters for the virus, accelerating its spread. The war turned a local outbreak into a global pandemic. Evidence also suggests that influenza's infectiousness worsened the German army's already depleted state and contributed to its offensive failures in 1918. The pandemic was certainly a cataclysmic event but as a breath-borne disease the virus was only marginally environmental and thus not included in this collection.[21]

[20] For the latest debates on the pandemic's origins, see Mark Humphries, Paths of Infection: The First World War and the Origins of the 1918 Influenza Pandemic. *War in History* 21 (1) (2014), 55–81; Ann H. Reid and Jeffery K. Taubenberger, The Origin of the 1918 Pandemic Influenza Virus: A Continuing Enigma. *Journal of General Virology* 84 (2003), 2285–2292; Dennis G. Shanks, No Evidence of 1918 Influenza Pandemic Origin in Chinese Laborers/Soldiers in France. *Journal of Chinese Medical Association* 79 (2016), 46–48; and Viroj Wiwanitkit, 1918 Influenza Pandemic Origin in Chinese Laborers/Soldiers: Medical Historical Analysis. *Journal of Chinese Medical Association* 79 (2016), 116.

[21] See David Killingray and Howard Phillips, eds., *The Spanish Influenza Pandemic of 1918–1919: New Perspectives* (New York: Routledge, 2013); Carol Byerly, *The Fever*

The high rates of death and destruction from industrial warfare on a global scale taught military planners that carefully managing natural resources was crucial; so too was safeguarding them from overexploitation. Civic nature protection groups arose in many industrializing countries during the late nineteenth century. Largely bourgeois and elite in social composition, these associations struggled, often vainly, to reduce industrial pollution. The First World War granted greater political legitimacy to these organizations through collusion with state governments to administer natural resources, but the conflict upset the trajectory of international environmentalism. Raf De Bont and Anna-Katharina Wöbse show how the war disrupted international preservationist networks. They argue that the conflict is partly to blame for the failure of elite environmental networks to function in the world of intergovernmental diplomacy. Distrust among nature protectionist elites seemed to prevent the League of Nations from initiating environmental reform. But witnessing the devastation of industrial warfare also galvanized international environmentalism in terms of which nature protection projects received priority and who promoted them. The unspoken military-industrial angle of nature conservation remained a tacit feature of environmental agendas long after the war's end.

The desire to protect natural resources and repair ruined lands reflected emotional attachments to nature, as much as military priorities and agricultural needs. Lush lands connoted innocence, peace, and a return to normalcy. The use of nature to mask death and destruction became increasingly popular after the armistice. Poppies, heroes' groves, and memorial trees symbolized resurrection and rejuvenation. Described as "clothed in the finest of human sentiment . . . a simple symbol to keep forever green the memory of those in whose honor it is planted," memorial trees became especially popular in the United States.[22] The American Legion worked together with the American Tree Association to distribute seedlings. Some groups started a "Roads of Remembrance" campaign, planting shade trees along highways. This was a timely effort since many states had begun to plan extensive systems of roads. Others traveled to France to plant memorial trees in honor of those who never made it home. Recent centennial commemorations have likewise

---

of War: The Influenza Epidemic in the US Army during World War I (New York: New York University Press, 2005); John Barry, *The Great Influenza: The Epic Story of the Deadliest Plague in History* (New York: Penguin, 2004); and Alfred Crosby, *America's Forgotten Pandemic: The Influenza of 1918* (New York: Cambridge University Press, 2003).

[22] Charles Lathrop Pack, *Trees as Good Citizens* (Washington, DC: The American Tree Association, 1922), 108.

employed nature to symbolize the cycles of death and rebirth. Among the more notable tributes was a public art installation, "Blood Swept Lands and Seas of Red," at the Tower of London. Between July and November 2014, organizers gradually planted 888,246 ceramic red poppies, each of which represented those who died serving the British Empire between 1914 and 1918. A few art critics accused the installation's designers of masking the war's horror with pretty flowers instead of presenting gory scenes with barbed wire and bones, but that did not stop an estimated 5 million people from visiting the memorial. Nearly as many visitors also attended Michael St Maur Sheil's *Fields of Battle – Lands of Peace* commemorative photographic exhibits in London and Paris. A professional photographer and battlefield tour guide, his contemporary pictures of the Somme, Ypres, and Messines, among dozens of famous battlegrounds, captured the eeriness of outwardly tranquil lands still haunted by hidden armaments.[23]

Reactions to the poppies and photographs, what John Edward Masefield foresaw as "a romance in memory," speak to Frank Uekötter's call to view the environment not only as a reflection of memories but also as a distinct mode of memory. Environmental historians have long emphasized that nature is more than a backdrop to human history. However, as Uekötter observes, the discipline of memory studies has remained largely unimpressed; it rests firmly within the province of cultural studies. Cultural historian Jay Winter wrote that "remembrance is part of the landscape," but he meant war memorials and cemeteries.[24] In his stark and unsentimental poem, published posthumously in 1916, Charles Hamilton Sorley instructed mourners not to give praise, spend tears, or bestow honor on the fallen, yet the "millions of the mouthless dead" do indeed give meaning to nature.[25] Soldiers' cemeteries consecrated former sites of carnage. War graves commissions collected human remains and organized parcels of land, such as Tyne Cot in Belgium, the largest British Commonwealth war cemetery in the world. Authorities from all the former belligerent countries established war ceme-teries throughout Europe, as well as in India, Australia, New Zealand, and

---

[23] Mark Brown, Blood-Swept Lands: The Story behind the Tower of London Poppies Tribute. *The Guardian*, December 28, 2014, www.theguardian.com/world/2014/dec/28/blood-swept-lands-story-behind-tower-of-london-poppies-first-world-war-memorial (accessed July 31, 2017). See Michael St Maur Sheil, *Fields of Battle – Lands of Peace, 1914–1918* (Baden: Edition Lammerhuber, 2016).

[24] Jay Winter, *Sites of Memory, Sites of Mourning: The Great War in European Cultural History* (New York: Cambridge University Press, 1995), 1.

[25] Tim Kendall, ed., *The Poetry of the First World War: An Anthology* (New York: Oxford University Press, 2014), 191.

the Middle East, and across North America. Burial sites provided enduring oases of memory amid recuperating lands. Designed to withstand ecological change caused by natural succession and placed on land granted in perpetuity, the cemeteries soon became sites of pilgrimage and a century later remain lasting fixtures in the countryside. But one need not amble contemplatively through quiet cemeteries on the old front lines to try to comprehend the catastrophe of the First World War. As the essays in this volume show, reminders of the conflict's environmental legacies are all around us; we need only look.

PART I

EUROPE AND NORTH AMERICA
Battle Zones and Support Systems

2

Beans Are Bullets, Potatoes Are Powder

Food as a Weapon during the First World War

Alice Weinreb

The First World War was defined, both in individual soldiers' experiences and in collective memory, by the mass deployment of chemical weapons. Of all forms of battlefield suffering that distinguished the war from prior conflicts, poison gas was the most infamous. Although relatively few of the millions of soldiers who died during the war were killed by chemical warfare, the symbolic and strategic importance of poison gas transformed scientists into crucial players in military strategy. Indeed, the war has often been referred to as the chemist's war for this reason.[1] While all major belligerents experimented with chemical weaponry, it was the German chemist Fritz Haber whose work on poison gas earned him the dubious honor of being dubbed the "father of chemical weapons." Despite his crucial research in the battlefield deployment of chlorine and other gases, Haber's 1918 Nobel Prize in chemistry did not mention his key research in battlefield weaponry. Instead, the prize was awarded for what was considered the greatest chemical breakthrough of modern agricultural science: the Haber-Bosch process of ammonia production.

This new method of nitrogen-fixing promised a near-limitless supply of nitrogen, which became a key military resource because it was a crucial component of explosives as well as providing fertilizer. Indeed, governments around the world had recognized the importance

---

[1] See Chapter 4 by Gerard Fitzgerald in this anthology.

of nitrogen supplies for maintaining an industrial war since the nine-teenth century. When Haber was awarded the Nobel Prize, there had been substantial public outrage; many claimed that his invention, like his research on poison gas, had prolonged the war. (His first wife had purportedly committed suicide out of guilt at his involve-ment in the development of poison gas.) Nonetheless, in the award speech delivered by the president of the Royal Swedish Academy of Sciences, Dr. A. G. Ekstrand described Haber's work as exclusively agricultural; according to Ekstrand, Haber's technique of ammonia production had been motivated by the goal of "improving the standards of agriculture" and was of "universal significance for the improvement of human nutrition and so of the greatest benefit to mankind."[2] Haber similarly avoided any mention of war or munitions in his acceptance speech, describing nitrogen-fixing as the key to the industrialization of the modern food system. Despite nitrogen's role in the production of the millions of tons of explosives used in the just-past war, the scientist poetically described his innovation as evidence for how the "chemical industry comes to the aid of the farmer who, in the good earth, changes stones into bread."[3]

Less than a year after the Armistice finally brought an official end to armed conflict, Haber and Ekstrand's description of ammonia as a feeder of the masses seems disingenuous. Hundreds of thousands of dead soldiers and civilians, countless acres of fertile land pock-marked by bombs, and the rubble-filled streets of Europe's cities all bore witness to the deadly power of nitrogen-based explosives. At the same time, however, these chemists' claims are inarguably true – nitrogen was most important source of fertilizer at the time, and its availability was one of the primary limiting factors on food production in Europe and much of the world. Nitrogen thus offers a prime example of the complex environmental legacy of the war, encompassing both the decimated soils of the Western Front and the fertile wheat plains of the American Midwest. As a key resource

---

[2] Nobel Prize in Physics 1920 – Presentation Speech. *Nobelprize.org.* Nobel Media AB 2014, www.nobelprize.org/nobel_prizes/physics/laureates/1920/press.html (accessed June 6, 2015).

[3] Fritz Haber, The Synthesis of Ammonia from Its Elements: Nobel Lecture. In *Nobel Lectures, Chemistry 1901–1921* (Amsterdam: Elsevier, 1966), 327, 329.

in the production and destruction of both food and human lives, nitrogen-fixing marked a turning point in the history of warfare. It symbolized the "absolute dependence of the modern fighting man upon chemistry" since, as a 1917 article on "Chemistry and the War" noted, "the soldier at the front can be provided with neither munitions nor food by those nations which have not at their command large supplies of nitrogen. Nitric acid is essential for explosives, and nitrates for the fertilizer which produces food."[4]

Most participant nations in the First World War asserted at one point or another that "food will win the war." This chapter unpacks this slogan in order to understand more fully the relationship between the world's food system and the First World War. Many historians have noted how the war changed the ways in which people acquired food as well as the nature of those foods themselves.[5] This work has rarely explored this issue from an environmental perspective, however. Such an environmental approach to the history of the war is especially helpful for conceptualizing the ramifications of this new codependence of food production and military conflict. Surprisingly, environmental history has been relatively slow to focus attention on food, despite a long-standing recognition of the centrality of the topic.[6] Environmental histories have generally explored aspects of the food economy through studies of agriculture and changing strategies of land management.[7] Scholars have recently published a number of environmental histories of specific commodities.[8] This chapter is a first attempt to conceptualize food *qua* food as a way of linking environmental history and the history of warfare. It does so by using the lens of war to explore changes in global food production, consumption, and distribution.

[4] Chemistry and the War. *The Outlook* 117(5) (October 3, 1917), 159.

[5] See, for example, Ina Zweiniger-Bargielowska, Rachel Duffett, and Alain Drouard, eds., *Food and War in Twentieth Century Europe* (Surrey: Ashgate, 2011).

[6] Robert Chester and Nicolaas Mink, Having Our Cake and Eating It Too: Food's Place in Environmental History, a Forum. *Environmental History* 14(2) (2009), 309–311.

[7] Cameron Muir, *The Broken Promise of Agricultural Progress: An Environmental History* (London: Routledge, 2014); Mart Stewart, "Whether Wast, Deodand, or Stray": Cattle, Culture, and the Environment in Early Georgia. *Agricultural History* 65(3) (1991), 1–28.

[8] John Soluri, *Banana Cultures: Agriculture, Consumption, and Environmental Change in Honduras and the United States* (Austin: University of Texas Press, 2006); Kendra Smith-Howard, *Pure and Modern Milk: An Environmental History since 1900* (New York: Oxford University Press, 2014).

Such a perspective reveals not only that the transnational food economy was transformed by the war but also that the war itself was shaped by the rise of a new food system.

Scientific innovations linking munitions and agriculture new military strategies that exploited global trade networks to regulate food imports and exports, and the rise of a new geopolitical humanitarianism all meant that making food and making war became inseparable from one another. Indeed, the varied functions assigned to food during the conflict proved one of the war's most significant legacies. Specifically, both food shortages (blockades) and food surpluses (aid) continued long past the end of the conflict. They not only defined lived experience during the interwar years, but represented a permanent change in the regulation of the world's food supply. Many scholars have noted the rise to global hegemony of the United States, the most powerful food-surplus nation in the world, at this time.[9] Less attention has been paid to Germany's multifaceted role in the rise of a new global food system. In fact, Germany played a crucial role, emerging as both preeminent victim and primary perpetrator of the militarized food economy that came into existence during the First World War.

FEEDING WAR: THE MILITARIZATION OF THE GLOBAL FOOD SYSTEM

In 1917, newly appointed US Food Administrator and future US president Herbert Hoover announced that "food has gradually, since the war began, assumed a larger place in the economics, the statesmanship and the strategy of the war until it is my belief that food will win this war – starvation or sufficiency will in the end determine the victor. The winning of the war is largely a problem of who can organize this weapon – food."[10]

Hoover's dramatic declaration elides the fact that the war was the culmination of a long process of industrialization that had remade the production, consumption, and distribution of foodstuffs throughout

---

[9] See, for example, Bill Winders, *The Politics of Food Supply: U.S. Agricultural Policy in the World Economy* (New Haven, CT: Yale University Press, 2009).

[10] Herbert Hoover, The Weapon of Food. *National Geographic Magazine* (September 1917), 197.

the world. Few parts of the world were untouched by this new industrial food system. Over the course of the nineteenth century, food had become a core commodity in a transnational network that linked continents and hemispheres in relationships of mutual dependence. Most nations exported and imported vast quantities of foodstuffs, fodder, or fertilizer. Food autarchy or self-sufficiency increasingly seemed an old-fashioned and unnecessary aspiration. While these networks allowed some Western nations to accumulate massive wealth and to reshape the consumption habits of their citizens, they also meant that any restriction on trade and exchange would profoundly affect food supply across the world. Even domestically, foods were rarely consumed where they were produced, as elaborate processing systems developed to standardize foods across urban and rural landscapes. Farmers increasingly turned to monoculture, as remarkable improvements in transportation technologies made vast crop surpluses newly profitable, in turn placing increased demands on soil and water. By the early twentieth century, demand for fertilizer and pesticides newly bound farmers to chemists in highly profitable relationships of interdependency.

The outbreak of a world war in 1914 exploited and modified these developments. The war hinged upon systems of global food exchange. Certainly the most obvious impact of the war was its restrictive impact on food consumption; between 1914 and 1918, food regulation and increasingly severe food shortages shaped civilian lives throughout Europe. German economist and statistician Ernst Wagemann, in a 1917 essay titled "The Foreign Food Economy," focused on limitations on food production as a major consequence of the war. He reported:

[T]he war has had a three-fold impact on the world's food supply. It has weakened the productivity of agriculture through the requisitioning of labor and draft animals; it has created the massive food demands of million-strong armies; and, most dramatically, it has destroyed the international division of labor, it has separated the global economy, which made up a single economic entity, into three distinct productive regions – Russia, the Central Powers, and the rest of the world [resulting in] a dramatic decline in crops.[11]

The actual impact of the war on the world's food supplies was far more complex than this narrative suggests. Wagemann, for example, does not mention the near-limitless fertilizer made available through nitrogen-fixing. The Haber-Bosch process remade the twentieth-century food economy, causing remarkable increases in crop yields in the

[11] Ernst Wagemann, Die Nahrungswirtschaft des Auslandes. In *Beiträge zur Kriegswirtschaft* (Berlin, 1917), 53.

United States and enabling the Green Revolution of the 1960s in much of the developing world, but also introducing the devastating impacts of nitrogen run-off for the world's water sources and the rapid depletion of topsoil. Similarly, the war redistributed food in new ways, creating new ways of feeding people and of starving them. This meant that, rather than being a necessary *precondition* of conflict (necessary to ensure that soldiers were capable of fighting), food was directly implicated in combat maneuvers. This new way of conceptualizing food as a weapon meant that food became a key military resource, rather than, as Wagemann implies, something that existed in an antithetical relationship to war (more war means less food).

While nitrogen continued to be the most significant link between battlefields and grain fields, countless components of peoples' everyday diets were reimagined as a crucial part of the war effort. Surging demand for glycerin meant that all forms of fats suddenly became strategic military resources. Noted British economist Sir William Beveridge, in his analysis of the First World War *Blockade and the Civilian Population*, claimed that "fats are, literally, not guns indeed, but the favorite food of guns in the form of propellant ... fats are more nearly munitions than are other foods."[12] Wartime propaganda in all sides of the conflict pressured civilians to reduce their fat consumption. An English campaign for the "Bone and Fat Bucket" explained that "bones and fat provide glycerin for making explosives, glue for making aeroplanes, fertilizers for food production. Save them for munitions," while American housewives were taught that "fats are fuel for fighters. Bake, boil and broil more – fry less."[13] Allied media reported that in Germany, "the civilian population is dying in large numbers because of the lack of [fat] ... von Hindenburg's men will lose out on the basis of fat rather than on the basis of munitions or military organization."[14] Even food waste was integrated into the war effort; peach pits proved a source of the especially absorptive form of charcoal needed to construct gas masks,[15] so children were encouraged to collect them by the bushel-full.

Food promised to win the war in more indirect ways as well. Or, more accurately, depriving people of food promised to win the war. Regulating

[12] William Beveridge, *Blockade and the Civilian Population* (Oxford: Clarendon Press, 1939), 9–10.
[13] Charles Houston Goudiss, *Foods That Will Win the War and How to Cook Them* (New York: World Syndicate Company, 1918), 73.
[14] Ibid., 74.
[15] See Gerard Fitzgerald's work on coconut and peach pit gathering in the United States, in his essay in this volume.

the global flow of foodstuffs by preventing food imports was one of the most widely used weapons of the war. Precisely because of food's importance to military strategy, and the vulnerable nature of the global food system, wartime blockades of foodstuffs targeted numerous countries during and after the war. The collapse of the Ottoman Empire was directly associated with internal food shortages. Some historians have argued that state-sanctioned food seizures and the internal rerouting of foodstuffs were responsible for the devastating food crises that rocked the Austro-Hungarian Empire as well. Strategic food blockades resulted in severe food shortages as far away from Europe as Lebanon and Syria.[16]

Despite its naval supremacy, England's small size and dependence on food imports made that country a target of blockade. German military experts had estimated that the country could last a maximum of five months before collapsing if it were cut off from its food imports.[17] Based on these statistics, Germany's U-boat campaign expected to rapidly starve the English into submission. Germany's propaganda machine eagerly claimed hunger as its most effective weapon, reporting that "England is about to starve ... in the near future England will lie on the ground: unconscious, hungry, beaten with the same weapon with which it attempted to defeat the dutiful German people."[18] The introduction of unlimited submarine warfare did initially devastate British food supplies; the loss of hundreds of thousands of tons of merchant ships decimated the country's wheat and sugar stores.[19] However, the island nation successfully remade its international trade network by importing vast quantities of American foods; by 1918, England was receiving almost two-thirds of its food supply from North America.[20] As a result, the German submarine

---

[16] See the chapters by Ernst Langthaler (Chapter 3), Graham Auman Pitts (Chapter 9), Zachary J. Foster (Chapter 10), and Steven Serels (Chapter 11) in this anthology for more on food shortages throughout the world caused by disruptions in international distribution networks.

[17] Holger Herwig, Total Rhetoric, Limited War: Germanys U-boat Campaign, 1917–1918. In Roger Chickering and Stig Forster, eds., *Great War, Total War: Combat and Mobilization on the Western Front, 1914–1918* (Cambridge: Cambridge University Press, 2000), 195.

[18] Cited in Jeffrey Verhey, *The Spirit of 1914: Militarism, Myth, and Mobilization in Germany* (Cambridge: Cambridge University Press, 2006), 194.

[19] David Monger, *Patriotism and Propaganda in First World War Britain: The National War Aims Committee and Civilian Morale* (Liverpool: Liverpool University Press, 2012), 21.

[20] Helen Veit, *Modern Food, Moral Food: Self-Control, Science, and the Rise of Modern American Eating in the Early Twentieth Century* (Chapel Hill: University of North Carolina Press, 2013), 61.

campaign ironically resulted in the stabilization of England's government, as the relative egalitarianism of the country's rationing program won over the poorer segments of society whose faith in the state had been sorely tried by long food queues and looming shortages.[21]

England's ability to successfully withstand a food blockade was largely due to its long familiarity with this tool of war. Since the eighteenth century, Great Britain, relying upon its naval supremacy, had become particularly adept at using trade blockades as a strategy for maintaining military and economic power. This practice culminated in the British "Hunger Blockade" of Germany, which aimed to prevent Germany from importing foodstuffs for its civilian population. In this aim, the English were quite successful; food imports sank dramatically over the course of the war, until by 1917 the country was almost entirely reliant upon domestically produced foods.[22] Unlike England's new trade relationships with the United States, Germany could not find adequate alternative sources for food importations, and protests and bread riots spread throughout the cities and towns of the country. Germany's defeat came to be nearly universally attributed to the British "Hunger Blockade."

British observers were fond of claiming that the use of military power to restrict the flow of goods into an enemy territory was an age-old strategy of war. In a 1918 article defending the ethics of the blockade, British journalist Margaret Jourdain cited approvingly "the antiquity and respectability of the [military] method of starvation and the parallel between siege and blockade."[23] This rationale was historically inaccurate – the trade relations and shipping technologies that made a modern food blockade possible were a recent innovation having little in common with medieval sieges. Nonetheless, this claim of antiquity resolved possible ethical objections to a style of warfare that unabashedly targeted civilians, especially women and children on the home front. It also obscured the fact that Britain had been calculating Germany's vulnerability to a food blockade for decades. Germany's well-known dependence on food imports seemed a strategic weakness that, with the outbreak of war, begged to be exploited. As the *New York Times* noted in 1916:

[21] Ina Zweiniger-Bargielowska, *Austerity in Britain: Rationing, Controls, and Consumption, 1939–1955* (Oxford: Oxford University Press, 2000), 13.

[22] Belinda Davis, *Home Fires Burning: Food, Politics, and Everyday Life in World War I Berlin* (Chapel Hill: University of North Carolina Press, 2000), 22.

[23] Margaret Jourdain, Air Raid Reprisals and Starvation by Blockade. *International Journal of Ethics* 28(4) (July 1918), 550.

"Germany's food supply has all along been one of the great questions of the war."[24]

Although before the war the average German consumed more calories than the average European – around 4,000 calories a day – imports directly made up almost half of these calories, and, through fodder and fertilizer, another half of Germans' total meat and fat consumption.[25] Of these imports, the vast majority – 74% – was shipped.[26] As a result, the British blockade was expected to be the decisive weapon of the war, bringing Germany to its knees rapidly and absolutely and with devastating consequences. British nutritionists promised military leaders that "the physical and mental weaklings produced by starvation are likely to beget their kind ... to the detriment of the next generation."[27] This form of blockade changed the definition of war expanding legitimate targets of warfare – now including women and children – and changing the nature of wartime conflict, which reached beyond direct acts of violence to include deliberate starvation that was expected to impact future generations.

This deliberate manipulation of wide-scale hunger and transnational food trade represented a key military innovation as well as providing a crucial impetus for the rise of new wartime food economies. The German government embarked on a restructuring of its food economy within months of the war's beginning with the August 1914 creation of the Wartime Raw Materials Department (*Kriegsrohstoffabteilung* or KRA). The KRA, headed by Walter Rathenau, was a new government unit charged with the central organization and regulation of all war-related goods and products, including food. It was this program that inspired England's declaration of food as contraband, claiming that the creation of the KRA made clear that food was "as essential to the forces as bullets and therefore equally seizable; there is really no difference with regard to the consideration of food as contraband of war."[28] This declaration marked the official beginning of the British blockade.

---

[24] How Germany's Food Problem Was Met. *New York Times* (April 16, 1916), 6.

[25] William Van der Kloot, Ernest Starling's Analysis of the Energy Balance of the German People during the Blockade, 1914–19. *Notes and Records of the Royal Society of London* 57(2) (May 2003), 190–191.

[26] Alan Kramer, *Dynamic of Destruction: Culture and Mass Killing in the First World War* (Oxford: Oxford University Press, 2007), 154.

[27] Suda Lorena Bane and Ralph Haswell Lutz, *Organization of American Relief in Europe, 1918–1919* (Stanford, CA: Stanford University Press, 1943), 527.

[28] Jourdain, Air Raid Reprisals and Starvation by Blockade, 551.

Although Britain managed to almost entirely cut off food imports to
Germany initial impacts were not as great as expected. Accumulated
food stores, wartime food seizure, and the initial well-fed state of the
population meant that basic nutrition was not seriously threatened for
the first two years of the war. Contrary to expectations, the primary
threat posed by the blockade was not to the country's actual food
supply, but its nitrogen supply. When the war broke out, the vast
majority of the world's – and Germany's – nitrates were imported from
Chile.[29] The British blockade put an end to this, and Germany's stores
of munitions threatened to run short without a new source of nitrogen.
This threat seemed even more dire as it became clear that a new style
of conflict – trench warfare – required unprecedented quantities of
munitions, making a reliable supply of nitrates a matter of immediacy,
and inspiring the creation of an official Nitrate Commission in
Germany.[30] It was clear that Germany would not be able to maintain
its war effort if it did not find an alternate source of nitrogen to
produce explosives. Fritz Haber's discovery of a method of synthesizing
ammonia meant that nitrogen could be domestically produced in massive quantities. This remarkable technique of extracting nitrogen from
air meant that Germany's production skyrocketed almost overnight,
growing from about 7,000 tons in 1913 to about 215,000 tons in
1918.[31] Without this new technology, experts calculated that
Germany would have run out of munitions by the spring of 1915: in
1916, American chemists claimed that "had it not been for the air-
nitrogen industry that Germany has brought to such a high state of
development, there is no doubt but that the Allies' 'plan of starvation'
would long ago have brought the war to a conclusion."[32] In the early
months of the blockade, British boats threatened to starve German
guns rather than German stomachs – and it was German chemists,
rather than German farmers, who challenged the success of the British
blockade. This was to change as hunger spread throughout Europe,
transforming food itself into a uniquely powerful weapon of war.

---

[29] Edward Melillo, The First Green Revolution: Debt Peonage and the Making of the
Nitrogen Fertilizer Trade, 1840–1930. *The American Historical Review* 117(4) (2012).
[30] Daniel Charles, *Master Mind: The Rise and Fall of Fritz Haber, the Nobel Laureate Who
Launched the Age of Chemical Warfare* (New York: Ecco, 2005), 147.
[31] Grinnell Jones, Nitrogen: Its Fixation, Its Uses in Peace and War. *The Quarterly Journal
of Economics* 34(3) (May 1920), 419.
[32] E. J. Pranke, The Cyanamid Industry – World Status, *The American Fertilizer Handbook*
(April 1916), 80.

FEEDING THE HUNGRY AS A STRATEGY OF WAR

Alongside military regulation of food to force a nation's surrender, optimize soldiers' fighting, and produce munitions, the First World War's transnational war economy exploited the power of food through the development of a system of global food aid. Although the military value of food deprivation seemed obvious – starving civilian populations was expected to hamper weapons production and destabilize enemy governments – the strategic provisioning of specific populations became for the first time crucial to the war effort as well. Shaped by the powerful vision of Herbert Hoover, international food relief programs flourished during the war and postwar years, creating a rhetoric for framing food relief that is still relevant today. Existing alongside, rather than in opposition to, the "hunger weapon" of the blockade, this particular form of food aid merged an apolitical humanitarian gesture based on an empathetic sense of shared humanity with a strategic use of food as political pressure and ultimately as weapon of war.

The first food relief program to emerge out of the World War was the Committee for the Relief of Belgium (CRB), a program that existed for almost the entire duration of war and extended into the postwar years. Cast as a project of pure humanitarianism, the CRB won support from both Triple Entente and Central Powers, who all saw the desire to feed hungry people as proof of their own humanity and of the cruelty of the war.

In August 1914, the German army invaded Belgium, a highly urban nation with limited capability for domestic food production. In a military takeover that became infamous for atrocities committed against the civilian population, the "Rape of Belgium" focused international attention on victims of German brutality. However, while the media initially focused on graphic stories of mutilation, mass executions, and sexual assault, it was Germany's control over Belgium's food supply that most threatened Belgian civilians – and that inspired international action. In Belgium, the normal hardships of military defeat and occupation were compounded by the German military's policy of aggressive food requisitioning. As one officer explained in a letter home:

In November [1914] we village commandants were given the instruction to confiscate all grain, have it threshed, and send it to Germany in so far as it was not needed by the army. The population was to be left with nothing, and was to be provided with food by Switzerland. In December this was changed so that the population was allowed 200 grams of wheat per day until May 1. Now in January

[1915], the order arrives for all troops to take over the task of tilling the fields with wheat, oats, etc. so that we get the benefit of the next harvest.[33]

Although the German occupation was the initial cause of the country's food shortage, the growing hunger of the civilian population quickly became intertwined with the larger food-war economy of the First World War. Occupied by Germany, Belgium was now enemy territory, and the British blockade explicitly prevented attempts by the Belgian government to purchase food internationally. Within months of the outbreak of the war, the increasingly dire situation in Belgium was drawing sympathetic international attention. On October 22, 1914, Herbert Hoover, at the time working in Europe to help organize the evacuation of American citizens, announced the official formation of the CRB, which aimed to distribute private food donations to hungry Belgian civilians.[34]

In order to achieve his goals, Hoover needed to create an independent organization that could secure cooperation from the main belligerents. The British government had to allow neutral shipments through the block-ade, while the German government promised not to seize the food for its own population; the American public had to approve the costs. Through careful negotiation, Hoover convinced all sides to support the delivery and distribution of foodstuffs to Belgium and, in 1915, to allow direct subsidies from the Triple Entente governments. By the end of the war, the CRB was supplying about two-thirds of Belgium's civilian food needs.[35] In 1917, Germany's declaration of unrestricted submarine warfare led to the United States' entry into the war; nonetheless, the CRB managed to retain its de facto status of neutrality. The organization became the main channel of communication between Germany and Great Britain, granting the United States a unique kind of political power through humanitarian action. By the time the program officially ended in August 1919, the CRB had become, as a laudatory 1929 essay proclaimed, "an organization without precedent in international relations."[36]

Especially impressive was Hoover's success in gaining the support of the American public for a massive relief program targeting a little-known

---

[33] Kramer, *Dynamic of Destruction*, 42.

[34] Benjamin Weissman, *Herbert Hoover and Famine Relief to Soviet Russia, 1921–1923* (Stanford, CA: Hoover Institution Publications, 1974), 23.

[35] Isabel Hull, *Absolute Destruction: Military Culture and the Practices of War in Imperial Germany* (Ithaca, NY: Cornell University Press, 2005), 230.

[36] George Gay, *Public Relations of the Commission for Relief in Belgium*, vol. 1 (Stanford, CA: Stanford University Press, 1929), v.

European nation, convincing the population that "great as the sacrifice may be on our part, we should find ample compensation in the carrying on of this task in the prestige which it would win for our country and its ideals."[37] Within this new rhetoric of humanitarianism, hunger was redefined. Rather than being a weapon of war, hunger itself became the enemy. Posters and benefits for the CRB reminded the American public that "for three years America has fought starvation in Belgium. Will you eat less wheat, meat, fats and sugar that we may still send food in ship loads?" Popular journals and newspapers reproduced letters from food aid recipients, explicitly and implicitly suggesting future returns for present American generosity. American food aid deliberately emphasized children as recipients because they embodied the idea that this aid would reap long-term profits, as children grew into grateful and politically conscious adults.

The CRB was the only food-aid program that existed parallel to the war itself, where it served as a direct counterpart to the British food blockade. Though rarely described in those terms, food aid was thus as much a part of the war machine as the blockade, signaling a new strategy of war within which the provisioning of food could have as much significance as the deliberate starving of enemies. Recent scholarship on the First World War has challenged the conventional chronology and geography of the war, pointing out that violence and political upheaval continued for years after the official cessation of hostilities in November 1918. The new wartime food economy clearly illustrates this, as the signing of the Armistice ended neither food aid nor food blockade. Germany's military defeat only encouraged countries around the world to continue seeing food as an effective means of regulating political power and economic strength. Thus, while both blockade and aid initially emerged as part of the war effort, their continued existence after war's end reveals how central they had become to the global food economy.

The devastating food shortages that spread throughout much of the world at war's end made Hoover's early experimentations with feeding Belgians seem especially well timed. From an American perspective, the end of hostilities meant a looming economic crisis as vast markets for millions of pounds of wheat and corn threatened to disappear. Compounding the problem was the sudden glut in nitrogen. When the war ended in 1918, economists and scientists in both Europe and the United States were deeply worried over how to dispose of their

---

[37] Ibid., 236–237.

tremendous supplies of nitrogen now that bombs and other explosives were no longer required in such vast quantities. Farmers were the lucky recipients, seeming to illustrate the world's limitless appetite for nitrogen, which provided, in the enthusiastic words of an American economist, "fertilizer in peace and munitions in war."[38] International food aid meant that America's food surplus – initially sustained by wartime exports to Britain and Belgium – could be transformed into postwar political power and economic wealth.

By continually emphasizing the economic and political gains for Americans of feeding hungry people, Hoover envisioned a new sort of charity that garnered the giver substantial profits and took advantage of war-induced hunger. Hoover gained the support of President Wilson for a large-scale postwar food aid program by emphasizing its financial rewards leading Congress to approve the funding of the American Relief Administration (ARA) in February 1919. The ARA ensured that American food became, in Hoover's proud words, "the medium of exchange between the United States and the liberated nations of Europe."[39]

Even more important than financial profit was the political leverage gained by regulating postwar food consumption. Indeed, this was at the heart of Hoover's particular vision of food aid, wherein

it was hoped that the effect of food arriving suddenly from a distance, by an unseen hand, without price or compensation, would do much to develop their ideals of justice, altruism and citizenship and perhaps obliterate in a large part the influences of the degrading environment of the war.[40]

"Altruism" and "citizenship" were not simply generic humanitarian or economic values, but specific political ones. Food promised to gain support for democracy and capitalism and weaken support for communism. In a powerful mingling of fearmongering with the language of Christian brotherhood, Hoover evoked "scenes of long lines of emaciated women and children" throughout Central Europe, while insisting that "not only should this pull at our hearts, but beyond this it is a menace to our very safety."[41] He deliberately equated hunger with a threat to American prosperity and political stability, and suggested that food was an effective

[38] Jones, Nitrogen, 428.
[39] Bane and Lutz, *Organization of American Relief in Europe, 1918–1919*, 416.
[40] Frank Surface and Raymond Bland, *American Food in the World War and Reconstruction Period* (Stanford, CA: Stanford University Press, 1931), 84.
[41] Herbert Hoover, *Food in War* (London: W. H. Smith & Son, 1918), 11.

way of controlling foreign nations' political development. As Wilson explained to Congress in January 1919: "Bolshevism cannot be stopped by force, but it can be stopped by food."[42] Thus, the political demands of the postwar moment demanded a reconfiguration of the CRB's initial brand of humanitarian food aid. The war seemed to prove that both hunger and satiety could be manipulated to determine the fate of nations and of peoples.

GERMANY AS ENEMY AND VICTIM

The close connections between food deprivation and food provisioning are most obvious in the case of Germany, the country that was the primary target of hunger blockades as well as the major recipient of American food aid. Both blockade and aid were used to shape Germany's political and economic landscape, militaristic food projects that were only conceivable in the emergent economy of Total War.

The armistice that Germany signed in 1918 unequivocally stated that "the existing blockade conditions set up by the allied and associated powers ... remain unchanged."[43] At the time of the Armistice, both the British and the French argued that only the continuation of civilian hunger would ensure that the German government acquiesce to the harsh demands of the Versailles negotiations. In February 1919, a fact-finding commission organized by Winston Churchill recommended that, as long as "Germany is still an enemy country, it would be inadvisable to remove the menace of starvation by a too sudden and abundant supply of foodstuffs. This menace is a powerful lever for negotiation at an important moment."[44] Thus, the blockade was reinterpreted from being a "weapon of war" to a guarantor of peace. Deliberately induced hunger shifted from a strategy to destabilize the German war effort to a method of political pressure.

The signing of the Versailles Treaty in June 1919 finally opened up Germany for international aid, and Hoover immediately began advocating for food distribution programs. Unsurprisingly, there was initially widespread resistance among the Allies to sending foodstuffs to the

---

[42] Bane and Lutz, *Organization of American Relief in Europe, 1918–1919*, 691.

[43] Surface and Bland, *American Food in the World War and Reconstruction Period*, 193.

[44] Cited in N. P. Howard, The Social and Political Consequences of the Allied Food Blockade of Germany, 1918–19. *German History* 11(2) (April 1993), 183.

enemy. In typically hysterical language, the English *Sunday Times* warned "the sentimental folk who cry out for pity for the German children" lest they "forget that Germany used most of her milk for munitions purposes."[45] Nonetheless, despite popular resistance in both Europe and the United States, in the summer of 1919 Hoover asked the Society of Friends to take on this relief. Between 1919 and 1925, the European Children's Fund (ECF) distributed a total of $3 million worth of food donated by the American public in Germany. German-Americans sent an estimated $120,000,000 in private aid between 1919 and 1921.[46] Between 1923 and 1924 American philanthropists independently formed the American Committee for the Relief of German Children. The program raised more than $4 million in private donations to allow for the continuation of feeding programs, which at their peak reached more than a million German children as well as pregnant and nursing women.[47] Ultimately, amongst all European nations devastated by postwar food shortages, Germany received the largest amount of American food relief, totaling approximately 1,215,000 tons.[48]

The remarkable scale of food aid sent to Germany implies that the British blockade had been successful at starving the German people. However, the impact of the blockade upon the civilian population is difficult to ascertain and more variable than often assumed. Ironically, Germany proved susceptible to the British blockade because of the country's especially modern food economy, which was entirely dependent upon markets and trade and an advanced infrastructure system. Densely packed cities were non-sustaining in foodstuffs, making them particularly vulnerable to disturbances in transportation and distribution. In contrast, small cities and towns generally maintained stable health during the war despite widespread discontent with the food situation, while rural areas often showed little reduction in food intake. As a result, urban populations, especially those that lived in large cities, suffered disproportionately. The consequences of inadequate diets especially ravaged the inhabitants of institutions and the elderly, who had high mortality rates

---

[45] Bane and Lutz, *Organization of American Relief in Europe, 1918–1919*, 797–798.

[46] Cited in Charles Strickland, American Aid to Germany, 1919 to 1921. *The Wisconsin Magazine of History* 45(4) (Summer, 1962), 257.

[47] Merle Curtis, *American Philanthropy Abroad* (New Brunswick, NJ: Rutgers University Press, 1963), 277.

[48] William Arnold-Forster, *The Blockade 1914–1919: Before the Armistice – and After* (Oxford: Clarendon Press, 1939), 31.

because of their isolation and inadequate access to social services and familial support.[49]

In fact, despite hyperbolic claims by the German media that the British blockade had murdered millions of civilians, recent statistical analysis suggests that blockade-induced food shortages did not directly cause mass starvation.[50] Nonetheless, during the war years Germany reported a total of 762,796 "extra" civilian deaths – that is to say, deaths in excess of what would have been expected based on prewar rates.[51] These increased mortality rates were primarily due to a wide array of sicknesses ranging from TB to dysentery, almost all of which were influenced by the inadequate food supply.[52] The most deadly was the outbreak of the Spanish Influenza, which infected 20 million people in Europe and North America between 1918 and 1920.[53] Influenza and related pneumonias ravaged a weakened Germany in the wake of the war and were responsible for the deaths of more than 200,000 men and women – giving the (postwar) winter of 1918 a higher civilian mortality rate than any month during the actual war.[54]

Ultimately, one of the most important consequences of the blockade was not the biologic harms caused by malnutrition, but the political instability caused by a population outraged at its government for not better protecting it against the harms of the blockade.[55] Food aid targeted Germany specifically because of this political instability. Hunger had been expected to bring the country to its knees during the war; food was supposed to nullify the threat of a "prostrate Germany" during the

---

[49] Richard Sautmann, *Dann bleibt er besser an der Front: Kommunalverwaltung, Kriegsfürsorge und Lebensmittelversorgung in Oldenburg 1914–1918* (Isensee: Florian, 2012), 176.

[50] Avner Offer, *The First World War: An Agrarian Interpretation* (Oxford: Oxford University Press, 1991), 38.

[51] Eckart Schremmer, Deutsche Lebensmittelimporte und ihre Finanzierung zwischen Waffenstillstand und Friedensvertrag. Das Hungerjahr 1918–19. *Beiträge zur Wirtschaftsgeschichte* 6 (1978), 629.

[52] Anne Roerkohl, *Hungerblockade und Heimatfront: Die kommunale Lebensmittel-Versorgung in Westfalen während des Ersten Weltkrieges* (Stuttgart: F. Steiner, 1991), 309.

[53] Wolfgang Eckart, The Most Extensive Experiment That Imagination Can Produce: Violence of War, Emotional Stress and German Medicine. In Roger Chickering and Stig Forster, eds., *Great War, Total War: Combat and Mobilization on the Western Front, 1914–1918* (Cambridge: Cambridge University Press, 2000), 138.

[54] Monica Black, *Death in Berlin: From Weimar to Divided Germany* (Cambridge: Cambridge University Press, 2000), 22.

[55] See Davis, *Home Fires Burning*, for a detailed discussion of the political consequences of food shortages for the German wartime and postwar governments.

chaos of the postwar period. The Russian Revolution had seemed to prove a link between hunger and communism – and no European nation seemed both as radical and as hungry as Germany. Journalist Henry Brailsford traveled through the former enemy nation in the wake of the war, warning that hunger was ensuring that "the whole current of political thought is 'to the left.'"[56] British diplomat Harold Nicholson warned in March 1919 that the Germans "have always got the trump card, Bolshevism. They will go bolshevist the moment they feel it is hopeless to get good terms. The only hope, therefore, is to give them food and peace at once."[57] Ultimately, Germany's postwar relief program was to become paradigmatic for the new politics of food aid.

American food aid to Germany is still today seen as a tremendous success. Hundreds of thousands of lunches were distributed in schools to children deemed needy enough to qualify, and an entire generation of Germans fondly remembered its "Hoover lunches." Both the German public and the German government believed that food aid was indispensable for restoring popular health in the wake of the British blockade. Between 1919 and 1924, German medical, religious, and political leaders called for American food aid in particular, citing particular cultural and economic benefits to both Germany and the United States.[58] Germany's recovery and reintegration into Europe after its ignominious defeat – above all the fact that it did not "go communist" – seemed to validate Hoover's strategic food aid policies. (The country's embrace of Nazism in the 1930s never challenged the assumed success of food aid to Germany.) During the chaos of the war and postwar years, Hoover's ability to present food aid as a universal humanitarian concern that transcended local politics shaped subsequent food aid projects as well as inspiring a new vision of global security that saw scarcity as a real threat to American peace and prosperity.[59]

CONCLUSION

By the end of the war, the idea that food was a weapon had been so oft repeated that it had become a cliché. Citizens around the world

---

[56] Henry Noel Brailsford, *Across the Blockade: A Record of Travels in Enemy Europe* (New York: Harcourt, Brace and Howe, 1919), 122.

[57] Colin Storer, *Britain and the Weimar Republic: The History of a Cultural Relationship* (London: I. B. Tauris, 2010), 46.

[58] See Bundesarchiv (BArch) R 431 / 1253 and BArch R 431 / 1256.

[59] Nick Cullather, *The Hungry World: America's Cold War Battle against Poverty in Asia* (Cambridge, MA: Harvard University Press, 2010), 22.

understood that inadequate food supply was equivalent to military defeat; at the same time, they had learned to see the contents of their dinner plates as directly linked to military resources as diverse as glycerin, nitrogen, and poison gas. In turn, regulating civilian food distribution and consumption had become as crucial to the war effort as training soldiers or munitions production. The widespread usage of food blockades during the war, most famously the British "Hunger Blockade" of Germany, confirmed that hunger was the only effective weapon in a Total War of constant stalemates and unfathomable scales of loss. At the same time, the emergent economy of global warfare incorporated strategies of food provisioning that coexisted alongside such strategies of restricting food's circulation.

Blocking food and shipping food were thus at the heart of the First World War, leaving lasting legacies for modern warfare as well as the modern food economy. The "deployment" of food as both a political and military weapon inspired the development of food aid and blockade programs, two quintessentially modern methods of regulating food consumption. Both strategies developed in relation to one another during the First World War, but both also extended into peacetime. The British blockade against Germany continued for almost a year after the Armistice, not officially ending until the signing of the Versailles Treaty in 1919; Hoover's food aid programs continued to feed populations across Europe until 1924. Different as food aid and food blockade initially seem, their parallel development over the course of the war and postwar years reveals that they were both crucial components of the new food economy that developed during the First World War. Examining the war from an environmental perspective helps to explain the many ways in which food promised to win the war. Naval technologies that remade the oceans enabled the movement of foods around the world; scientific innovations, most importantly nitrogen-fixing, crafted a new relationship between agriculture and military technology; and food was at the heart of the increasingly elaborate networks that linked nations and peoples around the world, placing home fronts and war fronts, and belligerent and neutral countries, in relationships of codependence. While it was not exactly true that, as a Georgia State College of Agriculture poster claimed, "beans are bullets [and] potatoes are powder," the First World War did mark a crucial turning point in the history of how, what, and why the world ate. This is one of the most important and durable legacies of the war – food might not have won the war, but it ultimately changed the meaning of war.

3

Dissolution before Dissolution

The Crisis of the Wartime Food Regime in Austria-Hungary

Ernst Langthaler

INTRODUCTION

During the First World War food became a scarce – and thus decisive – resource for the Habsburg Empire's warfare, with regard to the armed forces behind the war front as well as the people at the "home front."[1] For contemporaries this was rather surprising, since the Dual Monarchy was normally self-sufficient in basic foodstuffs; substantial imports were only necessary in years of bad harvests. While historiography has evaluated the food crisis as a key factor of Austria-Hungary's wartime society,[2] the environmental implications have been largely disregarded so far. This chapter argues that a full account of the wartime food crisis has to move beyond the nutrition of soldiers and civilians. Human nutrition is based upon animal and plant nutrition via a multitude of food chains – and the erosion of this nutritional basis became decisive for the crisis of Austria-Hungary's food regime during the war. Thus, human, animal, and plant nutrition are conceived as integral parts of the wartime food regime. The food regime in general and the food chains in particular comprise material and energetic flows between production and consumption as well as the regulatory framework of formal and informal institutions.[3]

---

[1] I would like to thank the editors of this volume, especially Martin Schmid, and two anonymous referees for their suggestions.
[2] See Zdeněk Jindra, Der wirtschaftliche Zerfall Österreich-Ungarns. In Alice Teichowa and Herbert Matis, eds., *Österreich und die Tschechoslowakei 1918–1938* (Vienna: Böhlau, 1996), 17–50.
[3] See Philipp McMichael, *Food Regimes and Agrarian Questions* (Halifax/Winnipeg: Fernwood Publishing, 2013).

FOOD PRODUCTION

According to the official figures, agricultural production in Austria-Hungary dramatically deteriorated during the war (Table 3.1). The agricultural component of the gross domestic product (GDP), i.e. the total value of marketed agricultural products and services, decreased from 9,430 to 5,639 million crowns in absolute terms or by 40% in relative terms in the period 1913–1917. Compared to the Hungarian part of the Dual Monarchy (–34%), the contraction proved even more severe in the Austrian part (–48%). According to the figures of selected crops, both components of arable production – acreage and yields per hectare – decreased during the war (Tables 3.2 and 3.3). However, considerable regional differences emerged: whereas acreage declined by nearly one half in Austria, it was quite stable in Hungary. Although both territories experienced declining yields per hectare, the shortfalls in Austria were more dramatic than those in Hungary. For instance, the loss in bread grain yields in the period 1913–1917 amounted to 38% for wheat and 44% for rye in Austria compared to 20% for wheat and 19% for rye in Hungary. The deterioration of agricultural resources affected the livestock as well, especially in Austria with declining numbers of cattle (–20%), pigs (–61%), and sheep (–15%) in the period 1910–1917.[4]

TABLE 3.1 *Agricultural GDP in Austria-Hungary, 1913–1917*

	1913	1914	1915	1916	1917
Austria					
million crowns (1913 prices)	4,256	3,687	3,221	2,910	2,211
index (1913 = 100)	100	87	76	68	52
Hungary					
million crowns (1913 prices)	5,174	4,565	4,789	3,943	3,428
index (1913 = 100)	100	88	93	76	66
Austria-Hungary					
million crowns (1913 prices)	9,430	8,252	8,010	6,853	5,639
index (1913 = 100)	100	88	85	73	60

Source: Max Stephan Schulze, Austria-Hungary's Economy in World War I. In Stephen Broadberry and Mark Harrison, eds., *The Economics of World War I* (Cambridge: Cambridge University Press, 2005), 77–111, here 85ff.

---

[4] See Hans Löwenfeld-Russ, *Die Regelung der Volksernährung im Kriege* (Vienna: Hölder-Pichler-Tempsky, 1926), 198ff.

TABLE 3.2 *Production of selected crops in Austria, 1913–1917*

	1913	1914	1915	1916	1917
Acreage	Size (1,000 ha)		Index (1913 = 100)		
Wheat	1,213	55	61	67	51
Rye	1,964	65	76	80	59
Barley	1,092	64	69	73	54
Oats	1,905	60	70	77	49
Maize	284	65	71	51	–
Potatoes	1,276	56	71	78	69
Yields	Size (100 kg/ha)		Index (1913 = 100)		
Wheat	13.4	115	88	69	62
Rye	13.8	108	75	59	56
Barley	16.0	114	63	66	41
Oats	14.1	118	57	67	71
Maize	11.9	122	120	83	–
Potatoes	90.6	119	106	69	73

Ibid., 92.

TABLE 3.3 *Production of selected crops in Hungary, 1913–1918*

	1913	1914	1915	1916	1917	1918
Acreage	Size (1,000 ha)		Index (1913 = 100)			
Wheat	3,453	104	104	95	98	98
Rye	1,102	105	103	96	97	95
Barley	1,232	94	97	89	83	80
Oats	1,277	91	92	91	86	83
Maize	2,916	98	99	92	89	91
Potatoes	565	101	104	97	99	79
Yields	Size (100 kg/ha)		Index (1913 = 100)			
Wheat	13.2	68	91	76	80	62
Rye	12.2	82	89	77	81	68
Barley	14.7	84	75	72	55	63
Oats	12.1	96	88	94	63	56
Maize	18.4	96	84	55	62	56
Potatoes	78.7	107	109	88	59	77

Ibid., 93.

Military concentration areas experienced even more dramatic losses. In the crown land of Tyrol near the southwestern frontline, for instance, farming families were heavily hit by military requisitions of hay and livestock.[5] Despite regional differences, the Habsburg Empire's agro-systems lost much of their performance during the war period.

Beyond the national scale, regional developments in the crown land of Lower Austria – the hinterland of the capital city of Vienna – indicate the considerable variation of land use and productivity (Figure 3.1). From the eve to the end of the war, the bulk of the 71 regional agro-systems severely reduced yields per hectare and slightly shifted from feed to food crops such as grain and potatoes in the period 1914–1917. The Alpine district of Gaming showed low land productivity and a strong emphasis on feed

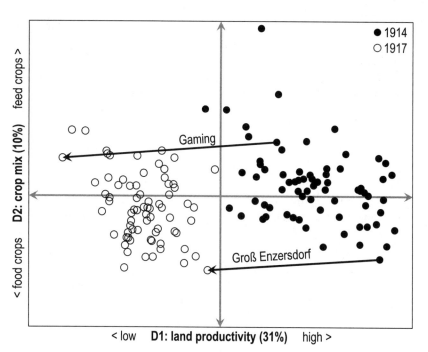

FIGURE 3.1 Land use and productivity in 71 districts of Lower Austria, 1914–1917
Source: Principal Components Analysis of Provincial Archives of Lower Austria, Anbau- und Erntestatistik nach niederösterreichischen Gerichtsbezirken 1909–1918. See Bauer, Alles für die Hauptstadt?.

[5] See Matthias Rettenwander, *Stilles Heldentum? Wirtschafts- und Sozialgeschichte Tirols im Ersten Weltkrieg* (Innsbruck: Universitätsverlag Wagner, 1997), 80–92.

crops compared to the more productive and breadstuff-oriented district of Groß Enzersdorf in the lowlands near Vienna. The farming community of Gaming, disfavored with regard to climate, soil, and relief as well as market connection, strongly cut back the cultivation of arable crops; consequently, land productivity fell from 16 to 4 wheat units[6] per hectare of cultivated area and fallow land increased from 3 to 45% of the acreage. Their counterpart in the favorable area of Groß Enzersdorf was able to keep up arable farming on a higher level; thus, land productivity decreased from 25 to 12 wheat units per hectare cultivated area and fallow land rose from 3 to 13% of the acreage. Both cases indicate the increasing diversity of regional agro-systems with regard to land use and productivity under war conditions.[7]

Since agriculture can be conceived of as a sort of "colonization" of nature by humans,[8] the deterioration of food production resulted from societal as well as environmental impacts, both more or less related to warfare. A purely societal impact was the devastation of agricultural land by the hostilities on the northeastern front. In the early stages of the war the Russian occupation of parts of the Austrian territory – Galicia, which accounted for about one-third of the country's grain harvest, and Bukovina – ran dry an important source of domestic food supply. Due to widespread devastation through Russian capture and Austrian recapture, these crown lands never regained their full agricultural performance until the end of the war. An environmental impact is indicated by the 1914 fall in crop yields in Hungary – in contrast to their rise in Austria – as a result of adverse climatic conditions.[9]

The most decisive impact on wartime agricultural production – the erosion of animal and plant nutrition – was both societal and environmental in essence. The mobilization of resources for the war effort led to a persistent labor shortage, lack of draught animals, and scarcity of organic and mineral fertilizers. The assignment of prisoners of war, though impressive in numbers, was no efficient solution to the lack of domestic farm holders, servants, and laborers conscripted to the armed forces. According to contemporary estimations, the performance of Russian

---

[6] Wheat units are used as basic units for the aggregation of different agricultural products.

[7] See Martin Bauer, Alles für die Hauptstadt? Agrarproduktion im Land um Wien während des Ersten Weltkrieges. In Elisabeth Loinig and Reinelde Motz-Linhart, eds., *Fern der Front – mitten im Krieg 1914–1918. Alltagsleben im Hinterland* (St. Pölten: NÖ Institut für Landeskunde, 2016), 45–67, here 57–67.

[8] See Marina Fischer-Kowalski and Helmut Haberl, Metabolism and Colonization: Modes of Production and the Physical Exchange between Societies and Nature. *Innovation: The European Journal of Social Science Research* 6 (1993), 415–442.

[9] See Schulze, Austria-Hungary's Economy in World War I, 92–94.

prisoners of war amounted to about 30–50% of that of the experienced domestic workforce.[10] The livestock was threatened not only by the conscription of horses but also by the shortage of feeding stuffs. Since imports of oilseeds ran dry and domestic feed grains and root crops were redirected for human uses, farm animals were relegated to inferior ersatz matter. Straw and hay meal, dried blood from slaughterhouses and kitchen waste, instead of concentrates (e.g., oilseed cake), as well as corn stover and heather, instead of roughage (e.g., meadow hay), were promoted by scientists, bureaucrats, and companies. Many of these dubious products were marketed under fanciful brand names such as "Triumph," "Ideal," and "Lucrative." As a consequence of inferior feed rations, the animals' traction force, slaughter weight, and milk yield, as well as the quantity and quality of manure, deteriorated.[11]

The shortage of manure due to impoverished animal nutrition had an adverse impact on plant nutrition. Austria-Hungary's crucial prewar sources of nitrogen fertilizer – Chile saltpeter from overseas and ammonium sulfate from coking plants – soon ran dry due to the sea blockade and armaments efforts. In 1916 the authorities decided to build plants for the production of lime-nitrogen according to the Frank-Caro procedure at suitable locations in Bohemia (brown coal), Styria (hydropower), and Transylvania (natural gas), but without any significant effect on agricultural production. The provision of phosphor fertilizers (guano, ground basic slag, superphosphate, etc.) proved precarious as well. The large-scale excavation of bone repositories in Stone Age caves to be used as phosphor-rich fertilizer did not start before the end of the war.[12] The substitution of domestic fertilizers (e.g., lime-nitrogen) or ersatz matter (e.g., crushed bones) for fertilizers imported prior to the war proved as ineffective as the mobilization of soil nutrients through additional application of lime. In the crown land of Tyrol, for instance, the application of mineral fertilizers in the period 1913–1918 decreased from 3,800 to 1,710 tons; this absolute decline coincided with the relative decline of nitrogen and phosphor in favor of potash, the use of which more than quadrupled.[13] In combination with the overuse of potash, the underuse of

[10] See Die Verwendung der Kriegsgefangenen in der Landwirtschaft. *Wiener Landwirtschaftliche Zeitung* 66(1) (January 1, 1916), 1–3.

[11] See Hubert Weitensfelder, Nähr-Stoffe: Nahrungsmittel, Tierfutter und Dünger in der Kriegswirtschaft. In Elisabeth Loinig and Reinelde Motz-Linhart, eds., *Fern der Front – mitten im Krieg 1914–1918. Alltagsleben im Hinterland* (St. Pölten: NÖ Institut für Landeskunde, 2016), 183–198, here 192–194.

[12] Ibid., 183–198, here 194–198. [13] See Rettenwander, *Stilles Heldentum?*, 77.

organic fertilizers due to the reduced and underfed livestock posed a threat to soil organisms, therefore reducing soil fertility.[14] Not surprisingly, in 1919 the agronomic journal *Wiener Landwirtschaftliche Zeitung* complained about the massive "depletion" (*Raubbau*) on the fields during the war period.[15]

The bottlenecks of the material and energetic flows in the regional agro-systems were further narrowed by the actors' farming strategies within the regulatory framework. The attempts of the state authorities to set maximum food prices in favor of the consumers had adverse effects on the producers' motivation to enlarge or at least stabilize farm outputs, especially cereals. In addition to the negative impact of limited absolute prices of cereals at the farm gate, the wartime shifts in the relative prices of arable and animal products led large farmers and estate owners to respond by moving out of bread grain and into animal feed production, converting arable land into meadows and pastures and even using crops needed for human consumption as livestock feed. Such state-induced market incentives had less impact on the subsistence-oriented survival strategies of small and medium peasant families; the families often adjusted their production efforts to the consumption needs of the reduced household.

FOOD DISTRIBUTION

Although the Dual Monarchy as a whole was normally self-sufficient in basic foodstuffs in the prewar period, the degree of self-sufficiency in the two parts, separated by the River Leitha – therefore called "Cisleithania" and "Transleithania" – diverged significantly (Figure 3.2). While Austria was nearly self-sufficient in dairy products, only two-thirds of the bread grain and four-tenths of the maize consumed were domestically produced; compensations for the shortfalls were for the most part imported from Hungary. Moreover, Austria's meat balance was even worse than its grain balance: only one-half of the pigs and three-tenths of the cattle slaughtered were domestically fed; the rest of the meat was of Hungarian origin. These proportions indicate the division of labor between the two parts of the empire that had fostered uneven regional development at least since the mid-eighteenth century: Austria with its industrial cores in Lower Austria,

---

[14] See Frank Uekötter, *Die Wahrheit ist auf dem Feld. Eine Wissensgeschichte der deutschen Landwirtschaft* (Göttingen: Vandenhoeck & Ruprecht, 2010), 183–190.
[15] See Düngemittelnot und Volksernährung. *Wiener Landwirtschaftliche Zeitung* 69(74) (September 13, 1919), 572.

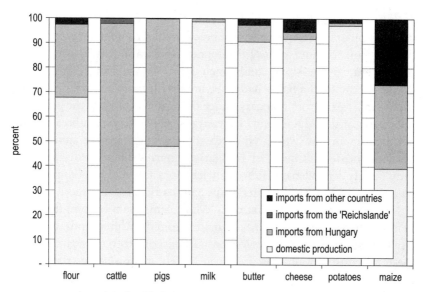

FIGURE 3.2 Austria's food balance, 1909/13
Source: Löwenfeld-Russ, *Die Regelung der Volksernährung im Kriege*, 31. The *Reichslande* comprise Bosnia and Herzegovina, which were occupied by Austria-Hungary in 1878.

Styria, Bohemia, Moravia, and Silesia delivered textiles and technological equipment; these regions were surrounded by agrarian peripheries with predominant peasant communities and scattered estates. Hungary, as an agrarian periphery dominated by large estates with wage laborers, delivered arable and livestock products. This interregional division of labor was prompted by the 1850 Austro-Hungarian customs union that had opened up the Viennese food market with its ultimately 2 million consumers to Magyar food producers, processors, and traders. Thus, flour mills and other branches of food processing formed the most dynamic sector of Hungary's industry, which, as a whole, faced fierce competition from Austria's export-oriented industry.[16]

Feeding the 2 million inhabitants of the imperial capital was one of the key tasks of the Austro-Hungarian food regime in the prewar era. Depending on the kinds of foodstuffs, the regions of origin of Vienna's food provision lay close to or far from the city. Despite highly productive

[16] See John Komlos, *Die Habsburgermonarchie als Zollunion. Die Wirtschaftsentwicklung Österreich-Ungarns im 19. Jahrhundert* (Vienna: Österreichischer Bundesverlag, 1986), 89–99, 137–141.

arable regions in the flat and hilly lands, Austria was far from meeting its urban population's requirements of bread grain. From the average annual consumption of flour of 144.6 kilograms per capita in Austria in the prewar era, in the Alpine lands, including Vienna, 77.5 kilograms per capita – more than a half – had to be imported; these imports originated for the most part from Hungary. Since the arable regions of the plain and hilly parts of the Alpine lands were largely self-sufficient in bread grain, Vienna's import rate was surely much above average. In short, most of the Viennese bread was made of Hungarian flour. Vienna's provision with meat largely depended on Hungarian deliveries as well. In 1914 more than half of the animals for slaughter – especially cattle, pigs, and sheep – on the city's central livestock market of St. Marx came from beyond the River Leitha, whereas only one-third originated from the Alpine lands. Only the city's provision with milk was for the most part of Austrian origin: in 1908 the total consumption was produced largely in Lower Austria (71%), followed by adjacent Moravia (17%); Hungary only delivered a small fraction (12%).[17]

All in all, two spaces of Viennese food provision interfered with each other: a ring around the city encompassing Lower and Upper Austria, southern Moravia, and western Hungary, especially for milk provision, and a corridor connecting the city with the interior of Hungary, especially for grain provision. Both spaces were limited by the relation of retail prices and transportation costs of foodstuffs. Within the ring around Vienna, the short and therefore cheap network of roads between places of production and consumption had acted in favor of branches such as dairy farming. Within the Austro-Hungarian corridor, arable farming and livestock breeding had been promoted through long but – thanks to steam-engine technology – relatively cheap transport connections: the River Danube and the emerging railroad network with links via Temesvár/Timişoara and Debrecen to the southern and eastern Hungarian regions highly favorable to agricultural uses. In short,

---

[17] See Ernst Langthaler, Food and Nutrition (Austria-Hungary). In Ute Daniel et al., eds., *1914–1918-online. International Encyclopedia of the First World War*, http://dx.doi.org/ 10.15463/ie1418.10796 (accessed April 17, 2017); Ernst Langthaler, Die Großstadt und ihr Hinterland. In Alfred Pfoser and Andreas Weigl, eds., *Im Epizentrum des Zusammenbruchs. Wien im Ersten Weltkrieg* (Vienna: Metroverlag, 2013), 232–239; Ernst Langthaler, Vom transnationalen zum regionalen Hinterland – und retour. Wiens Nahrungsmittelversorgung vor, im und nach dem Ersten Weltkrieg. In Stefan Karner and Philipp Lesiak, eds., *Erster Weltkrieg. Globaler Konflikt – lokale Folgen. Neue Perspektiven* (Innsbruck/Vienna/Bolzano: Studienverlag, 2014), 307–318.

Vienna's hinterland prior to the war was shaped both regionally and transnationally.[18]

Vienna's highly effective food provision network dramatically deteriorated during the war. The stream of foodstuffs through the transnational corridor more and more ran dry. By 1917 Austrian imports from Hungary compared to the prewar level had declined to 2% for grain, 3% for flour, 29% for cattle, 19% for pigs, and 17% for milk (Figure 3.3). Deliveries to the municipal animal market in the period 1914–1918 shrank by 70% (Figure 3.4). At the same time, the regional distribution of the Viennese sources of food changed as indicated by the different percentages of the decline of deliveries from Hungary (–76%) and the Alpine lands, especially Lower Austria (–56%). All in all, Vienna's area of food provision was relocated from the Austro-Hungarian corridor to the Lower Austrian ring – except for milk flows from the city's regional hinterland, which nearly ran dry by the end of the war (Figure 3.5).

Vienna's shrinking food basis reflected not only the declining amount of foodstuffs available to the Habsburg Empire but also their unequal distribution, especially between "Cisleithania" and "Transleithania." This

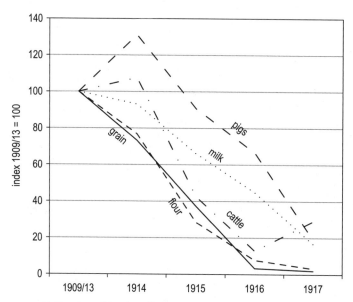

FIGURE 3.3 Deliveries of foodstuffs from Hungary to Austria, 1909/13–1917
Source: Löwenfeld-Russ, *Die Regelung der Volksernährung im Kriege*, 61.

[18] See Langthaler, *Die Großstadt und ihr Hinterland.*

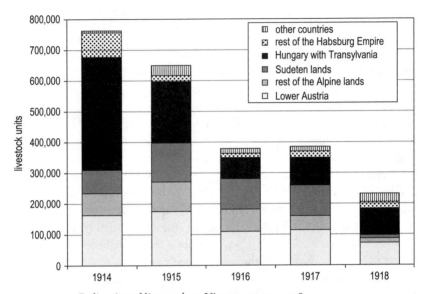

FIGURE 3.4 Deliveries of livestock to Vienna, 1914–1918
Source: Bundesministerium für Volksernährung, ed., *Das österreichische Ernährungsproblem* (Vienna, 1921), 167–173.

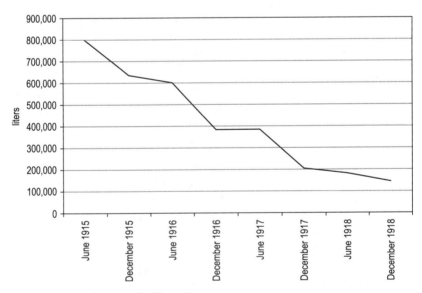

FIGURE 3.5 Deliveries of milk to Vienna, 1915–1918
Source: Löwenfeld-Russ, *Die Regelung der Volksernährung im Kriege*, 222.

FIGURE 3.6 Cartoon by Theo Zasche on the Austrian-Hungarian food conflict in the *Österreichische Volkszeitung*, 1917
Source: Österreichische Volkszeitung, October 21, 1917, 9.

problem was debated by the cartoon "Cis und Trans" published 1917 in the Viennese press (Figure 3.6). It contrasts the Austrian part ("Cis") with the Viennese mayor, Richard Weiskirchner, and the federal minister of food, Anton Höfer, desperately begging for food deliveries and – divided by the River Leitha – the Hungarian part ("Trans") with a fat bloke stone-heartedly withholding his multitudinous herd of animals. The inscribed message reflects the Viennese popular sentiment toward "the Hungarians" who violated the values of "moral economy" for nationalist and capitalist motives. However, the wartime balance of bread grain not only proves Austria as a deficit region but also disproves Hungary as a land of plenty (Table 3.4). In Austria the gap between domestic supply of and demand for bread grain even widened. Contrary to the prewar surpluses of bread grain, Hungary's production lagged behind the normal level of consumption with hardly any amounts left to export – except for 1915 when remarkable deliveries went to Germany. Due to the Allied sea blockade, imports were insufficient to fill the empire's food gap – even in 1916 and 1917, when substantial amounts of bread grain were brought from the Habsburg-occupied territories of Romania and Ukraine. Accordingly, material shortage rather than moral hazard explains the unequal distribution of foodstuffs between the two parts of the Habsburg Empire.

TABLE 3.4 *Balance of bread grain in Austria-Hungary, 1909/13–1918*
(*1,000 tons*)

Year	Net Output Austria	Net Output Hungary	Net Imports	Total Consumption	Balance Austria*	Balance Hungary*
1909/13	3,868	5,078	234	9,180	−1,472	+1,148
1914	2,542	3,737	522	6,801	−2,798	−193
1915	2,103	4,707	68	6,878	−3,237	+777
1916	1,765	3,642	541	5,948	−3,575	−288
1917	1,703	3,728	1,164	6,596	−3,637	−202
1918	1,649	3,134	190	4,973	−3,691	−796

* Difference between annual net output and prewar total consumption (Austria: 5,340;
Hungary: 3,930)
Source: Schulze, Austria-Hungary's Economy in World War I, 94; Gratz and Schüller, *Der wirtschaftliche Zusammenbruch Österreich-Ungarns*, 40–46.

However, in Hungary the average calorific value of rations was considerably higher than in Austria, therefore nourishing anti-Magyar sentiments among German and Slavic ethnic groups in the multinational empire.[19]

The Austrian-Hungarian food conflict nourished permanent dispute between the two administrations that was never resolved until the end of the war. The overarching problem was the inefficient institutional framework of coordination between the separate Austrian and Hungarian authorities, involving several subproblems. According to the 1850 customs union, Hungary was allowed – but definitely not obliged – to deliver its food surpluses to Austria. Thus, any delivery commitment was subject to bilateral negotiations via direct correspondence between the two premiers.[20] Moreover, no arrangements had been made for meeting the food requirements of the armed forces and the civilian population in case of war. According to the initial wartime agreement of 1915, the joint army's needs were to be met by the two states in proportion to their respective grain output. This stipulation – which neither party ever fully met – disregarded Austria's dependency on food imports from Hungary. In the face of Austria's deteriorating food situation, Hungary agreed to deliver

---

[19] See Richard Gratz and Richard Schüller, *Der wirtschaftliche Zusammenbruch Österreich-Ungarns. Die Tragödie der Erschöpfung* (Vienna: Hölder-Pichler-Tempsky, 1930), 37–91.
[20] See Gratz and Schüller, *Der wirtschaftliche Zusammenbruch Österreich-Ungarns*, 225–307.

the army's total requirements of bread grain from 1916.[21] Besides the burden of the army's food provision, Hungary had some more arguments to trim back food exports to Austria. Severe food shortages raised the risk of urban riots that might have threatened the Magyar domination of a country predominantly populated by other ethnic groups (Slavs, Romanians, Germans, etc.). Moreover, the food question provided Budapest with a means for raising a protest in Vienna against the disproportionate conscription of domestic peasants to the joint army, expressing concern over its adverse effect on agricultural production.[22] Finally, the Habsburg monarchy never succeeded in establishing a supranational agency for food distribution with adequate executive power. Even the Joint Food Committee (*Gemeinsamer Ernährungsausschuss*), formed in early 1917 after Emperor Franz Joseph's death on the initiative of his successor, Karl, was largely a toothless institution lacking power over the national food administrations in the two halves of the empire.[23]

The struggle for food reached far beyond the Austrian-Hungarian conflict; it also affected the provincial, regional, and local levels.[24] In response to input shortages and price controls, market-oriented farmers underreported actual harvests to the authorities, withheld their grain stocks from delivery to the official distribution channels, and sold considerable proportions of their outputs at far higher prices on the black market. The emergence of a "shadow economy" aggravated the inequality of food distribution between surplus and deficit regions, between countryside and towns, and between wealthier and poorer classes.[25] Moreover, the implementation of central public-private organizations for food

---

[21] See Schulze, Austria-Hungary's Economy in World War I, 95ff.

[22] See Holger H. Herwig, *The First World War. Germany and Austria-Hungary 1914–1918* (London: Bloomsbury Academic, 1997), 277.

[23] See Ottokar Landwehr, *Hunger. Die Erschöpfung der Mittelmächte 1917/18* (Zurich/Leipzig/Vienna: Amalthea Verlag, 1931).

[24] See Matthias König, Ernährungslage und Hunger. In Hermann J. W. Kuprian and Oswald Überegger, eds., *Katastrophenjahre. Der Erste Weltkrieg und Tirol* (Innsbruck: Universtitätsverlag Wagner, 2014), 135–153; Martin Moll, Die Steiermark im Ersten Weltkrieg. *Der Kampf des Hinterlandes ums Überleben 1914–1918* (Vienna: Styria, 2014); Thomas Hellmuth, "Acker und Wiesen wissen nichts von Patriotismus." Kriegswirtschaft im Ersten Weltkrieg. In Oskar Dohle and Thomas Mitterecker, eds., *Salzburg im Ersten Weltkrieg. Fernab der Front – dennoch im Krieg* (Vienna/Cologne/Weimar: Böhlau Verlag, 2014), 47–60; Rudolf Kučera, *Rationed Life. Science, Everyday Life, and Working-Class Politics in the Bohemian Lands, 1914–1918* (New York: Berghahn Books, 2016).

[25] See Gratz and Schüller, *Der wirtschaftliche Zusammenbruch Österreich-Ungarns*, 51–54.

distribution, beginning with the War Grain Distribution Institution (Kriegs-Getreide-Verkehrsanstalt) in 1915, proved rather ineffective with regard to equality. Provided with the double status of public agency and private merchant, this and similar organizations for other foodstuffs (potatoes, sugar, coffee, legumes, fruits, etc.) found that their tasks comprised the purchase of the producers' surpluses at official prices, the storage of the acquired stocks, and their distribution to processors and retailers according to official consumption plans. Incompetence, overload, and corruption prevented the "centrals" (*Zentralen*) from tackling the problem of uneven food distribution. Rather than orderly distribution, a chaotic competition prevailed between crown lands, districts, municipalities, enterprises, and military units – each against all – for any accessible food stock.[26] Finally, the state's attempt to restrain these centrifugal forces by the foundation of central food agencies in Austria (*Amt für Volksernährung*) and Hungary (*Landes-Volksernährungsamt*) in 1916 with subagencies at provincial, district, and municipal levels had limited effect due to lack of executive power.[27]

FOOD CONSUMPTION

The deteriorating production and unequal distribution of food resulted in declining quotas of consumption. The average consumption of bread grains per head in the Habsburg Empire decreased steadily compared to the prewar level (1909/13: 184 kg, 1914: 134 kg, 1915: 136 kg, 1916: 118 kg, 1917: 132 kg, 1918: 101 kg). However, stark differences between and within the two halves of the monarchy emerged; the quota Austrian civilians consumed in 1917 was probably 30% below that of their Hungarian counterparts. The armed forces in general and frontline troops in particular drew on higher – though also declining – allocations of foodstuffs.[28] In order to contain public unrest, the authorities attempted to tackle the scarcity and unequal allocation of food by rationing basic foodstuffs, including bread grains (since 1915), sugar, milk, coffee, fats (since 1916), potatoes, jam (since 1917), and meat (since 1918). The civilian population was classified into "self-supporters" with access to agricultural land and livestock and "non-self-supporters" depending on food purchases. The declining calorific value of the rations in Vienna reflects the worsening food situation in the Habsburg Empire, especially in the Austrian part (Table 3.5). Compared to the average

[26] See Löwenfeld-Russ, *Die Regelung der Volksernährung im Kriege*, 125–130.
[27] Ibid., 290ff.   [28] See Schulze, Austria-Hungary's Economy in World War I, 94–96.

TABLE 3.5 *Calorific value of the daily food ration of "non-self-supporters" in Vienna*

Foodstuffs	At the Time of the Introduction of Food Ration Cards	At the End of War
Flour	300	107
Bread	350	450
Fats	154	51
Meat	29	18
Milk	83	–
Potatoes	171	57
Sugar	166	100
Jam	48	48
Total	1,300	831

Ibid., 335.

intake of a Viennese worker of 2,845 kilocalories in the prewar era, the official ration at the end of the war had shrunk dramatically to 831 kilocalories (–71%) for normal "non-self-supporters" and 1,293 kilocalories (–55%) for "heavy workers." However, the amounts allocated by the food ration cards were rarely available in the retail stores; the real calorific value provided by the food administration was thus considerably lower.[29]

In addition to declining quantities, scarce foodstuffs such as wheat and rye flour were replaced by organic and synthetic surrogates, thus worsening food quality. The more wartime society faced food scarcity, the more scientists proposed alternatives to normal foodstuffs, often with a moralizing undertone. One among many others was chemist Julius Stoklasa, who made a virtue out of necessity by criticizing the prewar middle-class obsession with white bread made from wheat flour as an unhealthy custom; he instead proposed to make dark flour from bran a basic ingredient of bread.[30] Soon after the outbreak of war, the comminution rate of bread grains was raised by order of the authorities. Moreover, the content of wheat and rye flour in the "war bread" was stepwise limited to 50%; the gap was to be filled by barley, oats, and maize flour, as well as potatoes

[29] See Löwenfeld-Russ, *Die Regelung der Volksernährung im Kriege*, 327–360.
[30] See Julius Stoklasa, *Das Brot der Zukunft* (Jena: Gustav Fischer, 1917).

and swedes, thereby diverting scarce resources from animals to humans. Among the livestock, pigs were hardest hit by these measures: as consumers of potatoes and maize, they were conceived as serious competitors of human consumers and thus exceedingly slaughtered.[31] The proposals, experiments, and attempts for "stretching" (*Streckung*) bread and other foodstuffs hardly knew any limitations: even wood dust was used to stretch the "war bread"; though somehow satiable, this surrogate lacked any nutritional value.[32] Besides organic surrogates, a multitude of synthetic ersatz foodstuffs was developed, marketed, and sold: tea ersatz, juice ersatz, egg ersatz, cacao ersatz, goulash ersatz, and so on. An exhibition of ersatz matter in Vienna in summer 1918 addressed the wider audience. It is, however, hard to estimate to what extent these dubious products were actually consumed. More importantly, such makeshifts under wartime pressures fostered the postwar development of food technology.[33]

The quantity and quality of the actual food intake by urban and rural dwellers is difficult to grasp. According to housekeeping files, Viennese working-class families experienced fundamental dietary changes during the war. Two cases highlight the main tendency (Figure 3.7): the lower-middle-class family A experienced a dramatic decline of real income per head by 1917/18. The upper-lower-class family B, though also getting poorer by the end of war, managed to stabilize income in the first years. The per capita food intake reflects the development of family income (Figure 3.8): while for family A the calorific value of the food consumed steadily declined by 19% in total, family B initially improved access to food – probably through access to an allotment garden – until the sharp decline in 1917/18 by 26% in total. In both families the share of protein- and fat-rich food declined in favor of carbohydrate-rich food such as bread, potatoes, and legumes (family A: 76%; family B: 84%). The deteriorating food quantity and quality hit children and juveniles hardest. According to medical examinations of Viennese children soon after the war, 23% were severely undernourished,

---

[31] See Löwenfeld-Russ, *Die Regelung der Volksernährung im Kriege*, 117–125.

[32] See Martin Franc, Bread from Wood: Natural Food Substitutes in the Czech Lands during the First World War. In Ina Zweiniger-Bargielowska and Rachel Duffet, eds., *Food and War in Twentieth Century Europe* (Farnham: Ashgate, 2011), 73–83; Weitensfelder, Nähr-Stoffe, 183–187.

[33] See Franz Vojir, Ersatzlebensmittel im Ersten Weltkrieg in Österreich. In Herbert Matis, Juliane Mikoletzky, and Wolfgang Reiter, eds., *Wirtschaft, Technik und das Militär 1914–1918. Österreich-Ungarn im Ersten Weltkrieg* (Wien/Münster: Lit Verlag, 2014), 253–283.

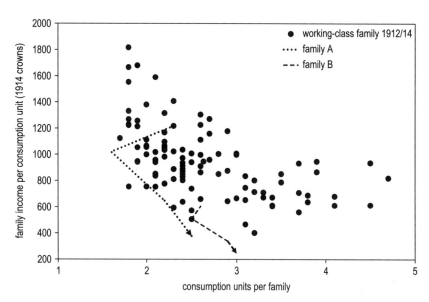

FIGURE 3.7 Size and income of two Viennese working-class families, 1912/14–1917/18

Family A: man: born 1874, plumber helper, 1914/15 military service; woman: no information; daughter: born 1900

Family B: man: born 1865, helper; woman: born 1876, housemaid; son: born 1902

Source: Arbeitsstatistisches Amt im Handelsministerium, ed., Wirtschaftsrechnungen und Lebensverhältnisse von Wiener Arbeiterfamilien in den Jahren 1912 bis 1914, Vienna 1916, 162–166; Helmut Rumpler and Anatol Schmied-Kowarzik, eds., *Weltkriegsstatistik Österreich-Ungarn 1914–1918 (Die Habsburgermonarchie 1848–1918, vol. XI/2)* (Vienna: VÖAW, 2013), 260–269.

56% were undernourished, and 21% were normally fed, with great differences between working- and middle-class districts. The nutritional status of schoolchildren was equally bad or even worse in Lower Austrian industrial cities. However, there was no clear distinction between urban and rural areas: while the arable farming regions in the flat and hilly lands (Vienna neighborhoods, Weinviertel and Waldviertel) showed better results, in the mountainous grassland farming areas (Bucklige Welt and northern fringe of the Alps) the situation was nearly as bad as in most cities (Figure 3.9). The unequal nutritional status of Lower Austrian regions reflects the rural dwellers' uneven access to staple food.

Dealing with food as both material and ideal became the focal point of everyday life in wartime Vienna, as represented in individual and collective memories of the "war bread": it crumbled into thousands of

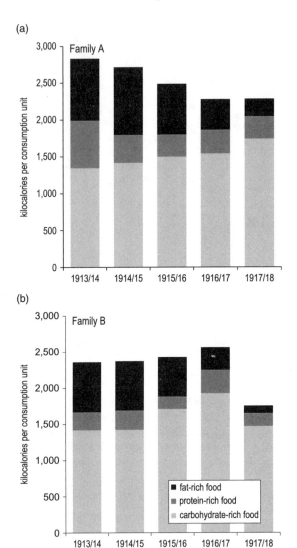

FIGURE 3.8 Calorific intake of two Viennese working-class families, 1913/
14–1917/18
Source: Rumpler and Schmied-Kowarzik, *Weltkriegsstatistik Österreich-Ungarn
1914–1918*, 260–269.

breadcrumbs while cut, because scarce bread grains were substituted by
inferior surrogates. A crucial disparity emerged between landowning
households who could produce food for their own consumption ("self-
supporters") and people without sufficient access to land ("non-self-

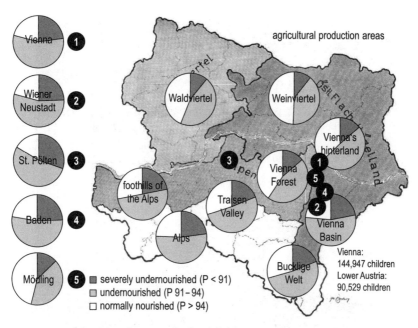

FIGURE 3.9 Nutritional status of schoolchildren in Lower Austria, 1920
Source: Clemens Pirquet, Schülerspeisung als Teil der allgemeinen Ernährungsfürsorge. In Clemens Pirquet, ed., *Volksgesundheit im Krieg*, vol. 1 (Vienna: Hölder-Pichler-Tempsky, 1926), 273–362, here 304.

supporters"). Whereas the poorer classes of the landless population were basically confined to the official rations at limited prices, the wealthier classes could provide their families with additional foodstuffs from the "black market" at high prices. In any case, collecting food became a most time-consuming activity, especially for women and children, queuing up for half a day – or even half a night – in front of retail stores. Despite surveillance by the police, the queues of hundreds of customers often led to rumor, protest, and food riots, involving activists not only from the proletariat but also from the bourgeois milieu. Many proletarian and middle-class families could make their living neither on the official nor on the unofficial urban market. One nonmarket survival strategy was to lay out vegetable gardens and feed livestock on small plots, either legally, through communal and cooperative support (1914: 36 hectares; 1919: 978 hectares), or illegally, through appropriation of uncultivated parcels. Civilians, especially schoolchildren under the guidance of their teachers, were commanded in a military rhetoric to cultivate each available parcel: "Grow vegetables everywhere!" (*Bauet überall Gemüse!*) (Figure 3.10).

FIGURE 3.10 Viennese magazine promoting urban vegetable gardens, 1917
Source: Wiener Bilder. Illustriertes Familienblatt, May 20, 1917, 1.

Another nonmarket strategy was to move to the near countryside in order to collect ears of corn or potatoes on the harvested fields or to barter objects of utility and value for foodstuffs. In contrast to "war cookbooks" that addressed housewives as patriotic fighters at the "kitchen front," the worsening lack of resources led family members to frequent factory canteens and charity kitchens.[34]

Undernutrition of the Viennese population had raged already prior to the war, especially among working-class families. The wartime food crisis enforced the chronic undersupply of macro- and micronutrients, which severely affected human bodies. Civilians' life expectancy decreased in all age groups by four to six years. Their death rate rose considerably; the war-induced surplus mortality in the period 1915–1919 amounted to about 40,000 persons (excluding military personnel). While pure starvation occurred rather rarely, many of these deaths were caused by nutrition-related diseases. Most narrowly correlated with the nutritional status was tuberculosis, the so-called Viennese disease, followed by nephritis, enteritis, anemia, heart disease, and edema. Women were more frequently affected by nutrition-related diseases; male mortality due to tuberculosis was 30% lower in 1919. The survivors of the wartime food crisis were unmistakably stamped from the years of chronic undernutrition. Most obvious was the retarded growth of the children's bodies, as drastically visualized in 1919 by the documentary film *The Misery of Children in Vienna* (*Das Kinderelend in Wien*). According to a physician, 12- to 14-year-olds looked like 8- to 10-year-olds. The average body height of children in postwar Vienna had shrunk to that of their counterparts in the late eighteenth

---

[34] See Ernst Langthaler, Mangel und Moral – Ernährungsalltag in Stadt und Land. In Elisabeth Loinig and Reinelde Motz-Linhart, eds., *Fern der Front – mitten im Krieg 1914–1918. Alltagsleben im Hinterland* (St. Pölten: NÖ Institut für Landeskunde, 2016), 170–182; Reinhard Sieder, Behind the Lines: Working-Class Family Life in Wartime Vienna. In Richard Wall and Jay Winter, eds., *The Upheaval of War: Family, Work and Welfare in Europe, 1914–1918* (Cambridge: Cambridge University Press, 1988), 109–138; Hans Hautmann, Hunger ist ein schlechter Koch. Die Ernährungslage der österreichischen Arbeiter im Ersten Weltkrieg. In Gerhard Botz et al., eds., *Bewegung und Klasse. Studien zur österreichischen Arbeitergeschichte* (Vienna/Munich/Zurich: Europaverlag, 1978), 661–681; Christian Mertens, Die Auswirkungen des Ersten Weltkriegs auf die Ernährung Wiens. In Alfred Pfoser and Andreas Weigl, eds., *Im Epizentrum des Zusammenbruchs. Wien im Ersten Weltkrieg* (Vienna: Metroverlag, 2013), 161–171; Andrea Brenner, Das Maisgespenst im Stacheldraht. Improvisation und Ersatz in der Wiener Lebensmittelversorgung des Ersten Weltkrieges. In Alfred Pfoser and Andreas Weigl, eds., *Im Epizentrum des Zusammenbruchs. Wien im Ersten Weltkrieg* (Vienna: Metroverlag, 2013), 140–149.

century. Given the disastrous state of the Viennese children's bodies and minds, contemporaries lamented a "lost generation."[35]

The daily experience of the scarcity and unequal distribution of foodstuffs in Vienna reinforced the city dwellers' impression of being victimized by selfish, incompetent, and corrupt perpetrators – local farm owners, Austrian bureaucrats, and "the Hungarians." This popular feeling delegitimized the official propaganda of the civilians' sacrifice at the "home front" to be subordinated to the soldiers' sacrifice at the war front; rather, the urban population felt its wartime sacrifice – for which it had not received a just return – to be of equal or even higher value. In summer 1918, this politicized "moral economy" was given rein in a "potato war," culminating in violent confrontations between tens of thousands of starving city dwellers, mostly women, children, and furloughed soldiers, and farm owners in the surrounding villages. All in all, the permanent struggle for food fostered the fragmentation of Viennese wartime society: inwardly, it led to accumulated denunciations, disputes, and violence within and between socioeconomic, ethnic, and religious groups, above all "the Jew"; outwardly, it accentuated the tensions between city and countryside, producers and consumers, "working class" and "peasantry," with a long-lasting resonance in the postwar society.[36]

CONCLUSION

In the wartime food crisis of the Habsburg Empire, several problems along the food chain of production, distribution, and consumption culminated. First of all, there was a *material* crisis with respect to the scarcity of agricultural products, especially in the Austrian half of the Dual Monarchy. Moreover, there was a *social* crisis with respect to distributional conflicts at macro, meso, and micro levels. Finally, there was a *symbolic* crisis with respect to the delegitimization of the public order in the minds of victimized consumers. Given that human nutrition is based upon animal and plant nutrition via a multitude of food chains, the erosion of this nutritional basis became decisive for the crisis of the imperial food regime. The "anthropocentric" diversion of resources

---

[35] See Andreas Weigl, Eine Stadt stirbt nicht so schnell. Demographische Fieberkurven am Rande des Abgrunds. In Alfred Pfoser and Andreas Weigl, eds., *Im Epizentrum des Zusammenbruchs. Wien im Ersten Weltkrieg* (Vienna: Metroverlag, 2013), 62–71; Maureen Healy, *Vienna and the Fall of the Habsburg Empire: Total War and Everyday Life in World War I* (Cambridge: Cambridge University Press, 2004), 255–257.

[36] See Healy, *Vienna and the Fall of the Habsburg Empire*, 31–86.

from plants and animals to humans led to a nutritional vicious circle that escalated the food crisis. The intersection of societal and environmental problems was crucial in all domains of the food chain: the undersupply of crops and livestock with nutrients due to the mobilization of farm resources for the war effort in the domain of production; the erosion of supra-regional food chains due to conflicts about the allocation of scarce resources for human, animal, and plant nutrition in the domain of distribution; the mass infection of human bodies by tuberculosis bacteria due to chronic undernutrition in the domain of consumption. With regard to the imperial food regime, the Austrian-Hungarian monarchy had begun to dissolve long before its legal dissolution in 1918.

4

The Chemist's War

Edgewood Arsenal, the First World War, and the Birth of a Militarized Environment

Gerard J. Fitzgerald

INTRODUCTION

In 1921, Major General Amos Fries, chief of the US Chemical Warfare Service (CWS), and Major Clarence J. West, a reserve officer under Fries also employed by the National Research Council (NRC), coauthored a book entitled *Chemical Warfare*, the first major textbook published in the United States for American military and industrial personnel interested in the fledgling art of using chemicals to gain victory on the battlefield.[1] While the United States was formally at war only from April 2, 1917 to November 11, 1918, the First World War had a considerable impact in forging a more intimate and dynamic relationship between government, industry, and academe in the United States. For instance, the creation of the CWS on June 28, 1918, and the NRC on June 19, 1916, the organizational homes of authors Fries and West, respectively, reflected in part the infrastructure of government institutions needed to successfully wage and manage the newly ascendant scientific and technical resources required for global war.

The new weapons systems of the Great War such as aircraft, poison gas, submarines, and tanks demonstrate the complete industrial and economic commitment of the various belligerents in addition to the unprecedented scientific and technological expertise applied by scientists, engineers, and physicians who served the military needs of the state. The first large-scale use of chemical weapons occurred at the Second Battle of Ypres on April 22, 1915. On that day special units of the

---

[1] Amos A. Fries and Clarence J. West, *Chemical Warfare* (New York: McGraw Hill, 1921).

German army released 160 tons of chlorine gas against Allied trenches killing more than 1,000 French and Algerian troops, wounding an additional 4,000, and forever changing the calculus of modern warfare. By the time of the Armistice on November 11, 1918, the use of chemical weapons such as chlorine, phosgene, and mustard gas had resulted in more than 1.3 million casualties and approximately 90,000 deaths.[2] Over the course of the next century, both the cultural legacy and environmental impact of chemical weapons use during the Great War continued to evolve, although gas warfare would personify for many the darkest and most sinister legacy of the war.

Fries, who succeeded Major General William Sibert in June 1920 as the second director of the CWS, was concerned in the early postwar years about the immediate needs of his command within the now much smaller peacetime army. Perhaps more importantly, Fries also focused on the continued success of this newly created branch of the service. While this new specialty service was granted permanent status as a separate branch of the US Army in 1920 – in part because of the success of the CWS during the First World War – questions remained about the long-term viability of the service. Ongoing internecine struggles with other branches of the army, not to mention larger questions raised by many politicians and civilians concerning the efficacy and morality of these new weapons, provided Fries with numerous challenges from both inside and outside the army.[3]

---

[2] On the history of the Second Battle of Ypres and its relationship to gas warfare see the following: Jeffery K. Smart, History of Chemical and Biological Warfare: An American Perspective. In Frederick R. Sidell, Ernest T. Takafuji, and David R. Franz, eds., *Medical Aspects of Chemical and Biological Warfare* (Washington, DC: Office of the Surgeon General, 1997), 15; Ludwig F. Haber, *The Poisonous Cloud: Chemical Warfare in the First World War* (New York: Clarendon Press, 1986), 31–32; James McWilliams and R. James Steel, *Gas! The Battle for Ypres, 1915* (St. Catherine, Ontario: Vanwell Publishing, 1986); Tim Cook, Creating the Faith: The Canadian Gas Services in the First World War. *Journal of Military History* 62(4) (October 1998), 755–786; Jonathon Krause, The Origins of Chemical Warfare in the French Army. *War in History* 20(4) (November 2013), 545–556; George H. Cassar, *Trial by Gas: The British Army at the Second Battle of Ypres* (Lincoln, NE: Potomac Books, 2014); and Ryan B. Flavelle, The Second Battle of Ypres and 100 Years of Remembrance. *Canadian Military History* 24 (1) (Winter/Spring 2015), 209–245. Finally, the overall causality figures of the Great War remain a subject of contention with gas warfare numbers especially problematic. On analysis of chemical weapons casualties see Haber, *The Poisonous Cloud*, 31–39.

[3] The history of the early years of the US Chemical Warfare Service is surprisingly complex for both political and institutional reasons and is beyond the scope of this chapter. After the United States' entrance into the war, responsibility for chemical warfare was divided and shared by the US Bureau of Mines, the army's Medical and Ordnance Departments,

Fries was particularly anxious about obtaining the commitment of the governmental and commercial resources necessary to make chemical weapons a permanent fixture in the national arsenal, and the book helped achieve that end. While not by any means an environmental history, *Chemical Warfare* does introduce readers to the construction of the chemical weapons production facility at the Edgewood Arsenal through a military-environmental lens. Two photographs, both taken at the same location nine months apart, dramatically illustrate the scale and scope of the industrial power the US government applied to create the first true weapon of mass destruction. In the first photograph, taken October 24, 1917, a single tree is centered in a field, a bucolic setting that reflected the farm fields, pastures, and rolling hills of the rural Maryland countryside.[4] The second photograph shows the same area now transformed into an industrial landscape by military engineers, a scene more reminiscent of the steel mills that defined Pittsburgh, Pennsylvania than the agricultural fields, forests, and wetlands nestled snugly along the shorelines of the Chesapeake Bay. An army engineering report described these changes in a capsule review of construction: "Situated in the most thickly populated district of the United States (the Atlantic Seaboard), this territory before the War was a little wilderness, the home of wild ducks, geese, and game of all kinds. Today it holds a maze of chemical plants, is covered with a network of roads, railroads, pipelines and all that goes with a huge manufacturing plant and proving ground for chemical warfare agents."[5]

The first photograph is seemingly familiar to those cognizant of earlier militarized landscapes in the mid-Atlantic region. It is similar

the Signal Corps, the Corps of Engineers, and the American Expeditionary Force, resulting in a variety of complications. For an analysis of the Service, see Thomas Faith, *Behind the Gas Mask: The U.S. Chemical Warfare Service in War and Peace* (Urbana: University of Illinois Press, 2014). See also Brooks E. Kleber and Dale Birdsell, *The Chemical Warfare Service: Chemicals in Combat* (Washington, DC: Center for Military History, United States Army, 2003), 1–24.

[4] Fries and West, *Chemical Warfare*, 54. This photo also appeared in the March 1919 issue of *The Edgewood Arsenal*, the installation's monthly in-house magazine. This special edition celebrated the history of the construction of the Edgewood Arsenal and the facility's contributions to the Allied victory during the First World War. Apparently, it was the only edition of the magazine ever published in hardcover, albeit in a very limited release. *The Edgewood Arsenal* 1 (March 1919), 7.

[5] NARA RG 175: Chemical Warfare Service, Entry 8: Technical Document, Files 1917–1920, Box 21: Miscellaneous Issuances Edgewood Arsenal – Range Tables, "Edgewood Arsenal the Seat of Chemical Warfare," 1.

FIGURE 4.1 Two photographs taken of the Edgewood Arsenal chemical weapons complex at Gunpowder Neck along the Chesapeake Bay in Maryland. The upper view shows the site on October 24, 1917. The lower image captures the same location nine months later.
Source: Reproduced from Amos A. Fries and Clarence J. West's *Chemical Warfare* (New York: McGraw Hill, 1921), 56.

in kind to a genre of photographs of devastated battlefields taken during the American Civil War at places such as Antietam and Gettysburg. The image of a lone bullet-riddled tree, the only "natural" survivor still standing but now shorn of branches and foliage, signified how war quickly and violently scarred the land.[6] However, these "before and after" photographs taken 50 years later at Edgewood illustrate a different evolutionary dimension of modern warfare: the successful application of American economic, industrial, military, and scientific resources to meet the demands of a new scale of global war.[7] Here the militarized landscape is created not by the

[6] On the cultural meaning of trees and forests in militarized landscapes during the American Civil War see Megan Kate Nelson, *Ruin Nation: Destruction and the American Civil War* (Athens: University of Georgia Press, 2012), 103–159. On the general military-environmental history of the Civil War see Lisa Brady, *War upon the Land: Military Strategy and the Transformation of Southern Landscapes during the American Civil War* (Athens: University of Georgia Press, 2012).

[7] To simplify matters, this chapter refers to the chemical weapons production facility at Gunpowder Neck Reservation, which was itself part of the much larger Aberdeen Proving Ground complex, as the Edgewood Arsenal or simply Edgewood. During the First World War, the facility was not formally designated as the "Edgewood Arsenal" installation by the Army Ordnance Department until May 4, 1918. See Leo B. Brophy, Wyndham D. Miles, and Rexmond C. Cohrane, *The Chemical Warfare Service: From Laboratory to Field* (Washington, DC: Office of the Chief of Military History, Department of the Army, 1959), 16.

violence of armies fighting or deadlocked on the battlefield but, instead, through the rapid construction of a massive new workscape thousands of miles from the fighting driven by wartime mobilization deadlines.

EDGEWOOD ARSENAL: MILITARY MOBILIZATION, THE ENVIRONMENT, AND HEALTH

This chapter briefly analyzes the creation of the Edgewood Arsenal chemical weapons production facility as a militarized industrial workscape. Spurred by a demanding mobilization timetable, the construction of Edgewood between November 1917 and November 1918 provides a window into various environmental and public health issues that were mediated by the interplay of both military and industrial culture brought on by a national emergency.

The army first broke ground in Maryland on October 28, 1917, and by October 1, 1918, the Edgewood facility contained 585 buildings, a 259-bed hospital, cantonment and barracks for 8,500 officers and enlisted men, 11 miles of roads, 21.25 miles of standard gauge railroads, 6.45 miles of narrow gauge railroads, 7.6 miles of industrial track,

FIGURE 4.2 View of the largest chlorine plant in the world at the Edgewood Arsenal taken on November 11, 1918
Source: Reproduced from *The Edgewood Arsenal* 1(5) (March 1919), 19.

3 powerhouses, 3 shell-filling plants, and separate plants for the manufacture of chloropicrin [trichloro(nitro)methane (CCl_3NO_2)], phosgene [Carbonyl Chloride ($COCl_2$)], chlorine [(Cl_2)], and mustard gas [ββ'-Dichlorethyl Sulfide ($ClCH_2CH_2$)2S], the four major gases of the Great War. By the time of the Armistice, Edgewood was the most advanced chemical weapons facility in the world and the only facility capable of producing all four of the Great War's war gases.[8]

The environmental dimensions of the construction of the Edgewood Arsenal draws upon recent work by a number of scholars in military-environmental history such as Chris Pearson, who defines "militarized environments" as "simultaneously material and cultural sites that have been partially or fully mobilized to achieve military aims."[9] The US Army

---

[8] On general construction numbers see NARA RG 175: Chemical Warfare Service, Entry 11: Construction of the Edgewood Arsenal, 1919, Box 11: Lt.-Col. Edward B. Ellicott Report on the Construction of the Filling Plants at Edgewood Plant of the Edgewood Arsenal, March 1919. On railroad construction see NARA RG 175: Chemical Warfare Service, Entry 11: Construction of Edgewood Arsenal, 1919, Box 11: Report on Railroad Construction of the Edgewood Plant of the Edgewood Arsenal, March 1919, 2; On plant construction see NARA RG 175: Chemical Warfare Service, Entry 11: Construction of the Edgewood Arsenal, 1919, Box 11: Lt.-Col. Edward B. Ellicott Report on the Construction of the Chemical, Mustard Gas and Refrigeration Plants at Edgewood Plant of the Edgewood Arsenal, March 1919.

[9] Chris Pearson, *Mobilizing Nature: The Environmental History of War and Militarization in Modern France* (Manchester: Manchester University Press, 2012), 1. For other insights on militarized locations beyond the "battlefield," see Edmund Russell, Afterword: Militarized Landscapes. In Chris Pearson, Peter Coates, and Tim Cole, eds., *Militarized Landscapes: From Gettysburg to Salisbury Plain* (London: Continuum, 2010), 230–233; and Edwin A. Martini, Bases, Places, and the Layered Landscape of American Empire. In Edwin A. Martini, ed., *Proving Grounds: Militarized Landscapes, Weapons Testing, and the Environmental Impact of U.S. Bases* (Seattle: University of Washington Press, 2015), 2–18. On the environmental consequences of war and militarized landscapes, see the following: Peter Coates, Tim Cole, Marianna Dudley, and Chris Pearson, Defending Nation, Defending Nature? Militarized Landscapes and Military Environmentalism in Britain, France and the United States. *Environmental History* 16(3) (2011), 456–491; Chris Pearson, Researching Militarized Landscapes: A Literature Review on War and the Militarization of the Environment. *Landscape Research* 37(1) (2012), 115–133; Marianna Dudley, *An Environmental History of the UK Defense Estate 1945 to the Present* (London: Continuum, 2012); Chris Pearson, *Scarred Landscapes: War and Nature in Vichy France* (Houndmills: Palgrave Macmillan, 2012); David Havlick, Militarization, Conservation and US Base Transformation. In Chris Pearson, Peter Coates, and Tim Cole, eds., *Militarized Landscapes: From Gettysburg to Salisbury Plain* (London: Continuum, 2010), 113–134; James R. McNeil and Corinna R. Unger, eds., *Environmental Histories of the Cold War* (Washington, DC: German Historical Institute, and Cambridge University Press, 2010); Charles E. Closmann, ed., *War and the Environment: Military Destruction in the Modern Age* (College Station: Texas A&M University Press, 2009); Richard P. Tucker and Edmund P. Russell, eds., *Natural Enemy, Natural Ally: Toward an*

has historically defined "mobilization" as "the assembling and organizing of troops, materiel, and equipment for active service in time of war or other national emergency; it is the basic factor on which depends the successful prosecution of any war."[10] The rapid design and construction of the Edgewood facility by the US Army beginning in the winter of 1917 is a useful case study of military mobilization from a weapons design and production standpoint. Beginning in November 1917, army engineers and civilian contractors were forced, on the fly, to design and build a much larger state-of-the-art and integrated production facility for the simultaneous production of multiple types of chemical weapons at a location chosen to meet the needs of a single shell-filling plant rather than a chemical weapons manufacturing complex.

Analysis of the birth of Edgewood also requires placing the facility in a broader historiographical context with respect to the scale and scope of scientific and technological manufacturing advances in 1917–1918, and,

---

Environmental History of War (Corvallis: Oregon State University Press, 2004); John Childs, *The Military Use of the Land: A History of the Defense Estate* (Bern: Peter Lang, 1998); and Seth Shulman, *The Threat at Home: Confronting the Toxic Legacy of the US Military* (Boston, MA: Beacon Press, 1992). On the environmental and cultural ramifications of chemical warfare see Hugh Slotten, Humane Chemistry or Scientific Barbarism? American Responses to World War I Poison Gas, 1915–1930. *Journal of American History* 77 (September 1990), 476–498; and Edmund P. Russell, *War and Nature: Fighting Humans and Insects with Chemicals from World War I to Silent Spring* (New York: Cambridge University Press, 2001). For a detailed technological and economic analysis of US chemical manufacturing activity during the First World War, see: Kathryn Steen, *The American Synthetic Organic Chemical Industry* (Chapel Hill: University of North Carolina Press, 2014), 95–112.

[10] Marvin A. Kreidberg and Merton G. Henry, *History of Military Mobilization in the United States Army, 1775–1945. Department of the Army, Pamphlet No. 20–212* (Washington, DC: Department of the Army, 1955), v. On First World War mobilization see pages 175–376. The most useful general source on industrial mobilization, logistics, and weapons production examining American efforts during the First World War remains the 1921 six-volume series written by Assistant Secretary of War and Director of Munitions Benedict Crowell and Captain Forrest Wilson, US Army. See the following by Crowell and Wilson: *The Giant Hand: Our Mobilization and Control of Industry and Natural Resources, 1917–1918* (New Haven, CT: Yale University Press, 1921); *The Road to France I: The Transportation of Troops and Military Supplies 1917–1918* (New Haven, CT: Yale University Press, 1921); *The Road to France II: The Transportation of Troops and Military Supplies 1917–1918* (New Haven, CT: Yale University Press, 1921); *The Armies of Industry I: Our Nation's Manufacture of Munitions for a World in Arms, 1917–1918* (New Haven, CT: Yale University Press, 1921); *The Armies of Industry II: Our Nation's Manufacture of Munitions for a World in Arms, 1917–1918* (New Haven, CT: Yale University Press, 1921); and *Demobilization: Our Industrial and Military Demobilization after the Armistice, 1918–1920* (New Haven, CT: Yale University Press, 1921). On chemical warfare see *The Armies of Industry II*, 488–537.

from an industrial landscape standpoint, within the evolution of government-sponsored American arms manufacture. This chapter builds upon
the path-breaking work of Daniel Kevles on American scientific research
and development activities during the First World War.[11] The focus by
Kevles and others on physics-based research and engineering projects in
the First World War, the Second World War, and the Cold War has to
some extent limited the historiographical impact of the success of chemical weapons research in the United States during the Great War, to say
nothing of the possible environmental consequences. While much of the
recent historical and geographic literature on militarized landscapes in the
United States examines the seismic changes brought forth by large-scale
Big Science projects during the Second World War and the Cold War –
projects dealing primarily with nuclear weapons production – the successful construction of the chemical weapons facilities at the Edgewood
Arsenal during the last year of the First World War provides a window
into very large-scale, militarized, science-based weapons production
a generation earlier.[12] The success of research and development activities

---

[11] The cornerstone of the political and cultural history of scientific research and development activities in the United States during the First World War remains Daniel Kevles's
early work on the American physics community. On the creation and evolution of the
National Research Council, various physics- and engineering-based research projects,
and other war-related scientific and technological activities in the United States during the
period see Daniel Kevles, *The Physicists: The History of a Scientific Community in
Modern America* (New York: Knopf, 1995), 102–154. On chemical warfare see pages
137–138.

[12] Most work in Big Science is related to the Second World War and the Cold War, focusing
on the creation and maturation of the academic-military-industrial complex, while the
First World War is usually ignored. Interwar work in the 1930s on the rise of large-scale
laboratories pioneers like Ernest Lawrence at the University of California, Berkeley, or
Wallace Carother's nylon group at DuPont, are mentioned on occasion but often as
a foundation for later work in some capacity during the Second World War.
On Lawrence see Robert Seidel, The Origins of the Lawrence Berkeley Laboratory.
In Peter Galison and Bruce Hevley, eds., *Big Science: The Growth of Large Scale
Research* (Stanford, CA: Stanford University Press, 1992), 21–45. On DuPont see
David A. Hounshell, DuPont and the Management of Large-Scale Research and
Development. In Peter Galison and Bruce Hevley, eds., *Big Science: The Growth of
Large Scale Research* (Stanford, CA: Stanford University Press, 1992), 236–265. For an
introduction, see Peter Galison and Bruce Hevley, eds., *Big Science: The Growth of Large
Scale Research* (Stanford, CA: Stanford University Press, 1992); and Arnold Thackray,
ed., *Science after '40, Osiris*, Second Series, 7 (1992). On the cost of Big Science see: James
H. Capshew and Karen A. Rader, Big Science's Price to the Present. *Science after '40,
Osiris*, Second Series, 7 (1992), 3–25. For recent work on the environmental history of
American nuclear weapons production facilities, test sites, and waste disposal, see the
following: Jacob Darwin Hamblin, *Radioactive Waste in the Oceans at the Dawn of the
Nuclear Age* (New Brunswick, NJ: Rutgers University Press, 2008); Ryan Edgington,

at Edgewood between 1917 and 1918, the accelerated timetable for project completion, and most importantly for this volume, the damage done to both the Maryland landscape and various worker bodies – not to mention those exposed to chemical weapons used on the battlefield – makes a proper understanding of the history of the construction of the chemical weapons production facilities at Edgewood during the First World War crucial for understanding the evolution of military environmental history in the United States. In addition, Edgewood provides a useful bridge from a technological and scientific munitions production perspective, linking the evolution of earlier, smaller, more traditional, and less toxic government-sponsored arms manufacture such as the nineteenth-century federal armories at Springfield, Massachusetts, Harpers Ferry, West Virginia, and Rock Island, Illinois, with the generation of twentieth-century facilities that followed Edgewood such as the Manhattan Project's enormous plutonium-manufacturing complex at Hanford, Washington. As such, Edgewood provides a useful historical juncture for looking both back and ahead to appraise the evolution of government-sponsored arms production during the second decade of the past century.[13] Finally, Edgewood illuminates that from an American perspective, the First World War was to a degree less about "Total War" and more about the cultural, economic, and political embrace of "total industrialization."

Fragmented Histories: Science, Environment and Monument Building at the Trinity Site, 1945–2005. In Chris Pearson, Peter Coates, and Tim Cole, eds., *Militarized Landscapes: From Gettysburg to Salisbury Plain* (London: Continuum, 2010), 189–208; Brett L. Walker, *Toxic Archipelago: A History of Industrial Disease in Japan* (Seattle: University of Washington Press, 2010); Mark Fiege, *The Republic of Nature: An Environmental History of the United States* (Seattle: University of Washington Press, 2012), 281–317; and Kate Brown, *Plutopia: Nuclear Families, Atomic Cities, and the Great Soviet and American Plutonium Disasters* (New York: Oxford University Press, 2013).

[13] On the federal arsenal system and mass production in the United States see Merritt Roe Smith, *Harpers Ferry Armory and the New Technology: The Challenge of Change* (Ithaca, NY: Cornell University Press, 1974); Otto Mayr and Robert Post, eds., *Yankee Enterprise: The Rise of the American System of Manufactures* (Washington, DC: Smithsonian Institution Press, 1981); David Hounshell, *The American System of Mass Production, 1800–1932* (Baltimore, MD: Johns Hopkins University, 1984); and David R. Meyer, *Networked Machinists: High Technology Industries in Antebellum America* (Baltimore, MD: Johns Hopkins University, 1996). For an analysis of the role of science-based research in the US arsenal system, see Thomas C. Lassman, Putting the Military Back into the History of the Military Industrial Complex: The Management of Technological Innovation in the U.S. Army, 1945–1960. *Isis* 106 (2015), 109–118.

In understanding the process by which the landscape at Gunpowder Neck was militarized during the First World War, and remains militarized today, it is important to see how the industrial landscape was altered not just by observing what the Army *took* from the site, such as large amounts of fresh- and saltwater, but perhaps more significantly from the view of what the army chose to *put there.* For it was in this latter process that the army truly began to change the environment at Edgewood over the course of the next century. As such, this chapter also analyzes public health aspects of the Edgewood environment, examining the impact of site selection on the lack of freshwater, the approach to sewage and waste management practices, and the dangers posed to workers from mustard gas manufacture, drawing upon the work of scholars such as Nancy Langston, Gregg Mitman, Linda Nash, and Christopher Sellers, among others who focus on the relationship between industrialization and the body.[14]

SITE LOCATION AND THE EVOLUTION OF THE EDGEWOOD ARSENAL MISSION PROFILE

The decision to build Edgewood on Gunpowder Neck in coastal Maryland, a 4,500-acre parcel within the newly acquired 35,000-acre Aberdeen Proving Ground, began with a presumption within US Army Ordnance Department planning circles about the future of

---

[14] On the historical question of the interaction between bodies, illness, and the environment in the context of modern industrialization see Christopher Sellers, *Hazards of the Job: From Industrial Disease to Environmental Health Science* (Chapel Hill: University of North Carolina Press, 1997); Steve Sturdy, The Industrial Body. In Roger Cooter and John Pickstone, eds., *Medicine in the Twentieth Century* (Amsterdam: Harwood Academic Publishers, 2000), 217–234; Christopher Warren, *Brush with Death: A Social History of Lead Poisoning* (Baltimore, MD: Johns Hopkins University Press, 2000); Gregg Mitman, In Search of Health: Landscape and Disease in American Environmental History. *Environmental History* 10 (April 2005), 184–210; Michelle Murphy, *Sick Building Syndrome and the Problem of Uncertainty: Environmental Politics, Technoscience, and Women Workers* (Durham, NC: Duke University Press, 2006); Linda Nash, *Inescapable Ecologies: A History of Environment, Disease and Knowledge* (Berkeley: University of California Press, 2006); Gregg Mitman, *Breathing Space: How Allergies Shape Our Lives and Landscapes* (New Haven, CT: Yale University Press, 2007); Jody A. Roberts and Nancy Langston, Toxic Bodies/Toxic Environments: An Interdisciplinary Forum. *Environmental History* 13 (2008), 629–635; and Nancy Langston, *Toxic Bodies: Hormone Disrupters and the Legacy of DES* (New Haven, CT: Yale University Press, 2010).

chemical weapons procurement.[15] In the early summer of 1917, Brigadier General William B. Crozier, chief of ordnance, was quite aware of advances in weaponry and technological innovation taking place in the European war and he was preoccupied with making sure that the United States did not fall too far behind the other warring nations. His primary interest, however, was not on the new phenomenon of chemical warfare. Instead, Crozier focused on more mainstream artillery matters.[16] Crozier and his officers were convinced that the Sandy Hook Proving Ground at Fort Hancock, New Jersey, established in 1874, was too small and unable to meet the army's

[15] An Act of Congress on October 6, 1917 provided authority for land acquisition of the 35,000-acre Aberdeen Proving Ground. The property was acquired by proclamation of the president on October 16, 1917 under the Urgent Efficiency Act, which cleared the way for army engineers to break ground at Aberdeen five days later. This was the first of three presidential proclamations. On Aberdeen see: NARA RG 175: Chemical Warfare Service, Entry 11: Construction of the Edgewood Arsenal, 1919, Box 11: R. C. Marshall Jr. Brigadier General (Chief of Construction Division) and Edward, B. Ellicott, Lt.-Col. (Construction Officer), Introduction to the Report on the Construction of the Edgewood Plant of the Edgewood Arsenal, March 1919, 4. See also Katherine Grandine, William R. Henry Jr., and Irene Jackson Henry, "Historic American Engineering Record, Aberdeen Proving Ground (Edgewood Arsenal), MD-47, Herford and Baltimore Counties, MD," National Park Service, Department of the Interior (Washington, DC, 1985), 22–25. On federal land seizure for base construction during the Second World War see Brandon C. Davis, Defending the Nation, Defending the Land: Emergency Powers and the Militarization of American Public Lands. In Edwin A. Martini, ed., *Proving Grounds: Militarized Landscapes, Weapons Testing, and the Environmental Impact of U.S. Bases* (Seattle: University of Washington Press, 2015), 19–42. As for the history of the location with respect to the use of the word "gunpowder," the origin of the use of "Gunpowder River" and later "Gunpowder Neck" by European colonizers dates back to an August 29, 1658 land survey of the area and long predates any organized manufacturing at that location, including weapons manufacture. The use of the term remains unclear. The geographic identifications of Gunpowder River, Gunpowder Island (now Carroll's Island), and Gunpowder Neck all date back to at least 1658, if not earlier, and are exclusive of indigenous Native American traditions and culture. On the 1658 survey see William B. Marye, Early Settlers of the Site of Havre De Grace. *Maryland Historical Magazine* 13(3) (September 1918), 197–200. See also by William B. Marye, The Place Names of Baltimore and Harbor Counties. *Maryland Historical Magazine* 25(3) (December 1930), 325–327, 337–342, 362–364.

[16] During the first two decades of the twentieth century the US Army was primarily interested in the research, development, and procurement of more conventional nitrogen-based explosives. William Hayes noted "official interest in the nitrogen problem was sparked in 1903 by General William Crozier." See William Hayes, *American Chemical Industry: A History: The World War I Period: 1912–1922* (New York: D. Van Nostrand Company, 1945), 89. On the history of the Ordnance Department through the First World War see Constance McLaughlin Green, Henry C. Thomas, and Peter C. Roots, *The Ordnance Department: Planning Munitions for War* (Washington, DC: Department of the Army, 1955), 13–29. For a detailed analysis of US chemical manufacturing activity during the First World War, including nitrates, see Steen, *The American Synthetic Organic Chemical Industry.*

technical needs as a modern ordnance test ground. Aberdeen was created to fill this gap. Chemical weapons production at Gunpowder Neck was not discussed or planned since Ordnance Department officers were confident they could purchase these weapons from domestic commercial manufacturers.

Understanding the evolution of the militarized environment at Edgewood must begin with an appreciation that the location was chosen not because of its suitability as a potential industrial *production* site but instead because the primary consideration for US military planners in the summer of 1917 was *logistical*. The land designated for chemical weapons operations in the Aberdeen Proving Ground was chosen because it offered ready access to national rail, coastal, and oceanic transportation systems to send chemical weapons to France and Great Britain. To facilitate shipping: "a 12 ft. channel about a quarter mile in length was dredged through Bush River to the Bay."[17] The logistical advantages of the Gunpowder Neck site are central to the army's description of the location.

The great plant of the Chemical Warfare Service, is located on the main line of the Pennsylvania Railroad twenty miles north of Baltimore. The territory occupied by the Arsenal is known as Gunpowder Neck, a peninsula eight miles long, and averaging two miles wide, jutting into Chesapeake Bay between the mouths of the Gunpowder and Bush Rivers. The railway cuts across the entire width of the Neck forming the northern boundary of the Arsenal. On all other sides, the Arsenal is bounded by water. Thus excellent transportation facilities are afforded both by land and water.[18]

In the summer of 1917, Ordnance Department planning officers did not envision chemical weapons production on site in any form whatsoever, as they expected finished weapons to arrive in liquid or gaseous form transported by railroad tank cars from civilian chemical plants. Once unloaded, the chemicals would be carefully reloaded into artillery shells by onsite personnel in the new army shell-filling facility. Once the shell-filling process was completed, ammunition would be quickly shipped out by either rail or barge to major coastal ports along the Eastern Seaboard, or preferably

[17] Charles H. Hurty, Gas Offense in the United States: A Record of Achievement. *Journal of Industrial and Engineering Chemistry* 11(January 1, 1919), 7.

[18] NARA RG 175: Chemical Warfare Service, Entry 8: Technical Document, Files 1917–1920, Box 21: Miscellaneous Issuances Edgewood Arsenal – Range Tables, "Edgewood Arsenal the Seat of Chemical Warfare," 1.

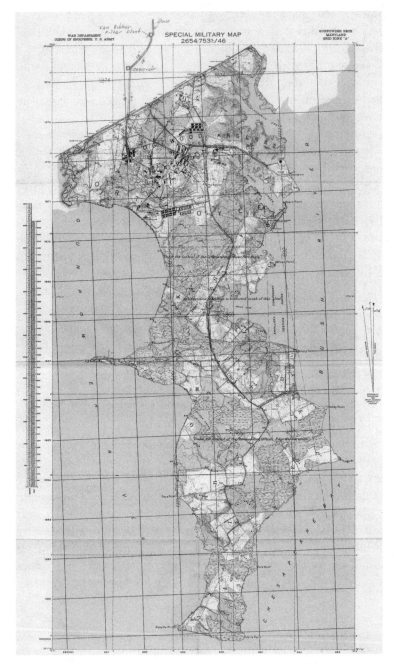

FIGURE 4.3 1923 Army Corps of Engineers map of the Edgewood Arsenal complex at Gunpowder Neck. The map includes additional drawings of the freshwater supply pipeline, dam, filter plant, and reservoir from Van Bibber to the arsenal's many chemical weapons production plants.

Source: NARA RG 92: Entry 1891: Office of Quartermaster General, General Correspondence, Geographic File, 1922–1935. Box 578: 333.1–600.1 Edgewood.

from the new deep-water dock complex at Edgewood, for shipment overseas.[19]

The bureaucratic confusion about exactly what type of facility the army planned to build along the Bush River in late 1917 is perhaps best encapsulated in the opening sentences of the official army engineering history of the project, which state: "No specific authorization for this project can be found. Its conception seems to have been in a proposed experimental filling plant for gas-shells decided upon by the Ordnance Department in June 1917, and approved verbally by General Crozier."[20] Initial army plans to build only a small artillery shell-filling plant at Gunpowder Neck was thwarted by two factors: a chemical industry initially unwilling to expand existing facilities, or build expensive new plants, to manufacture exceedingly dangerous products with no postwar product marketability – not to mention possible future public relations problems – and a ruling by the Director General of Railroads that toxic loads involving poison gas could only be moved by expensive special trains.[21] Both responses apparently blindsided army planners, although national rail service around the country, and especially in the eastern United States, was already in serious disarray and on the verge of collapse as construction at Edgewood's construction commenced that winter. To deal with the ongoing and increasingly desperate national transportation crisis President Woodrow Wilson nationalized the US railway system in December 1917 and created the US Railroad Association.[22]

---

[19] In 1918, engineers constructed a dock complex at the Bush River "in order to be able to make direct shipments overseas, thus eliminating the extra handling of gas and shells if shipped via rail. Shipment via water direct eliminates the extra hazard to communities by containers breaking or leaking while in transit." NARA RG 175: Chemical Warfare Service, Entry 11: Construction of the Edgewood Arsenal, 1919, Box 11: Lt.-Col. Edward B. Ellicott Report on the Construction of the Filling Plants at Edgewood Plant of the Edgewood Arsenal, March 1919, 153.

[20] NARA RG 175: Chemical Warfare Service, Entry 11: Construction of the Edgewood Arsenal, 1919, Box 11: Lt.-Col. Edward B. Ellicott Report on the Construction of the Filling Plants at Edgewood Plant of the Edgewood Arsenal, March 1919, 1.

[21] On industrial resistance to chemical weapons production see Hurty, Gas Offense in the United States, 6–7. On the railroad question see Fries and West, *Chemical Warfare*, 53.

[22] On the issue of railroad transportation difficulties in the United States during the war see Robert B. Cuff, United States Mobilization and Railroad Transportation: Lessons in Coordination and Control, 1917–1945. *Journal of Military History* 53 (January 1989), 33–50; and K. Austin Kerr, Decision for Federal Control: Wilson, McAdoo, and the Railroads, 1917. *The Journal of American History* 54 (December 1967), 550–560.

The difficulty in moving chemical weapons by rail during the First World War was shaped by passage of the Explosives and Combustible Act of 1908 that "authorized the Interstate Commerce Commission [ICC] to issue regulations covering the packing, marking, loading, and handling of explosives and other dangerous substances in transit."[23] Adopted formally in 1911, these regulations were drawn from earlier studies carried out by investigators in the Bureau of Explosives, a research branch of the Association of American Railroads founded in 1905. In 1917, the movement of chemical weapons, a dangerous and brand new commodity, presented challenges to transportation and military officials alike, frustrating Ordnance Department planners. While familiar industrial chemicals such as sulfuric acid were shipped in great bulk by rail, it would take time for the federal government to categorize and study this new class of dangerous, toxic, and potentially life-threatening liquids and gases and provide useful protocols to guide loading and transportation.[24]

To facilitate chemical weapons production at Edgewood, there were a number of so-called civilian outside plants around the country that were controlled and funded to varying degrees by the army through the Edgewood Arsenal. These chemical plants either manufactured chemical weapons on site or produced various chemicals that were integral to the production of toxic war gases at Edgewood during the war.[25] While some of these chemical manufacturers

[23] US Congress, Office of Technology Assessment, *Transportation of Hazardous Materials, OTA SET-304* (Washington, DC: US Government Printing Office, July 1986), 146.

[24] On the rail shipment of acids and other dangerous substances in the United States in the years immediately prior to the First World War see Mark Aldrich, *Death Rode the Rails: American Railroad Accidents and Safety, 1828–1965* (Baltimore, MD: Johns Hopkins University Press, 2006), 217–236.

[25] The history of each of these facilities is as complex as Edgewood itself and well beyond the scope of this chapter. Some were quite successful, others failed to achieve their wartime production goals, and others fell somewhere in between. The facilities included a chloropicrin plant in Stamford, Connecticut; a phosgene plant in Niagara Falls, New York; a bromine plant in Midland, Michigan; a phosgene plant in Bound Brook, New Jersey; a sulphur monochloride plant in Charleston, West Virginia; a proposed mustard gas plant in Hasting-on-Hudson, New York; a mustard gas plant in Buffalo, New York; a sodium cyanide plant in Saltville, Virginia; a brombenzylecyanide plant in Kingsport, Tennessee; a diphenychloroarsine plant in Croyland, Pennsylvania; and a lewisite plant in Willoughby, Ohio. Taken together, these facilities and Edgewood represent an integrated system that reflected the increasing sophistication of weapons production through the US Army's arsenal-based model of production. See NARA RG 175: Chemical Warfare Service, Entry 8: Technical Documents Files 1917–1920, Box 11: Memos-Plants Folder: Plant Edgewood.

The Outside Plants:
Edgewood Arsenal Toxic Gas Plants in the United States, 1918

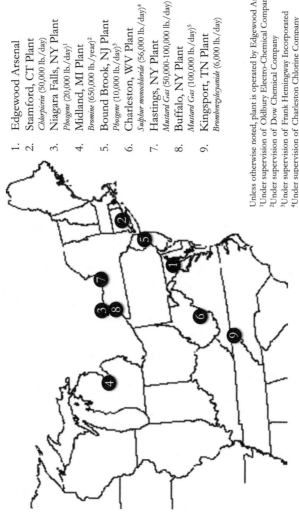

1. Edgewood Arsenal
2. Stamford, CT Plant
   Chlorpicrin (50,000 lb./day)
3. Niagara Falls, NY Plant
   Phosgene (20,000 lb./day)[1]
4. Midland, MI Plant
   Bromine (650,000 lb./year)[2]
5. Bound Brook, NJ Plant
   Phosgene (10,000 lb./day)[3]
6. Charleston, WV Plant
   Sulphur monochloride (56,000 lb./day)[4]
7. Hastings, NY Plant
   Mustard Gas (50,000-100,000 lb./day)
8. Buffalo, NY Plant
   Mustard Gas (100,000 lb./day)[5]
9. Kingsport, TN Plant
   Bromobenzylcyanide (6,000 lb./day)

Unless otherwise noted, plant is operated by Edgewood Arsenal
[1]Under supervision of Oldbury Electro-Chemical Company
[2]Under supervision of Dow Chemical Company
[3]Under supervision of Frank Hemingway Incorporated
[4]Under supervision of Charleston Chlorine Company
[5]Under supervision of National Alinine & Chemical Company

FIGURE 4.4 Map of the so-called civilian outside plants that were part of chemical weapons production in the United States during the war
Source: NARA RG 175: Chemical Warfare Service, Entry 8: Technical Documents Files 1917–1920, Box 11: Memos-Plants Folder: Plant Edgewood.

shipped chemical weapons in limited quantities to Edgewood during
the war, it was not until July 12, 1919 that the ICC formally imple-
mented safety specifications dictating the movement and loading of
the first chemical weapons by rail.[26]

CONSTRUCTION: WATER, WASTE, AND MUSTARD GAS

Ground breaking commenced at Edgewood on October 24, 1917 with "the
construction of a railroad spur connecting the grounds with the Pennsylvania
Railroad" mainline and on November 15, work was started on the first
building, Filling Plant No. 1.[27] Army engineers and civilian contractors
moved quickly and with great purpose to build the Edgewood facility.
The swiftness with which the chemical weapons facilities were designed,
constructed, and made operational is even more impressive as engineers and
laborers found themselves starting construction "during the worst part of one
of the worst winters this section of the country has ever known."[28]

[26] The first authorization by the ICC for rail movement of "cylinders for the shipment of
phosgene gas and other such poisonous gases and liquids" began July 12, 1919 following
ICC Specification 33 (image 6418). See *Supplement No. 1 to Regulations for the
Transportation of Explosives and Other Dangerous Articles, Dangerous Articles by
Freight and Express, and Specifications for Shipping Containers.* US Interstate
Commerce Commission (Washington, DC: US Government Printing Office, 1919), 20.
By 1959, toxic agents shipped by rail included nerve gases, lewisite, mustard gas, and
diphosgene, among others. See "Chemical Corps Safety Directive No. 385–2: Shipping
Criteria for Chemical Agents Chemical Ammunition, Poisons, and Other Dangerous
Articles," Headquarters, Department of the Army, Office of the Chief Chemical Officer
(Washington, DC: US Government Printing Office, February 1959), 1–3.

[27] NARA RG 175: Chemical Warfare Service, Entry 8: Technical Document Files
1917–1920, Box 14: Laboratory Summary – National Electrolytic Folder: 1918–1920
Tech. Subject Mustard Oil, Trench Sprayers, Mustard Gas, Phosgene Gas.

[28] NARA RG 175: Chemical Warfare Service, Entry 11: Construction of the Edgewood
Arsenal, 1919, Box 11: Lt.-Col. Edward B. Ellicott Report on the Construction of the
Temporary Structures at Edgewood Plant of the Edgewood Arsenal, March 1919, 2.
Construction delays and difficulties due to the terrible weather are often mentioned in the
description of the construction of the arsenal. The severity of the winter on the American
war effort in 1917–1918 remains an important but relatively unexplored military environmental research topic. Heavy storms and freezing temperatures significantly impacted
wartime construction projects across the nation and also impeded rail, road, riverine, and
oceanic traffic on the Eastern Seaboard, delaying shipments of war materials and food to
the Allies. On transportation issues see George H. Nash, *The Life of Herbert Hoover:
Master of Emergencies, 1917–1918* (New York: W. W. Norton, 1996), 197–226.
On weather conditions see Charles F. Brooks, The "Old-Fashioned" Winter of
1917–1918. *Geographic Review* 5 (May 1918), 405–414; and Preston C. Day,
The Cold Weather of 1917–1918. *Monthly Weather Review* 46 (December 1918),
570–580.

The construction engineers recalled that even such mundane tasks as "digging sewers and water lines" became impossible.[29] To build the Edgewood water system "it was necessary to build fires all along the proposed line before commencing to excavate. The ground was frozen so hard that it was necessary to blast for a considerable amount of the excavation."[30] In addition to meteorological roadblocks, the project presented engineers and contractors with a seemingly never-ending series of increasingly complex technological challenges as the project expanded enormously in just a few short months. As the war progressed, the number of chemical weapons Edgewood was charged to produce increased from two to three to four. Plans to build a chloropicrin plant and a phosgene plant were decided by December 1, 1917, with construction of the chloropicrin plant beginning on January 25, 1918 while work on the phosgene facility began on March 1, 1918. Production of both chloropicrin and phosgene required large amounts of highly pure chlorine, volumes that placed limits on overall national production in terms of both quality and quantity. On May 11, 1918, a chlorine plant with "capacity of 200,000 pounds per day," the largest in the United States, began and on May 18, work began on a mustard gas facility with a daily capacity of 100,000 pounds per day.[31] The expanding number of chemical weapons being manufactured at Edgewood increased the number of buildings and support facilities that needed to be designed and constructed, multiplying not only the number of structures at the arsenal but also the volume of construction materials necessary to erect the complex, as well as the number of laborers, horses, and mules essential to completing Edgewood's new mission. While officers and contractors successfully met a daunting series of chemical engineering challenges in the first few months, it was a much more

---

[29] NARA RG 175: Chemical Warfare Service, Entry 11: Construction of the Edgewood Arsenal, 1919, Box 11: Lt.-Col. Edward B. Ellicott Report on the Construction of the Temporary Structures at Edgewood Plant of the Edgewood Arsenal, March 1919, 2.

[30] Ibid.

[31] On the entirety of Edgewood's construction see NARA RG 175: Chemical Warfare Service, Entry 11: Construction of the Edgewood Arsenal, 1919, Box 11: Lt.-Col. Edward B. Ellicott Report on the Construction of the Filling Plants at Edgewood Plant of the Edgewood Arsenal, March 1919, 1–25. For specific construction dates for chloropicrin, phosgene, and mustard plants, see NARA RG 175: Chemical Warfare Service, Entry 8: Technical Document Files 1917–1920, Box 14: Laboratory Summary – National Electrolytic Folder: 1918–1920 Tech. Subject Mustard Oil, Trench Sprayers, Mustard Gas, Phosgene Gas. On chlorine construction dates see NARA RG 175: Chemical Warfare Service, Entry 11: Construction of the Edgewood Arsenal, 1919, Box 11: Lt.-Col. Edward B. Ellicott Completion Report on Chlorine Plant at Edgewood Plant of the Edgewood Arsenal, March 1919, 2.

straightforward problem in civil engineering and resource management that caused them the greatest concern.

As the project accelerated and expanded in December 1917, it became apparent that the amount of freshwater available within the confines of the Edgewood site was completely inadequate to meet the needs of the much larger permanent industrial facility that was quickly rising out of Maryland's brackish marshes and rolling hills. There was very little groundwater on Gunpowder Neck, and it was clear to Edgewood engineers and contractors that the wells that were dug to meet immediate human, animal, and industrial needs during the initial construction phase would soon run dry. While the amount of well water available might not have been an issue for the relatively small number of personnel needed to build and operate the original shell-filling plant, the groundwater stores were not even remotely viable for the large-scale facility now under construction. Lead construction engineers decided that "the water supply [was] the most important requirement and was to be given immediate attention."[32] Two possibilities presented themselves: a small stream two miles from the site at Winter's Run at Van Bibber, Maryland, and another much larger water supply on the Gunpowder River five miles from Edgewood.[33] While the Gunpowder River location was three miles farther away, it was also at a much higher elevation than Winter's Run, a crucial factor with respect to how much pumping infrastructure needed to be built to supply Edgewood with water. A complicating factor for army engineers was that Van Bibber was also the primary water source for the 1,500 people in the small village of nearby Belair, Maryland, a situation that raised significant questions about future water availability at the arsenal.[34] The feasibility of Winter's

[32] NARA RG 175: Chemical Warfare Service, Entry 11: Construction of the Edgewood Arsenal, 1919, Box 11: Lt.-Col. Edward B. Ellicott Report on the Construction of the Filling Plants at Edgewood Plant of the Edgewood Arsenal, March 1919, 26.

[33] The Winter's Run stream at Van Bibber "had a drainage area of approximately fifty square miles." See NARA RG 175: Chemical Warfare Service, Entry 11: Construction of the Edgewood Arsenal, 1919, Box 11: Lt.-Col. Edward B. Ellicott Report on the Construction of the Water System at Edgewood Plant of the Edgewood Arsenal, March 1919, 4.

[34] Army engineers later noted that the chief engineer of the Maryland State Department of Health at Belair "had plans prepared for a sewer system and this system will carry the drainage to another watershed," thus eliminating this as a sewage problem that complicated plans for Edgewood. NARA RG 175: Chemical Warfare Service, Entry 11: Construction of the Edgewood Arsenal, 1919, Box 11: Lt.-Col. Edward B. Ellicott Report on the Construction of the Water System at Edgewood Plant of the Edgewood Arsenal, March 1919, 5.

Run stoked considerable debate among the various army engineers designing the facility. The construction report explained:

The objection to this source of supply [Winter's Run] was due to the possible limited quantity of water that could be obtained, because there were other users of the waters of this stream, and the necessary expense of pumping the water to an elevation of 140 feet, from which point it could be delivered to the reservation by gravity. This latter project also involved the building of a dam of 1,300 feet in length and the purchase of considerable property that would be overflowed by back water from the dam.[35]

Despite intense time pressure, the "location of the fresh water supply for use on the Reservation was not decided until March 27, 1918" with Winter's Run finally winning out.[36] This was not, however, the end of delays for this project as the weather continued to impede progress and access to the land for the pipeline led to even more complications. The snow and sleet of earlier winter storms gave way to exceptionally heavy rains in the first two weeks of April, impeding construction on almost every project at Edgewood. Once the skies cleared on April 15, work on the freshwater pipeline project was stymied once more because at that "time no rights of way had been secured for the necessary pipe line [sic] to conduct the water across private property to the reservation, and no property had been purchased or options secured thereon for the site of the dam, pumping station or reservoir."[37] Unable to take advantage of the presidential and congressional power that had created the Aberdeen Proving Ground in 1917, in the spring of 1918, the army found itself unable, and on occasion unwilling, to work with small landowners and farmers, who with the exception of one holdout, were willing to part with their property for $100 an acre to make way for a water pipeline.

Between April 16 and July 3, army lawyers in the office of the Judge Advocate General pleaded and cajoled with the Maryland Attorney General, the Attorney General of the United States, and the lawyers of the various landowners before finally taking possession of the various parcels during the early summer.[38] Because of time constraints and the increasing need for freshwater: "it was decided that a temporary plant should be installed and to make the supply available at the earliest possible

---

[35] NARA RG 175: Chemical Warfare Service, Entry 11: Construction of the Edgewood Arsenal, 1919, Box 11: Lt.-Col. Edward B. Ellicott Report on the Construction of the Water System at Edgewood Plant of the Edgewood Arsenal, March 1919, 2.

[36] Ibid.   [37] Ibid.

[38] On the legal aspects of the pipeline's land acquisition see NARA RG 92: Office of the Quartermaster General, General Correspondence, Geographic File: 1922–1935: 601.1–601.5, Edgewood Folder: War Department Real Estate Service, Number I Ordnance Reservoir and Pipe Line Right of Way at Edgewood Arsenal, Baltimore Md., 1918.

time one pipe line was to be laid on top of the ground, and lowered when
the second line had been installed in permanent manner."[39] Using this
temporary aboveground system, freshwater first flowed to the complex
from Winter's Run on May 15.[40] Army engineers spent the rest of the
summer working on completing a permanent system and "the dam,
powerhouse, and reservoir were completed on August 15 while the filter
system had not been completed and the electric and gasoline driven
pumps had not yet arrived."[41] The Winter's Run water-pumping station,
first operated September 1, 1918, had a "capacity of 2,000,000 gallons
daily," although work on the system continued until October 1.[42]
Figures 4.2 and 4.3 illustrate the placement of the "Van Bibber Filter
Plant," dam, and reservoir and the 10-inch and 14-inch pipes that
brought water down into the Edgewood facility. Once on base, a series
of smaller pipes carried water into the key facilities such as the chlorine
plant and the other weapons production buildings for industrial use in
addition to water carried to all areas of the base for "domestic, sanitary,
and fire purposes."[43]

The freshwater that was purified at the Van Bibber filtration complex
satisfied the freshwater requirements for various public health and

[39] NARA RG 175: Chemical Warfare Service, Entry 11: Construction of the Edgewood
Arsenal, 1919, Box 11: Lt.-Col. Edward B. Ellicott Report on the Construction of the
Filling Plants at Edgewood Plant of the Edgewood Arsenal, March 1919, 27.

[40] Ibid., 43. "A temporary steam plant was purchased and installed, a temporary dam
constructed, and combined 8-and 10-inch pipe line laid for a distance of over two miles
and water delivered to the Reservation on May 15."

[41] NARA RG 175: Chemical Warfare Service, Entry 11: Construction of the Edgewood
Arsenal, 1919, Box 11: Lt.-Col. Edward B. Ellicott Report on the Construction of the
Water System at Edgewood Plant of the Edgewood Arsenal, March 1919, 4.
"Bacteriological analyses of raw water" at Van Bibber indicated "that the water is mildly
but continuously polluted" and so the army installed a state-of-the-art purification system
involving mechanical and chemical filtration. Ibid., 5–10. On the technological details of
water purification technology in the United States during this time see Martin V. Melosi,
The Sanitary City: Urban Infrastructure in America from Colonial Times to the Present
(Baltimore, MD: Johns Hopkins University Press, 2000), 103–175.

[42] NARA RG 175: Chemical Warfare Service, Entry 8: Technical Document Files
1917–1920, Box 14 Laboratory Summary – National Electrolytic Folder: 1918–1920
Tech. Subject Mustard Oil, Trench Sprayers, Mustard Gas, Phosgene Gas "Historical
Sketch of the Development of Edgewood Arsenal." See also NARA RG 175: Chemical
Warfare Service, Entry 11: Construction of the Edgewood Arsenal, 1919, Box 11: Lt.-Col.
Edward B. Ellicott Report on the Construction of the Water System at Edgewood Plant of
the Edgewood Arsenal, March 1919, 4–6.

[43] NARA RG 175: Chemical Warfare Service, Entry 11: Construction of the Edgewood
Arsenal, 1919, Box 11: Lt.-Col. Edward B. Ellicott Report on the Construction of the
Water System at Edgewood Plant of the Edgewood Arsenal, March 1919, 5.

FIGURE 4.5 The Van Bibber pumping station and forebay
Source: NARA RG 77: Office of the Chief of Engineers, Entry 391: Construction Reports, 1917–1943. Box 93 Edgewood Arsenal Vols. 1–2.

industrial needs across the facility. This system was, nonetheless, inadequate to meet larger overall manufacturing demands, including significant problems with heat transfer as the various production facilities came on line. Turning to the more convenient Bush River, engineers "decided to use salt water for all cooling water in both the Filling Plants and the Chemical and Mustard Oil Plants; for condensing water in the Power Plant; for wash water in all the Scrubbing and Washing Towers in the Filling and Chemical Plants; and for the fire supply system in the Filling and Chemical Plants."[44] Construction of the Bush River Pump House

[44] NARA RG 175: Chemical Warfare Service, Entry 11: Construction of the Edgewood Arsenal, 1919, Box 11: Lt.-Col. Edward B. Ellicott Report on the Construction of the Water System at Edgewood Plant of the Edgewood Arsenal, March 1919, 23. With respect to drawing water from nearby waterways, the 1985 Historic American Engineering Report (HAER), unlike other government and military publications, noted that the larger Aberdeen facility, of which Edgewood was but one small part, was composed of "approximately 78,042 acres of property of which 39,100 acres are water and 38,942 acres are land." This included the Bush River and other areas such as Spesutie

FIGURE 4.6 Interior of the Van Bibber pumping station showing the water filtration tanks
Source: NARA RG 77: Office of the Chief of Engineers, Entry 391: Construction Reports, 1917–1943. Box 93 Edgewood Arsenal Vols. 1–2.

allowed for "'full capacity' that was 22,920 gallons per minute against a 60-foot head," and, by September 1918, Edgewood drew 9.5 million gallons of saltwater per day to support chemical production.[45]

The success of the various chemical weapons manufacturing processes and the evolving industrial landscape at Edgewood in 1918 were not only shaped by natural resources such as freshwater and saltwater extracted from nearby streams and rivers and pumped *into* the facility, but Edgewood was also defined by waste by-products that were processed and deposited *back out* to the local environment. Waste management

Island, Pooles Island, and Carroll Island. See Grandine, Henry, and Henry, "Historic American Engineering Record," 2.
[45] NARA RG 175: Chemical Warfare Service, Entry 11: Construction of the Edgewood Arsenal, 1919, Box 11: Lt.-Col. Edward B. Ellicott Report on the Construction of the Water System at Edgewood Plant of the Edgewood Arsenal, March 1919, 23, See also Fries and West, *Chemical Warfare*, 55.

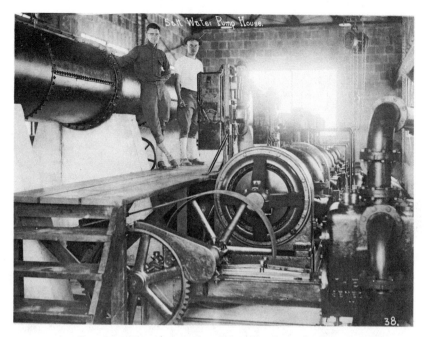

FIGURE 4.7 Interior view of the saltwater pump house showing motors and pumps
Source: NARA RG 77: Office of the Chief of Engineers, Entry 391: Construction Reports, 1917–1943. Box 93 Edgewood Arsenal Vols. 1–2.

practice at Edgewood reflected the engineering culture of the time and as the numerous plants and systems came on line over the course of 1918, and the production of chloropicrin, phosgene, chlorine, and mustard gas began, the army devised strategies to deal with dangerous and sometimes toxic liquids, solids, and gases that were left over. Engineers originally framed waste management at Edgewood during the construction phase as a problem of human waste: "before it was possible to make any provisions for sewer lines, it was necessary to take care of the excreta of about 10,000 persons who were employed in the construction of the arsenal."[46]

That bitter cold winter, engineers jerry-rigged "vaults [that] were excavated and provided with frame latrines consisting of about 10 to 12 seats with wooden covers and a urinal trough made of galvanized iron and wood

[46] NARA RG 175: Chemical Warfare Service, Entry 11: Construction of the Edgewood Arsenal, 1919, Box 11: Lt.-Col. Edward B. Ellicott Report on the Construction of the Sewer System, Steam and Air Lines at Edgewood Plant of the Edgewood Arsenal, March 1919, 2.

FIGURE 4.8 Spray pond for the evaporator building at the Edgewood chlorine plant taken December 2, 1918
Source: NARA RG 77: Office of the Chief of Engineers, Entry 391: Construction Reports, 1917–1943. Box 93 Edgewood Arsenal Vols. 1–2.

frame. The latrines were subject to frequent inspection by the sanitary department and were disinfected and filled in upon authority of the sanitary officers."[47] The design of a single installation-wide sewage system was discussed and rejected: "[O]wing to the location of the various plants and the contours of the ground it was found more economical to have separate sewage systems."[48] Once the sewage systems were installed, the marshes, creeks, and waterways that anchored the ecological base of the Gunpowder Neck peninsula once again came into play. Engineers concluded, for instance: "as there was very little excreta in the sewage system of the filling plant, it was decided to flow the effluent direct[ly] into Canal Creek."[49]

[47] Ibid., 3.
[48] Ibid. Because of the Maryland climate, "all sewage lines were laid below the frost line and consisted entirely of good grade vitrified clay tile sewer pipe."
[49] Ibid.

The disposal of more toxic materials brought more creative solutions that involved chemical treatment of wastewaters, or, in other cases, mixing waste streams of various chemicals together in the hope of neutralizing possible ill effects. The construction report explained that: "The effluent of this plants consisted mostly of wash waters from the turbines, surface drainage, and other waters such as sour batches of chemicals which [sic] were discharged from time to time into the sewage system."[50] Strikingly, the operations officers decided: "As the percentage of dilution of phosgene, chlorpicrin, mustard oil and other toxic gases was very large ... the effluent would have to be chemically treated."[51] Given that "the wash waters of the scrubbing and washing towers consisted of from one to ten per cent caustic soda solution," officers decided that the scrubbing and washing tower water would "neutralize some of the deleterious chemical in the sewage systems."[52]

The disposal system evolved as toxic waste accumulated because of production errors. Engineers noted: "The only time that any gas was liberated through the sewage system was when a whole batch of spoiled chloripicrin was dumped at one time into the sewer. Later when a sour batch was about to be discharged it was neutralized in the stills and allowed to flow gradually into the sewers with a large volume of wash water and no further inconveniences were suffered from the liberation of toxic gases."[53] Waste management and public health complications stemming from the production of all four of the major war gases in the same complex created numerous technical hurdles for the engineers, contractors, and enlisted personnel working at the various plants although only one weapon required a different worker safety system for its manufacture.

On the battlefield, mustard gas was so toxic and environmentally destructive that battlefield use raised troubling questions for military planners. The manufacture of mustard gas was in many ways just as dangerous and toxic for those working at Edgewood as it was for soldiers on the battlefield.[54] General Fries called the "introduction of mustard gas ... probably the greatest single development in gas warfare," noting that

---

[50] Ibid.   [51] Ibid.   [52] Ibid.   [53] Ibid., 2.

[54] Mustard gas "is a combination of ethylene and sulfur chloride as the ethylene gas is bubbled up through sulphur chloride in what is known as a reactor." NARA RG 175: Chemical Warfare Service, Entry 11: Construction of the Edgewood Arsenal, 1919, Box 11: Lt.-Col. Edward B. Ellicott Report on the Construction of the Chemical, Mustard Gas and Refrigeration Plants at Edgewood Plant of the Edgewood Arsenal, March 1919, 69. For a detailed analysis of mustard gas production both at Edgewood and also among the Allies and Germany during the First World War, see Fries and West, *Chemical Warfare*, 150–179. See also Haber, *The Poisonous Cloud*, 167–170.

"very low concentrations of vapor are capable of 'burning' the skin and producing casualties which require from three weeks to three months for recovery."[55] Moreover, mustard gas persisted in the environment for days or weeks at a time depending upon the landscape and weather, contaminating locations where shells exploded, requiring battlefield remediation if troops or animals moved through the area. The army noted that mustard gas's "chief value lies in the burning effects when it comes in contact with the flesh, and the fact that one never knows that he has come in contact with it until a burn commences to show."[56] The relatively long-term environmental contamination and health effects of mustard gas undermined its tactical utility for seizing ground after gas barrages. Edgewood officers explained: "A section of ground sprayed with mustard gas is uninhabitable for a period varying from two weeks to six months, as it is a very stable compound and will penetrate most any protective material such as rubber, leather, wood, etc."[57] In forward areas, soldiers, civilians, horses, and any other living creature could be injured by contact with mustard gas-permeated soil and suffer serious harm or burns, hindering the war effort for both man and beast.[58]

Not surprisingly, the safe manufacture and handling of mustard gas was extremely difficult from a chemical engineering standpoint. In an otherwise laudatory 1919 article in the *Journal of Industrial and Engineering Chemistry*, Charles H. Hurty, one of the nation's foremost inorganic chemists and a booster for the industry, described the mustard gas production process at Edgewood as "a cranky one" and extremely "difficult to control."[59] Producing mustard gas was not a simple straightforward

---

[55] Fries and West, *Chemical Warfare*, 150.

[56] NARA RG 175: Chemical Warfare Service, Entry 11: Construction of the Edgewood Arsenal, 1919, Box 11: Lt.-Col. Edward B. Ellicott Report on the Construction of the Chemical, Mustard Gas and Refrigeration Plants at Edgewood Plant of the Edgewood Arsenal, March 1919, 69.

[57] Ibid.

[58] On the environmental effects of mustard gas in the field and factory see Haber, *The Poisonous Cloud*, 239–258; and Gerard J. Fitzgerald, Chemical Warfare and Medical Response during World War I. *American Journal of Public Health* 98 (April 2008), 619–621. On the medical aspects of vesicants, in general, and mustard gas, in particular, see Frederick R. Sidell, Ernest T. Takafuji, and David R. Franz, eds., *Medical Aspects of Chemical and Biological Warfare* (Washington, DC: Office of the Surgeon General, 1997), in particular Sidell, Takafuji, and Franz, Vesicants, 197–228, and Frederick R. Sidell and Charles G. Hurst, Long-Term Heal Effects of Nerve Agents and Mustard, 229–246.

[59] Hurty, Gas Offense in the United States, 10. Charles H. Hurty became the editor of the *Journal of Industrial and Engineering Chemistry* following his two-term presidency of the

FIGURE 4.9 The Edgewood mustard gas plant during construction on July 2, 1918
Source: NARA RG 77: Office of the Chief of Engineers, Entry 391: Construction Reports, 1917–1943. Box 94 Edgewood Arsenal Vols. 3–4, Vol. 3.

chemical reaction but rather one that could easily set off dangerous side reactions. Hurty went on to explain that "the reaction is highly exothermic and a large cooling surface must be maintained."[60] If the temperature was not precisely controlled: "a batch 'goes wild' [and] great volumes of hydrochloric acid are given off, accompanied by highly toxic gases of an unknown composition," creating perils for those working in or near the plant.[61] "As the gas is strongly lachrymatory," Hurty noted, "such accidents produce great discomfort," understating how painful exposure to mustard gas really was.[62]

American Chemical Society in 1915–1916 and his observations are quite interesting in light of his support of the industry and the war effort. See Germaine M. Greer, *Crusading for Chemistry: The Professional Career of Charles Holmes Hurty* (Athens: University of Georgia Press, 1995).
[60] Hurty, Gas Offense in the United States, 10.   [61] Ibid.   [62] Ibid.

While production vexed engineers, the process of loading mustard gas into artillery shells, an operation that was highly automated to increase safety, was nevertheless quite dangerous. This led to the construction of Building No. 617, the "Operators' Building or Laundry Locker and Wash Room," a structure unique to the mustard gas facility.[63] The dangers of producing mustard gas were clear to the army. The official construction report said as much: "It was necessary to have this laundry and washroom because of the contamination of the men's clothing by the highly-dangerous material made. The suits and clothing worn by the men while working around the Mustard Gas Plant would become saturated with the fumes and had to be thoroughly washed and chlorinated before they would be safe to wear again."[64] To help and ensure the men's safety the "building was designed and erected with the advice and co-operation of the Gas Defense and was approved by them for the handling of contaminated clothing for the care of men who worked in the Mustard Gas Plant."[65]

Producing mustard gas caused 674 of the 925 reported injuries at Edgewood in 1918 (see Figure 4.10). The difficulties involved in mustard gas production also extended to quality control and waste management for bad production runs. Mixing Building No. 603 had a 700-foot pipeline "installed to take care of bad charges of Mustard Gas and permit [the] same to be pumped to [the] swamp and thus disposed of."[66] Another complicating factor that created both environmental and health hazards was the texture of mustard oil. The equipment used to make mustard gas, which often clogged pipes during production, led to the demolition of the entire facility after the war. These contaminated structures were simply dumped at Edgewood because it was impossible for the army to safely or economically solve the contamination problem.

Official documents explained: "The Mustard Oil, commonly known as Mustard 'Gas' Plant, which was used during the War, was torn down and all the equipment thrown in the swamp. This was necessary because the equipment became clogged when shut down and it was impossible to clean it because of the dangerous nature of the material."[67] After

---

[63] NARA RG 175: Chemical Warfare Service, Entry 11: Construction of the Edgewood Arsenal, 1919, Box 11: Lt.-Col. Edward B. Ellicott Report on the Construction of the Chemical, Mustard Gas and Refrigeration Plants at Edgewood Plant of the Edgewood Arsenal, March 1919, 95.
[64] Ibid., 96.   [65] Ibid., 95.   [66] Ibid., 125.
[67] NARA RG 175: Chemical Warfare Service, Entry 8: Technical Document, Files 1917–1920, Box 21: Miscellaneous Issuances Edgewood Arsenal – Range Tables, "Edgewood Arsenal the Seat of Chemical Warfare," 21.

Gas Casualties at Edgewood Arsenal, 1918								
Toxic agent	*June*	*July*	*August*	*September*	*October*	*November*	*December*	*Total*
Mustard gas	14	41	190	153	227	47	2	674
Stannic chloride	...	3	8	15	21	3	...	50
Phosgene	...	...	3	7	22	17	1	50
Chlorpicrin	...	14	18	9	3	...	...	44
Bleach chlorine	...	2	39	2	1	...	...	44
Liquid chlorine	...	1	3	2	7	5	...	18
Sulphur chloride	...	...	2	1	6	...	...	9
Phosphorus	...	2	7	5	1	...	...	15
Caustic soda	...	...	3	...	3	4	...	10
Sulphuric acid	...	...	4	3	1	...	...	8
Picric acid	...	...	2	...	...	...	...	2
Carbon monoxide	...	...	...	...	1	...	...	1
Totals	14	63	279	197	293	76	3	925

FIGURE 4.10 Medical data on industrial injuries resulting from chemical weapons production at Edgewood for the year 1918
Source: Table reproduced from Benedict Crowell and Robert Forrest Wilson, *The Armies of Industry Volume II. Our Nation's Manufacture of Munitions for A World In Arms, 1917–1918* (New Haven, CT: Yale University Press, 1921), 496.

jettisoning the defunct plant in nearby wetlands, the army built: "A new plant, capacity fifty tons per day, which embodies the best experience gained during the War, had been erected and is now ready for operation."[68] While this solved a problem in the short run, the decision to begin dumping toxic waste and contaminated machinery on site set a precedent that eventually devastated portions of Gunpowder Neck for the rest of the century. Over time these extremely dangerous pollutants made their way into the waters of the Chesapeake Bay and impacted the fragile marine ecosystems that provided oysters and other forms of sea-food to dinner tables all across the United States.[69]

[68] Ibid.
[69] Research to date has shown no evidence within primary or secondary military or civilian records of a massive fish kill or damage to the fragile oyster beds and aquaculture that were intrinsic to the Chesapeake Bay maritime economy during the war years, which is puzzling. Increased public interest in the ecological health of the Chesapeake Bay began to accelerate in the 1970s when the Chesapeake Bay was identified as containing a large marine dead zone resulting from increasing industrial and agricultural runoff following the Second World War from within the much larger Chesapeake Bay Watershed. The direct role of chemical waste from Edgewood in the health of the Bay is yet unknown aside from various Superfund studies beginning in the late 1990s. On the ecological history of the Bay during this time period see Christine Keiner, *The Oyster Question: Scientists, Waterman, and the Chesapeake Bay since 1880* (Athens: University of Georgia Press, 2009). On Superfund activity see footnote 71.

Although the army constructed new facilities at Edgewood, the future
of mustard as a tactical weapon had its limits. While mustard gas both
inflicted casualties on the enemy and contaminated enemy territory, the
public health and environmental difficulties were just as problematic for
trench warfare use because mustard gas lingered as each side advanced or
retreated through the same contaminated spaces. Engineers noted:
"although mustard gas was a very effective gas to make a trench or series
of fortifications uninhabitable, yet, after its use, it was impossible for
investing troops to occupy such positions. With Phosgene, on the other
hand, an offensive action could be carried on and the investing troops
could occupy the positions vacated."[70] When the war ended
in November 1918, the question about what to do with the many tons
of chemical weapons that had either never left Edgewood, or would soon
be returning from Europe, shaped the future of Gunpowder Neck.

CONCLUSION: THE ENVIRONMENTAL LEGACY OF
"DEMOBILIZATION"

Today the value of scientific, technological, and material contributions
made by the United States to its allies in the First World War is seen as at
best limited, especially since it is viewed in comparison to the unprecedented American military innovation and industrial production during
the Second World War and the Cold War. The success of the chemical
warfare project at Edgewood Arsenal stands out as a high point when
American military, governmental, and industrial planners were almost
completely unprepared to wage a modern global war. The successful
creation of the chemical-weapons production facility at Edgewood
Arsenal in less than one year marked an important step forward in
American arms manufacture and academic-military-scientific-industrial
practice, and a major milestone in the history of the chemical engineering
and US industrial chemistry.

---

[70] NARA RG 175: Chemical Warfare Service, Entry 11: Construction of the Edgewood
Arsenal, 1919, Box 11: Lt.-Col. Edward B. Ellicott Report on the Construction of the
Filling Plants at the Edgewood Plant of the Edgewood Arsenal, March 1919, 58. Mustard
might have been replaced, in 1919, by lewisite if the war continued. Synthesized by
America chemists, lewisite was the only "new" chemical weapon produced during the
war. While causing similar bodily damage as mustard gas, lewisite also broke down
quickly, so it eliminated serious decontamination issues. On the history of the development of lewisite see Joel A. Vilensky, *Dew of Death: The Story of Lewisite, America's
World War I Weapon of Mass Destruction* (Bloomington: Indiana University Press,
2005).

Unfortunately, Edgewood's material success was superseded by the military's failed stewardship of the land during the frenzied period of construction in 1917 and 1918. The decades of expansion and contraction that followed the Second World War and the Cold War created a site of environmental collapse that resulted in the Environmental Protection Agency (EPA) designating Edgewood as a Superfund site, initiating costly and extensive remediation that continues to this day.[71] On April 10, 1985, the EPA proposed that Edgewood be added to the National Priorities List as one of the most seriously uncontrolled or abandoned hazardous waste sites in the United States. This designation not only mandated long-term remediation but also elevated Edgewood to a Superfund Site on February 21, 1990. While destruction of stored chemical weapons, including mustard gas, was "completed" in February 2006, even today more than 100 contaminated areas continue to undergo study, decontamination, and remediation. The EPA completed a third five-year review in late 2013 to guide future work.

---

[71] For an introduction to the history of the government's response, or lack of response, regarding toxicity, groundwater contamination, and general public health concerns at Edgewood, in addition to the ongoing remediation problem, see the following: Scott E. Downing et al., Edgewood Arsenal: "An Installation Environmental Impact Assessment," National Technical Information Service, US Department of Commerce, Edgewood Arsenal, Aberdeen Proving Ground, Maryland, July 1975; "Public Health Assessment for U.S. Army Aberdeen Proving Ground, Edgewood Area, Aberdeen, Harford County, Maryland, EPA Facility ID: MD2210020036," US Department of Health and Human Services, Public Health Service, Agency for Toxic Substances and Disease Registry, 20 May 2008; "U.S. Army Garrison, Aberdeen Proving Ground, Aberdeen, MD, Aberdeen Proving Ground," Installation Restoration Program, Other Edgewood Areas Study Area, Record of Decision, Remedial Action at the Western Shore, Investigation Area (EAOE12) Final, August 2011; Global Security.org, Edgewood Chemical Activity (ECA) Aberdeen Proving Ground, Maryland. *Weapons of Mass Destruction*, www.globalsecurity.org/wmd/fa cility/edgewood.htm (accessed September 25, 2016). On the modern remediation of the Edgewood site see Richard D. Albright, *Cleanup of Chemicals and Explosive Munitions: Locating Identifying Contaminants and Planning for Environmental Remediation of Land and Sea Military Ranges and Ordnance Dumpsites* (Norwich, NY: William Andrew, 2008). On restoration and remediation of other militarized landscapes in the United States see David G. Havlick, Restoration and the Meaning of Former Military Lands in the United States. In Edwin A. Martini, ed., *Proving Grounds: Militarized Landscapes, Weapons Testing, and the Environmental Impact of U.S. Bases* (Seattle: University of Washington Press, 2015), 265–287. On military superfund sites see Jennifer Liss Ohayon, Addressing Environmental Risks and Mobilizing Democracy? Policy on Public Participation in U.S. Military Superfund Sites. In Edwin A. Martini, ed., *Proving Grounds: Militarized Landscapes, Weapons Testing, and the Environmental Impact of U.S. Bases* (Seattle: University of Washington Press, 2015), 175–210.

By the November 11, 1918 Armistice, Edgewood had produced chlor-opicrin, phosgene, chlorine, and mustard gases although output was limited. This was not because of any technical difficulties within the facility but because the Ordnance Department was unable to secure enough artillery shells and boosters to meet demand. The postwar world arrived quickly at Edgewood and on November 29, 1918, the director of the CWS received official notice that "the amount of such [chemical warfare] equipment for the needs of the Army after the passing of the present emergency will be zero."[72] Benedict Crowell's and Robert Forest Wilson's 1921 book *Demobilization: Our Industrial and Military Demobilization after the Armistice, 1918–1920* noted that the "Edgewood Arsenal was retained, at first in stand-by condition, with all machinery cleaned and oiled, all outdoor equipment housed in safe storage, and all surfaces subject to deterioration painted. The subsidiary [those outside of Edgewood] plants, buildings, and equipment, were sold, principally to manufacturers of chemicals and dyes. The sales were conducted by the auction method, and the Government received good prices."[73] The facility at Edgewood cost approximately $30 million and, in 1918, the Army had no plans to part with the property or its state-of-the-art facility.[74] The Edgewood Arsenal not only contained the largest and most up-to-date chemical weapons facility on Earth, mothballed, for now, but easily placed back in production as a turnkey operation, but Edgewood had also become the only major storage facility in the United States for chemical weapons on the Eastern Seaboard. The logistical imperatives that drove site selection in 1917, making Gunpowder Neck convenient for sending chemical weapons to the Western Front, made it just as useful a locale for shipping weapons back to the United States once the war was over. And there many of the weapons stayed.

---

[72] Crowell and Wilson, *Demobilization*, 220.   [73] Ibid., 221.

[74] The exact cost of the project is somewhat hard to verify. Although $20–25 million seems reasonable, some have estimated Edgewood's cost to be as high as $30 million. During construction in 1918, army engineers noted: "The sum of $19,040,000 has been set aside on the books of this office for the construction and initial operation of filling plants, chemical plants, and a chlorine plant, and additional power installation, as well as the necessary cantonments, hospital, storehouses, etc., and a gas-shell proving ground with laboratory and animal farm." The cost was surely higher since the army expanded the scale of the project beyond this initial figure. NARA RG 175: Chemical Warfare Service, Entry 11: Construction of the Edgewood Arsenal, 1919, Box 11: Lt.-Col. Edward B. Ellicott Report on the Construction of the Filling Plants at Edgewood Plant of the Edgewood Arsenal, March 1919, 11.

In 1921, "nearly 1,400 tons of phosgene, chloropicrin, mustard, and other deadly gases made during the war" were stored at the Edgewood Arsenal, "in addition to 51,000 Livens projectors, 88 trench mortars, 3,000,000 unfilled gas shells, and 700,000 unfilled hand grenades," and military experts assumed long-term storage could be readily accomplished for years to come.[75] Over the rest of the twentieth century, in addition to First World War weapons such as mustard gas, Cold War weapons such as the nerve agent sarin also found their way to Edgewood for storage, until the 1990s when some agents were incinerated. While the Edgewood Arsenal was demobilized after the Armistice, and reactivated in varying degrees over the course of the twentieth century, the environment of Gunpowder Neck was never demobilized. The land was militarized in such a dramatic fashion that it has limited use in any capacity other than for military uses. Unlike other types of military bases, weapons production sites such as Edgewood or Hanford, Washington remain "mobilized" because toxic changes to the land there hold fast in a much more permanent way than, say, the roots of the tree that was photographed guarding the empty fields at Gunpowder Neck prior to construction in October 1917.

In 2018, Edgewood is part of the US Army Edgewood Chemical Biological Center (ECBC) and is "the nation's principal research and development resource for non-medical chemical and biological (CB) defense" and operates as a thriving and well-funded biological/chemical warfare research facility employing both government scientists and engineers and various corporate military contractors.[76] Closely guarded and not open to the general public, the Edgewood facility hides in plain sight

---

[75] NARA RG 175: Chemical Warfare Service, Entry 11: Construction of the Edgewood Arsenal, 1919, Box 11: Lt.-Col. Edward B. Ellicott Report on the Construction of the Filling Plants at Edgewood Plant of the Edgewood Arsenal, March 1919, 11. "It is estimated that the [chemical weapons containers] will not deteriorate in storage for at least ten years, a fact indicating that poison gases are as durable in storage as smokeless powder. There are also stored at Edgewood large loaded gas shells manufactured during the war. ... The experts now estimate that the loaded gas shells will exist in good condition as long as a battleship can give service, from the time of commissioning the ship to the time when it is declared obsolete."

[76] For information on the ECBC, see www.ecbc.army.mil (accessed September 26, 2016). The larger Aberdeen Proving Ground is the center for more than 50 government laboratories and command facilities including the US Army Test and Evaluation Command, the US Army Chemical and Biological Defense Command, the US Army Medical Research Institute of Chemical Defense, the Program Manager for Chemical Demilitarization and various components of the Army Research Laboratory. On the remediation of the Edgewood site see Albright, *Cleanup of Chemicals and Explosive Munitions*.

from those who pass by on Amtrak's Northeast Corridor. Each day, passengers speed back and forth along the facility's northern edge, riding along the busiest passenger rail system in the nation. Unlike more famous weapons and waste storage facilities such as Hanford, Washington or Yucca Mountain, Nevada, Edgewood is located not in the vast and more sparsely populated spaces of the far west, but rather is bounded on one side by the suburban environs between Baltimore, Maryland and Philadelphia, Pennsylvania and on the other by the ecologically fragile Chesapeake Bay watershed. As environmental engineers and scientists struggle to contain and repair the damage to the land caused by the legacy of the First World War at Gunpowder Neck, the Edgewood Arsenal exists today less as a symbol of wartime mobilization success and chemical engineering expertise and more as an invisible and seemingly irreparable environmental disaster almost a century since the guns of August were silenced.

PART II

WAR'S GLOBAL REACH

Extracting Natural Resources

5

"The Mineral Sanction"

The Great War and the Strategic Role of Natural Resources

Roy MacLeod

INTRODUCTION

By the close of 1914, following the collapse of the Schlieffen Plan, and the failure of the German offensive, a complex and almost immovable line of trenches stretched on both sides from the English Channel to the Swiss border.[1] A conflict that was to be over by Christmas had instead seen the industrialized nations of the world catapulted into a struggle that would last for the next four years. The Great War has earned the sobriquet of the "chemist's war," but with the advent of tanks, submarines, and aircraft there were roles for other scientific disciplines, including meteorology, mathematics, physics, geology, and metallurgy. A world war that would redraw the map, destroy empires, create new alliances, and shatter certainties brought with it the concept of war as a contest of machines, governed by intelligence and communication, and based on a continuing supply of critical raw materials. A war in which new disciplines were born and new industrial organizations were created depended increasingly upon an understanding of Nature and the methods of science.

This was evident in Britain in the early months of 1915, when shortages of manufactured materials and chemicals for which the Allies had depended upon Germany were the shared experience of everyday life. Less forgivable were the shell scandals of February and March 1915, which brought disaster to the British army in France, and helped bring

[1] This chapter forms part of a larger study of strategic minerals and minerals strategies supported by the Australian Research Council. The author wishes warmly to acknowledge the assistance of Dr. Kimberley Webber, Dr. Eckart Krause, and Mr. Stuart Rollo, and the advice and comments of Professors John McNeill and Richard Tucker.

down the Asquith government. Before the war, British strategic planning focused on securing imperial control of the seas, the selective use of naval blockades, and (outside India) the occasional use of a small expeditionary force, trained and supplied to fight a short war. Lord Kitchener, Secretary of State for War, was among the first in government to foresee a long war and the need to mobilize and plan for it.

Before the war, Russia produced 56% of the world's manganese, against British India's 35% and Brazil's 5%. Britain historically imported from Russia; now, with transport shortages, India could not satisfy the British demand, and London was forced to buy on the international market. Similarly, before the war, Britain imported much of what it needed – even from the Central Powers – for example, magnesite bricks from Austria needed to line British steel furnaces. Now, Britain was obliged to seize the minerals of the Greek island of Euboea, where magnesite deposits could be worked under the guns of the Royal Navy.

Similar diplomatic embarrassment surrounded Burma's deposits of tungsten ore, vital to steel making, which were mined by British companies, but sent to Germany for processing. Until April 1915, much of Britain's sophisticated steel industry depended on the skill and refinement of German metallurgy.

The omnipresent but largely unspoken war of "minerals" forms a neglected branch of environmental history, not least because it throws light on the use of natural products that created the tortured landscapes of Europe. Rediscovering the role and impact of "strategic minerals" opens a new way of viewing the Great War, as science and industry fostered ever more efficient ways of exploiting and hurling substances of nature against Nature herself.

THE MINERALS WAR

The minerals war on the Western Front is conveniently seen in three phases – a makeshift start, leading by the spring of 1915 to the mobilization and creation of new agencies, transforming relationships between public and private, civilian and military. A second phase began in late 1916–1917, with the advent of Kitchener's Army, preparations for the Somme, and the massive industrialization implicit in the Hindenburg Program. From 1917 to the end of the war, the world saw the reality of "Total War," in material and environmental terms, much of it bought at considerable cost to the civilian population.

Industrial warfare in 1914 turned on wheels of iron and steel, fortified by coal. In prewar Germany, with plentiful coal and access to iron, industry grew quickly. In the decade preceding the war, Germany's iron and steel manufactures exceeded those of Britain, France, Russia, and Italy combined; and in the early months of 1914, well before the guns of August, American observers saw record imports of iron ore going to Germany, as well as huge stocks of manganese, brass, nickel, tin, aluminum, sulphur, graphite, and mica "so far in excess of previous rates" that British intelligence concluded that "some exceptional use was (being) planned."[2] Germany could obtain magnesite from Austria, but outside coal and potash, Germany was not blessed with raw materials. The German war machine faced the urgent task of securing new sources of raw materials.

The political significance of mineral acquisition was beyond doubt. After the war was declared, rumors circulated that France had deliberately withdrawn its troops ten kilometers from the border, and ceded the mines and steel works of Lorraine to Germany, so as to make it appear that it was Germany, rather than France, that began hostilities. Whatever the intent, the occupation of Lorraine swung the balance immediately in Germany's favor.

Within the first days of war, Germany had occupied the territory that produced 30 million tons of the 41 million tons of coal that France had produced in 1913.[3]

The synergy of blood and iron (*Blut und Eisen*) was a maxim of military planning, and for the next four years, Germany produced enough coal and iron ore by domestic production and neutral trade. But so-called tonnage minerals were not enough; industry needed also "pound" quantities of other substances.[4] In 1913, Germany imported 680,000 tons of manganese ore – 447,000 tons from Russia and 178,000 from India. Before 1914, German specialty steels contained up to 30% tungsten, but the blockade of wolfram ore imports from British Burma forced German industry to cut this by half. Molybdenum was a possible substitute, but was in short supply and seldom used.[5] The blockade brought further

[2] Frank Chambers, *The War behind the War, 1914 to 1918* (London: Faber and Faber, 1939), 141.

[3] Edwin C. Eckle, *Coal, Iron and War* (London: George Harrap, 1920), 78–80; Clifford Singer, *Energy and International War* (Singapore: World Scientific, 2008), 72.

[4] H. Foster Bain, Mineral Resources and Their Effect on International Relations. *Journal of the Royal Institute of International Affairs* 9(5) (September 1930), 664–679 at 671.

[5] Ronald Limbaugh, *Tungsten in Peace and War, 1918–1946* (Reno: University of Nevada Press, 2010), 24.

shortages in manganese and chromium, as well as in nonferrous metals such as copper, nickel, tin, and mercury, and in many other materials, including phosphates, rubber, lubricants, and asbestos.[6] Stories were told of spies smuggling in their baggage from overseas quantities of "the secret substance," platinum, an essential catalyst in explosives manufacture.[7] Thanks to Walter Rathenau's planning, the ferro-manganese stockpiles accumulated by August 1914 lasted for more than 20 months, but by 1917, German steel output began a slow decline.[8]

Data collected by the Board of Trade and the Ministry of Munitions, kept secret for decades, suggest that by 1917, Germany faced the probability of defeat not on the Front, where military eyes were focused, but at home, despite (or because of) the total militarization of its natural resources. Had Churchill's spring munitions offensive of 1919 materialized, with American material arriving in ever-increasing quantities, the Allies' superiority in resources would have taken them to Berlin.

OF MINERALS AND MEN

As the war continued into 1915, a new kind of war emerged, whose secrets were shared by small numbers of experts on either side. This "secret war" went to the supply of raw materials without which nations could not win. In particular, modern warfare needed steel, and steel-making depended upon a steady supply of minerals and metals that were essential to its production.

The mineral war – a struggle fought below ground, across the oceans, in factories, research laboratories, and commodity markets – brought to prominence a generation of scientific administrators quite as distinguished as those better known for their skill in science – less conspicuous than Fritz Haber, Arnold Sommerfeld, Ernest Rutherford, William Bragg, and even the young James Conant – and their rise was as rapid as it was unexpected.[9] In British circles, these included Sir Richard Redmayne in London, Archibald Liversidge of Sydney,[10] and Sir Thomas Holland of Delhi and London, and in the United States, George Otis Smith of the

---

[6] Chambers, *The War behind the War, 1914 to 1918*, 144–145.

[7] Bain, Mineral Resources and Their Effect on International Relations, 664–679.

[8] Anonymous, German Industry and the War II. *Nature* 102 (October 3, 1918), 87.

[9] Roy MacLeod, Scientists. In Jay Winter, ed., *Cambridge History of the First World War*, vol. 5 (Cambridge: Cambridge University Press, 2014), 434–459, 704–708.

[10] Roy MacLeod, *Imperial Science under the Southern Cross: Archibald Liversidge, FRS* (Sydney: University of Sydney Press, 2009).

United States Geological Survey (USGS) and Charles Kenneth Leith of the University of Wisconsin. In Europe, there was Walther Rathenau in Berlin and Albert Thomas in Paris. Bernard Baruch began his long career in American resources administration supervising minerals for the War Industries Board.[11] Their personal histories were diverse, but they found remarkably common ground, as industrial warfare everywhere forced attention to the strategic use of resources.

Even before the guns of August, the remarkable Walther Rathenau – engineer, businessman, and political reformer, later chairman of the Allgemeine Elekrizitäts-Gesellschaft (AEG), the biggest industrial combine in Europe – sensed the likelihood of a long war, and used his considerable influence to persuade the German War Ministry to establish a "War Raw Materials Department" (*Kriegsrohstoffabteilung*, or KRA) for the supply of strategic materials. Rightly surmising that Germany would be short of essential materials by the summer of 1915, he launched a policy of sequestration, adroitly avoiding the costs of stockpiling tons of confiscated goods by using private warehouses subject to government order. Sub-departments of War Industry Companies (*Kriegswirtschafts-Gesellschaften*) were created, staffed by professionals and businessmen who organized transfers of raw materials to manufacturers at given times and prices.[12]

In October 1916, the KRA was combined with imperial labor, munitions, and war food offices into an *Oberstes Kriegsamt*, or Supreme War Office, which assumed the preparation of the Hindenburg Program – foreshadowing the *Materialschlacht* of unprecedented intensity that was to be the harbinger of Total War. The program cost Germany dearly, and by 1917, the KRA was reduced to sponsoring the production of ersatz materials, some of which kept German armies in the field and postponed disaster at home. In response to shortages caused by the Allied blockade, German scientists extracted aluminum from native clays, and replaced iron and steel for copper in fuses and electric fittings. Similarly, calcium carbide replaced metals required for steel production; wood pulp was proposed to rescue the textile industry; glycerin was produced from beet sugar; and oils were made from seeds.[13] The coal tar industry, which sustained Germany's prodigious explosives industry, also supplied a host of substitutes; one account lists 446 synthetic products used in

---

[11] Bernard M. Baruch, *American Industry in the War* (Washington, DC: US Government Printing Office, 1921).

[12] Chambers, *The War behind the War, 1914 to 1918*, 147.   [13] Ibid., 150.

medicine and food.[14] Buttons, cartridges, shell bands, facings for helmets, and belt buckles – all could be, and were, made from scrap metals. Gasoline was replaced by benzol, and petroleum by acetylene. Shipbuilders replaced bronze fittings with iron or steel coated with bronze.[15]

In France, the organization of raw materials was dominated by the Ministry of War, but in October 1914, Albert Thomas, a socialist member of the French Parliament, was given the task of mobilizing the factories in northern France that had escaped German occupation. In 1915, Thomas became the minister of munitions, and the following year, the minister of armament, and within the next two years, performed a "miracle" in transforming the French war machine. In particular, he secured vast quantities of essential materials from the United States and Britain, which involved working closely with Britain's first minister of munitions, later the prime minister, David Lloyd George.

Under Lloyd George's administration, the Anglo-American connection became one of the most significant features of the war. Britain's first measures to control raw materials focused on the restriction of imports and the tightening of controls, both born (as Joel Hurstfield later put it, in describing the Second World War) of "scarcity and improvisation."[16] As early as October 1914, when materiel contracts proved slow and inadequate, Britain turned to the United States. In 1915, Lloyd George became the minister of munitions and assumed the task of "making order out of chaos and plenty out of shortage." In retrospect, his grasp of the situation was complete:

The making of a gun or shell-case, for instance, involves the metal trades, blast-furnaces, steel works, iron and steel foundries, forges, stamps, drops and dies, rolling-mills, drawn rod and wire works – and behind them, the colliery and the iron-ore quarry. It requires factories, and these in turn require machinery, covered electrical plant, factory equipment and machine tools; engines, pumps, turbines, road and rail transport; boiler-making and constructional engineering work. The explosives for filling and propelling the shell from the gun involve the output of chemical works, dye works, gas works, and a great deal of very careful laboratory experiment, investigation and testing.[17]

[14] George A. Schreiner, *The Iron Ration: Three Years in Warring Central Europe* (New York: Harper, 2012), 155.
[15] Anonymous, Copper in Germany. *The Engineering and Mining Journal* (January 30, 1915); Anonymous, What Germany Is Doing in the Chemical and Metallurgical Industries. *Engineering and Mining Journal* (May 8, 1915), 829.
[16] Joel Hurstfield, *The Control of Raw Materials: History of the Second World War* (London: HMSO, 1953).
[17] David Lloyd George, *War Memoirs*, vol. 6 (London: Ivor Nicholson & Watson, 1936).

These features of modern war were the essence of modern weaponry. Although, as Ronald Limbaugh has shown, nickel steel had replaced carbon steel, wrought iron, and bronze in the construction of rifle and cannon barrels, weapons were prone to erode and lose accuracy in the heat of fire. Metallurgists discovered that by lining the barrels with tungsten or molybdenum these effects were greatly reduced.[18] In this secret war, neither side was more prudent, nor much prepared. Germany began the war without stockpiles of tungsten, and was forced to substitute molybdenum imported from Norway. But by mid-1915, Britain was fully alive to the problem, and outflanked Germany by buying up all Norway's molybdenum and by threatening Sweden's entire system of oil imports if Sweden sold its steel to Germany. Not all such tactics were successful.

In April 1915, facing stalemate on the Western Front, First Lord of the Admiralty Winston Churchill persuaded Prime Minister Asquith's Cabinet to attempt to knock Turkey out of the war, so as to neutralize Austria-Hungary and protect the passage to British India. The disaster of Gallipoli was the result. Recrimination flowed, but unmentioned in Cabinet papers, and unnoticed by the press, the Allied failure to take Istanbul compounded another disaster, of even greater magnitude. Only a few at the Board of Trade knew that failure to clear the Dardanelles – closed by the Turks since the previous October – meant the loss of tons of Russian manganese ore that were vital to the Allied effort. Without these supplies, France and Britain were hard-pressed to find the alloy steel needed for artillery.

To Britain's war industry, the empire made a vast contribution. Prompted by the Imperial Conference of 1911, the British government established a Royal Commission (the "Dominion Commission") to investigate the supply of empire resources. The expertise of Canadians and Australians was always respected; with the coming of war, it was essential. In 1917, the Commission's final report coincided with a range of proposals – endorsed by the Imperial Institute and the War Minerals Committee of the Institute of Mining and Metallurgy[19] – to survey and "audit" the natural reserves of the entire empire, and to apply the resources of science to their conservation and use.

---

[18] Limbaugh, *Tungsten in Peace and War, 1918–1946*, 19.
[19] William Young Westervelt, Bill to Control War Minerals. *Engineering and Mining Journal* 105(2) (January 12, 1918), 149–150.

But the fruits of this research were to come slowly. Until at least 1917, the Allies were deeply indebted to American sources of aluminum and other minerals, coupled with imports from Portugal and Sicily. In the United States, from 1914 onward, the resulting domestic and export demand for raw materials produced a boom in prospecting and mining. Prices were forced upward by Allied procurement, and America itself faced shortages. From 1917, the initiative in American strategic mineral planning fell to Professor Charles Leith and George Otis Smith,[20] both of whom worked with the Shipping Board and the Bureau of Mines; and to the War Industries Board (WIB), directed by Bernard Baruch. The WIB oversaw the sources and mining of chromite, gypsum, graphite, ferroalloys, sulphur, manganese, and pyrites[21] and worked with mineral producers to increase domestic output against established prices and credits. The war led to a broader appreciation of what constituted industrial minerals, and stimulated government to gather data to serve "as a sound basis for planning a proper distribution and use of raw materials of the earth."[22] Clearly, keeping future reserves of strategic minerals required consideration not only of mineralogy and geology but also of transport, trade, and diplomacy.

APRÈS LA GUERRE

The conclusion of the war began a long period of rethinking about the conduct of the mineral campaign, and the improvisations of 1914–1918. During and after Versailles, in parallel with the postwar settlement, British and American geologists and geographers began to argue for surveys of world mineral reserves, and for audits of resources available in the event of another war. Mineral resources were to become a key source of geopolitical calculation.[23]

The Great War had demonstrated that no single country – not even the United States, nor the British Empire, which together controlled three-

[20] George Otis Smith, Public Service Opportunity and the Oil Geologist. *Engineering and Mining Journal* 109(13) (March 27, 1920), 759.

[21] Sylvia Wallace McGrath, *Charles Kenneth Leith, Scientific Adviser* (Madison: University of Wisconsin Press, 1971), 99.

[22] Charles K. Leith, *Mineral Supplies and the War* (1918). Quoted in Sylvia Wallace McGrath, *Charles Kenneth Leith, Scientific Adviser* (Madison: University of Wisconsin Press, 1971), 106.

[23] For a comparative account, see Andrea Westermann, Geology and World Politics: Mineral Resource Appraisals as Tools of Geopolitical Calculation, 1919–1939. *Historical Social Research* 40(2) (2015), 151–173.

fourths of the world's production of minerals – could ever be self-contained in industrial minerals; that while the British Empire could eventually supply all essential minerals if freedom of transport were assured, it could not always do so in sufficient quantities. Before the war, and when neutral, American industry traditionally experienced shortages of ferro-manganese, magnesite, and antimony for which it relied upon imports.[24] When the United States entered the war, these shortages worsened; and in early 1918, the War Department drew up its first list of 28 essential materials (the "Harbord list"), which was later divided into two groups – 14 "strategic materials essential to the national defense, the supply of which must be based on sources outside the US," and 15 other "critical materials" whose procurement would be difficult. By the Armistice, the language both of strategic minerals and mineral strategy was fully in place.

So too was the recognition that the relative strength of different nations in the possession of strategic minerals was itself a potential cause of war. In preparation for the Peace Conference in 1919, Bernard Baruch, who led the Economic Section of the American Commission, proposed a plan to equalize international access to war materials, including minerals. The French and English representatives submitted similar proposals, but for reasons that remain unclear the subject was sidelined by the Conference. What is clear is that the issue created political divisions between the Allies and the United States, which, it was widely believed, was in a position to find a solution if it so wished. However, the American standpoint was clearly set out in instructions issued in October 1918 by Herbert Hoover, with State Department approval, that applied to all raw materials: "The Government will not agree to any program that even looks like inter-Allied control of our [i.e., American] resources after peace. . . . Our only hope of securing justice in distribution, proper appreciation abroad of the effort we make to assist foreign nations, and proper return for the service that we will perform will revolve around complete independence of commitment to joint action on our part."[25]

Subsequently, Europeans took up the issue of mineral security at the Miners Congress in Geneva in 1920, the International Chamber of

---

[24] See Anonymous, Some Deficiencies in Mineral Resources. *Engineering and Mining Journal* 98(10) (September 5, 1914), 450.

[25] *Papers Relating to the Foreign Relations of the United States, 1918*, Supp. 1, vol. 1, 616. Quoted in Gerd Hardach, *The First World War, 1914–1918* (London: Allen Lane, 1977), 253.

Commerce in 1921, the Economic and Financial Committee of the League of Nations in 1922, the World Economic Conference in 1927, and the Diplomatic Conference of the League of Nations, in 1927, but to no avail.[26] If no one disagreed about the importance of the issues, given the postwar world of tariffs, there was also no consensus about the way of securing or regulating access to raw materials, whether in the interests of strategy, welfare, or conservation.

Into this political wilderness, few ventured, but one stands out: Charles Leith, professor of geology at the University of Wisconsin and veteran chairman of the Mineral Advisory Committee of the Army and Navy Munitions Board, chairman of the Planning Committee for Mineral Policy of the National Resources Board, and mineral adviser to the War Industries Board and to the American Commission in Paris. War service had taken Leith from pre-Cambrian geology to international geopolitics. From the early 1920s he wrote a series of papers, extending his war experience to international affairs. Few grasped as well as he the dynamics of what he called the "three primary units" – the United States, the British Empire, and Western Europe – in managing "the logical effects of the development of natural resources upon international affairs."[27]

For Leith, there was no escape from the need for an international agreement on the sourcing and stockpiling of strategic minerals – perhaps a "commercial League of Nations."[28] Leith was not uncritical of the United States, which produced 40% of the world's minerals, but consumed much more than this, and relied upon the rest of the world for up to 15 industrial minerals for its own economy. For decades, American mineral policy had been slow, piecemeal, and contradictory. There was, he believed, a role for the United States in regulating domestic commerce, and in tightening public supervision of monopolies, but also in developing foreign policy to inspire not "super-national," but "partnership control" of scarce materials among the nations.[29]

In some ways, Leith caught the temper of the times – and won the support of the "preparedness" party. In 1921, for example, he chaired

[26] Charles K. Leith, *Minerals in the Peace Settlement* (Washington, DC: The Geological Society of America, 1940), 3.

[27] Charles K. Leith, The World Iron and Steel Situation in Its Bearing on the French Occupation of the Ruhr. *Foreign Affairs* 133 (1922–1923), 136–151 at 151.

[28] Charles K. Leith, Mineral Resources in Certain International Relations. *Journal of the Royal Institute of International Affairs* 5(3) (1926), 155–159 at 156.

[29] Charles K. Leith, The International Aspect of the Mineral Industry, *Annals of the American Academy of Political and Social Science* 150 (1930), 98–104 at 104.

a committee of the Mining and Metallurgical Society of America and the American Institute of Mining and Metallurgical Engineers to assess the "industrial preparedness" of the United States. This committee agreed that it was impossible for any single country to be self-contained, urged an "open door" for American exploitation and exploration, and asked the American government to increase its investment in mineral intelligence both at home and abroad. A world of potential "strategic scarcities" soon brought even longer lists of "essential" materials, all of which America would be bound to contain or control.

THE WAY TO END ALL WARS

Across the Atlantic, Leith found an ally in Sir Thomas Holland, the prewar director of the Geological Survey of India, who put a similar case to the Empire Congress of the Institution of Mining and Metallurgy, meeting at Montreal in 1927. Holland, a graduate of the Royal School of Science, imperial geologist, and professor of geology at Manchester, had been the wartime director of the Indian Munitions Board – the central authority for controlling munitions supplies to British forces across India, Mesopotamia, and Egypt. Since 1922 he had been the rector of Imperial College, London, and was later to be the principal of the University of Edinburgh (1929–1944). He spoke with the unusual authority of a geologist who knew, better than Macaulay, whether an acre in Middlesex might be richer than a principality in Utopia.[30]

Holland met Leith in 1919 and in 1926, when they both spoke to the Royal Institute of International Affairs. Both agreed on the need for intelligence about world resources, and more discussion about national monopolies,[31] about the pace and direction of technical change in the use of materials, and about means of international accounting and control. However, it fell to Holland, rather than Leith, in the depths of the Depression, and amidst economic fears for the future of manufacturing, to exploit the logic of "international movements of mineral products" in a dangerous world.

As part of the wider effort to overhaul the realm of imperial science, an imperial audit of resources, followed by careful management, was vital. Holland rested his case on the experience of the war. First, he surmised, victory in the industrial war had gone not to the bravest, but to the best

---

[30] Roy MacLeod, Sir Thomas Henry Holland (1868–1947). *Oxford Dictionary of National Biography* (Oxford: Oxford University Press, 2004), 1–5.

[31] Leith, Mineral Resources in Certain International Relations, 156.

equipped and the best organized, who had made the most intelligent use of industrial and domestic resources. Second, the war demonstrated that most munitions depend upon minerals. Of the 80 known chemical elements, 30 were required in modern warfare. In many cases, the absence of small quantities of key elements could render large factories useless. Despite deep shortages in copper, nickel, aluminum, tin, antimony, manganese, and petroleum, Germany had kept the war going for its final two years only by virtue of careful stockpiling, massive investment in applied research, careful mining of low-grade deposits, and extensive imports from neutrals.[32]

Looking to the future, the uneven geographical distribution of key minerals was destined to play a role in political settlements. What was known about the location and distribution of strategic resources influenced the recasting of boundaries at Versailles The resources of Russia and China and elsewhere in Asia remained largely uncanvassed, and would make an important difference in the future. But in the meantime, Allied governments knew that the basis of international trade – material, capacity, and consumption[33] – must remain global and be kept international. The concern was that, if the demand for minerals was historically an underlying cause of war, then peacetime commerce could only compound the problem, and further conflict could result.

Such reflections required a reversal in strategic thinking. Future policy for national security must rest not merely upon stockpiles, but upon international policies to restrict the supply of materials. This theme was taken up by Holland in his Presidential Address to the British Association in Johannesburg in 1929,[34] and elaborated in the Trueman Wood Lecture to the Royal Society of Arts in London in 1930, in which Holland set out a plan for a "mineral sanction" – an instrument to prevent war, without interfering with other necessities, which could be adopted with the minimum of interference with commerce or finance, and which would not arouse "international jealousies by the usurpation of deserted markets."[35]

---

[32] Joseph E. Pogue, Mineral Resources in War and Their Bearing on Preparedness. *The Scientific Monthly* 5(2) (August 1917), 120–134 at 121.

[33] Bain, Mineral Resources and Their Effect on International Relations, 672.

[34] Thomas Holland, "The International Relationship of Minerals," Presidential Address, British Association for the Advancement of Science. *Report of the Ninety-Seventh Meeting, Johannesburg, 1929* (London: British Association, 1930), 22–37.

[35] Thomas Holland, "International Movement of Mineral Products in Peace and War," Trueman Wood Lecture, Royal Society of Arts, London, January 29, 1930, reprinted in *The Straits Times*, March 7, 1930, 2.

Over the next five years, Holland warmed to his theme, suggesting there should be a new mineral sanction clause in the Covenant of the League of Nations, and that the United States and the British Empire should act together to keep the peace, by restricting their exports of war-making minerals to other countries within the knowable limits of their peacetime requirements. The British debate coincided with growing American interest, which led in 1931 to the establishment of a so-called Mineral Inquiry, under the direction of William P. Rawles, with the task of making "factual studies of the mineral resources of the United States and the world in their political and international relations." The Inquiry reported to the Council on Foreign Relations in New York in 1933.

Critics were quick to point out the difficulties inherent in minerals data. For example, counting and control of Canada's nickel exports to neutral countries could be misleading and difficult, and financial control of minerals was often vested in international, rather than national, companies. Still, the idea turned and caught the light – there could be no doubt, as an Australian economist put it, that war might be averted – or at least its likely coming, well advertised – by the international supervision of trade figures and mineral production. The tools of science could serve as instruments of peace.[36]

For his agencies of enforcement, Holland looked to the world's two most recent innovations for the preservation of peace – the League of Nations and the Kellogg-Briand Pact of 1928. However, they suffered from the fact that, as Holland saw it, the Covenant was too comprehensive and too drastic to employ in specific cases without bringing vast political and economic repercussions. Article XVI, as he put it, was an "ill equipped workshop that has no hammer available but a steam hammer, which the mechanics are afraid even to use."[37] Sanctions could be used, but selectively.

This would be done by limiting a nation's capacity to wage war. This would be achieved not by financial sanctions, because offending nations could always default, and creditor nations would never agree to restrictions on their own commerce. To deter non-industrialized nations from war, embargoes might work. But for industrialized nations, a system was needed to refuse the export of war-relevant minerals to those countries in amounts beyond those required for civilian needs. Members of the League

---

[36] J. Macdonald Holmes. *Sydney Morning Herald*, October 26, 1935, 21.
[37] Thomas Holland, *The Mineral Sanction as an Aid to International Security* (Edinburgh: Oliver and Boyd, 1935), 9.

would be asked to impose an international minerals embargo against any industrial power that declared war on another.[38]

His case turned on what all knew, but few understood, of the nature of modern warfare. "It is evident," he said, "from the recent disarmament discussions that very few of those who influence our political commitments have the slightest conception of the enormous strides which have been made in recent years in, for example, the utilization of ferroalloys."[39] "The use of metals ... is developing without visible limit to its possibilities. We have indeed to recast fundamentally our mental estimates of what is necessary for war; we have to realize that mechanization – and therefore the use of a wide range of mineral products – requires a complete change of our estimates of speed and power, as well as of material, in problems of tactics and strategy."[40]

From this assessment followed Holland's recommendation of a "Mineral Sanction," a principle – or a norm of conduct – that looked beyond the familiar discourse of economic sanctions, to what might be called environmental control. Minerals were unevenly distributed throughout the world. No nation was self-sufficient in every mineral. Therefore, the prospect of mineral misapplication to war lay in the restriction of mineral supplies, in accordance with agreements by parties to the Covenant. The cooperation of the United States, he felt, could be achieved by granting countries the right to prohibit the export of mineral products to any country that broke the peace with any other.

Holland's argument turned on a set of plausible assumptions:

1) The progress of mechanization had made world powers dependent on a supply of minerals and metals that had grown from 5 to 25 times their prewar peacetime requirements;

2) No country can carry on industrial war without a continuous and sufficient supply of minerals and metals;

3) No country – not even the United States or Britain – is self-contained as regards minerals; none could produce the necessary variety and quantity of minerals from its own resources; nor will any country ever be able to do so, "for minerals, unlike vegetable products, cannot be transplanted, cannot be reproduced synthetically and cannot be replaced by artificial substitutes";[41]

---

[38] Thomas Holland, The Mineral Sanction as a Contribution to International Security. *International Affairs* 15(5) (1936), 735–752 at 746.
[39] Holland, *The Mineral Sanction as an Aid to International Security*, 21.   [40] Ibid.
[41] Ibid., 17.

4) Global audits of natural resources – to be conducted under international control – would establish transparent accounts of mineral resources, from which supervision would follow; this supervision would contribute to global conservation;

5) Suggestions that the progress of science would at any time soon produce substitutes for natural minerals – say, in the hydrogenation of coal and the production of alcohol to offset shortages in petroleum – were "nonsense." Wars (as currently conceived) were likely to require far more of these materials than countries could presently produce, and at far greater cost;

6) There was nothing to prevent the United States from adopting the plan in unison with the League, as it was consistent with the Kellogg-Briand Pact; and

7) The force of the Mineral Sanction had the force of Nature: "Minerals cannot be made artificially or be replaced by substitutes." Given this "law of nature," international regulation was both scientifically and politically feasible. In principle, the Mineral Sanction would bring about both mineral security and economic development, and would contribute to the prevention of war.

Moreover, the establishment of a Mineral Sanction offered other advantages. For example, it would not require updating, for "mechanisation would continue with the development of science"; and quotas of minerals allowed each country would be adjusted accordingly. It would contain the ambitions of the great powers, while not interfering with the trade of weaker nations.[42] No blockading force would be required; exporting nations would merely refuse to give port clearance. Authorization to enable regulation would receive "careful definition by the League, and appropriate legislation in every member country."

SANCTIONS VERSUS SHORTCOMINGS

In the early 1930s, the concept of the Mineral Sanction enjoyed a rational appeal, especially among the scientific community. After a decade of gestation, it marked the public arrival of the geosciences as a factor in geopolitics. The political and military relevance of natural resources was made explicit in a way never before put so clearly. In international relations, the concept had many virtues. It created a prescriptive norm – and in

[42] Ibid., 10.

certain circumstances, might force a potential aggressor to think twice. It was proleptic, and could promote a range of restrictions in other fields. Today, the international "Australia Group" (15 countries in 1985, and 40 today) – which exists to monitor the export of materials, including dual-use precursors, that are relevant to the production of chemical and biological weapons – uses remarkably similar language.

Regrettably, the idea was ahead of its time. The economic sanctions adopted by the League when Italy invaded Abyssinia in October 1935 were precarious – three nations (Austria, Albania, and Hungary) backed out because they could not afford to lose a customer – and the League's admonitions omitted to deny key minerals and petroleum, in the absence of which Italy could not have proceeded. If, as Holland told Chatham House in June 1936, "the League had done no more than impose at once an oil embargo, the Italian submarines, aeroplanes and tanks would have been powerless."[43]

The failure of the League to levy sanctions underlined flaws that were well recognized at the time.[44] Enforcement was not made easy by the language of Article XVI. Mineral sanctions could not "stop" a country going to war, but could inhibit that country from waging war. While such a constraint might logically oblige a country to reconsider, war would inevitably follow a period of planning and stockpiling; and once declared, there could be a long time before stockpiles ran out (and assuming the belligerent failed to obtain materiel from elsewhere).

Such flaws in conception were worsened by the fact that the act of sanction relied upon peacetime calculations of trade, consumption, and production that were not reliable indicators of wartime activity. Sanctions could even be counterproductive, if they drove the peacetime accumulation of stocks, intensified rivalries, and fostered protective tariffs, import restrictions, and economic nationalism. Worse, a mineral sanction would not prevent a quick war of movement, the prospect of which would increase insecurity overall. Finally, there remained the consistent argument against sanctions – that they can do more damage to the giver than the receiver, and force distress upon those who least deserve it.

By 1939, the coming of war again reversed the narrative of prevention, and revisited the discourse of stockpiling and acquisition. Romanian oil, Swedish steel, and the resources of the Middle East became targets. The Sanction seemed to disappear.

---

[43] Holland, The Mineral Sanction as a Contribution to International Security, 738.
[44] See M. J. Bonn, How Sanctions Failed. *Foreign Affairs* 15(1) (January 1937), 350–361.

For Holland, however, the fight was not over. As late as 1942, five years before his death, Holland continued to argue for the "international exchange of minerals" as a way of dealing with "tensions that cannot be relieved except by war." No country, he said, can ever be self-contained, and no nation could contribute its share to civilization without operating the principles of the Atlantic Charter. The problem, he saw, was "national exclusiveness" – the solution was international cooperation.[45]

Against this, however, stood political realities. The USSR and the United States saw no alternative to stockpiling strategic minerals in the interests of national security. The British Empire and the United States, who owned two-thirds and controlled three-quarters of the minerals of the world, failed to agree on a cooperative plan. There was even less prospect of agreement among the minerals-rich members of the post-war Commonwealth.

What of the future? Holland's fear was, as Eugene Staley put it, "There is nothing for which states will fight more quickly than those things which affect their power to fight."[46] Holland's response was:

The development of an international conscience about the hoarding of mineral deposits was not a question of [mere] academic interest. Unless it is settled, and settled quickly at the end of the War, by an intelligent understanding among the successful Powers, newly concocted aggressive attempts to enforce control will lead intermittently to further outbreaks of war. Delay for more mature consideration may be the rashest step to take.[47]

CONCLUSION

In the short term, and in a narrow sense, Holland's proposal failed: mineral sanctions were never pursued. Whether they could work remains an untested proposition. Admittedly, the prospect is doubtful. Today, with the advance of science, many factors drive military and industrial development – and setting any limit on the acquisition of materials merely forces the discovery of new materials and promotes innovation. Holland's generation could not know of the uses of lasers and rare earths in electronics and telecommunications, and had little conception of the vast

---

[45] Thomas Holland, Relation of Mineral Resources to World Peace. *Nature*, 150 (3804) (September 26, 1942), 364–366 at 366.

[46] Eugene Staley, *Raw Materials in Peace and War* (New York: Council on Foreign Relations, 1937), 29.

[47] Holland, Relation of Mineral Resources to World Peace, 366.

resources awaiting discovery in Central Asia, Siberia, Australia, and Africa, let alone on the high seas and in outer space.

But in other ways, the principle of a mineral sanction was successful. The Great War debate gave rise to a new global polity of strategic minerals, as well as a new discipline of mineral economics, and brought new forms of expertise to the care and conservation of minerals of strategic value.

The end of the war saw the beginning of a new wave of resources nationalism, framed by national self-interest, which is still with us. A century on, with our strategic future increasingly framed by Asia, we await an international consensus on the conservation and control of strategic minerals in the interests of world peace. As we move into the minerals-rich domains of outer space, and revisit the implications of astropolitics for mankind, we will have reason to look more deeply into its history. But that is another story, for another time.

6

Something New under the Fog of War

The First World War and the Debut of Oil on the Global Stage

Dan Tamïr

In October 2014, helicopters, minesweepers, and 200 service personnel of the Swedish armed forces were mobilized for searches in the waters off Stockholm after what was suspected to be a Russian submarine.* Russia, for its part, rejected all allegations of hostile activity.[1] The searches revealed nothing at the time. But in July 2015 a Swedish oceanic exploring company found the wreck of an unidentified submarine off the coast of the country, with Cyrillic letters engraved on the hull.[2] Indeed it was Russian, but a bit older than expected: it was a submarine that belonged to the Imperial Russian Navy, last seen in 1916.[3]

Exactly 101 years after the outbreak of the Great War, one of its shadows showed up from the abyss. The war in the Baltic Sea was only a sideshow during that war: the more intensive naval activity took place in the North Sea and the Atlantic Ocean. But while its contribution to the outcome of that particular war itself was marginal, the introduction of the

* This chapter is based on work supported by the Swiss National Fund grant PBZHP1_141503 *War Resources: Oil Availability as an Explanatory Historical Factor, 1890–2000.* The research was cordially hosted by Prof. Alexander Nützenadel, at Humboldt University of Berlin.

[1] Peter Walker, Sweden Searches for Suspected Russian Submarine off Stockholm. *The Guardian*, October 19, 2014, www.theguardian.com/world/2014/oct/19/sweden -search-russian-submarine-stockholm (accessed August 1, 2017).

[2] Doug Bolton, Sweden Submarine: Investigation Underway into Wreck of Unidentified Warship Found Off Coast. *Independent*, July 27, 2015, www.independent.co.uk/news/ world/europe/investigation-underway-into-wreck-of-an-unidentified-submarine-found -off-the-coast-of-sweden-10420209.html (accessed August 1, 2017).

[3] Dan Bilefsky, Sweden Spots a Russian Submarine, 99 Years Late. *New York Times*, July 29, 2015, www.nytimes.com/2015/07/30/world/europe/sweden-spots-a-russian -submarine-99-years-late.html?mcubz=2 (accessed August 1, 2017).

submarine to battle during the First World War, together with other technological innovations of the time – the armored vehicle and the air-plane – marked a significant shift in the history of warfare.[4] All these military machines had one thing in common: they were fueled solely with petroleum.

The First World War was a decisive moment in petroleum's role in the global arena; it was then when petroleum became the resource *par excellence* of the twentieth century. The rise of petroleum society was a long – and not at all straightforward – historical development, which began in the late nineteenth century at the latest. Even the most revolutionary social and technological novelties are deeply rooted in the past. But if we are looking for a "watershed" in the environmental history of war, or indeed the history of war more generally, this is a good place to start.

Prior to 1914, war planners and thinkers in Europe were mostly of the opinion that the next war would be short, offensive, and decisive.[5] They were offering human solutions – national spirit, élan, and so forth – to technical problems and innovations in the battlefield – a strategy that resulted in carnage. One reason for sticking to old assumptions might have been the conservative stance inherent in military high echelons; another reason might have been political: military planners, who were members of a social and economic elite, believed that a prolonged war would cause massive social upheaval among both conscripts and civilians.[6] A short war of the familiar sort was more comforting to contemplate.

But by 1914 technology, supply, and infrastructure were sufficient and ready for manufacturing and maintaining large mechanized navies, armies, and air forces. It took the military commanders and strategists a while to fully comprehend that the old tactics of flank attack, envelop-ment, and annihilation are futile when confronted with the massive fire power of well-entrenched defenders, armed with modern machine guns

---

[4] Timothy Mitchell, *Carbon Democracy: Political Power in the Age of Oil* (London: Verso, 2011), 66.

[5] Later on, Ivan Bloch became known as one of the prophets who warned humanity of the danger of a prolonged, all-encompassing war. His view, however, was an exception. See Margaret MacMillan, *The War That Ended Peace: The Road to 1914* (New York: Random House, 2013), 270ff.

[6] Andrew Liaropoulos, Revolution in Warfare: Theoretical Paradigms and Historical Evidence – The Napoleonic and First World War Revolutions in Military Affairs. *The Journal of Military History* 70 (2006), 363–384. Such was indeed the case in Russia in 1917 and – in a somehow different manner – in Germany and in some of the successor states of the Austro-Hungarian Empire.

and state-of-the-art ammunition.[7] The way out of the standstill was to use a modern trident: attrition of the enemy's supplies, enhancing the speed of movement and transportation, and rendering the old two-dimensional war a three-dimensional one. This trident was all but oil driven.

The importance of the First World War for the use of petroleum can be seen in two parallel channels: the *quantity* of energy available and the *quality* of its practical usage and technical implementation. The first part of this chapter, therefore, briefly reviews the place of energy research in historical analysis. The second part of the chapter examines the quantitative meaning of the introduction of petroleum to the art of war, while the third part examines petroleum's qualitative aspects. Finally, the chapter concludes with an assessment of the meaning and significance of that petroleum's military debut for our perception and understanding of the historical era born out of the agony of that war: the twentieth century.

OIL IN HISTORY

Many studies concerning energy questions have been conducted during the past several decades in the fields of sociology and politics; the *history* of energy and its uses has been researched by various historical subdisciplines. Prominent among them is environmental history, which tends to be more open toward interdisciplinary research than other historical branches.[8]

Environmental historians regard energy mostly as a part of the relationship between humans and nature, as well as a historically changing basis for human existence. At the same time, the history of energy is also accepted as a part of the history of technology.[9]

---

[7] Jonathan B. A. Bailey, The First World War and the Birth of Modern Warfare. In MacGregor Knox and Williamson Murray, eds., *The Dynamics of Military Revolution, 1300–2050* (Cambridge: Cambridge University Press, 2001), 132–153. While the image of the trenches was epitomized in the battlefields of France and Belgium, similar standstills and dead-ends were present in other fronts as well, from Poland to the Sinai desert.

[8] The best examples are probably Alfred Crosby, *Children of the Sun: A History of Humanity's Unappeasable Appetite for Energy* (New York: Norton, 2006); Rolf Sieferle, *The Subterranean Forest: Energy Systems and the Industrial Revolution* (Cambridge: White Horse Press, 2001); John McNeill, *Something New under the Sun: An Environmental History of the World in the 20th Century* (New York: Norton, 2000). For a recent overview by a historically minded geographer, see Vaclav Smil, *Energy and Civilization: A History* (Cambridge, MA: MIT Press, 2017).

[9] For a short review of the historiography of energy, see Hendrik Ehrhardt and Thomas Knoll, Einleitung. In Hendrik Ehrhardt and Thomas Knoll, eds., *Energie in der modernen Gesellschaft: Zeithistorische Perspektiven* (Göttingen: Vandenhoeck & Ruprecht, 2012), 5–11.

Historians usually divide the energy history of humanity roughly into two eras, based on two "energetic regimes": the "old regime," which is based on annually renewable solar cycles, and the "new regime," involving fossil fuels.[10] While the temporal distinction between the two is varied (the two still coexist in various parts of our world), the "new regime" is perceived as representing the modern world. This regime can be further subdivided, in accordance with the three main fossil fuels humans use: coal, gas, and petroleum. Coal was available and in broad use from the eighteenth century; petroleum from the late nineteenth century; and the broad commercial use of gas began just recently, in historical terms.

Although their chemical and natural origins are similar, oil has a series of operational advantages over coal and gas. First, oil used to be relatively easily extracted: during the booming years of cheap, accessible oil, the drilling of oil wells, the shipping of crude, and its final refining demanded a very small investment of energy and a few workers compared to the inputs required to operate coal mines.[11] Second, the transportation of oil – be it in barrels, pipelines, or tankers – is easy, compared with the transportation of coal (which is bulky and holds less combustible energy per unit of volume or weight) and with gas (which has to be either liquefied or very well sealed before it is transported). Last but not least, oil can be processed quite easily into a variety of different products: from gasoline to plastic toys and from lubricants to fertilizers. It is not surprising, therefore, that oil was recognized as the prime mover of twentieth-century industrial societies.[12] Cheap, flexible, and abundant, it

---

[10] Edmund Burke, The Big Story: Human History, Energy Regimes, and the Environment. In Edmund Burke III and Kenneth Pomeranz, eds., *The Environment and World History* (Berkeley/Los Angeles: University of California Press, 2009), 33–53; Sieferle, *The Subterranean Forest*, 4–34.

[11] This was the situation during most of the twentieth century, when oil was abundant and easily accessible. For the current trend of depletion in the reserves of easily accessible and cheap oil, see Colin Campbell and Jean Laherrere, The End of Cheap Oil. *Scientific American* (March 1998), 78–83; Robert Hirsch, The Inevitable Peaking of World Oil Production, *Atlantic Council Bulletin* 16(3) (2005); Richard Heinberg, *The Oil Depletion Protocol* (Gabriola Island: New Society Publishers, 2006); and Ian Chapman, The End of Peak Oil? Why This Topic Is Still Relevant Despite Recent Denial, *Energy Policy* 64 (2013), 93–101.

[12] A good introduction to this theme is Vaclav Smil, *Prime Movers of Globalization: The History and Impact of Diesel Engines and Gas Turbines* (Cambridge, MA: MIT Press, 2010).

endowed modern industrial societies an immense quantity of readily available energy.

FOSSIL FUELS AVAILABLE FOR INDUSTRIAL WARFARE

Like all human activities, the waging of war consumes energy, the sources of which varied throughout human history. The availability of energy – combined with technological innovation – continuously influences the methods, the extent, and the magnitude of wars.[13]

The nineteenth century was already shaped, to a large extent, by a fossil fuel. With coal, humanity suddenly had energy at its disposal on a scale that far exceeded what is available in regenerating biomass.[14] Accordingly, it was coal that made the big difference between ancient wars and nineteenth-century wars. By the century's end, coal became an integral part of warfare; modern armies of the time could not do without it.

But if one asked an army general in 1912 whether he could imagine a war without petroleum, his answer might well have been positive. On land, infantry soldiers were transported by coal-fueled trains; the cavalry used horses; cannons were dragged by horses or mules (or even large dogs, in some cases); trains, donkeys, and camels were used for supply and logistics.[15] At sea, the navies of the early twentieth century were faster, stronger, and more reliable than their predecessors – but were still mostly fueled with coal.[16] Aerial warfare was negligible, and, except for a tiny number of airplanes, was based on Zeppelins and some balloons. Oil scarcely mattered.

On land, the early battles of the First World War were in a sense the last battles of the nineteenth century: railways brought men, horses, and ammunition to the front – and left them there to fight on their own

---

[13] Crosby, *Children of the Sun*; for specific case studies, see Philippe Le Billon, The Political Ecology of War: Natural Resources and Armed Conflicts. *Political Geography* 20 (2001), 561–584. A theoretical framework for the relations between war and available energy is provided by Joseph A. Tainter, Archeology of Overshoot and Collapse. *Annual Review of Anthropology* 35 (2006), 59–74.

[14] Sieferle, *The Subterranean Forest*, 44. For the role coal played in giving birth to the industrial era, see also John F. Richards, *The Unending Frontier: An Environmental History of the Early Modern World* (Berkeley: University of California Press, 2003), 194–233.

[15] See Gene Tempest, *The Long Face of War: Horses and the Nature of Warfare in the French and British Armies on the Western Front* (PhD dissertation, Yale University, 2013).

[16] James Goldrick, Coal and the Advent of the First World War at Sea. *War in History* 21 (2014), 322–337.

devices.[17] Warfare in 1914 was linear, centered on the contact battle of masses of infantry soldiers and cavalry troops, supported by artillery shooting at the enemy in the open, usually from short range.[18] This strategy, however, quickly exposed the main problem of the war: the strong defensive abilities of modern industrial armies. The old school did not assess well enough the firepower of well equipped, entrenched troops. The war that was supposed to be won swiftly by an attack (in the case of the German Schlieffen Plan) or a counterattack (to be executed by French and British forces) came to a halt when facing these defensive formations: the rapid development of firearms and weapons during the late nineteenth century granted an infantry squad the ability to thwart the advance of an entire battalion. Instead of "coming home before Christmas," the belligerents found themselves in a prolonged stalemate.

This stalemate created one major quantitative challenge: the sending of millions of soldiers to the front and the huge logistic apparatus that supplying these troops required. This challenge contributed to the introduction of internal combustion engines to the battlefield: commanders gradually understood that railroads alone would not suffice for supplying the large armies involved in the war. Thus cars and trucks were deployed in the field. As the war progressed, oil-powered vehicles became increasingly important in combat.[19]

The US Army, in combat by March 1918, relied more heavily on motor transportation than any other: the American Expeditionary Force (AEF) had 40,000 trucks at the armistice, with the lowest ratio of men to machines. The French army had about 95,000 vehicles at that time, but had many more troops: French commanders viewed motorized vehicles as a supplement for railroads and horses; their infrastructure and logistic planning remained dependent on animals until the end of the war. In a similar vein, the British Expeditionary Force (BEF) relied initially on rails for transportation, and had to move to trucks in 1916, after conscription increased tremendously the number of troops sent to the front, as wheeled vehicles could manoeuver much better than light-rail trains near the front. However, while many field commanders quickly saw the potential for motor transportation, conservative elements in the British and French armies still favored

---

[17] W. G. Jensen, The Importance of Energy in the First and Second World Wars. *The Historical Journal* 11 (1968), 528–554.

[18] Bailey, The First World War and the Birth of Modern Warfare, 132–153.

[19] Bruce Podobnik, *Global Energy Shifts* (Philadelphia, PA: Temple University Press, 2006), 70. A second challenge – the need to overcome ground defenses – contributed to the invention of the tank. It is discussed later in this chapter.

keeping the horse and the mule; this dispute was settled only after the war. American officers, on their part, were still making plans for a military railway network in France in 1918.[20]

The shift from coal-fueled trains to petroleum-fueled trucks wasn't a swift one on the German side either. At the peak of the war, the German military still relied heavily on coal-fueled trains: on average, 162 trains left Germany daily to the Western Front, 52 to the Eastern Front and 9 to the Italian Front.[21] This was a rational choice for German decision-makers, as Germany had much more coal than oil. However, Germany's abundant quantities of coal were not enough to maintain a long war effort, and production actually declined during the war: in 1913, German coal mines yielded 190 million tons (MT) of coal; in 1917 the amount declined to 168 MT and in 1918 only 158 MT. The main reason for this was labor shortage, as miners were recruited to military service. Furthermore, the coastal areas of northern Germany were supplied until 1914 with coal imported from Britain: the cutting of these supply lines put even more stress on German coal reserves, affecting also Germany's allies. Coal exports from German mines to Austria declined from 44 MT in 1913 to 16 MT in 1918.[22]

The German shortage of oil was even more severe. With limited oil resources of its own (some small fields in Silesia), Germany had to import oil from abroad. The cutting of imports from Western countries set a clear quantitative limit to its qualitative advantages: although the German war industry managed to multiply the number of airplanes it produced tenfold, the German air force simply lacked the oil needed for keeping these planes flying.[23]

Another push toward petroleum-fueled transportation came not from the technical limitations of the iron horse, but from the biological limitations of the horses of flesh: the AEF in France suffered a chronic shortage of animals, mostly horses.[24] Another war casualty, therefore, was the

---

[20] See Matthew McCoy, Grinding Gears: The AEF and Motor Transportation in the First World War. *War in History* 11 (2004), 193–208.

[21] Jensen, The Importance of Energy in the First and Second World Wars.   [22] Ibid.

[23] In 1914 the German army had 1,348 airplanes; in 1916 it had 8,180 and in 1918 about 14,100. However, no more than about 4,000 airplanes could operate simultaneously, because of oil shortage. Jensen, The Importance of Energy in the First and Second World Wars.

[24] Furthermore, horses needed fuel even when not working, unlike trucks; occupying scarce transports with horse feed made little sense when munitions and other military supplies were needed. I would like to thank John McNeill for this remark.

centuries-old tradition of the elevated, aristocratic officer, keeping an eye on his troops from horseback.[25]

A similar change emanating from availability and quantity took place on the high seas, where navies shifted gradually from coal to oil. Ironically, the first major fleet to shift systematically from coal to oil was the last one to enter the war: in the decade before the Great War, the United States began converting its coal-burning battle fleet to one that used oil for fuel. While oil provided several advantages over coal all around the world – such as a higher speed at sea and a faster refueling process – the shift to oil was a result of specific geopolitical considerations of the United States. At the end of the nineteenth century, the United States increased its political and military involvement in the Pacific Ocean. Accordingly, US naval activity was focused to the West Coast – a part of the continent with little coal, but a lot of oil.[26]

With oil, American ships were able to travel faster and for longer distances before having to refuel. The British and French navies soon followed suit, trusting that fuel for their navies would come from the New World. For instance, French imports of oil during the war were as follows:

TABLE 6.1 *French oil imports during the war*

Year	Tons of Imported Petroleum[27]
1914	276,000
1915	457,000
1916	640,000
1917	610,000
1918	1,000,000

US support of the Allies during the war was crucial: over the course of the war, the United States provided more than 80% of the Allies' oil requirements.[28] This "flood" of oil (and coal, to a smaller degree) from North America guaranteed the French and the British armies, air forces, and navies the resources needed for maintaining their war efforts.[29]

---

[25] In what today seems an environmental friendly solution, General John Pershing, commander of the AEF, suggested that the troops would use bicycles as a substitute in some of their other missions, such as surveillance rides. See McCoy, Grinding Gears.

[27] Jensen, The Importance of Energy in the First and Second World Wars.

[26] David S. Painter, Oil and the American Century. *The Journal of American History* 99(1) (June 2012), 24–39.

[28] Ibid.

[29] Of course, oil was not the only resource coming from the new world to the old one during the war: so were also cereals and horses.

The German navy, on the other hand, was in real distress. It was building mighty battleships from the beginning of the twentieth century, and German diesel-electric motors technology enabled it to build efficient submarines that could travel slowly but steadily. During the war, German shipyards produced more than 450 light attack vessels, in addition to the large battleships already in service. But here again, as with airplanes, the limit to German potential was set by the lack of oil in the prolonged war. By October 1918 there were only a few weeks' reserves of oil in the German Reich.[30]

Altogether, the quantity of available oil – or the lack thereof – became a factor in deciding the outcome of the war gradually, during its last stages. But even beyond matters of quantity, oil had other qualities that first showed up during the First World War and changed modern warfare and modern societies in general.

QUALITATIVE EFFECTS

The main changes oil brought to warfare during the First World War were qualitative in nature. These changes can be divided into direct changes and indirect ones. The first and probably most decisive change oil made possible was in the air, although the first documented usage of aerial warfare was during the run-up for the Great War, in Libya in 1911, and in the first Balkan War of 1912–1913. In Libya, Italian forces used several small airplanes mostly for reconnaissance missions and occasionally for dropping bombs from the air or spreading leaflets; Bulgarian, Greek, and Serbian pilots used their machines for more or less the same purposes. Although airships and balloons were in service already, the integration of airplanes marked a turning point: the airplane's relatively small size and high speed were soon to change the entire perception of aerial warfare. This new phase would not have been possible without petroleum.[31]

It is noteworthy how military and aviation experts perceived the new technology at the time. In Italy the public celebrated the part airplanes played in the success of the Libyan campaign. Among their opponents,

---

[30] Jensen, The Importance of Energy in the First and Second World Wars. This oil shortage was well engraved in the memory of German strategists and planners during the 1930s; getting control of oil fields in Eastern Europe was therefore one of the main goals in their Blitzkrieg strategy during the Second World War.

[31] Michael Paris, The First Air Wars – North Africa and the Balkans, 1911–1913. *Journal of Contemporary History* 26 (1991), 97–109. For the social aspects of the rise of aerial warfare, see Michael Paris, The Rise of the Airmen: The Origins of Air Force Elitism, c. 1890–1918. *Journal of Contemporary History* 28 (1993), 123–141.

however, although the Ottoman government already had airplanes and trained pilots at its disposal at the time, there was no attempt to ship them to Africa to counterbalance the Italian airplanes.[32]

This difference in attitudes was prevalent among observers in other countries too. Although amateur British pilots were fascinated by the military possibilities airplanes opened up, in 1912 the British War Office ignored suggestions to integrate airplanes into future war plans, let alone forming any squadrons. The advantages of aerial warfare were either ignored or simply dismissed as a "German bogey," in the words of one high-ranking British official.[33] Indeed, some German officers noted the military capabilities that airplanes possessed, but in Germany too, until 1914, high echelons continued to concentrate mostly on Zeppelins and their improvement, believing they had an excellent first strike capability.[34]

At the beginning of the war, German and British general staffs were interested in airplanes mostly as platforms for reconnaissance missions. Their French counterparts were just as unconvinced of the possible contribution of airplanes to the war effort. Although some French officers contemplated as early as 1910 the use of airplanes for bombing, in 1913 French General Ferdinand Foch asserted that aviation is "fine as a sport," but "as an instrument of war it is worthless." Five years later, in 1918, he probably had changed his mind.[35]

Second to the introduction of aerial warfare was the change of fuel used for war at sea. Here, the clearest innovation brought by oil was the submarine. Modern submarines evolved gradually over decades before becoming a truly effective naval craft around 1910: their functioning became feasible only with the introduction of kerosene, diesel, and electric engines – all derivatives of oil. Smaller and slower than modern submarines, these vessels were nonetheless capable of carrying out missions of coast defense in friendly water, attrition of the enemy's naval force, and commerce warfare directed at civilian vessels.[36]

During the First World War, however, their effect was still more psychological (and qualitative) than practical (or quantitative): fleet commanders on

[32] Paris, The First Air Wars.   [33] Ibid.
[34] John H. Morrow Jr., Expectation and Reality: The Great War in the Air. *Airpower Journal* (Winter 1996), 27–34.
[35] Ibid.
[36] Karl Lautenschläger, The Submarine in Naval Warfare, 1901–2001. *International Security* 11 (1987), 94–140. France first put submarines into service in 1901, followed by Britain in 1902, the United States in 1903, and Russia in 1904. These were, however, only the first prototypes, hardly operational.

both sides suffered considerable anxiety over submarines, and gave orders to their fleets accordingly, in spite of the fact that their losses to submarine attacks were minimal. Submarines therefore contributed more to defense through dissuasion of the enemy rather than actual sinking enemy ships.[37] Nonetheless, this was enough to make them a new factor in naval warfare.

Another naval change was less revolutionary, but still important: shifting battleships from coal and steam to oil. This American innovation quickly inspired British ministers, providing a classical example of the connections between resources, politics, and economy. From February 1910 to October 1911, while serving as Home Secretary of the British government, Winston Churchill witnessed the beginning of the "Great Unrest" – a series of closures, stoppages, and strikes in which workers demanded what today seems to be the basics of welfare policy: minimum wages, pensions, and social insurance. Involving mostly workers in coal mines, docks, and railways, these protests exposed the vulnerability of the formidable infrastructure that made Great Britain the industrial and commercial power it was: the closures and strikes demonstrated how dependent the British economy was on a constant, continuous flow of coal. "Shipping, coal, railways, dockers etc. are all uniting and breaking out at once," Churchill noticed, understanding that "a new force has arisen in trade unionism." Concerned with the possible long-term effect organized labor might have on the prevailing political system so cherished by British conservatives, it became clear to him that "the general strike 'policy' is a factor which must be dealt with."[38]

When Churchill became First Lord of the Admiralty in October 1911, it did not escape his mind that the ability of coal workers on land to cause problems for the swift functioning of the British economy – if not to sabotage it and destroy it completely – had its parallel on the high seas. Though the strikes and riots in civilian industries were dealt with gradually by the British government, a similar "strike" in the navy during war could be hazardous, indeed paralyzing.[39]

---

[37] This was to a large extent because of the poor navigation tools, ammunition, and armaments submarines had until the 1920s. During the Second World War this situation changed. See ibid.

[38] Randolph S. Churchill, *Winston S. Churchill: Young Statesman 1901–1914* (London: Heinemann, 1967), 365. Cited in Mitchell, *Carbon Democracy*, 23.

[39] In August 1911 Churchill actually deployed military troops to maintain control of railways in Britain: Mitchell, *Carbon Democracy*, 62. One should also remember that the building of the infrastructure for the use of oil was not an instantaneous one: many were skeptical about the possibility, as the first experiments in fueling British ships with oil were unsuccessful. See Brian

Furthermore, the number of sailors needed to maintain the engines of oil-driven ships was much smaller than the number of boiler room workers with shovels and dusty hands required to keep the old coal steamers going. With the shift from coal to oil, the number of embittered sailors decreased, and so did the probability of mutinies. Furthermore, this mechanization enabled the British government to shift more young men from the navy to the army, from the dark boiler rooms to the muddy trenches. And in those trenches the soldiers of the First World War met another qualitative innovation of the age of oil: the armored vehicle, or – as it was known – the tank.

Providing troops with good mobile protection and strong firepower has been a goal since ancient times. The tank, however, was the first such instrument in the era of firearms. It was the outcome of the combination of an armor plate, light cannons and machine guns, and an internal combustion engine. Like the submarine and the airplane, tanks were the result of a long development process. An armor-carrying car made its debut in 1904, but it required roads. It was the installation of the caterpillar treads that provided armored vehicles with independent, all-terrain mobility.

The first models of tanks were slow and clumsy, easily bypassed and out-flanked by infantry or cavalry. Disadvantageous in the open fields, they were first used as an answer to the stalemate imposed on the Western Front by the trench warfare of the years 1915–1916: their combination of armor, mobility, and fire was invaluable in that context of slow, frontal encounters.

The first tank battle in history took place in September 1916, on the Somme. The British innovation was soon copied by Britain's French allies; within a few months, Renault tanks joined the battles.[40] Totally dependent on the supply of oil, the German military hardly used tanks, although plans to produce German equivalents were already made for the end of 1918. The Germans simply lacked the oil needed to move them.[41]

The Great War ended before the belligerents could fully put into practice all the lessons they had learned about mechanization, the internal

C. Black, *Crude Reality: Petroleum in World History* (Lanham, MD: Rowman & Littlefield, 2012), 60–62.

[40] Altogether, Great Britain produced about 2,600 tanks during the war; the French firm Renault produced around 3,000 pieces. The US troops in France also used Renault tanks; the American production of this innovative instrument began only at the end of the war.

[41] Jensen, The Importance of Energy in the First and Second World Wars.

combustion engine, and motor transportation. But the experience accumulated with these inventions demonstrated that the new weapons required the planning and organization of a new infrastructure in order to be effective.[42] Such military planning and organization were the technical heralds of an entire new society, the society of oil. In this new society and novel social order one can also see some indirect qualitative impacts of the introduction of oil not only to the art of war, but to human life in general.

INDIRECT QUALITATIVE IMPACTS

The history of the twentieth century reveals at least two indirect social and political impacts on modern societies caused by the introduction of oil into warfare during the First World War. The first impact is a shift in social structure, as the distance between commanders and subordinates became less rigid within military organizations; the second is a shift in global geopolitics, toward regions with the much sought after resource.

The First World War awakened the Western world to the demands of industrialized warfare, not only as logistical requirements for a small-scale experiment or in the context of a local, limited, and contained campaign – but as a challenge to the entire social and political capacities of the warring parties.[43] The war deeply altered (and in some cases, as in Russia, broke) old and established social structures and hierarchies. At the front, the "flattening" of the social order took visual shape as officers found themselves stuck in the same mud with their soldiers; at the same time, a new order of "cavaliers" was taking shape 5,000 feet in the air, as aviation added an entire new dimension to human experience.[44]

Coming back home, the veterans saw how oil took an ever greater part in human life, at the expense of older energy sources: the muscles of humans and animals alike were replaced by engines. The process of replacement of animals by machines was gradual, but the massive use of animals as a source of energy began to diminish rapidly in industrialized countries after the war: streets once roamed by horses soon became motorways.[45] A new era began in human–animal relations, made possible by oil.

---

[42] McCoy, Grinding Gears.   [43] Ibid.; Mitchell, *Carbon Democracy*, 66–67.
[44] Paris, The Rise of the Airmen.   [45] See Tempest, *The Long Face of War*.

Last but not least is the social change caused by the shift *within* the realm of fossil fuels. Whereas the coal economy was labor-intensive – from the mines to the boiler rooms and locomotives and everywhere in between – the oil economy demanded less manpower. In a manner not unfamiliar to the once mounted officers, miners and sailors saw their socioeconomic specialization washed away by the advantages of the black liquid. This process did not take place overnight, but took place over the entire twentieth century, as central governments worked to weaken the strong labor unions of the coal economy, by switching from coal to oil.[46]

SHIFT OF GLOBAL GEOPOLITICAL AIMS AND FOCI

Petroleum influenced not only the organizational structure of societies going to war, but the aims of war as well. The British Empire provides a prominent example. The naval rivalry between Great Britain and Germany had begun during the last decade of the nineteenth century, but gained speed and became obvious from 1905 on, with the official inauguration of the dreadnoughts and heavy cruisers building program. The British planners saw the German navy as their main future enemy; for the Germans, the ambition to rival Britain on the high seas became clear when Admiral Alfred von Tirpitz became the minister of the navy in 1897.[47]

With the conversion of the British fleet's engines from coal to oil, securing the constant flow of petroleum became crucial to all aspects of running the empire. The control – either direct or indirect – over the sources of that liquid became a central consideration in imperial strategic planning. With hardly any oil available near the British Isles, the presence of oil in the Middle East – halfway between the British crown in England and its precious jewel of India – did not escape the attention of planners in Westminster. With the initial Middle Eastern oil boom, which began in

---

[46] Britain makes a good example, both of the essence of the process and of the long time it took to be completed: 70 years after Churchill recognized the political threat posed by the coal workers' unions, the Conservative government broke the backbone of what Margaret Thatcher named "the Enemy Within" in the early 1980s. Her determination to withdraw from coal and rely more on petroleum was supported and encouraged by the discovery of large oil fields in the North Sea. Mitchell, *Carbon Democracy*, 236–237. See also Podobnik, *Global Energy Shifts*, 38–43.

[47] For a detailed description of the geopolitical context of the naval race between Great Britain and Germany and the diplomatic steps and intrigues that accompanied it, see MacMillan, *The War That Ended Peace*, 110–142.

Iraq in 1908, the region gained imperial importance. The Persian Gulf became as crucial as Sunderland for the maintenance of the empire; what Newcastle was for the ships of the nineteenth century, Basra was for the naval and aerial forces of the twentieth. With all the fierce battles waged on Europe's Western Front, the British Ministry of War did its utmost to get hold of this region too.[48]

The interest in Middle Eastern oil did not come out of the blue in August 1914: the oil politics in Mesopotamia had already developed in the decades before the Great War. Furthermore, as would happen many times during the following century, geopolitical and financial interests were intertwined: specifically, investments of German banks collided with those of British oil companies in the region.[49] The war, however, transformed a business competition into a matter of global domination. Hence another aspect of the war as a *world war*: all over the globe belligerent forces needed the same resources, which were found only in a limited number of places, far fewer than was the case with coal. This geopolitical feature, drawing international attention to oil-rich areas, became a characteristic of the entire twentieth century, and the beginning of the twenty-first.[50]

LEGACIES

Fond of the opportunities opened by modern technologies, Archduke Franz Ferdinand made his tour of Sarajevo in July 1914 not by a horse-towed chariot but by a motorcar.[51] He was probably the first high-ranking political (even if not official) personality to be assassinated while sitting in one. The resource that enabled the archduke to take his deadly ride also shaped the war that followed his murder. During the ensuing century, millions more were killed for oil and because of it.

Although commercial drilling for oil was already under way during the 1860s and the pumps in Pennsylvania were already working intensively during the American Civil War,[52] it took several decades until both

---

[48] Karl Meyer and Shareen Blair Brysack, *Kingmakers: The Invention of the Modern Middle East* (New York: Norton & Company, 2008), 130–131.

[49] See Mitchell, *Carbon Democracy*, 54–59; Daniele Ganser, *Europa im Erdölrausch: Die Folgen einer gefährlichen Abhängigkeit* (Zürich: Orell Füssli, 2012), 52–58.

[50] Mitchell, *Carbon Democracy*, 86–108, especially 94–98; Ganser, *Europa im Erdölrausch*, 52–54, 281–282; Black, *Crude Reality*, 134–135.

[51] A moving report of the day of the assassination is brought by MacMillan, *The War That Ended Peace*, chapter 18: Assassination in Sarajevo.

[52] Black, *Crude Reality*, 25–37.

technology and supply were ripe for a wide application of that liquid. As is usually the case with technological innovations, there were several time lags between the consequent stages of using the resource: first the discovery of the new resource or possibility, then the theoretical framing of its practical usage, and finally its actual implementation and its mass production.

Gradually but surely, oil made its way to the center of the arena. To be sure, oil did not play a central role in the First World War in what regards *quantity*: the tanks and the airplanes had only a limited effect on the practical outcomes of campaigns and battles. The submarines, for their part, provide us with a telling example of the mixture of quantity and quality: the German decision to pursue unrestricted submarine warfare (knowing that would most probably bring the United States into the war) was probably the gamble that decided the war. The Germans thus used an oil-based weapon in their strategic gamble, and its failure – the U-boats could not starve out Britain and France before the United States got mobilized – ended the war.[53]

The substantial influx of petroleum into human society and the exponential growth in its extraction and consumption did not take place until after the Second World War.[54] But on the *qualitative* aspect, military innovations such as the submarine, the airplane, the tank, and motorized transport were and are all oil dependent.[55] Air-to-air combat, strategic bombing, submarine warfare, tanks and anti-tanks, internal combustion engines for logistics: altogether, the years 1917–1918 marked the birth of the "modern style of conflict": all-encompassing and three-dimensional. Almost all the developments that showed up in 1937–1945 may be viewed

[53] Whereas the German U-boats initially had a frightening effect on Atlantic shipping and transportation, a tactical solution was soon found, by gathering vessels into convoys. I would like to thank Roger Chickering and John McNeill for this point.

[54] This sudden increase in the input of energy into human societies shaped what Christian Pfister termed "The 1950s Syndrome": the great increase in material wealth that altered all parts of industrial human societies on our planet. See Christian Pfister, Das "1950er Syndrom": Die umweltgeschichtliche Epochenschwelle zwischen Industriegesellschaft und Konsumgesellschaft. In Christian Pfister, ed., *Das 1950er Syndrom: Der Weg in die Konsumgesellschaft* (Bern: Haupt, 1996), 51–95. For an abbreviated version in English, see Pfister, The "1950s Syndrome" and the Transition from a Slow-Going to a Rapid Loss of Global Sustainability. In Frank Uekoetter, ed., *The Turning Points of Environmental History* (Pittsburgh, PA: University of Pittsburgh Press, 2010), 90–118. For the North American peculiarities of oil consumption trends, see Brian Black, Oil for Living: Petroleum and American Conspicuous Consumption. *The Journal of American History* (June 2012), 40–50.

[55] Painter, Oil and the American Century. A partial exception is the nuclear submarine.

as improvements upon the revolutionary conceptual model laid down in 1917–1918 rather than totally new innovations.[56] By the outbreak of the Second World War, the usage of petroleum was crucial to all aspects of modern warfare.[57]

The shift from coal to oil also had indirect social implications in the industrialized societies, geopolitical consequences among them. Socially, the shift from coal to oil made governments less vulnerable and less prone to strikes and protests, thus enjoying a larger space to maneuver socially and politically. On the geopolitical sphere, some regions of the world – those rich with petroleum – gained greater importance, rapidly changing their status from that of forgotten backwater to the center of political considerations.

Like all energy shifts, the shift surrounding the First World War was a complex process. In 1914, France lost some large coal mines and was cut off from its supply of coal from Belgium by the first German attacks. This drove French planners to rely more heavily on hydroelectricity from plants in the southern part of the country, away from the battlefields, providing a strong impetus to the development of French hydroelectric power (and electricity in general) – a development that lasted after the war. A similar process took place in Germany.[58] Another example of nonlinearity in the introduction of oil was the Russian navy: with a shortage of available and transportable coal and enough petroleum, the Russian fleet started burning oil under the boilers of its old steamers.[59]

In its various forms, petroleum enabled humans to overcome limits, particularly those of time and space.[60] The importance of the Great War

---

[56] To be even more precise, the birth of modern warfare may be dated to July 1918: the British offensive in Hamel, although small in size and with limited success, probably was the first time that artillery, tanks, infantry, and aircrafts functioned together efficiently, in an organized manner. See Bailey, The First World War and the Birth of Modern Warfare, 132–153.

[57] Morrow, Expectation and Reality.

[58] For the German story, see Marc Landry, Environmental Consequences of the Peace: The Great War, Dammed Lakes, and Hydraulic History in the Eastern Alps. *Environmental History* 20 (2015), 422–448; noteworthy is his assertion that the Great War created a political consensus in Germany about the need for state-supported industrialization. The situation in Austria was just as severe, as the Austro-Hungarian Empire ceased to exist as one political and economic unit; the impetus given to hydroelectric power there was accordingly considerable. The rise of electricity was motivated not only by the loss of coal mines but by the loss of manpower too, as cohorts of coal miners were killed or wounded; see Podobnik, *Global Energy Shifts*, 69–70.

[59] Jensen, The Importance of Energy in the First and Second World Wars.

[60] Black, Oil for Living.

was not only in space, as it extracted resources globally, but in time as well: in what concerns patterns of energy usage, the four years of belligerence mark the beginning of a new era of mobile, mechanized warfare – namely, the age of oil. The Great War's energy regime can therefore serve as a model for all other modern wars waged during the following century.[61]

In his seminal work summarizing the twentieth century, Eric Hobsbawm periodized it from 1914 to 1991: from the outbreak of the Great War to the fall of the Soviet Union in 1991.[62] Hobsbawm concentrated on ideology, not on resources, but his political periodization runs parallel to that of oil. The double-edged sword – or the vicious circle – of petroleum can be seen here in all its might: the waging of the First World War in 1917–1918 was made possible to a large extent by the growing availability and expanding uses of petroleum in Europe and North America; the waging of the Gulf War in 1991 was necessary to quench the thirst of Europe, North America, and Japan for oil.[63] Petroleum became both a means for waging modern wars and their aim. Here is another trick of history: isn't the dependency on oil one of the main features of modern wars? While insurgency by its mere definition needs few fossils, counterinsurgency demands much more carbon inputs. Is the shift from "old wars" to "new wars" equivalent to a shift from oil-rich to oil-poor conflicts?[64] With Peak Oil already here and the end of the Age of Oil looming, "energy insecurity" becomes ever more present in political and international considerations.[65]

The remote British military airfields built in the aftermath of the Great War, whose task was to protect oilfields and pipelines, became Iraqi

[61] Painter, *Oil and the American Century*.

[62] Eric Hobsbawm, *Age of Extremes: The Short Twentieth Century, 1914–1991* (London: Abacus, 1995). Hobsbawm hardly refers to oil availability in his book. In his description and analysis of the "golden age" of the twentieth century he refers to oil almost entirely (except two sentences on p. 262) as a tool in the hands of world politicians.

[63] David Harvey, *The New Imperialism* (Oxford: Oxford University Press, 2003); Ganser, *Europa im Erdölrausch*, 230–236.

[64] Mary Kaldor, *New & Old Wars: Organized Violence in a Global Era* (Stanford, CA: Stanford University Press, 2012). For a critical view of that concept, see Sinisa Malesevic, The Sociology of New Wars? Assessing the Causes and Objectives of Contemporary Violent Conflicts. *International Political Sociology* 2 (2008), 97–112. For oil in new wars specifically, see Paivi Lujala, Jan Rod, and Nadja Thieme, Fighting over Oil: Introducing a New Dataset. *Conflict Management and Peace Science* 24 (2007), 239–256.

[65] Richard Heinberg, *Peak Everything: Waking up to the Century of Decline in Earth's Resources* (Gabriola Island: New Society, 2007); Chapman, The End of Peak Oil?, 93–101.

strongholds in the 1991 war over the Gulf's petroleum resources. Today, these airfields and the oil infrastructure they were supposed to protect are once again the bone of contention between rival factions in Iraq and Syria. In April 2017, concerns increased regarding the probability of an escalating conflict between superpowers, as US vessels and missiles joined their Russian counterparts in attacks on local armed forces in the paramilitary hodge-podge of what used to be the states of Syria and Iraq.[66] In 1917 the availability of oil enabled the great powers to wage wars and determine their outcome; one hundred years later oil draws powers great and small into war. This is the political history of energy in the twentieth century in a nutshell.

---

[66] Anonymous, Syria War: US Warns of "More" after Missile Strikes. *BBC News*, 7 April 2017, www.bbc.com/news/world-middle-east-39529264 (accessed August 3, 2017); Bethan McKernan, Syria Air Strikes: Russia Sends more Warships to Assad-Controlled Port of Tartus. *The Independent*, April 11, 2017, www.independent.co.uk/news/world/middle-east/syria-air-strikes-russia-send-warships-tartus-port-bashar-al-assad-support-us-chemical-attack-a7678261.html (accessed August 3, 2017).

7

The First World War and the Beginning of Overfishing in the North Sea

Ingo Heidbrink

Any attempt to write an environmental history of the First World War would be incomplete without a maritime environmental history of the various naval theaters of the First World War and in particular the North Sea. The North Sea was one of the most relevant theaters of naval warfare during the First World War. It was also the body of water that had been affected most by the introduction of steam trawling and thus an industrialized distant-water fishery in the decades prior to the outbreak of the war. With the first steam trawlers working the fishing grounds of the North Sea in the mid-1880s,[1] catch capacity increased exponentially.[2] Furthermore, with the introduction of public fish auctions and markets, as well as the development of distribution schemes to take fish inland, consumption of sea fish was no longer restricted to the immediate coastal regions.[3]

Although the term *overfishing* was not used in the period between the introduction of the first steam trawlers in the mid-1880s and the outbreak of the war, a declining ratio between the ever-increasing fishing capacity and catch results clearly demonstrated that at least some kind of relative

---

[1] Wolfgang Walter, *Deutsche Fischdampfer: Technik, Entwicklung, Einsatz, Schiffsregister* (Hamburg: Die Hanse, 1999).

[2] Georg H. Engelhard, One Hundred and Twenty Years of Change in Fishing Power of English North Sea Trawlers. In Andrew I. L. Payne, John Cotter, and Ted Potter, eds., *Advances in Fisheries Science: 50 Years on from Beverton and Holt* (Oxford/Ames, IA: Blackwell Publishing/Cefas, 2008), 6.

[3] Ingo Heidbrink, Werner Beckmann, and Matthias Keller, ... *Und Heute Gibt Es Fisch!: 100 Jahre Fischindustrie Und Fischgroßhandel in Schlaglichtern 1903–2003* (Bremen: H. M. Hauschild, 2003).

overfishing had already begun within the very first decades of steam trawling. This continued until competing fishing fleets of nations like Germany and Great Britain were replaced by battle fleets of the very same nations.[4] Note that the effects of this early overfishing remained limited, as the fish stocks at large were not affected, but the impact was felt mainly on individual species in specific fishing grounds. Thus, relative overfishing could be easily compensated for by exploring new fishing grounds, like those off Iceland or the north Norwegian coast, and by shifting target species.

Prior to discussing the effects of the First World War on the North Sea fisheries, it might be helpful to introduce at least some of the main characteristics of the North Sea marine ecosystem and more importantly the main target species of the North Sea fisheries. The North Sea is characterized by a high biological productivity, diverse coastal regions, and a wide variety of different habitats.[5] With a total biomass of 10 million metric tons for an area just under 750,000 km^2 (as of 2002), the North Sea provides extremely good fishing conditions for species like cod, haddock, whiting, saithe, plaice, and sole, but also for pelagic species like herring and mackerel.[6] For the time period under review in this chapter there is no reliable total biomass estimate available as fisheries science was only beginning to understand the complex ecosystem of the North Sea, but it is safe to assume that the total biomass was at least at the same level as today, probably even a little higher. Intensive fisheries had already been developed during the age of sail, given that primary production was spread over the North Sea, in coastal regions and in areas like the Dogger Bank. This intensified after the advent of steam trawling. Extremely simplified, it might be stated that at the end of the nineteenth century the North Sea was one of the most important fishing regions of the globe. More importantly in the context of this chapter, it was the single most important region for steam trawler operations.

While all nations around the North Sea participated in the fisheries at the end of the nineteenth century, only some developed steam-trawling industries at this time. In particular, British and German fishing companies began introducing steam trawlers to their fishing fleets, as they had

---

[4] Ingo Heidbrink, *"Deutschlands Einzige Kolonie Ist Das Meer!": Die Deutsche Hochseefischerei Und Die Fischereikonflikte Des 20. Jahrhunderts* (Hamburg: Convent, 2004).

[5] Jacqueline M. McGlade, The North Sea Large Marine Ecosystem. In Kenneth Sherman and Hein Rune Skjoldal, eds., *Large Marine Ecosystems of the North Atlantic: Changing States and Sustainability* (Amsterdam/Boston, MA: Elsevier, 2002).

[6] Ibid.

the markets to accept the increased landings and the industrial base required for the development of steam trawler fleets. Nations like the Netherlands or Scandinavia lacked either one or both of these prerequisites for large-scale steam trawler operations. Consequently, this chapter focuses mainly on the British and German trawler operations during the First World War, especially as they were also the main belligerent nations in the war of the North Sea nations.

While the outbreak of the hostilities did not come completely unexpectedly for the fisheries, aware as they were of the July 1914 international crisis, fishing companies and trawler crews were ultimately caught by surprise by the actual outbreak of the First World War, which put an immediate end to all fishing activities in the North Sea. For example, the complete fleet of 23 herring boats from the small German city of Elsfleth was working on the North Sea fishing grounds on the day of the German general mobilization and declaration of war on Russia on August 1, 1914.[7]

Immediately after the outbreak of war the North Sea became a theater of war, and during the Battle of Heligoland Bay on August 28, 1914, the first major encounter between German and British cruisers and battle cruisers.[8] There were not many actual naval battles between major men-of-war of the belligerent nations, in particular not after the indecisive Battle of Jutland on May 31 and June 1, 1916. Thereafter the German surface fleet almost never ventured out to sea. Instead, U-boats, fishing vessels converted into auxiliary warships, and, most notably, mine warfare became characteristic for the First World War in the North Sea theater.[9]

With the North Sea now a theater of war, the fishing activities of the nations involved in North Sea fisheries prior to the war came more or less immediately to a complete stop during the second half of 1914. A continuation of fishing activities was considered too risky, in particular due to the threat of mine warfare. For a fishing vessel trawling its fishing gear below the surface, this was even more dangerous than for a traditional ship not trawling any kind of gear. In addition, fishing trawlers and their crews became part of the navies of the belligerent nations. Together with

[7] Adolf Blumenberg, *Elsfleth: Stadt Und Hafen an Der Weser* (Oldenburg: Holzberg, 1989).
[8] Eric W. Osborne, *The Battle of Heligoland Bight* (Bloomington: Indiana University Press, 2006).
[9] Friedrich Lützow, Konteradmiral A.D., *Der Nordseekrieg: Doggerbank-Skagerrak* (Oldenburg: Gerhard Stalling, 1931).

many other small and auxiliary naval vessels, they took over the burden of everyday maritime warfare,[10] leaving the battleships, heavy and light cruisers, and other naval vessels alike of both sides to face the expected clash with the same types of ships of the enemy.

Numerous historical publications have dealt with the role of fishermen and fishing vessels during the First World War on both sides of the conflict,[11] and most publications on the history of the North Sea fisheries of the twentieth century include at least a chapter on the First World War. The majority of these publications have focused on the question of how the outbreak of the war ended the rapid development of steam trawling from the previous three decades, the conversion of fishing vessels to auxiliary warships, civilian fishermen becoming crew members of these now naval vessels, and the very limited continuation of fishing activities under the permanent threat of mines and encounters with enemy ships.

Other publications such as the well-respected two-volume *History of the North Atlantic Fisheries* published by the North Atlantic Fisheries History Association (NAFHA)[12] or *England's Sea Fisheries*[13] provide long-term overviews on the history of fisheries in the North Sea and North Atlantic region but do not engage with short-term developments like the ones discussed in this chapter. The same basically applies to books like Bolster's *Mortal Sea*,[14] which also falls short of discussing the rapid

---

[10] Robb Robinson and Ian Hart, *Viola: The Life and Times of a Hull Steam Trawler* (London: Lodestar Books, 2014).

[11] For example Walter Wood, *Fishermen in War Time* (London/Edinburgh: S. Low, Marston & Co. Ltd., 1918); A. Bückmann, *Die Schollenbevölkerung Der Helgoländer Bucht Und Die Einschränkung Der Fischerei Während Der Kriegsjahre 1914–1918 Und 1939–1942*, Counseil Permanent International pour l'Exploration de la Mer (Rapports et Procès-verbaux des réunions, vol. 114) (Copenhague: Andr. Fred. Høst & Fils, 1944); Board of Agriculture Great Britain and Fisheries, *Fisheries in the Great War, Being the Report on Sea Fisheries for the Years 1915–1918 of the Board of Agriculture and Fisheries* (London: HMSO, 1920); Günther K. Anton and Zentral-Einkaufsgesellschaft-Berlin, *Der Einfluss Des Weltkrieges Auf Die Seefischerei Der Niederlande Und Seine Folgen Für Deutschland* (Jena: G. Fischer, 1918); Robinson and Hart, *Viola*.

[12] David J. Starkey, Jon Th. Thor, and Ingo Heidbrink, eds., *A History of the North Atlantic Fisheries: Volume 1 – From Early Times to the mid-19th Century* (German Maritime Studies 5) (Bremerhaven/Bremen: Hauschild Verlag, 2009); David J. Starkey and Ingo Heidbrink, eds., *A History of the North Atlantic Fisheries – Volume 2 – From the 1850s to the Early Twentieth-First Century* (German Maritime Studies 19) (Bremerhaven/Bremen: Hauschild Verlag, 2012).

[13] Neil Ashcroft, David J. Starkey, and Chris Reid, *England's Sea Fisheries: The Commercial Sea Fisheries of England and Wales since 1300* (London: Chatham Publishers, 2000).

[14] Jeffrey Bolster, *The Mortal Sea: Fishing the Atlantic in the Age of Sail* (Cambridge, MA: Belknap Press, 2012).

changes in the fisheries after the introduction of steam power to the fishing industries due to the focus of the book on the age of sail. While Bolster's book might consequently seem to be of no direct relevance for the topic discussed here, it is still a useful contribution as it also challenges the traditional narrative of overfishing.

More recent publications, in particular those based on research carried out in the context of environmental history–focused research projects like H-MAP (History of Marine Animals Populations – Project),[15] have focused on how and to what degree the First World War caused a respite for the fish stocks of the North Sea from an ever-increasing catch. Many of these confirm the well-accepted thesis of fisheries scientists, that the First World War was beneficial to the fish stocks of the North Sea as the war brought direct relief from fishing pressure. Originally developed immediately after the end of the First World War by renowned fisheries scientists such as Herman Henking, this thesis of war-related relief for the fish stocks included not only a total increase in stock but also an increase in average fish size.[16]

Thus, it might be concluded that the First World War caused direct positive effects on the fish stocks and environment of the North Sea, if only because fishing activities came to a stop at the beginning of the war. Most of the respective historiography until today is either confirming this interpretation or at least not challenging the idea that the First World War had a positive effect on the fish stocks of the North Sea. But is it really true that a maritime environmental history of the North Sea during the First World War should come to such a positive conclusion regarding the effects of the war on the environment and the fish stocks of the North Sea?

Of course, such an interpretation of the effects of the First World War on the North Sea might be considered common sense for those interested in a maritime environmental history of the First World War or at least the standard result of a conventional maritime/fisheries history. Indeed, even more sophisticated maritime environmental research approaches like the H-MAP approach seem to confirm such an interpretation. Nevertheless, it still needs to be questioned whether such an understanding of the effects of the First World War on the maritime environment is really the truth or if

---

[15] Henn Ojaveer and Brian R. MacKenzie, Historical Development of Fisheries in Northern Europe – Reconstructing Chronology of Interactions between Nature and Man. *Fisheries Research* 87 (2–3) (2007), 102–105.

[16] Hermann Henking, Die Wirkung Des Krieges Auf Den Fischbestand Der Nordsee. II Und III. Der Schellfisch Und Der Wittling. *Berichte der Deutschen wissenschaftlichen Kommission für Meeresforschung, Neue Folge* 1 (1919–1923) (1923), 137.

the situation might have been much more complex. Perhaps consequences of the First World War for the North Sea were even negative, at least when looking at long-lasting consequences?

Should the First World War, then, be understood as the key element of a postwar scenario with heavily increased fishing capacity, substantially improved fishing technology, and, consequently, massive overfishing of the fish stocks of the North Sea and thus a situation that clearly needs to be marked as negative? Or to rephrase the question: Do we need to understand the First World War as an unexpected, and probably paradoxical stimulus for overfishing in the years after the armistice? Might a maritime environmental history of the First World War not need to look at the period of the actual hostilities, but also the immediate postwar period?

It is an obvious, well-known fact that fishing efforts decreased substantially once the North Sea had become a theater of war and fishermen and trawlers served for the navies of the belligerent nations. It is also well known that the few fishing vessels that had not been requisitioned to naval service started fishing again on a limited scale after the first couple of months of the war and even some trawlers converted to naval vessels and other auxiliary warships set out fishing gear during routine patrol duty without any real risk of encountering the enemy. The Bild- und Filmamt, a German military department set up in 1916 in charge of using film and radio for propaganda and psychological warfare,[17] even produced a 21-minute documentary in 1918 on these fishing activities of the German navy.[18] While the documentary clearly needs to be classified as propaganda, demonstrating that the navy was helping with securing food supplies for the general population at a time when large groups of Germans were starving and the caloric value of food supplies available to the average German was down to 1,000 kcal per day,[19] it also shows that fisheries were continued during the war and not only by the few trawlers not requisitioned but even by trawlers now primarily acting as auxiliary warships. Thus the simplified statement that the First World War basically ended fishing activities in the North Sea needs to be put into perspective.

---

[17] Hans Barkhausen, *Filmpropaganda Für Deutschland Im Ersten Und Zweiten Weltkrieg* (Hildesheim/Zürich/New York: Olms, 1982).

[18] Hochseefischerei Der Deutschen Marine (1918), Deutsches Bundesarchiv. (The 21-minute, black-and-white documentary is available via the European Film Gateway web portal: www.europeanfilmgateway.eu/de/detail/Hochseefischerei%20in%20der%20Deutschen%20Marine/barch::884e49fa9f949448fc2fb4deb2c8cebb [accessed August 23, 2017]).

[19] Hans-Ulrich Wehler, *Deutsche Gesellschaftsgeschichte* 4(4) (München: Beck, 2003), 61.

Less well known is what happened in detail to the fishing fleets and trawlers converted to naval trawlers or other types of auxiliary warships, and more importantly how many new fishing vessels and/or trawler type naval vessels had been built during the war. While naval authorities of several nations on both sides of the war enlisted or requisitioned existing fishing vessels and used them as auxiliary warships, the major belligerent naval powers of the First World War, in particular Germany and Great Britain, also requisitioned fishing trawlers under construction directly from the shipyards and completed these hulls as naval trawlers instead of fishing trawlers. Finally and probably most importantly, they began designing and building naval trawlers or *Vorpostenboote* (VP-Boats).[20]

These ships were standard constructions based on the same basic hull and engine designs as prewar fishing trawlers, but equipped with all kinds of naval weaponry and equipment instead of a trawl winch, and additional crew quarters instead of the holds for fish.[21] In contrast to repurposed fishing trawlers, the hull, frames and bulkheads were designed to bear the foundations of heavy armament or other kinds of military equipment. A naval trawler was thus often a more powerful weapon than a repurposed fishing trawler, normally characterized by all kinds of compromises when it came to the installation of guns and other military equipment.

Furthermore, and important for the long-term effect of the First World War on the marine environment of the North Sea, the trawler designs used for the development of the naval trawlers were the most up-to date designs available and thus substantially larger and far more sophisticated than many of the older trawlers that operated on the fishing grounds of the North Sea when the war broke out.

The rationale for utilizing the trawler design for auxiliary warships was an easy one. On the one hand, the fishing trawlers had already proved a successful design for operations in the North Sea, being well suited to the North Sea's challenging navigational requirements. In addition, vessels of the trawler type required only a small number of crew members, of the utmost importance when the war took so many men. Trawlers, moreover, had an easy-to-handle, reliable technology, and could be operated year-round during all weather and sea conditions of the North Sea.

---

[20] The term *Vorpostenboot* is originally the German language term used for a naval trawler, but became also used in English language.

[21] John Rushworth Jellicoe, *The Crisis of the Naval War* (London/New York: Cassell, 1920).

Furthermore, the design could be easily converted and amended for naval purposes. Converting a former fishing trawler to an auxiliary minesweeper did not require much more than replacing the trawl winch with the equipment required for towing the minesweeping gear. It was even easier to build in this converted design, as frames and bulkheads could be constructed in such a way that they could carry the foundations of guns without additional reinforcements.

With mine warfare becoming a major element of the naval activities of the First World War in the North Sea area, the number of trawler-type vessels in the North Sea reached previously unknown levels, but of course almost none of these ships were used for any kind of fishing besides the aforementioned limited fishing activities carried out by the crews of some naval trawlers during war patrols. Besides the sheer number of trawler-type ships operating in the North Sea during the First World War, for example, the more than 200 British "castle-class" naval trawlers,[22] these ships quickly became much larger and more sophisticated than the average fishing trawlers used prior to the outbreak of the war.[23] Notably enough, naval trawlers like the "castle class" were designed and constructed to be easily reconfigured into ordinary fishing trawlers after the end of the war. A very similar development took place in Germany when nearly 180 *Vorpostenboote* were built. Like the British naval trawlers, the *Vorpostenboote* were based on standard trawler designs, but again were large and sophisticated in comparison to the average prewar fishing trawler. Thus the total number of trawler-type ships operating in the North Sea region increased substantially despite war-related losses of these ships.

But as already mentioned, the German *Vorpostenboote* and British naval trawlers were built and/or used as auxiliary warships and not as fishing boats even if some of them engaged in limited fishing activities. Thus the question needs to be raised if naval trawlers and *Vorpostenboote* had any direct relevance for a marine environmental history of the First World War.

While arguably such relevance might have been very limited during the war itself, the mere existence of these ships caused dramatic changes to the North Sea fisheries after the end of the war and might even be considered

---

[22] Despite conflicting numbers in various publications, there were at least circa 200 castle-class trawlers built for the Royal Navy during the course of the First World War. Richard Worth, *Fleets of World War II* (Cambridge, MA: Da Capo Press, 2001), 128.

[23] Walter, *Deutsche Fischdampfer*.

the unexpected stimulus for the beginning of substantial overfishing of the North Sea in the early postwar period.

Traditional fisheries history for the First World War describes a drastic reduction of the number of fishing vessels due to war-related losses and includes roughly 200 British and an equal number of German fishing trawlers lost during the war.[24] With the majority of the surviving trawlers being older and technologically outdated,[25] it is safe to assume that fishing capacity was greatly reduced by the war and thus the assumption of the war causing a relief period for the fish stocks of the North Sea seems to be correct. Nevertheless, such an interpretation of the development during the First World War seems incomplete, as it does not take into account that the development in the immediate years after the war was determined by a number of developments during the war, most notably the construction and availability of a substantial number of naval trawlers on both sides of the conflict.

With the end of the war, the navies no longer had any use for these ships and tried to get rid of them as quickly as possible. As naval trawlers were basically identical to fishing trawlers in ship design, the naval trawlers could be as easily converted to fishing trawlers as fishing trawlers had been converted to auxiliary warships. Thus the best solution for the navies was as simple as offering the surplus of naval trawlers built during the war to fishing companies as a replacement for their ships lost during the war.

Thus the war itself was a double-edged sword for the fishing companies of the belligerent nations: they had to face substantial losses of their prewar fishing fleets, but at the end of the war they had an opportunity to purchase for comparatively little money a substantial number of trawler type ships that could easily be converted to fishing trawlers. Furthermore, compared to the ships they had lost, the new vessels were all more or less recently built and state of the art in technology and catch capacity. In addition, as the navies had no longer any use for these ships, they were sold basically for scrap value: the asking price for the fishing companies was way below the cost of new fishing trawlers. Even if unintended, this mechanism needs to be understood as an enormous subsidy to the postwar fishing industries.

In other words, the war indirectly caused a substantial modernization of the North Sea fishing fleets, and after a short period of time it meant an increase in total catch capacity available and in average catch capacity per trawler, mainly due to larger size of the trawlers and increased engine

[24] Ibid. [25] Heidbrink, *"Deutschlands Einzige Kolonie Ist Das Meer!"*

power. Note that the fishing technology itself remained mainly unchanged during the First World War. The fishing companies substantially benefited from the various improvements in ship design, propulsion, and navigation technology that were made in the context of the construction of naval vessels,[26] but the actual catch technology remained more or less unchanged. Of course, this is easy to explain, as research and development capacities were focused on naval technology for obvious reasons and while the fisheries could benefit from these activities, they were not able to attract research funding for the development of catch technology, as there was no direct benefit for the war activities.

In addition to the modernization of the actual trawler fleet, the decommissioning of naval vessels, auxiliary or otherwise, at the end of the war resulted in tens of thousands of navy sailors having no employment and desperately looking for any kind of job. As many of the younger sailors had had no civilian job prior to the war, the only trade they had learned was war, a trade for which luckily there was no longer a need. For those members of the military who had served in the navy the war had at least given them some degree of training for all kinds of maritime professions, including the distant water fisheries. While a former crew member of a warship might have had no idea about the fisheries at all, he knew at least how to operate an oceangoing vessel and thus had half of the qualifications required for working onboard a fishing trawler. For the fishing industry, the decommissioning of war ships thus resulted in the unique situation that for the first time ever there was not a shortage of potential labor, but a surplus. As the fisheries did not require a formal education, but vocational training consisted mainly of training on the job,[27] crewing the trawlers was a comparatively easy task and by no means an obstacle for putting the now repurposed naval trawlers into service as fishing trawlers. In fact, working on a trawler was highly attractive in the immediate postwar period, as in addition to wages and percentages, crew members received an allowance of fish and train oil, a most welcome benefit in a period characterized by shortages of protein for large parts of society.

---

[26] Walter, *Deutsche Fischdampfer.*

[27] Ingo Heidbrink, Vocational Training in the German Deep-Sea Fishing Industry. *International Journal of Maritime History* 11(2) (1999); Martin Wilcox, The Role of Apprenticed Labour in the British Fisheries, 1850–1939. In Lars U. Scholl and David M. Williams, eds., *Crisis and Transition: Maritime Sectors in the North Sea Region 1790–1940* (Bremerhaven: Deutsches Schiffahrtsmuseum, 2008).

The number of fishing vessels reached prewar levels in most countries along the North Sea by 1919/20, despite the losses of trawlers during the war. The main reason for this extremely successful reconstruction of the fishing fleets was of course the previously mentioned conversion of naval trawlers to fishing trawlers. Interestingly enough, even the German trawler fleet reached its prewar level again in 1920 despite the regulations of the Versailles Treaty.[28] Four years later, the number of German trawlers reached its all-time maximum with more than 400 steam trawlers.[29]

It would seem logical to back up these findings with statistical data on the actual catch and landings of the North Sea fisheries during the First World War and the immediate postwar period. However, the available statistical materials for each country include a number of systematic differences that make it extremely difficult to draw any reliable conclusions.

The main problem with the statistical data available for the various nations participating in the North Sea fisheries is that some of the national statistics account for catch, while others account for landings. These different approaches result in the risk of some fish caught being counted twice. As it was common for German trawlers to land their catch in British ports, these catches might have been counted twice, in the German catch data as well as in the British landing records. Other methodological problems include the different measurement systems used in the United Kingdom and Germany or even the simple fact that different sets of species have been combined into one category for the respective statistical data. Finally, the question needs to be asked how reliable fisheries statistics have been overall during wartimes, as fish were channeled into grey or black markets, directly allocated to military food supply, or not accounted for due to a variety of other reasons. For example, it is uncertain whether any catch by fishing vessels now serving mainly as auxiliary warships but still occasionally setting out fishing gear was counted at all. In many cases, the catch was either directly consumed within the respective military unit or went into the black markets or local bartering. For all these reasons, catch data in the wartime and immediate postwar eras must be regarded with suspicion.

One of the few data sets available that seems to be at least reliable enough to support the argument presented are the annual statistical

[28] Roland Baartz, *Entwicklung Und Strukturwandel Der Deutschen Hochseefischerei Unter Besonderer Berücksichtigung Ihrer Bedeutung Für Siedlung, Wirtschaft Und Verkehr Cuxhavens* (Stuttgart: Steiner, 1991), 643.
[29] Ibid.

TABLE 7.1 *German steam trawling in the North Sea, 1905–1922*

| | North Sea | | |
	Number of Steam Trawler Journeys	Total Number of Trawler Days on Sea	Total Catch [t/year]
1905	1,943	16,405	12,522
1906	2,078	17,366	16,344
1907	2,387	21,266	19,683
1908	2,860	26,412	24,726
1909	2,997	28,141	27,643
1910	3,060	28,723	28,357
1911	3,230	29,725	31,623
1912	3,476	30,864	37,750
1913	3,563	32,318	36,861
1914	2,091	18,996	20,615
1915	809	6,269	11,752
1916	227	1,403	1,360
1917	710	4,808	5,678
1918	1,427	10,765	14,560
1919	3,913	34,694	57,352
1920	3,367	37,537	69,749
1921	4149	44674	68911
1922	3807	42029	66190

Source: Compiled by the author based on J. Lundbeck, *Statistische Jahres-Tabellen der deutschen Dampfhochseefischerei 1893–1922 bearbeitet und herausgegeben nach den Unterlagen des ehemaligen Deutschen Seefischerei-Vereins* (Mitteilungen aus dem Institut für Seefischerei der Bundesforschungsanstalt für Fischerei, Heft 7) (Hamburg, 1955).

reports about the German steam trawling industry prior to 1922 collected by the *Deutscher Seefischerei-Verein* that were compiled and edited in the 1950s by J. Lundbeck.

Even if considering that the data might be incomplete and include at least some of the systematic issues mentioned before, it can be calculated that for the German fishing fleet the average catch per trawler day on the ocean never reached a value above 1.2 t prior to the First World War, while after the war the catch per trawler day on the ocean was at least 1.5 t and the maximum reached in 1920 was nearly 1.9 t, clearly showing the

increased catch capacity per vessel due to the average trawler now being
larger and more sophisticated. There is no reason to assume that the
trends that characterized the German development were unique, and
thus the paradoxical effect of an increased catch capacity and consequently total catch would be the same if comparable statistical data of
other nations were available.

Any historical analysis of the fisheries of a certain period and region,
that is to say a marine environmental history, would be incomplete without at least some comments on the markets, consumption patterns, or
demand for fish. While in Great Britain the situation when peace returned
might be simply characterized as "back to normal," e.g., returning to
patterns that existed prior to the war, the situation in Germany was
completely different.

Despite the successful development of marine fisheries and in particular
the trawling industry in the period between the 1880s and the outbreak of
the First World War, fish remained largely unknown as a part of the daily
diet to the majority of people living in Germany. The term *Toter Seefisch*
(dead sea fish) was a well-established stereotype, in particular in the areas
far from the North Sea landing ports, and fish was often accepted only as
a (cheap) surrogate for pork and to a lesser degree beef and poultry, when
these protein sources were not available.

As the First World War caused a major food supply crisis in Germany
and in particular all kinds of protein became scarce, people became willing
to accept alternative protein sources[30] such as fish. By late 1917, most
citizens of Germany and Austria were eager for anything edible they could
get. Moreover, the introduction of marine fish into military food supplies
and other forms of institutionalized food supplies like hospital diets,
school menus, soup kitchens, etc. during the war[31] had helped to lower
the threshold for acceptance of fish throughout large circles of the population and thus established an increasing demand for fish. While this
increased market demand was fragile, in particular after the end of the
war and especially when other protein sources like pork and beef became
available again, the scarcity of traditional protein sources during the First
World War had helped to develop the market for fish to a level of demand
never seen prior to the war. In addition, even during the period of inflation

[30] Belinda J. Davis, *Home Fires Burning: Food, Politics, and Everyday Life in World War
I Berlin* (Chapel Hill: University of North Carolina Press, 2000).
[31] Heidbrink, Beckmann, and Keller, ... *Und Heute Gibt Es Fisch!*

(1918–1922) and hyperinflation (1923) in Germany, the fish industries remained less affected than other food industries, again resulting in an increasing demand for fish at least in comparison to other protein sources.

When imports of other protein sources were reestablished, mainly the import of frozen beef from South America,[32] the German fish industry did not simply accept the loss of market share gained during the war, but developed a number of products to compensate. The most successful product was *Seelachs in Öl*, literally translated as sea salmon in oil, actually smoked and colored pollock.[33] Within short time *Seelachs in Öl* became accepted in the German market not only as a surrogate for imports of real salmon but also as a new fish product in its own right.[34] *Seelachs in Öl* was particularly important as it provided the German trawling industry an opportunity to distribute a species to consumers in Germany that had not been accepted prior to the outbreak of the First World War. Thus another North Sea species had become a main target species of the German North Sea fisheries as an indirect consequence of the war.

Another development that helped the fishing industry retain market share once other sources of protein became available again was the fish filet. While fish was traded prior to the war basically only as headed and gutted fish, now it was traded as filet and thus preparation of fish no longer required special knowledge. The fish filet could be prepared in the same way as any piece of beef or pork.[35] These changes in fish preparation resulted in a continuation not only of fish consumption in Germany after the war at the same levels as during the war but also of the fishing activities themselves. Sufficient demand now existed to bring all catches to market, including species that before 1914 found no buyers. Again, even with these changes actually occurring only after the war, the First World War needs to be understood as the main driving factor for the change. Consumers in Germany had learned during the First World War that fish was not only a surrogate for other sources of protein, but a highly attractive protein source in itself.

---

[32] August Dierks, *Männer, Trawler, Meere August Dierks* (Bremerhaven: Verband d. deutschen Hochseefischereien, 1961), 34.

[33] Fritz Lücke, *Fischindustrielles Taschenbuch* (Braunschweig: Serger & Hempel, 1940), 155.

[34] Even today *Seelachs in Öl* can be found easily in most German grocery stores, although nobody would consider the product any longer as a surrogate for real salmon.

[35] Lücke, *Fischindustrielles Taschenbuch*, 34.

In the end, the final outcome of the First World War for the fishing industries of Great Britain was a substantial modernization of the fishing fleets indirectly subsidized by the state, as the trawling companies could acquire modern ships at scrap value despite the fact that the ships were fully functional naval trawlers, easily fitted out with equipment for fishing purposes. For the German fishing companies the result of the First World War was to a certain degree comparable; in addition, the war had created an increased acceptance of fish and, consequently, an increased demand for fish. Looking at these developments from a marine environmental history perspective the consequences are obvious: while the war itself might have caused a short-lived relief period for the fish stocks of the North Sea from 1914 to 1918 it also caused a substantial increase in catch capacity and even market demand immediately after the end of the war.

With the North Sea already on the brink of overfishing at the outbreak of the First World War, the situation after the war almost automatically resulted in substantial overfishing. The war-related relief period for certain species of North Sea fish during the war itself did not change this situation, but may have postponed it for some years. The only reasons overfishing indirectly caused by the First World War has not become immediately visible were: the delay between cause and effect in the context of increased fishing activities and related negative effects on the fish stocks of a certain region, the option for the fishing companies to utilize new fishing grounds once traditional fishing grounds showed signs of depletion, and ultimately the Great Depression and the outbreak of the Second World War, resulting first in a decline and then once again in an almost complete stoppage of all fishing activities in the North Sea.

While Henking's observation that the First World War resulted in a relief period for the fish stocks of the North Sea, including not only a total increase in stock volume but also an increase in average fish size,[36] is definitely true for the period 1914 to 1918, this period is far too brief to understand the maritime environmental history of the North Sea during the First World War. A maritime environmental history of the North Sea during the First World War period cannot focus only on the actual years of the naval conflict, but needs to take the full range of consequences of the war into account. As these consequences included not only a substantial modernization of the fishing fleets around the North Sea, an increased number of trawlers working the fishing grounds of the North Sea, a near endless pool of crew members for manning the trawlers, and finally

---

[36] Henking, Die Wirkung Des Krieges Auf Den Fischbestand Der Nordsee.

a market starved for protein and food of any sort, the final effect of the war was paradoxical. The First World War was the reason for stopping nearly all fishing activities in late 1914, but also the reason for a substantial increase in fishing activities in the long run and thus over-fishing at levels previously unknown. Thus the short period of relief for the fish stocks might be described as a Pyrrhic victory.

8

The Political and Natural Eco-Footprint of the First World War in East Asia

Environments, Systems Building, and the Japanese Empire, 1914–1923

Jack Patrick Hayes

INTRODUCTION

This chapter outlines some of the short- and long-term environmental consequences of the Great War in East Asia. It examines facets of the global and regional environmental footprint of military actions and political and economic trends as they developed in East Asia, focusing primarily on the Japanese empire along the Asia Pacific Rim, with short introductions to some of the environmental systems in China, Taiwan, Korea, and the northern South Pacific islands that were damaged during and immediately following the Great War period (1914–1923). This analysis targets significant changes in international relations that reshaped resource development in the region. These included extractive development of mineral resources, forests, fisheries, and plantation agriculture – all with implications for land and marine systems. Japanese imperialism, bolstered by the unique strategic opening that the First World War offered Japan and the patterns of resource exploitation that developed out of the war period and its immediate aftermath, affected both dry-land (terrestrial) and water and marine (pelagic) environments. The extractive resource and international political systems that resulted bolstered domestic and external growth and ultimately provided a nursery for events that would make the greater Pacific War of the 1930s and 1940s possible.

The First World War sparked mostly indirect transformations of East Asia's physical environment, as fighting reached only a few locations. More importantly, the geostrategic opening that the war provided imperial Japan generated more thorough colonial exploitation of the region's various natural environments. Warlord Chinese and Japanese market and political demands shifted the empire's regional perspectives toward exploitation of landscapes and peoples in new ways and led to far-reaching changes in Japanese perceptions of resource values, exploitation, and management. The corporate, industry, and political systems that resulted from this new level of commodity complexity in turn increased the capacity of the Japanese empire to further exploit the eastern Pacific Rim region.

There are two ways to approach the First World War's environmental history and ecosystems impacts in East Asia: on one hand, as military environmental history, short-term effects (immediate effects of warfare on landscapes); and on the other hand, medium- and long-term effects or "ecological shadows"[1] (the environmental effects of practices and policies, economic regimes, and their development for industrial-level exploitation of natural resources) that resulted from the "strategic opening" that the First World War afforded the Japanese empire. The ecological shadow of the First World War in East Asia resulted in changes in both environmental systems and the political ecology of the region. Fisheries in East Asia were one of the first ecological spaces to experience the new growth of empire and industrial-level exploitation, and they experienced a variety of environmental consequences.[2] But this analysis takes into account land, air, sea, flora, and fauna, literally, the terrestrial and pelagic ecological footprint of the Great War. Imperial Japan at the outset of the Great War was on the cusp of a major industrial, metabolic transition that increasingly tapped all of the regional ecosystems in complex and transformative ways. This chapter introduces elements of this systems-building process

---

[1] For practical and theoretical overviews of the "ecological shadow effect" concept from an industrial perspective, see Robert Marks, *China: Its Environment and History* (Lanham, MD: Rowman & Littlefield, 2012); Peter Dauvergne, *Shadows in the Forest: Japan and the Politics of Timber in Southeast Asia* (Boston, MA: MIT Press, 1997). See also Mark Peattie, *Nan'yo: The Rise and Fall of the Japanese in Micronesia, 1885–1945* (Honolulu: University of Hawaii Press, 1988) and Chih-Ming Ka, *Japanese Colonialism in Taiwan: Land Tenure, Development, and Dependency, 1895–1945* (Boulder, CO: Westview, 1995), for more specific overviews of Japan's pelagic empire at this time.

[2] This account does not, however, tackle (except in brief) the sea or fisheries as William M. Tsutsui and Micah Muscalino have already effectively done so in their respective essays and books like Ian Miller, Julia Adeney Thomas, and Brett L. Walker, eds., *Japan at Nature's Edge* (Honolulu: University of Hawaii Press, 2013) and Micah Muscolino, *Fishing Wars and Environmental Change* (Cambridge, MA: Harvard University Press, 2009), respectively. In particular, see William M. Tsutsui, The Pelagic Empire: Reconsidering Japanese Expansionism. In Ian Miller, Julia Adeney Thomas, and Brett L. Walker, eds., *Japan at Nature's Edge* (Honolulu: University of Hawaii Press, 2013), 21–38.

and environmental footprint of the Great War in two stages – by first outlining the political and strategic openings the war provided Japan, and then introducing the longer-term environmental eco-footprint of the war through four examples of ecosystems change(s) in the Japanese empire.

THE FIRST WORLD WAR IN EAST ASIAN POLITICS AND THE 21 DEMANDS

The narrative of Japan's imperial presence in East Asia is usually traced through territorial acquisition of island chains and on the mainland, along with annexation of populations, expropriation of land, and natural resources, as well as efforts to gain recognition among international powers.[3] Claiming and then exploiting island landscapes (and importantly, the fisheries around them) set a general pattern for developing new territories by the empire, one that often started with military invasion, surveying and "dominating" the land, and then either government or private development of natural resources.[4] The Russo–Japanese War (1905) gained Japan the southern half of Sakhalin Island and the Liaodong Peninsula, and manufactured other disputes in Korea in 1910. The First World War brought new resources, peoples, and territory to exploit. In each stage of imperial pelagic and terrestrial expansion, the empire exploited areas while transforming natural landscapes.

The First World War gave Japan both the diplomatic and military opportunity to create new bilateral relationships with the Asian mainland and southern Pacific, one that fell outside the multilateral norms of imperialism typical of the turn-of-the-century Pacific Rim.[5] Prior to the outbreak of the First World War (1905–1914) the *defense* of the Japanese

---

[3] A chronology of military developments is at the core of this process, starting with the acquisition of the Ryukyu Islands in 1871, the Bonin Island group and Kuriles in 1875, and Taiwan in 1895.

[4] One formative way that this economic and ecological process unfolded in Manchuria *after* the Great War period was the work of the South Manchuria Railway and its researchers in studying, targeting, and exploiting the region under increasingly thorough Japanese control after the early 1920s. For the Great War and interwar period, see Patrick Fuliang Shan, *Taming China's Wilderness: Immigration, Settlement, and the Shaping of the Heilongjiang Frontier, 1900–1931* (Burlington, VT: Ashgate, 2014). For the later 1920s and 1930s, see John Young, *The Research Activities of the South Manchurian Railway Company* (New York: East Asia Institute, Columbia University, 1966); Bruce Elleman and Stephen Kotkin, eds., *Manchurian Railways and the Opening of China* (Oxon: Routledge, 2014).

[5] Standard discussions of the First World War and East Asia are often linked to Chinese labor on the Western Front and Japan, its 21 Demands on China, and Japanese

empire constituted the basis of Japan's strategic and diplomatic policies in the Far East. Control of resources was also an important area of analysis. The outbreak of the Great War radically altered the diplomatic and military context in East Asia and afforded the empire, its businesses, and resource-oriented capitalists an excellent opportunity to *expand* on the continent and in the northern half of the south Pacific at the expense of the Western powers. Both short and long term, this would also have tremendous implications for Asia's environment and ecosystems.

At the same time that the Great War provided military and political cover for imperial expansion, it also afforded industries and corporate-state systems new opportunities for systems-building.[6] Political and military cover were necessary in order to exploit the natural resources near the center of Japanese imperial expansion. With the cover in place with the Great War and Euro-American attention focused on the European theater, Japan still needed the systems to extract from its new imperial hinterland on the mainland and in the South Pacific. Systems-building by corporate and government research arms, and businesses and entrepreneurs exploring new opportunities before, during, and after the war, built up the capacity of the Japanese state to expand. The Great War in Asia was not just an ideal political and strategic opening; it was also a multilayered event over a slightly longer time frame (into the 1920s) that changed the nature of existing commodity chains across wider Asia.

involvement in the war. There are also many British and American "discussions" of the First World War in Asia that date from the immediate aftermath of the war. These materials often lack systematic analysis and borrow heavily from one another. This chapter takes a slightly different tack by merging more sustained discussions and analyses of issues related to natural environments and their exploitation to Japanese empire building and the opportunities afforded various individuals during and immediately following the Great War. For examples, see Michael Summerskill, *China on the Western Front* (London: Michael Summerskill, 1982); Xu Guoqi, *Strangers on the Western Front: Chinese Workers in the Great War* (Cambridge: Cambridge University Press, 2011); Paul H. Clyde and Burton Beers, *The Far East: A History of Western Impacts and Eastern Responses, 1830–1975* (New York: Prentice Hall, 1971); or Alvin Coox, ed., *China and Japan: Search for Balance since World War I* (New York: ABC-CLIO Inc., 1978). And for a representative example of British and American Great War literature, see Reginald W. Wheeler, *China and the World War* (New York, 1919).

[6] One of the best historical overviews of this kind of Japanese systems-building remains Tessa Morris-Suzuki, *The Technological Transformation of Japan: From the Seventeenth to the Twenty-First Century* (Cambridge: Cambridge University Press, 1994), 105–142. Before there was an effective or great push into Manchuria in the late 1920s and early 1930s, there was a push into the wider Pacific and coastal China during and after the Great War that made later military and political adventures, commercially and in resource terms, viable and palatable.

The expansion of the Japanese empire during the First World War took place in two distinct phases, 1914–1916 and 1916–1923. These gains for the Japanese empire do not fit the traditional periodization of the war as they include not only the war and treaty process in Europe, but the events and military adventures like the Siberian Intervention in East Asia. For Asia, the Great War was not over until the Siberian Intervention, ostensibly a military action to "rescue" wartime soldiers stranded in Soviet Russia by the wider political shifts,[7] stumbled to a close in October 1922. The military and political gains afforded during these two periods, and the political and economic systems-building made possible by Japanese imperial demands on China, were the human systems side of environmental transformations wrought by the Great War in East Asia. The outbreak of the Great War in Europe gave great momentum to expanding Japanese interests in China. It was apparent, from the very beginning of the war, that the hostilities in Europe would upset the balance of power in East Asia, leaving Japan free to pursue its ambitions almost without check. Under the cabinet of Okuma Shigenobu, Japan's Foreign Ministry and military pursued a program of territorial expansion and bilateral negotiations that secured a new position for Japan in China and the Pacific. Japan consolidated these gains and tried to further expand on the Asian mainland through a secret treaty process with the Western powers. This territorial expansion on the Asian mainland and in the South Pacific came at the direct expense of the Western imperial powers of Germany, Great Britain, France, Russia, and the United States because of their preoccupation with the European war effort, as well as Koreans, Chinese, and South Pacific islanders coopted by the empire.

Great Britain tried to limit potential Japanese expansion at the start of the war by asking Japan to join the Allied effort.[8] Great Britain did not preclude Japanese gains at Germany's expense in China, but London did try to limit what the Japanese government could do in wider Asia and the

---

[7] The classic and exhaustive overview and analysis remains James W. Morley, *The Japanese Thrust into Siberia, 1918* (New York: University of Columbia, 1957).

[8] Using the Anglo-Japanese Alliance of 1910, British Ambassador Greene made a formal request on August 7 that "the Japanese fleet should if possible hunt out and destroy the armed German merchant cruisers who are now attacking our [British] commerce." He added that such a course "means an act of war against Germany but this is, in our opinion, unavoidable." However, the British changed their tone by issuing a second memorandum on August 12 to the effect that Japanese actions should not extend beyond the China Seas to the Pacific Ocean, or to any foreign territory with the exception of the territory on the continent of East Asia immediately occupied by Germany. See Roy Hidemichi Akagi, *Japan's Foreign Relations: 1542–1936* (Tokyo: Hokuseido, 1936), 310.

South Pacific using the Anglo–Japanese Alliance of 1910.[9] However, the Japanese government, under the cabinet of Okuma Shigenobu and then several later party coalitions, had other plans in mind regarding Japanese actions in Asia. In 1914, the government and Council on National Defense[10] began to coordinate the budgets and planning of the two military services (army and navy) to deal with German forces in East Asia and the South Pacific.[11] And while the British sought only limited help in East Asia, the Okuma cabinet elected to go to war in order to seize the German possessions in China's Shandong Province (Kiaochow) and to establish control over the German islands in the Pacific. By early 1915, Japan captured and controlled the former German holdings in Shandong Province and German Micronesia north of the Equator. Other than these limited actions, Japan's active role as an "ally" in the First World War was limited to the use of some of its warships to patrol the Mediterranean Sea toward the latter part of the war.[12]

In the wake of the "war effort" in January 1915, the Japanese government issued the infamous "21 Demands" to China.[13] Through them, the Japanese government sought to extend Japanese influence in the provinces of Shandong, south Manchuria, Inner Mongolia, and Fujian. Interest and expansion (economic, and, to a lesser extent, military) into these provinces

---

[9] Charles Spinks, Japan's Entrance into the World War. *Pacific Historical Review* 5(4) (1936), 297–311, 308–309. In many respects, the Americans had even less leverage to deal with Japanese imperial gains, though President Wilson did view their gains as problematic from both military and economic standpoints. See Russell Fifield, *Woodrow Wilson and the Far East: The Diplomacy of the Shantung Question* (New York: Archon Books, 1965).

[10] This "Council on National Defense" was composed of various leaders of the government ministries and the chiefs of the army and navy general staffs. They agreed upon a defense program that sanctioned an increase in forces stationed in Korea, an expanded naval program, and a greatly increased financial package for the military.

[11] James Crowley, Japan's Military Foreign Policies. In James W. Morley, ed., *Japan's Foreign Policy, 1868–1914* (New York: Columbia University Press, 1974), 3–117, 30. See also Takeuchi Tatsuji, *War and Diplomacy in the Japanese Empire* (London: Russell & Russell, 1935).

[12] See Hidemichi Akagi, *Japan's Foreign Relations*, 314–315; Peattie, *Nan'yo*.

[13] In opposition to Okuma's agenda, certain elements of the Japanese imperial government and long-time politicians (*genro*) of the late Meiji period wished a reappraisal of Japan's war-time China policy based on racial and cultural affinities, a kind of Pan-Asianism. The object of this policy was to try to firmly attach China more closely to Japan in order to deal with the Western powers following the First World War. However, the Okuma cabinet and Ministry of Foreign Affairs issued a series of more popular, controlling, and diverse proposals that clearly gave Japan a great deal more power in China than the Western powers and the Chinese government of Yuan Shikai. See William G. Beasley, *Japanese Imperialism, 1894–1945* (Oxford: Oxford University Press, 1987), 110–111.

brought together elements of an imperialist policy toward China that
Japan had previously been unable to pursue because of the opposition of
the Western powers. With Western powers focused on the European
front, Japan had an almost free hand to demand of East Asia and China
whatever it wanted.

The 21 Demands were grouped under five headings. The first had to do
with the transfer of German rights in Shandong Province to Japan as well
as the right to construct a rail line there. The second heading concerned the
recognition of Japan's special position in south Manchuria and eastern
Inner Mongolia. The third group dealt with the establishment of
a Sino–Japanese company under the tutelage of the Japanese government
that would grant extensive and exclusive rights to mine in certain areas of
the Yangtze River region. The fourth group asked that no further harbors,
bays, or islands along the coast of China be ceded or leased to any other
imperial power, especially the Fujian coastline opposite Taiwan. Group
five asked a number of things specifically of the Chinese government: to
employ Japanese political, financial, and military advisors; to establish
joint Chinese–Japanese police forces where the Japanese felt them necessary; to purchase 50% or more of China's arms and armaments from the
Japanese, or else establish joint Chinese–Japanese arsenals that would
employ Japanese engineers and use Japanese materials; and to grant
Japan the right to build railroads in southern China.[14]

In effect, these demands would strengthen Japan's military position in
Korea and Taiwan and furnish the basis for a rapid extension of Japanese
commercial activities on the mainland. For these reasons, they met with
strong approval in Japan, but caused serious political and social upheaval
in China and ire among the Western powers. In particular, group five of
the 21 Demands was considered noxious to Chinese and foreign observers. The wider aspirations of the Japanese government were discernible
in the Japanese interest in influencing the Chinese government in a manner
carrying hints of an overall protectorate over China. By dropping group
five of the 21 Demands, the Japanese foreign minister to China was able to
secure acceptance of the rest, both in Tokyo and in Beijing.[15]
In May 1915, China signed treaties embodying with minor modifications
all of the demands except group five, thereby giving Japan most of its
imperialist gains of the First World War era.

---

[14] Ian Nish, *Japanese Foreign Policy, 1869–1942: Kasumigaseki to Miyakezaka* (London:
Routledge & Keegan, 1977), 96–99.
[15] Beasley, *Japanese Imperialism, 1894–1945*, 114.

As important or more important than the imperialist political gains of the invasion of German lease territories in Shandong and the South Pacific, the territorial and policy gains of the 21 Demands helped Japan obtain and then solidify its control of key strategic resources (coal and timber, for example) and resource regions from China to the South Pacific. With these resources, the empire began to create a larger environmental footprint in Asia, one premised on not just a war of words but also on exploiting natural resources for further Japanese territorial expansion. They also allowed the Japanese to supply the Allies with certain scarce and lucrative goods (minerals, copra, and licorice, for example), and to exploit resources and populations earlier dominated by the British. These actions left an indelible imprint traceable to the Great War.

THE FIRST WORLD WAR IN EAST ASIAN ENVIRONMENTAL HISTORY: THE ECO-FOOTPRINT OF THE GREAT WAR IN ASIA

William Tsutsui in his discussion of Japan's *Pelagic Empire* has outlined the nature of Japanese fisheries and maritime developments before and after the First World War.[16] This section of this chapter looks at the pelagic and terrestrial repercussions of the Great War in East Asia first from a fisheries point of view and then from a short-term structural and long-term, industrial-scale exploitation of specific resources. While not even close to an exhaustive list of the environmental shifts taking place in the wider empire, the five areas explored in what follows do highlight some of the key transformations.

The 21 Demands Era (1915–1918) and the Pelagic Eco-Footprint

With the relative success of the military in taking over new pelagic and continental territory and the 21 Demands, Japan had new opportunities to exploit maritime fisheries on a grander scale. Japan has a long and well-studied history of intensive coastal fishing and whaling. However, with the Great War, offshore fisheries reached a new milestone in their development.[17] Japan already had significant fishing concessions off the

---

[16] Tsutsui, The Pelagic Empire, 23–28.
[17] The fisheries were developed starting in the late nineteenth century – see ibid.; Muscolino, *Fishing Wars and Environmental Change*; and Micah Muscolino, The Yellow Croaker War. In Ian Miller, Julia Adeney Thomas, and Brett L. Walker, eds., *Japan at Nature's Edge* (Honolulu: University of Hawaii Press, 2013).

various island conquests of the early empire-building stage, but gaining access to northern South Pacific and coastal Chinese fisheries expanded both the reach and breadth of maritime exploitation as many Japanese fishing vessels had more advanced (and damaging) netting technologies than their competitors in the region.

Modern otter trawlers (first imported from the British in 1908) were among the new technologies, packed with larger nets and holds, that were more damaging to regional reef and aquatic systems. Utilizing the terms of the 21 Demands in 1915 helped Japan establish its fisheries well outside home waters (that already included Korean waters). The number of vessels grew (hundreds of otter trawlers and motor-powered tuna boats by 1915 in formerly and formally Chinese waters), as did numbers of Japanese fishermen (an employment spike) and the volume of catch (rapid expansion in 1915–1921 in tons of fish, a fivefold increase). The Japanese boats had entered the East China and Yellow Seas en masse by 1920 and were off the coast of Fujian and Zhejiang (Taiwan Straits) by 1921. They chased tuna in the northern South Pacific off the former German mandate in large numbers starting in 1918–1919. By the mid-1920s, the new Japanese fisheries were producing many times more processed fish than just a decade earlier.

The expansion of this fishing fleet and its activities were guided and underwritten by the Japanese state.[18] Exploratory missions during the First World War (and after the 21 Demands) led to large-scale trawling by the beginning of the 1920s in numerous locations. In the case of the yellow croaker fishery in the East China Sea, Japanese fishermen, using their new technologies and diplomatic means, displaced local Chinese fishermen and overfished the yellow croaker fishery to such an extent that it was effectively defunct after 1928, after serving numerous populations for several centuries. Japan successfully used its burgeoning military might, diplomatic arm twisting, and new technologies (like the boats) to expand aggressively into existing fisheries, and in a relatively short period of time, to overharvest to the point of international contention and permanent local damage. This limited set of examples, however, is still only part of the story. The pelagic expansion of the Japanese empire constituted only one eco-footprint related to the Great War.

The Terrestrial Ecological Footprint in East Asia (1914–1919/21)

The short-term terrestrial consequences of the Great War in Asia were more limited when they related to outright warfare. The military-environmental

---

[18] Tsutsui, The Pelagic Empire, 26.

footprint was light – but not invisible. In the short and medium terms, Shandong Province faced a series of large-scale fire disasters linked to shelling or human carelessness (campfires gone wrong and urban fires from shelling during the attacks on Qingdao and several other smaller cities). There were also a number of defensive works built around Qingdao that altered local landscapes for a short time, though many of them were already based on existing or older imperial defenses. As it unfolded, active warfare in Shandong was more or less confined to a 200-square-mile territory of Kiaochow (Jiazhou) in the Shandong lease (Qingdao to Jinan Fu along the German railway concessions in particular).[19] During the hostilities, approximately 3,800 volunteers and 2,700 professional German soldiers and some 22,000 Japanese and 2,600 British soldiers were deployed. These soldiers and support groups had to be fed, which put some strain on local agricultural resources. However, the military footprint was very small by comparison to other regions and the scale of war, battle, and landscape transformation elsewhere between 1914 and 1919. The pelagic footprint was hardly mentionable in the South Pacific islands, in contrast with the Second World War's island terraforming, defense works, aerial bombardments, sunken ships, and reef and island destruction.[20]

One area where the First World War and its trench warfare had a medium-term effect on East Asia was the development of trench warfare

---

[19] Japanese forces quickly occupied German-leased territories in the Far East. On September 2, 1914, Japanese forces landed in China's Shandong Province and surrounded the German settlement at Tsingtao (Qingdao). In the process of marching overland to Qingdao, the Japanese army took possession of various towns and cities in the interior, railroads, and then the provincial capital. They were the cause of or blamed for a number of fire disasters (*huozai*) described in local newspapers and later gazetteers. In one case, "bandits" (the Japanese army) were accused of burning down an entire village in Tancheng County when their cookfires got out of control. The siege of Qingdao concluded with the surrender of German colonial forces on November 16, 1914. See *Shandong sheng zhi*, 1921, 1984 (Jinan: Shandong renmin chubanshe, 1984); *Shandong sheng zhi*. Huang jin gong ye zhi [*Shandong Provincial Gazetteer: Mining*] (Jinan: Shandong renmin chubanshe chuban faxing, 1993); *Zhongguo huozai dadian* [*Grand Collection of Chinese Fire Disasters*], 3 vols. (Shanghai: Shanghai kexue jishu, 1998) vol. 3, 2973; Dagong bao, September 21, 1914.

[20] During October 1914, acting virtually independently of the civil government, the Imperial Japanese Navy seized Germany's island colonies in the Pacific, including the Mariana, Caroline, and Marshall Islands. The Japanese navy also conducted the world's first naval-launched air raids against German-held land targets in Shandong Province and ships in Qiaozhou Bay from the seaplane-carrier *Wakamiya*. See Wilhelm M. Donko, *Österreichs Kriegsmarine in Fernost: Alle Fahrten von Schiffen der k.(u.)k. Kriegsmarine nach Ostasien, Australien und Ozeanien von 1820 bis 1914* (Berlin: epubli, 2013), 4, 156–162, 427.

during the interwar period in Jiangxi. German and British military advisors of Chiang Kai Shek from 1928 to 1933 advised military personnel in their goal(s) to destroy the Communist presence in Jiangxi Province, and to use trench warfare and a sort of scorched-earth policy to break Mao Zedong and his supporters there. This Jiangxi Campaign led to widespread destruction of farmland from repeated shelling, fires, and trench and blockhouse warfare. Though on a smaller scale, this was reminiscent of the Western Front. This reshaped the landscape in fundamental ways, especially in fertile river valley regions and on semi-forested mountain slopes. Much of the damage was, however, largely dismantled and repaired by the late 1960s in various land restoration projects.

The Power of Terrestrial Imperialism and Industrial-Scale Resource Exploitation

Approximately 100 years after the end of the First World War, the environmental legacies of Japanese imperialism and terrestrial eco-footprints are more apparent in several specific and consequential resource settings. The strategic opening of the Great War, the 21 Demands, and the power of imperialism allowed Japan to penetrate and develop several key markets, agricultural zones, and the earth in extensive new ways with long-term consequences for the populations and ecosystems that Japanese businessmen and boosters exploited. Competition for possession and exploitation of maritime environments was only part of the story. Industrial exploitation of coal for railroads and steam power for steamships, mining on the mainland and islands, agricultural development in the archipelagoes, Taiwan, and Manchuria, and grassland resource and forest development in the terrestrial realm during and immediately following the Great War had significant short- and long-term consequences.

The reach and exponential growth of Japan's terrestrial and pelagic empire coincided with the First World War – its economic exploitation of the seas and land paralleled the nation's economic and military advances throughout Asia that were simply not possible until the other imperial powers were involved elsewhere – the British, Germans, and French in particular worked to block Japanese imperial and economic advances on the mainland through a variety of diplomatic and economic means. And this was not a short-term effect, but the acceptance of the 21 Demands and a series of power plays during and after the First World War (the Siberian Intervention, etc.), meant that Japan was in all these new locations for the long haul (and Siberia through 1922) – developing and exploiting them (and their resources) at an increasing then sustained industrial scale. Illustrating a few, but certainly not all, of this level of aggressive shaping and reshaping of natural environments and their various resources were four environmental footprints and resource production areas between 1914 and 1923: grasslands products from Inner Mongolia (licorice root); plantation agriculture development on Taiwan and Micronesia (sugar, rice, copra); coal mining in the Shandong and Liaodong regions (and gold in Korea); and forestry across the imperial periphery. While these examples barely scratch the surface of Japanese imperial resource exploitation in East Asia during and immediately following the Great War, they are indicative of some of the trends.

Medicinal Harvesting and Agriculture after the 21 Demands

In the midst of the First World War, the Allies scrambled to find new sources of licorice – used in medicines, tobacco, and sweeteners – after their main suppliers, the Ottoman Empire among others, sided with the enemy and open warfare sent existing prices upward and depleted stocks. British agents found new sources of licorice (*Glycyrrhiza uralnesis*, Ch. 甘草, Mo. *shikhir ebesü*) along the Yellow River in Shaanxi, Shanxi, and Suiyuan Province in Inner Mongolia. This set in motion a decade of licorice speculation led by Japanese companies and entrepreneurs in the wake of the successful geopolitical bid of the 21 Demands to attempt to control licorice production in East Asia.

Sakura Christmas's micro-history of the licorice industry in eastern Inner Mongolia (1915–1930)[21] traces the growth of the industry from negotiations between Japanese brokers and local princes, to the building of distillation factories in Chifeng and Zhengjiatun, and finally the production and distribution of the root in extract form on a mass scale. Extracting licorice as it was developed for industrial-scale purposes was highly destructive. Root removal left gaping holes in the ground several feet deep, encouraging erosion and desertification in eastern Inner Mongolia, permanently scarring county landscapes in ways still being faced today. In 1916, following the opening up of Mongolian territories based on elements of the 21 Demands, licorice extraction, in particular, intensified with the founding of two distillation factories run by Japanese.

[21] Used with the kind permission of the author. Sakura Christmas, *Roots of a Drug Economy: Licorice in the Desertification of Northern China, 1915–1930*, unpublished manuscript, presented at ASEH 2014.

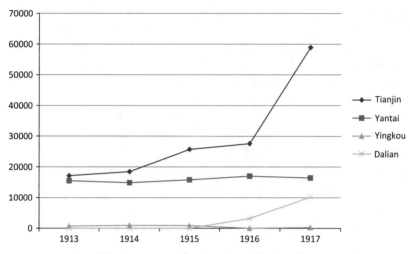

FIGURE 8.1 Licorice exports from major collection sites, 1913–1917

This was the year after Japan issued the 21 Demands to China, giving it significant economic rights in eastern Inner Mongolia for the first time. If we were to trace the licorice industry, it would begin among coolies, farmers, and herders on the steppe. They would pick licorice – about 12 to 24 kg per day per person – from the Khorchin Banner territory to the north, or from the uplands in Rehe (Jehol), and collect it in depots in the counties. Companies would transfer the bundles via rail or cart to factories, which would process them in Zhengjiatun or Chifeng. Then Japanese and Chinese trading firms exported the root or extract out of Tianjin and Dalian to cities like Osaka and then beyond. In the 1910s, exportation figures appear in the graph that follows: Tianjin and Dalian accelerated their exports while Yingkou remained steady and Yantai declined.

Weight of measurement: 斤 "jin" (1 jin = 596.8 gr/1.31 lb). From Sakura Christmas, *Roots of a Drug Economy: Licorice in the Desertification of Northern China, 1915–1930*, Unpublished manuscript, ASEH 2014, 3.

As Christmas has shown with her careful analysis of the development of the licorice industry during and immediately following the war, the Japanese individuals and firms involved in the region not only gained lucrative contracts and nominal authority in eastern Inner Mongolia, they actually accelerated collecting in the region. From 1916 to 1917, the amount of raw product coming out of the Khorchin Banners increased nearly seven times, and continued to soar to about 1.3 million pounds per year. The environmental consequences of this licorice rush were striking. Louis Edmonds, a historical geographer of China, speculated that collecting licorice and cutting ephedra contributed significantly to landscape degradation. Thus, Mongolian herders faced two threats during the First World War period: grazing zones diminished in surface area because of agriculturalization (usually by Han Chinese), and then the quality of those grazing zones worsened because of licorice digging (Han, Japanese, Mongols). The fact that agricultural scientists today plant licorice in the Khorchin Banners to stop the slow creep of the Gobi Desert suggests the crucial role this root plays in retarding erosion. The companies themselves rarely commented on the consequences of digging for licorice, but several sources note the repercussions of the licorice industry. For example, traveling across the steppe became complicated. Foreign explorers wrote, "Difficulties were increased by the numerous pits dug by licorice-root hunters ... which necessitated wide detours." These ditches, more importantly, posed risks to the herds of Mongols: "Not only have drought and disease occurred but cattle of every sort, [the] basis of our life, food, and taxes, have fallen into those holes dug by them. Not a few have fallen to their death."[22]

Licorice exploitation was only one facet of sector resource exploitation and landscape and agricultural development spurred by the Japanese empire during the war period. Expansion of agricultural zones and herds in Manchuria, driven at least in part by Japanese businesses and entrepreneurs active in the region in the wake of the 21 Demands, had immediate effects.[23] Chinese and Japanese exploitation of the grasslands, in terms of grazing and opening up new areas to the plow, increased during the Great War for both regional and global consumption, led to new levels of soil erosion from Heilongjiang to the Liaoning Peninsula by 1921.

Another area of terrestrial exploitation made possible and expanded by the Great War was the expansion of plantation culture and agriculture on Taiwan (sugar, rice) for domestic consumption as well as increased sugar exports abroad. The First World War disrupted sugar shipping from the

---

[22] W. R. Carles, Problems in Exploration: II. Ordos. *The Geographical Journal* 33(6) (June 1909), 668–679, 670.
[23] Sun Xiaoping, Blaine Chiasson, and others discussed this kind of imperial agricultural expansion at length in a recent conference on the environmental history of Manchuria. See Norman Smith, ed., *Manchuria: Environmental and Human History* (Vancouver: University of British Columbia Press, 2017).

Americas and over the course of the war, a relatively secure line of sugar for medical, military, and domestic consumption made its way to the empire from ramped-up sugar exports. While sugar production and exports were not new from Taiwan (as a Chinese province or colonial extension of Japan from 1895 to 1945), the scale expanded during the Great War.[24] Japanese firms and zaibatsu facilitated sugar (and other) exports in new ways to Western wartime markets. But expansion of plantation agriculture created its own problems with natural environments.[25] Sugar was a pure cash crop and in monocultures destructive of local flora. Sugar production itself used a great deal of water, producing not only large amounts of organic waste but significantly polluted water supplies as well (processes accelerated by the replacement of small-scale, artisanal, Chinese mills by large-scale, industrial Japanese ones). Localized deforestation to expand sugar plantations and to fuel (with firewood) sugar processing also made a lasting mark on Taiwanese lowlands, hillsides, and mountain areas during and after the war. A first major stage of soil exhaustion and landscape redevelopment ensued from this short-term emphasis on cash-crop sugar production in Taiwan.

In a similar fashion, with the seizure of Micronesia came an almost immediate ramp up in copra (coconut oil) production in the northern South Pacific Islands. As Mark Peattie demonstrates in his extensive study of Nan'yo (Japanese Micronesia), similar plantation culture developed in the island territories of Japan. Many of the same zaibatsu (and some of the Japanese boosters) active in Taiwan looked south and immediately (1916–1917) launched development projects in Micronesia. Widespread flora and fauna destruction resulted around copra/coconut oil plantations in easily accessible areas, and longer-term soil erosion and flora degradation set in by the mid-1920s.[26] The environmental price of colonial development developed fairly early, with increasing problems surrounding water supplies and soil erosion especially with rapid deforestation as well as introduction of alien species. Starting in 1916, Japanese entrepreneurs, businesses, and scientist-administrators introduced plant and animal life for domestic use. For example, cattle were introduced to Ponape; Japanese farmers brought "paddle grass" as feed, but it took over native species, and the tachinid fly was imported from Hawaii to prey on sugarcane borer but

---

[24] Ka, *Japanese Colonialism in Taiwan*, 64–68.
[25] An important issue raised by Chih-Ming Ka's research on Taiwan was that the major upward trend during the war and the commoditization of agricultural production precipitated increased specialization of agricultural production with resulting, localized environmental issues.
[26] Peattie, *Nan'yo*, 120–121.

swarmed the sugar mills. Farms, animals, and people, as well as crop-damaging imported toads, insects, and other flora, soon overran the roads and waterways of a number of islands.

Coal Mining and the Mining Environment

Japanese terrestrial, industrial, and shipping expansion followed the same trajectory of growth as Japan's shallow and deep sea fishing. Coal and other mining expanded rapidly in newly acquired Japanese territories, which had immense implications for local and regional environments, as well as long-term Japanese interests and perceived resource needs vis-à-vis other imperial states and economic systems. With the success of the 21 Demands, there was an almost immediate and immense expansion of Japanese coal mining interests in East Asia, and in China and Manchuria in particular. The initial wave of coal mining expansion started with Chinese collieries and joint ventures with British and Japanese coal businesses, but with the outbreak of the war in 1914, the joint ventures and Chinese-run coal-mining companies were increasingly sidelined by Japanese ones. After the 21 Demands, one of which specifically dealt with coal mining, Japanese concerns took control of specific coal-mining areas in southern Manchuria (Liaodong) and Shandong Province,[27] leading to massive coal development in these two regions, while others foundered during the wartime period.[28]

In terms of geographic distribution, large mine and expanding output and ownership in China during the war period was more or less concentrated in two areas: Liaoning, with 30.8% of coal output during the war period with more than 90% Japanese ownership, and Shandong coal mining with 27.7% of output and 48% Japanese ownership (up from 32% German ownership prior to the war).[29] The nature of longer-term output fluctuated with global

[27] See *Shandong sheng zhi*. Huang jin gong ye zhi [*Shandong Provincial Gazetteer: Mining*] (Jinan: Shandong renmin chubanshe chuban faxing, 1993).

[28] There is a bit of a complication to the statistics related to coal mining in China during the Great War. On the surface, coal output flatlined or stagnated depending on the source, but only in non-Japanese-controlled areas after 1915. Other coal-mining areas foundered in particular because of the First World War itself – with British and French interests otherwise occupied, East Asian collieries outside of Japanese interests had few commercial outlets. Conversely, Japanese areas not only had Japanese industry on the home islands, but Japanese coal-based businesses on the mainland to supply, as well as a rapidly expanding coal-driven merchant marine, and an expanding, partially coal-powered Japanese navy.

[29] See Julean Arnold, *China: A Commercial and Industrial Handbook* (Department of Commerce Trade Promotion Series No. 38) (Washington, DC: US Department of Commerce, 1926), 211–213, 737–741, 752–755. This commercial handbook is full

TABLE 8.1 *Output of coal by nationality/ownership of enterprise*

Coal Enterprises	1913	1919	1926	1936	1942
National Total	100.00	100.00	100.00	100.00	100.00
Chinese Enterprises	44.00	50.26	44.92	45.52	10.06
Joint Enterprises	32.37	26.54	23.5	19.8	0.6
Chinese–Japanese Enterprises	11.76	6.84	7.05	1.71	0.00
Japanese Enterprises	14.35	20.87	31.11	37.68	89.34

Source: From Timothy Wright, *Coal Mining in China's Economy and Society: 1895–1937* (Cambridge: Cambridge University Press, 1984): 118–121; Alexander Ikonnikov, *The Coal Industry of China* (Canberra: Research School of Pacific Studies, Australia National University, 1977), 22–24; Julean Arnold et al., *China: A Commercial and Industrial Handbook* (Washington, DC: US Government Printing Office, 1926), 211–212, 265–267, 268–269

and regional use and supply, but note (Table 8.1) the increase in wartime and in the immediate postwar period of Japanese coal enterprise output and the relative decrease of joint enterprise and Chinese–Japanese ventures in the same time period and afterward.[30]

In terms of environmental impacts, several issues stand out with the Japanese expansion of coal use. An immediate problem noted in regional and local gazetteers during the 1910s and 1920s was increased soil erosion in heavily mined areas, particularly in the Liaoning coal mining region under Japanese control. Most of the mines were shaft mines and shallow workings in either coal seams or outcrops. In both Manchurian mines and Shandong, water tables were relatively shallow, so water pollution was also a problem – not just for mining, but for local water supplies. Most mines averaged no more than 90 meters in depth as almost no pumps were used to drain them, leaving the open shafts or pits full of polluted water when seams played out.

of fascinating data on the Great War and immediate postwar period – and Japan (along with the United States) took center stage in developing a variety of natural resources in China. A significant portion of the data in the handbook was based on an earlier two-volume commercial handbook from 1919 to 1920 in the same series.

[30] Other key sources in English on China and imperial Japan in China's coal industry during and immediately after the Great War include Tim Wright, *Coal Mining in China's Economy and Society, 1895–1937* (Cambridge: Cambridge University Press, 1984); Elspeth Thomson, *The Chinese Coal Industry: An Economic History* (New York: Routledge, 2003); and Alexander B. Ikonnikov, *The Coal Industry of China* (Canberra: Australian National University, 1977).

Mining and its footprint were increasingly felt beyond the coal sector, though, and included other issues and territories related to Japanese expansion based on the Great War. Mining and resource degradation in the northern South Pacific and Taiwan under First World War–era Japanese imperialist exploitation, beyond the erosive power of land clearance for agriculture and cash crops, included increased mining of bauxite, copper, and phosphorus on the Pacific Islands and increased mining (and arsenic- and mercury-related issues) in Korea.[31] In particular, by the mid-to-late 1920s, serious problems developed around the industrial-scale exploitation of phosphorus in Micronesia, fouling water supplies on several islands. With increased mining and agricultural development came a related surge in forest destruction in Micronesia (Saipan, Tinian, Rota, and Palaus), Taiwan, and Manchuria in some places, as timber and trees were deemed significant impediments to the development of particular resources or cash crops. This forest destruction resulted in steadily increasing soil erosion and flooding in lower river valleys, as well as destruction or degradation of associated flora and fauna.

Timber and the First World War in East Asia

Finally, a timber exploitation shadow was felt throughout the regions associated with or near the wartime Japanese empire. Japan depended on quality timber just as much as other major imperial powers, and the Great War afforded a unique opportunity to exploit timber supplies throughout East Asia and the Pacific Islands in new ways. Initially, there were three primary areas for commercial and industrial-scale timber exploitation for the empire in China: Manchuria, Shandong (where it was quickly exhausted), and the Fujian coastline. In Manchuria and Fujian in particular, Japanese concerns sought *Pinus* and *cunninghamia* (Chinese fir) timber stands.[32] Some local gazetteers and newsprint describe damaged river systems in all three areas, not only from soil erosion and displacement, but as the primary means of moving the logs. Clear cutting and forest depletion were disproportionately high near rivers. In Shandong,

---

[31] See Peattie, *Nan'yo*. A recent and excellent analysis of mining and the Imperial Japanese Korean gold mining system can be found in Patricia Sippel, *Resource Exploitation as Imperial Power: Ecological and Human Consequences in the Development of Japan's Modern Mining Industry*, unpublished manuscript, presented at WCEH 2014 (Kagawa, Japan).

[32] See E. Elena Songster, Cultivating the Nation in Fujian's Forests: Forest Policies and Afforestation Efforts in China, 1911–1937. *Environmental History* 8 (2003), 452–473.

especially around Japanese-controlled port and mining areas, by 1918 Japanese officials and businesses were forced to import lumber for construction, fuel, and charcoal. In parts of southern Manchuria, throughout Shandong Province, and parts of coastal Fujian, the Japanese administrators were forced to enact despised timber-cutting restrictions by the early 1920s and to begin afforestation projects in Fujian after the late 1920s.[33] This was the "First Great Cutting" in Manchuria and Shandong from Japanese forestry operations, and it continued through the wartime 1940s. Along with Mao Zedong's Great Leap Forward (1958–1960), this was considered some of the most damaging forest destruction and exploitation of Chinese history.[34]

A similar pattern of forest exploitation and destruction was enacted on the islands in the wake of First World War–era exploitation. In their scramble to promote commercial agriculture, neither colonists nor companies were concerned with conservation of the islands' meager timber resources. Forest cover on the larger islands was seen only as an impediment, to be stripped away as quickly as possible. Taiwan fared better than the Pacific mandate, but had its own increasing problems with soil erosion and fouled water supplies. Within a decade the Pacific Islands, Saipan, Tinian, and Rota in particular, which had had good stands of timber before the Japanese takeover, were clear cut or burned over. Mangrove forests on the low-lying coastal areas were also stripped for Japanese colonists for their charcoal. Without their mangrove protection, beaches and coastal zones were increasingly eroded and washed away rapidly. Removal of sand for concrete – first for building projects and roads, then for the military by the 1930s – further badly damaged barrier reefs protecting a number of islands.[35]

SUMMARY

Imperial Japan's exploitation of natural resources across the East Asian region left various ecological legacies. Some included forest destruction,

---

[33] See Arnold, *China*, 118–121.
[34] Useful discussions of Japanese and Chinese exploitation of their timber reserves, especially from 1912 to the 1930s, include Patrick Caffrey, Transforming the Forests of a Counterfeit Nation: Japan's "Manchu Nation" in Northeast China. *Environmental History* 18 (2013), 309–332; Songster, Cultivating the Nation in Fujian's Forests. See also Patrick J. Caffrey, *The Forests of Northeast China, 1600–1960: Environment, Politics, and Society* (PhD thesis, Georgetown University, 2003).
[35] See Peattie, *Nan'yo*, 34–50, 136–149.

mining damage, great holes in the steppes, water pollution, soil erosion, beach and reef erosion, near species extinctions, and the introduction of invasive species. In the scramble to promote commercial agriculture and natural resource exploitation, and to achieve increased control of East Asia's economies and natural environments, imperial Japan was not concerned with conservation of resources or people.

The legacies of the Great War–era pelagic and terrestrial empire of Japan had a mix of short-term and long-term consequences. At their heart was imperial consumption of natural resources and creation of ecological shadows – legacies of empire building and modeling that would inspire a host of East Asian warlords and leaders well into the 1960s. Strengthening the nation through territorial and natural resource acquisition was central to the "modern" project of Japan during the Great War period and its aftermath. The First World War had provided the opening, and a voracious and ever expanding Japanese terrestrial and pelagic environmental footprint in East Asia was the result. The massive intensification of coal exploitation in Manchuria and Shandong Province tied directly to increased Japanese exploitation of coal resources for energy production, rail, and steam shipping use. Strip mining gold in colonial Korea helped pay for this expansion.

While this new industrial and resource regime unfolded in the 1920s, water and air quality issues were increasingly noted in popular media and administrative literature. Forest tree exploitation and degradation from Manchuria to Micronesia in the Japanese empire and its frontier zones also transformed natural systems. From at least the mid-to-late 1920s, timber destruction, exploitation, and related flora and fauna degradation (including reduced biodiversity on Pacific islands), joined with agro-forestry clearance to reshape Manchuria. Linked to agro-forestry clearance and clear cutting, soil and coastal erosion on the mainland and islands had increasing effects on water quality and irrigation. This aggressive industrial exploitation of natural resources helped to reshape the natural "spaces" of the expansive Japanese empire as well as the subject populations working for, in, and around it. The major environmental effects of the Great War in East Asia were about the war as affording Japan an opportunity to expand an empire, and setting up industrial-scale exploitation afforded Japan tremendous advantages in the 1910s and 1920s that did not simply end with relative "peace" in the 1920s or imperial implosion in the 1940s. Mao's China perpetuated many of the same methods of industrial extraction of resources and populations in a downward spiral of socialist development from the 1950s to the 1970s.

The geostrategic gains of the Great War for the Japanese empire left a fundamental eco-footprint. The technologies of peace and war built up during and following the Great War period expanded Japan's economy and territory, but this expansion did not stand alone and needed the support of a wide range of other industries producing materials, components, machinery, and above all natural resources to support workers in a growing empire. With the war, the Japanese state not only gained access to new resources, populations, and markets, it also gained greater and improved capacity to manage and exploit environments and ecosystems in new ways. From expanding agriculture and mining in a newly seized Pacific Island mandate to coal extraction on the mainland for shipping and industry, timber and grassland destruction extracting resources and industrializing fisheries with new technologies, the Japanese empire during the Great War went about transforming social and environmental systems. While the Great War started this process, it also set the stage politically, militarily, and especially environmentally for even further-reaching transformations during the 1930s and 1940s.

PART III

THE MIDDLE EAST AND AFRICA

Ecosystems, Refugees, and Famine

9

"Make Them Hated in All of the Arab Countries"

France, Famine, and the Creation of Lebanon

Graham Auman Pitts

Between April 1915 and December 1918, one in three Lebanese perished.[1] Nearly all died of starvation or disease stemming from the wartime conditions. Mount Lebanon, more than any other Ottoman province, relied on access to global markets. Once blockaded by the Triple Entente fleet, Lebanese farmers could no longer sell silk to France or receive remittances from Lebanese migrants in the Americas. The province's income fell as much as 80% in the wake of the Ottoman Empire's November 1914 declaration of war.[2] In turn, and despite the total absence of significant military combat, the war nevertheless produced a landscape of enormous violence in Lebanon, which suffered more casualties per capita than any other belligerent nation. This chapter aims to explore the international dimension of Lebanon's tragic wartime environmental history.

In no sense was the famine a "natural disaster." Drought and locusts, often cited in conjunction with the onset of famine,[3] cannot account for the excess mortality of the war years. Rain was short in 1916, but not

---

[1] The autonomous Ottoman province of Mount Lebanon had around 450,000 inhabitants in 1914. Approximately 150,000 of them died due to famine before the war's end. My dissertation discusses the demography of Mount Lebanon in more detail. Graham Auman Pitts, *Fallow Fields: Famine and the Making of Lebanon* (PhD dissertation, Georgetown University, 2016), 29–30.

[2] My calculations are based on Celal Bey, Al-Ahwal al-Zira'iyya wa al-Tijariyya wa al-Iqtisadiyya fi Jabal Lubnan [The Agricultural and Commercial and Economic Conditions of Mount Lebanon]. In Hakki Bek, ed., *Lubnan: Mabahith 'Ilmiyya wa Ijtima'iyya* [*Lebanon: Scientific and Social Investigations*] (Bayrut: 1918 [1993]), 88.

[3] See, for instance, Eugene Rogan, *The Arabs: A History* (New York: Basic Books, 2011), 149.

more than a 7% drop from the 100-year average.[4] Scarcity had set in before the arrival of locusts in 1915.[5] While the locust plague was unprecedented in its severity, the insects spared the grain crop of the Syrian interior (the region's breadbasket), which was bountiful.[6] In addition to starvation, the war also produced novel disease environments. An epidemic of typhus garnered the appellation in Arabic "military fever," revealing that the inhabitants of Lebanon understood that the massive troop movements entailed by the war had brought the novel epidemic. Typhus was all but unknown in Lebanon before the war.[7] The blockade appears responsible for other wartime disease outbreaks: quinine disappeared from pharmacy shelves, as did other imported medicines, and malaria abounded.[8] Bodies weakened by starvation easily fell victim to disease.

Lebanon was caught between warring empires. In addition to economic linkages, France imported Lebanese silk, and the autonomous province of Mount Lebanon also relied on French diplomatic support to maintain its special privileges. That reliance on France became a dangerous vulnerability once the Ottoman Empire entered the war. One of the

---

[4] Between 1875 and 1975, the observatory at the American University of Beirut (AUB) (founded as Syrian Protestant College) recorded an average yearly rainfall of 892.42 millimeters. In 1916, AUB's Observatory measured 832.9 mm of rainfall. Ghassan Halim Haddad, *Precipitation Trends and Modeling Case Study Beirut Region* (Master's thesis, American University of Beirut, Dept. of Land and Water Resources, 2005), 41–42.

[5] Despite the heightened wartime censorship of newspapers, Beirut's daily *al-Ittihad al-Uthmani* reported on the dire conditions faced by lower and middle-class Beirutis, who could no longer purchase grain. *Al-Ittihad al-Uthmani*, March 21, 1915.

[6] See, for instance, an Ottoman cable that reports the best harvest in 20 years for the Aleppo region, Halab Valisi [governor of Aleppo] to Dahiliyye Nazaretine [Interior Ministry], 9 Nisan 1331 [April 22, 1915], DH. ŞFR 469/45/2, Başbakanlık Osmanlı Arşivi (BOA). Northern Lebanon also reported record harvests for the war period. The years 1916–1918 saw record olive harvests according to Samih 'Abd al-Masih, Al Masa'lah al-Zira'iyah wa Masa't Harb al-Ju' fi Mutasarrifiyat Jabal Lubnan [The Agrarian Question and the Tragedy of the Great War in the Province of Mount Lebanon]. In Antoine Qissis, ed., *Lubnan fi al-Harb al-'Alamiyyah al-Ula* [*Lebanon in the First World War*] (Beirut: The Lebanese University, 2011), 557. A regional history of another region in north Lebanon also notes the exceptional quantity of the wartime harvests. See Sima'an Khazin, *Tarikh Ihdin al-Qadim wa-l-Hadith, tome 1, Tarikh Ihdin al-Madani* (Juniah: 1938), 264.

[7] Husni Bek, Al-Umur al-Sihhiyya fi Jabal Lubnan. In Hakki Bek, ed., *Lubnan: Mabahith 'Ilmiyya wa Ijtima'iyya* [*Lebanon: Scientific and Social Investigations*] (Bayrut: 1918 [1993]), 276.

[8] Interview with Dr. Ra'if Abi al-Lama'. In Nicolas Ajay, *Mount Lebanon and the Wilayah of Beirut, 1914–1918: The War Years* (PhD dissertation, Georgetown University, 1973), 409–410.

key motivations for the "Young Turk" Committee of Union and Progress (CUP) to join the Central Powers was ridding itself of concessions made to France, Britain, and Russia, such as Mount Lebanon's autonomy. Wartime Ottoman attempts to eliminate foreign influence and reengineer its society severely disrupted the normal functioning of the economy.

By early 1918, the famine had totally crippled the ability of the Ottoman state to retain its legitimacy to govern, in Lebanon as elsewhere in the Syrian provinces. For the French and British colonial project that replaced Ottoman rule, starvation conditions left the population desperate for effective administrators who could ensure the supply of grain. In that sense, the transition between Ottoman and French rule in Lebanon hinged on the ability of the French Empire to enforce a blockade for the duration of the war, and then arrive to relieve the famine its navy had helped create, with ships laden with grain. Lebanese nationalists also capitalized on the famine to demand an expansion of borders, exploiting French guilt about the tragedy. Recent scholarship on the war has neglected the centrality of the food crisis to the transition between Ottoman and French rule.

On top of the international context, the famine resulted from the particularities of Mount Lebanon's economy and ecology. Lebanon produced, according to the estimate of the minister of agriculture, only 6.3% of its own grain needs.[9] The conventional wisdom that Lebanese production accounted for one-fourth of grain requirements,[10] still repeated in 1914, was almost certainly dated by that time. For long centuries, the inhabitants of the Lebanon mountains, lacking a comparative advantage in the production of wheat, traded their tree crops with surrounding regions, especially Palestine and the Syrian interior.[11] Silk and olive production increased near the end of the eighteenth century, spurred by growing regional demand, and the Lebanese dependence on imported grain grew. With the inception of steamer traffic to the port at Beirut in 1835 and the consequent uptick of silk exports to Lyonnais factories, the

[9] That number is based on my calculation according to numbers provided in Bek, Al-Ahwal al-Zira'iyya wa al-Tijariyya wa al-Iqtisadiyya fi Jabal Lubnan, 85.

[10] Asad Rustum quotes the archive of the Administrative Council making this claim in 1880 in Asad Rustum, *Lubnan fi 'Ahd al-Mutasarrifiyyah* (Bayrut: al-Maktabah al-Bulusiyah, 1987), 208–209.

[11] References to Lebanese apples appear in poetry from tenth-century Baghdad, along with the much earlier references to Lebanese timber that appear frequently in the Old Testament. See Philip Hitti, *Lebanon in History from the Earliest Times to the Present* (London: Macmillan, 1957), 25–41.

Lebanese economy was transformed. Instead of growing its food, Lebanon's burgeoning rural population increasingly purchased grain. Instability in silk prices brought crisis in the 1880s and drove many Lebanese to emigrate to the Americas. By 1914, the largest sources of income for Lebanon were remittances from abroad followed by silk production. Both relied on access to global markets and were imperiled by the onset of the war, and in particular, the Entente blockade.

The consul at Beirut, François Georges-Picot,[12] the leading French envoy to the Middle East, boarded a steamer on November 1, 1914 to Alexandria, reportedly telling colleagues he would "see them in a couple weeks."[13] The Ottoman Empire had just entered the war on the side of the Central Powers and diplomats from the Entente nations had to flee Ottoman territory. Picot would not set foot in Beirut for nearly four years, despite his pledge of a swift return. It is unclear whether he expected the war to last no more than a couple of weeks or rather envisioned leading an invasion to "liberate" Beirut and Mount Lebanon from Ottoman rule. Once in Egypt, he lobbied for armed intervention in Lebanon.[14] His plan for an invasion fell on deaf ears in Paris.

Before the war, Picot had coordinated French influence in Beirut and Mount Lebanon, ensuring the implementation of the 1861 agreement to grant Mount Lebanon autonomy under a Catholic governor. France, among the signatories to the 1861 treaty, acted as the sponsor of Lebanon's autonomy. In turn, Mount Lebanon paid a lower tax rate than other Ottoman provinces and practiced self-government.[15] Lebanon's privileges stood among the "capitulations" of autonomy that had become the object of resentment for the Ottoman administration. In 1914, joining the Central Powers offered Young Turks the opportunity to do away with those affronts to their autonomy that, in their view, encouraged

[12] French diplomat Picot (1870–1951) signed what would come to be known as the "Sykes-Picot agreement" with British diplomat Mark Sykes in early 1916, agreeing to divide the Middle East into zones of direct and indirect French and British influence.

[13] See Yusuf Al-Hakim, *Bayrut wa-Lubnan fi 'Ahd Al 'Uthman* [*Beirut and Lebanon in the Ottoman Age*] (Beirut: 1964), 233.

[14] Defrance to Ministry of Foreign Affairs, November 4, 1914, Série Guerre 867, Ministère des Affaires Étrangères-la Courneuve (MAE).

[15] The Lebanese paid such a low tax rate, as little as 19% of the rates paid by surrounding regions, that even French diplomats – the guarantors of the autonomy that granted special tax status – occasionally lost sympathy for the economic demands of their erstwhile proxies. See John P. Spagnolo, *France & Ottoman Lebanon, 1861–1914* (London: Ithaca Press for the Middle East Centre, St. Antony's College Oxford, 1977), 273. See ibid., 285–286 for a discussion of self-government in Lebanon.

disloyalty.[16] Ottoman troops occupied Lebanon in November 1914, abrogating the province's autonomy.[17] Ottoman fears and Lebanese nationalist hopes aside, the detachment that occupied Lebanon met no resistance. For the political classes, the war was to be an ideological conflict between warring nations.

The Ottoman army – potentially aware of the machinations of French diplomats for a rebellion – began limiting grain shipments to the coast in order to deny provisions to a potential rebel or invading force.[18] That policy proved to be the proximate catalyst for the famine as prices soared in Beirut and Mount Lebanon, causing an integrated grain market to suddenly segment. Lebanese nationalists would later claim that the famine followed from an intentional Young Turk policy to starve the population. In the policy of grain limitation, there is some small truth to the claim of an active regime hand in the production of scarcity; however, no scholar has produced direct evidence of an Ottoman scheme to punish the "disloyal" Lebanese by starving them, despite the persistent claims of nationalist historians to that effect.[19]

A counter narrative that the Entente blockade should be held ultimately responsible[20] is equally simplistic. No party foresaw the coming of the famine, or intended it. For both the Ottoman regime and the Entente, the provisioning of the Lebanese was not a priority during the war. Meanwhile France and Britain actively fomented food scarcity among the populations of their adversaries. Aware that famine would undermine the loyalty of the populace to the Ottoman Empire and enable their

---

[16] See Djemal Pasha, *Memoirs of a Turkish Statesmen* (London: Hutchinson, 1922), 207.

[17] In practice, if not officially. Italy was signatory to the "protocol" guaranteeing Mount Lebanon's autonomy and therefore the Ottomans waited until after Italy had entered the war to officially abrogate the province's autonomy.

[18] Evidence for this policy of grain limitation comes from French diplomatic sources. See, for instance, Ottavi to Bompard, August 29, 1914, Constantinople Ambassade 275, CADN; Defrance to Declassé, April 24, 1915, Série Guerre 868, MAE.

[19] That narrative was first articulated by French diplomats and Lebanese exiles, who charged that the famine was a counterpart of the Ottoman Armenian policy; "the Armenians by the sword, the Arabs by starvation," they quoted Enver as saying, apocryphally. See Youssef Mouawad, Jamal Pacha, en une version libanaise: l'usage positif d'une legende noire. In Olaf Farschid, Manfred Kropp, and Stephan Dähne, eds., *The First World War as Remembered in the Countries of the Eastern Mediterranean* (Beirut: Orient-Institut, 2006), 432.

[20] Shakib Arslan, an Ottoman parliamentarian and later Arab nationalist who was close to Cemal Pasha during the war, makes this claim in his memoir, which also finds its way into other histories of Ottoman minority populations during the First World War. See his autobiography: Shakib Arslan, *Sirah Dhatiyah* (Bayrut: Dar al-Tali'ah, 1969), 225–235.

colonial project, they scuttled international relief efforts destined to bring food to starving populations in Lebanon and Syria. The French minister of foreign affairs wrote, in regards to the aid mission, that the famine represented a potential political opportunity for their colonial policy, as it would make the Ottoman Empire "hated in all of the Arab countries."[21]

Lebanon imported grain from other regions of the Ottoman Empire, primarily by sea. The Beirut–Damascus train line, completed in 1895, also brought grain to Beirut, and from there to Mount Lebanon. Grain arrived to the port at Beirut, and from there to Mount Lebanon. While lamenting the "absence of official statistics" a Lebanese official surmised that the "majority" of grain arrived to Lebanon via coastal barge traffic.[22] The latter would not have appeared in the tallies of consular officials and is thus difficult to quantify in retrospect. The reliance on water transport to connect the Ottoman grain market internally is indisputable. Just at the moment when the blockade meant that land transportation networks would have to compensate for the loss of access to the Mediterranean in the face of the blockade, the Ottoman army requisitioned what little coal was available along with draft animals from the interior.[23] The transport bottleneck enabled corruption as the flow of grain could be easily controlled by those well placed to do so.

On the ground, the mechanics of the famine, environmental and otherwise, were complex. An unprecedented plague of locusts in 1915 severely damaged summer crops in Lebanon along with the wheat crop in Palestine. In Beirut province (which encompassed northern Palestine), agricultural production fell 25% from the previous year in 1915, according to testimony before the Ottoman parliament.[24] Widespread conscription of men, along with the locusts, contributed to the fall. Nevertheless, in the Syrian interior, record harvests drove prices down, thereby segmenting an integrated grain market. Producers near Aleppo had no incentive to sell their harvest at unusually low prices, while the army had increasingly requisitioned draft animals and train cargo space, the means of transporting grain to the coast and Mount Lebanon. Bottlenecks in the flow of grain

---

[21] Jules Cambon, memorandum, July 4, 1916, *Série Guerre* 873, MAE.

[22] Salim al-Asfar, al-Zira'ah fi Lubnan. In Hakki Bek, ed., *Lubnan: Mabahith 'Ilmiyya wa Ijtima'iyya [Lebanon: Scientific and Social Investigations]* (Bayrut: 1918 [1993]), 26.

[23] M. Talha Çiçek, *War and State Formation in Syria: Cemal Pasha's Governorate during World War I, 1914–1917* (London: Routledge, 2014), 19.

[24] Ahmet Nesimi Bey (minister of agriculture and commerce), *Meclis-i Mebusan Zabıt* İ:14. 21 Kanunuevvel 1331 (January 3, 1916) C: 1, Büyük Millet Meclisi, http://acikarsiv .ankara.edu.tr/ (accessed August 23, 2017).

enabled corruption and Beirut's daily noted, in October 1915, that "a more salient reason for the rise of wheat prices in Beirut and Mount Lebanon than transport [difficulties], is a powerful ring of speculators enabled by some kind of monopoly [*qutb dairat al-mudaraba al-mashfu'a binaw' min al-ihtikar*]."[25]

Grain was available, but not effectively distributed. Lebanon's food crisis appears to conform to Amartya Sen's model wherein simple food availability decline (FAD) is insufficient to explain widespread starvation.[26] Prominent commercial figures, such as Alfred and Michel Sursock, persuaded the wartime military commander, Cemal Pasha, to let them coordinate the provisioning of Lebanon,[27] a privilege they exploited to criminal proportions. As time passed and the reality of mass starvation could no longer be denied, the Ottoman administration appears to have genuinely attempted to curtail the famine,[28] but lacked the administrative resources to do so. Thus, the famine defies simple characterization. In another sense, however, the origins of the famine are quite simple. War made the famine – in particular, a sustained, industrial conflict wherein food became contraband, and entire enemy populations became the legitimate targets of blockade. In this regard the Lebanese were almost innocent bystanders. The British had certainly not had them in mind when they hatched their policy of blockade.

Lebanese villagers experienced the war not as a political or military clash between nationalisms, but in terms of the catastrophic demise of their sources of income, followed by prolonged scarcity and disease outbreaks. On March 7, 1917, two priests reached one of Lebanon's highest villages, Tannourine, tasked by the Maronite Patriarch with distributing grain and money to the needy. Their aim was to hold mass, hear confession, distribute flour and money, and assess the damage famine had wrought over the three preceding years. They found villagers hoping to perform an "abbreviated confession," because so many of them had, according to the priests' report,

arrived at the doors of eternity due to extreme scarcity ... the closure of their sources of prosperity, and the death of many of them from hunger and infectious disease such as smallpox, typhus, lice and dysentery fevers. We tried to ascertain the number of destitute poor, which was close to 800 in need of daily provisions

---

[25] *Al-Ittihad al-Uthmani*, October 13, 1915.

[26] Amartya Sen, *Poverty and Famines: An Essay on Entitlement and Deprivation* (Oxford: Oxford University Press, 1981), 1.

[27] An edict of Cemal Pasha, translated from *al-Sharq* (October 14, 1916) reproduced in Defrance to Briand, November 11, 1916, Série Guerre 874, MAE.

[28] Cemal Pasha to BEO, 9 Receb 1335 [May 1, 1917], BEO 446/.334986, BOA.

and suddenly came to us the sight of half [of that number] and the reality hit us and we couldn't speak, because we saw the poor in their paltry numbers and their desperate state ... standing in the freezing rain and storm winds ... [that] which pains the heart, especially the sight of the naked among them ... we comforted the sick, offered our condolences, but, due to the destitution engulfing them, their ears do not hear, their eyes cannot see, and their hearts will not understand.[29]

The priests reckoned that 1,000 of the district's population (of approximately 3,000 before the war) had perished. Tannourine's experience encapsulates that of Lebanon more broadly during the war, in terms of the numbers dead and the causes of death: the cessation of commerce, starvation, and disease that followed, killing large numbers of people in a prolonged and gruesome manner. Like the majority of the inhabitants of rural Mount Lebanon, the people of Tannourine relied on alms from the church; no public relief came to their aid.

The implications of having to transport grain by land were stark for Mount Lebanon. "If not for the sea blockade," two bureaucrats transiting Mount Lebanon in 1917 wrote, a steamship could have taken them from Beirut to Tripoli in three hours. As it was, a carriage had to suffice them to cross the 90 kilometers between the two port cities. The journey took more than a day, and they stopped after the 60 kilometers between Beirut and Batrun for the night.[30] The poor condition of the road caught their attention.[31] Whatever animals pulled their carriage (they did not specify) were rare at that late point in the war; many had been requisitioned or starved. A permit was required to move freely with the draft animals.[32] Starvation was worst in the districts most isolated by the high Lebanon mountain range, the districts transited by the bureaucrats, who fell asleep in the town of Batrun to children crying, "hungry, hungry," in their "Mountain accent."[33] To the north, areas bordering Tripoli appeared to have escaped starvation, and to the south, the Shuf mountains, with easier access to the Bekaa, also avoided starvation until sometime in late 1916. In those districts (the *kazas* of the Matn, Batrun, and Kisrawan) administrators and police chiefs could take advantage of their power to exploit the

---

[29] Frs. Louis and Butrus, "Ziyarat al-Qura wa Tawziʻ Ihsanat [A Visit to the Villages and the Distribution of Alms]: 1917," Drawer Elias Huwwayik 32/270, Archives of the Maronite Patriarchate, Bkirki, Lebanon (Bkirki).

[30] Muhammad Rafiq al-Tamimi and Muhammad Bahjat al-Katib, *Wilayat Bayrut* (Judaydat al-Matn, Lubnan: Dar Lahd Khatir, 1979), 179.

[31] Ibid.

[32] *Sijil al-Yawmiyyat* [*Daily Register*]: "3 March 1917," Jamʻiyat al-Mursalin al-Bulusiyin [St. Paul Society of Missionaries], Harissa, Lebanon (Harissa).

[33] al-Tamimi and al-Katib, *Wilayat Bayrut*, 179.

populace, especially by selling grain that had been given to them by the Ottoman administration for distribution to the poor.[34]

The Empire's internal transportation network, as noted earlier, was largely seaborne. At the war's outset, no railroad line connected Istanbul with the Syrian provinces. Goods had to be off-loaded and transported over the Amanus Mountains to reach Syria. Coal production dropped 40% just as the Ottoman Empire needed it the most and could no longer import that key input into land-based transport. The 5,759 kilometers of railways in the empire were geared to interface with maritime transport, and not link Ottoman provinces directly. The Ottoman Empire's susceptibility to a naval blockade was thus significantly greater than the other Central Powers, and its consequences there were more lethal than elsewhere. In an agricultural economy that had seen very little mechanization, inputs other than labor (such as tractors and fertilizers) could not be inserted in the place of conscripted men to maintain production levels, as in countries with industrialized agricultural sectors. In the Ottoman Empire the production of food was not capital-intensive and the government had little money to pay producers. Its attempts to set low prices for staple grains had the unwelcome consequence of discouraging farmers from parting with their harvests.[35] In the countries where capital abounded, governments could afford to pay more for agricultural goods, and rural economies continued to function.[36]

The downturn in agricultural production across the empire impacted Mount Lebanon disproportionately. The province devoted a higher percentage of land to export crops than any other Ottoman province, perhaps even twice as much as the next-most commercialized province. Among the most vulnerable province to the cessation of commerce in grain, it was duly struck first by extreme scarcity, among all of the Ottoman provinces. On average, the Asian provinces of the Ottoman Empire only devoted 5% of cropped area to commercial crops.[37] Lebanon appears to have been a significant outlier in that regard, with only 12% of its land area devoted

---

[34] On this point see Pitts, *Fallow Fields*, chapter 3.

[35] Şevket Pamuk, The Ottoman Economy in World War I. In Stephen Broadberry and Mark Harrison, eds., *The Economics of World War I* (Cambridge: Cambridge University Press, 2005), 121.

[36] Stephen Broadberry and Mark Harrison, *The Economics of World War I* (Cambridge: Cambridge University Press, 2005), 19.

[37] Chris Gratien, *The Mountains Are Ours: Ecology and Settlement in Late Ottoman and Early Republican Cilicia, 1856–1956* (PhD dissertation, Georgetown University, 2015), 227. For land use in Lebanon, see later in this chapter.

to the production of staple grains, and the rest devoted to silk, olives, and tobacco.[38] Mount Lebanon was not the only province to suffer from famine, however, belying the idea that famine had been hatched as a special plan against Lebanese Christians. By 1917, starvation became a general phenomenon in the Syrian provinces.

In the end, the deprivations of the war snapped the loyalty of Arabic-speaking populations to the Ottoman Empire. Salim Tamari has noted that years of food scarcity soured public opinion toward the Ottomans in Palestine, and a whole body of scholarship has emphasized that an exclusive "Arab identity" only coalesced after the war among the region's intelligentsia. However, scholars have too often assumed that the Lebanese, and especially Christians, were already in favor of being colonized by France in 1914.[39] The inability of the regime to provide sustenance to its population and soldiers undermined its credibility among the populace and colored the entire legacy of Ottoman rule in the region. The collapse of Ottoman legitimacy was particularly dramatic in Lebanon; death rates in surrounding provinces did not generally exceed one in ten per capita, compared to the more than three in ten who lost their lives in Mount Lebanon.[40]

The clash of empires that determined Lebanon's future hinged on the French capacity to feed Lebanon's population and the Ottoman inability to do so. In that sense, Lebanon's experience conforms to the environmental history of the First World War more broadly: the Entente distributed grain effectively and prevented the Central Powers and the Ottoman Empire from doing so through a policy of blockade. Avner Offer's influential thesis has maintained that Germany's inability to mobilize primary commodities to compete with the Entente was the decisive factor in its defeat: "Germany did not run out of rifles or shells. It suffered badly from shortages of food. Likewise the Allies: their agrarian resources decided the war. So not only a war of steel and gold, but a war of bread and potatoes."[41] In that regard, the Ottoman Empire was extremely

---

[38] My calculation based on Paul Jouplain [Nujaym], *La question du Liban, étude d'histoire diplomatique et de droit international* (Beirut: 1961 [1908]), 495.

[39] According to Patrick Seale, "The Christians of Lebanon – especially the Maronites among them – linked to Europe by generations of association, impregnated with French language and culture, fearful of the surrounding Muslim world, looked to Paris for protection. So much was obvious." *The Struggle for Arab Independence: Riad el-Solh and the Makers of the Modern Middle East* (Cambridge: Cambridge University Press, 2010), 151.

[40] Pitts, *Fallow Fields*, 37–38.

[41] Avner Offer, *The First World War: An Agrarian Interpretation* (Oxford: Oxford University Press, 1989), 1. Alexander Watson's thick tome on the Central Powers'

vulnerable and experienced severe disruptions to its food distribution networks before its German and Austro-Hungarian allies. The Entente nations simply had superior capability to provision their armies and populations and the naval power to prevent their adversaries from doing so. The Lebanese became the first victims of the cordon imposed by the British and French navies.

News of the famine trickled out of Lebanon via Cairo's Syrian émigré community. The French *charge d'affaires* in Cairo, Jules-Albert Defrance, maintained close relations with the community of politically minded exiles, many of whom had fled on the eve of the war. He championed their cause, and in November 1914, advocated for French intervention in Lebanon before Ottoman troops could occupy the country. Defrance was fully apprised of the famine conditions in early 1916, as was the government in Paris. Quickly, the same news reached the global press and an international outcry began. Many political exiles had fled to Cairo to avoid the repression of Jamal Pasha's regime. "*L'émotion chez les Syriens est intense.* ... Here the Syrians are discussing a plan to send a delegation to Paris to implore France to send relief and influence the public opinion [in that regard]." Defrance did not see the need for them to make the voyage, however, and had assured the worried exiles that "the Government of the Republic is informed *le plus exactement possible* as to the situation in Syria." Faced with his Lebanese contacts on a daily basis, Defrance implored Paris to act, by forwarding letters from Lebanese recalling France's own claims to be "*protectrice séculaire du Liban.*" Defrance echoed their criticisms, noting France's "material and moral obligations [toward Lebanon]," as well as France's role in causing the famine: "it is certain that the blockade of the coast, established and maintained by a French squadron, is an obstacle to the provisioning of Lebanon."[42]

Picot also pressed the government of France to intervene. In the absence of decisive action, the reputation of France as the protector of Christians might suffer irreparable damage, he feared.[43] Paris and London never seriously considered a relief mission that might compromise the goals of

experience during the First World War testifies to the continued relevance of Offer's work: Writing nearly 30 years later, Watson also concludes that the Central Powers inferior resource base made their odds of defeating the powers arrayed against them "dreadful." Alexander Watson, *Ring of Steel: Germany and Austria-Hungary in World War I* (New York: Basic Books, 2014), 2.

[42] Defrance to MAE, May 25, 1916, Série Guerre 873, MAE.

[43] François Georges-Picot, memorandum, July 26, 1916, Série Guerre 873, MAE.

their blockade and "remedy the shortage of supplies which it is the very intention of the blockade to produce."[44] The United States lobbied the French and British administrations to allow relief missions in the summer of 1916. As soon as the potential relief mission of the US steamer *Ceaser* appeared on the diplomatic cables, the foreign ministers of France and Britain colluded to publicly entertain plans for a relief mission while privately courting a diplomatic dispute with the Ottoman administration over the details of distribution.[45] Ottoman officials eventually agreed to the mission and to let the American Red Cross distribute aid,[46] thereby calling the Entente's bluff. In January 1917, the *Caesar* reached Alexandria, having arrived from New York loaded with tons of cargo destined for Beirut and Mount Lebanon. Just as the *Caesar* was poised to sail for Beirut, the French Navy cabled US diplomats in Egypt, denying it permission to pass.[47]

Paris elected to wait for the ultimate military solution to the conflict: the British army would methodically advance from Egypt, slowly turning back the Ottoman army at the beginning of 1917.[48] After that moment, plans for "saving" the starving Lebanese and Syrians faded from the minds of French diplomats. Paris and London decided to focus on establishing a narrative wherein starvation had been intentional on the part of the Ottomans. Instructions had already been given to the French ambassador in Washington that President Wilson should be made to understand that the cause of famine was not a *lack of resources* but rather Cemal Pasha's intentional blockade of Lebanon.[49]

To what extent were the British and French aware of their own culpability? The Foreign Office tellingly denied that Britain had even declared a blockade in 1918, seeking to blame the French instead.[50] Britain had of course declared and enforced the blockade, and the British attempted denial reveals that the famine represented a potential political liability.

---

[44] Bertie (British Embassy, Paris) to Margerie, June 2, 1916, Série Guerre 873, MAE.

[45] Ibid.   [46] Defrance to MAE, September 29, 1916, Série Guerre 874, MAE.

[47] Garrels, Consul (Alexandria) to Secretary of State, January 29, 1917, Microcopy No. 353, Roll 52, Records of the Department of State Relating to the Internal Affairs of Turkey, 1910–1929, National Archives and Records Administration, College Park, Maryland (NARA).

[48] The British government announced its intention to launch a January offensive against Al-Arish, and encouraged French participation. De la Panouse (military attaché, London) to French General Staff, October 6, 1916, Série Guerre 874, MAE.

[49] Margerie [MAE] to Washington, September 25, 1916, Série Guerre 874, MAE.

[50] Harmsworth to Admiralty, February 26, 1919, FO 372/1273, the [British] National Archive (BNA).

In order to salvage their respective reputations, the ability of the Entente to provide the relief to end famine would be crucial. Years of starvation had snapped the loyalty of the populace to Ottoman regime.[51] The desperation of these inhabitants offered ripe conditions for the construction of new loyalties after the fall of the Ottoman military in Syria in October 1918.

In the wake of the November 1918 Ottoman withdrawal, French administrators enacted a plan carefully crafted by Picot to assert French influence based on systematic grain distribution. Instead of relying on elite intermediaries as had the Ottomans, supplies were to pass directly from the hands of soldiers to those of consumers, reducing the risk of fraud to a minimum. Meanwhile, the political impact of these operations loomed ubiquitously: "The free distribution of these ... goods, a welcome gift from France, indispensable to save one hundred thousand starving Lebanese from death, will produce a great impression in the country."[52] Twenty thousand relief cards were to be distributed to the "most needy families," as adjudged by local authorities. Returning with the French army to oversee the distribution of grain were Jesuit priests who had spent decades in Lebanon.[53] Their sophistication allowed relief to be quickly effective in Beirut and rural districts of Lebanon. "Monopolizers" subsequently released their stocks. French policy next aimed to remove the visible reminders of the horror of the famine from the public eye, providing shelter to orphans and gainful employment to women who had turned to prostitution.[54] Responding to objections about the expense involved in relief, Picot noted that foreign aid was "a political necessity of the first order."[55] By May 1919, French officials on the ground perceived that further shipments from France loaded with grain for free distribution were unnecessary.[56]

---

[51] Salim Tamari, *The Year of the Locust: A Soldier's Diary and the Erasure of Palestine's Ottoman Past* (Berkeley: University of California Press, 2011); Hasan Kayalı, *Arabs and Young Turks Ottomanism, Arabism, and Islamism in the Ottoman Empire, 1908–1918* (Berkeley: University of California Press, 1997).

[52] Coulondre to Ministry of Foreign Affairs, October 29, 1918, E-Levant 59, MAE.

[53] Comité de l'Asie française, La famine du Liban: et l'assistance française aux Libanais pendant la Grande Guerre (1915–1919). In *Supplément à l'Asie française: Documents économiques, politiques et scientifiques* (Paris: 1922).

[54] Ibid., 11, 14.   [55] Picot to Foreign Minister, March 4, 1919, E-Levant 59, MAE.

[56] Feer to Foreign Minister, May 7, 1919, E-Levant 59, MAE. Several relief ships had arrived from Marseille in the interim: the *Bosphore* on February 28, the *Waldeck Rousseau* on March 17, the *Ispahan* on March 20, the *San-Antao* on March 29. Additionally, the French authorities sourced grain locally from Alexandrette, Latakia,

At war's end Lebanese in the diaspora were anxious to learn the fate of their relatives. In response to a desperate plea for news of their country-men sent by the Lebanese émigré community of Buenos Aires, Picot cabled back denying that 30% of the population – the figure they had heard in Argentina – perished during the war.[57] Picot knew better and was even willing to use Lebanese suffering to pursue political goals when conveni-ent: a week after his denial to Buenos Aires he forwarded a petition suggesting that "half" the mountain had died from starvation during the war.[58] On the one hand, France's inability to protect the Lebanese during the war proved a political liability for France. Picot felt he needed to hide it from their Lebanese clients abroad; at the same time an exaggeration of the scale of the tragedy bolstered claims for a country with extended borders, the necessity for which appeared as a bulwark against the repeat of starvation. Without those districts, worried Picot, they would run the risk of "gravely disappointing our clients in Lebanon, by enclosing them in a circle of abrupt mountains where they will not be able to survive."[59] The specter of starvation infused the debates over Lebanon's future, and crucially bolstered Lebanese nationalist claims for extended borders.

Talk of the famine infused the negotiations around the creation of Greater Lebanon, which established modern Lebanon in its contemporary borders. Maronite Patriarch Elias al-Huwwayik and his deputy, Abdallah al-Khuri, led the three delegations to Paris until Prime Minister Millerand acceded to their demands in August 1920. In staking their claim for Lebanon to be a distinct national entity, they made persistent reference to the famine, playing on the conscience of the French diplomatic corps by reminding them that "more than a third of the Lebanese population" died because of a "Turkish" campaign of "terror and intentional starvation [*affamement*]." In turn, "Lebanon paid, during the war, the most formid-able, the most bloody tribute that a people has ever paid for the defense of a cause."[60] A chorus of voices made the same point. The Greek Catholic

and Hawran. British authorities had also delivered grain to Beirut. Picot to Pichon, July 7, 1919, E-Levant 59, MAE.
[57] Goussen to Picot, November 25, 1918; Picot to MAE, December 4, 1918, E-Levant 59, MAE.
[58] The petition was eventually distributed to French delegates to the Peace Conference in February 1919. Conseil Administratif du Liban, petition, December 19, 1918, E-Levant 5, MAE.
[59] Picot to Pichon, November 22, 1918, E-Levant 5, MAE.
[60] Elias al-Huwayyik, Les révendications du Liban. Mémoire de la Délégation Libanaise à la Conférence de la Paix. *La revue phenicienne* (Noël 1919).

archbishop wrote Millerand, "In effect, without the annexation [of additional territory], Lebanon would be condemned to die of starvation."[61]

Ultimately, On September 1, 1920, High Commissioner of the French Mandate Authority General Henri Gouraud declared, in Beirut, the creation of "Greater Lebanon." Lebanese nationalists celebrated and one of their number summed up their reaction "Everything is set. It is a total success. [Tout est réglé. C'est un succès total],"[62] even though they had acceded to French colonization. Not only had cities of the coast: Tripoli, Beirut, Sidon, Tyre (never part of the Ottoman province of Mount Lebanon) been adjoined, but so had the fertile plains of 'Akkar and the Bekaa valley. The southern border was to include the well-watered agricultural districts in the shadow of Mount Hermon. The main journal of Lebanese nationalists carefully quantified these districts in terms of their agricultural contribution to the new territory, noting that they would facilitate Lebanese "independence" from the rest of the Syrian hinterland.[63] The autonomous district of Lebanon had encompassed 3,200 square kilometers, Greater Lebanon, after 1920, expanded to more than 10,000.

France and Lebanese nationalists had reason to oppose the addition of territory to Lebanon. For the nascent French Mandate, the annexation of land presented an obvious political liability as such a measure was enormously unpopular through Syria and especially in the territories to be annexed. Those territories also contained majority-Muslim populations, thereby diluting the Christian majority. Along with fertile, grain-producing plains and port cities came many Muslim inhabitants. The liability that annexation would have presented for the Christian dominance of the country was a necessary evil; avoiding a repeat of the starvation of the war formed Lebanese nationalists' main priority. The contradictions between the demographic realties of the country created in 1920 and the Maronite monopoly on political power had fateful consequences for Lebanon in the twentieth century.

The First World War projected violence well past the European and Middle Eastern battlefields. War sustained a landscape of starvation, disease, and depravity in Lebanon for four years. No evidence suggests that any party relished the starvation that took place; it resulted as an

[61] Cyrille Mogabgab (Archevêque de Zahle) to Millerand, n.d., E-Levant 125, MAE.

[62] Sarhan al-Khoury to Yusuf al-Sawda, September 8, 1920, YS-12L-032 (-e), Archive Yusuf al-Sawda, Université Saint-Esprit de Kaslik, Lebanon (USEK).

[63] Paul Noujaim [Bulus Nujaym], La question du Liban: étude de politique economique et de statistique descriptive *La revue phenicienne* (August 1919).

"externality" of a military clash between empires. Lebanon, imperfectly colonized by either the French or Ottomans, fell victim to its relative lack of importance *vis-à-vis* the military goals of those empires. Picot, in particular, lamented that France could not live up to half a century of rhetoric that it was the protector of the Lebanese. France's policy did not intend for such evil to befall the country, but was nevertheless willing to take advantage of the crisis to establish the legitimacy of its Mandate. The blockade created a need for the colonialism France had for decades attempted to foist on Lebanon. It cannot be assumed that the Lebanese were destined to accept the imposition of French authority. They had suffered more than any other community and their acquiescence to the French Mandate must be understood in light of the famine. The starving populace was desperate for a savior when French ships arrived laden with grain in 1918 and early 1919. The famine, to a great extent, must account for the lack of resistance to the occupation by the French and the creation of an expanded Greater Lebanon under French auspices in September 1920.

10

Why Are Modern Famines So Deadly?

The First World War in Syria and Palestine

Zachary J. Foster

Famine must have seemed almost as natural a part of the life cycle as birth, childhood, and death before the nineteenth century in the Middle East. Various parts of the Arabian Peninsula, for instance, suffered from food shortages and famine on average once every 7.8 years from the mid-seventeenth to the early twentieth century.[1] Famine struck the cities of Aleppo or Damascus at least once every five and a half years in the seventeenth and eighteenth centuries, while bread riots were commonplace in Damascus throughout the 1730s–1750s.[2] Taken together, there were a dozen famines in Palestine, Iraq, Anatolia, the Hijaz, Yemen, Armenia, Iran, and Morocco from 1765 to 1769.[3] Famine was nothing unusual

[1] The region under examination included what are parts of Saudi Arabia, Jordan, Yemen, and Iraq. This must be considered an extremely rough estimation, because the source material for the study of environmental history of Arabia is quite sparse, but also because the figure includes food scarcity, famine, and widespread starvation, as well as periods of "continual famine." In some cases, the region may have gone for up to two decades or more without experiencing a famine, whereas at other times famine struck for nine straight years. However we interpret the ill-descript data, famine was common in premodern Arabia. During this period, it is also worth noting, locusts were explicitly implicated in at least six famines. See Muhammad A. H. Abdulla, Climatic Fluctuation and Natural Disasters in Arabia between Mid-17th and Early 20th Centuries. *GeoJournal* 37(1), *The Muslim World* (September 1995), 176–180.

[2] Yaron Ayalon, *Plagues, Famines, Earthquakes: The Jews of Ottoman Syria and Natural Disasters* (PhD dissertation, Princeton University, 2009), 240–245; on the bread riots, see James Grehan, *Everyday Life and Consumer Culture in Eighteenth-Century Damascus* (Seattle: University of Washington Press, 2007), chapter 2.

[3] This is based on a survey of the monthly diary of Yusuf Jahshan, a Christian notable from Ramla. See Yusuf Jahshan, *Waqa'i' Filastin: al-Ramla wa-Ghazza*, JER NLI AP Ar. 121 (1769) (Manuscript Section of the National Library of Israel, Jerusalem), see folios 42, 44, 55, 57–61, 63, 66, 77, 80.

before the nineteenth century; it was often caused by some combination of war, requisitions, drought, locust invasions, or crop failures.

By the nineteenth century, though, famine seems to have been on the decline across Syria and Palestine. A minor famine hit Jerusalem in 1833.[4] Prices skyrocketed after an 1865 locust attack decimated the summer crops, but we do not find widespread reports of starvation.[5] The El Niño famines of the 1870s may have been felt somewhat, such as a major drought in 1872.[6] But the fastest-growing city in the region, Beirut, did not experience any major episodes of famine in the nineteenth century.[7] The nineteenth century may have been the first century to pass without a major famine.

And then some 500,000 people (11–16% of the population) starved to death or died from starvation-related diseases like typhus during the First World War.[8] The death rates in Mount Lebanon and Beirut may have been as high as one-third, with reports of entire villages completely wiped out.[9] Jerusalem and Safed were hit hard, and so were coastal cities like

---

[4] See William T. Gidney, *History of the London Society for Promoting Christianity amongst the Jews* (London, 1908), 178.

[5] Zachary J. Foster, The 1915 Locust Attack in Syria and Palestine and Its Role in the Famine during the First World War. *Middle Eastern Studies* 51(3) (2014), 375.

[6] On the El Niño famines, see Ellsworth Huntington, *Palestine and Its Transformation* (Boston, MA: Houghton Mifflin, 1911), 364. Lebanese grain merchants diverted their stocks to Cyprus after they had experienced drought in 1871, causing wheat shortages in Mount Lebanon. See Mehmet Yavuz Erler, *Osmanlı Devlet'inde Kuraklık, 1800–1880* (Istanbul: Libra Kitap, 2010), 86. In fact, during the famine that befell central Anatolia in 1874, funds were raised from Syria (and even the Hijaz) and sent to Anatolia, which suggests these regions were not affected by the drought to the same extent. See ibid., 219.

[7] On Beirut, see Leila Fawaz, *Merchants and Migrants in Nineteenth-Century Beirut* (Cambridge, MA: Harvard University Press, 1983), 2.

[8] Linda Schilcher's oft-cited essay on the famine estimates that starvation or starvation-related diseases led to 500,000 deaths by the end of 1918. Linda Schilcher, The Famine of 1915–1918 in Greater Syria. In John P. Spagnolo, ed., *Problems of the Modern Middle East in Historical Perspective* (Oxford: Oxford University Press, 1992), 229, 231. Others placed the death toll somewhat lower at 200,000. See Fa'iz Ghusayn, *al-Mazalim fi Suriyya, wa-l-Iraq wa-l-Hijaz* (n.p.: n.p., 1918), 38. The population of the region has been estimated at 3.25–4.37 million people. See Foster, The 1915 Locust Attack in Syria and Palestine, 370.

[9] On the one-third figure, or roughly 150,000–200,000 people, see A Meeting of the General Committee for the Syria and Palestine Relief Fund (November 13, 1918), MS 2612, Lambeth Palace Library (LPL), London; Nagib Sadaka, *La Question Syrienne Pendant la Guerre de 1914* (PhD thesis, Université de Paris, 1940), 39–40; Adib Farhat, *Lubnan wa-Suriya* (Beirut: Maktabat Sadir, 194? [1924]), 331; Marie E. James, Life in Safed during the War. *Jewish Military Intelligence* 7(3) (1919), 68; in Batroun, for instance, the population diminished from 5,000 to 2,000; in Mar Na'ama, from 200 to 6; in Abdelli, from 2,000 to 100; in Rushih, from 160 to 30; in Ebrine, from 3,000 to 500;

Haifa.[10] The mountainous interior between Jerusalem and Hebron experienced death tolls in the thousands as well, especially because of typhus.[11] In the village of Salfit, for instance, located halfway between Ramallah and Nablus, two eyewitnesses claimed that between 32 and 44% of the 2,500–3,000 inhabitants had died by 1915–1916 as a result of plague and typhus.[12]

Although few could escape the spread of diseases, especially typhus, the populations least affected by nineteenth-century modernization seem to have fared better than others. Rural hinterlands were better off than urban areas, while inland cities, such as Homs and Hama, Nablus and Hebron, suffered less than the coastal cities.[13] The mountains were also dangerous, as many people in Safed left for the rural hinterlands where food was less scarce.[14] One eyewitness recalled the time when some of his friends took him to their village "because there we might get a fried egg for our lunch."[15] The breadbaskets of the region, including the Hawran, actually became sites of refuge and charity for tens of thousands of starving people.[16] Many nomadic pastoralists, especially camel herders, may

and in Dhuq, from 300 to 7. See Mas'ud Dahir, *Tarikh Lubnan al-'Ijtima'i, 1914–1926* (Beirut: Dar al-Farabi, 1974), 26. In 'Ashqut, 300 died; in Ba'albek, the majority died. Many other villages, such as Ra'shin, Wata al-Juz, Baqa'ata, Wadi al-Dilba, al-Mazra'a, Shahtul, al-Bawar, al-Ma'arib, 'Amshit, Jabil, and Haqil, were almost completely wiped out, in particular in the winter of 1916–1917. See 'Isam Kamal Khalifa, *Lubnan, 1914–1918* (Beirut: 'Isam Kamal Khalifa, 2005), 38. The town of Juba' was reduced from a population of 5,000 before the war to 500 by the war's end. See 'Ali Murawwa, *Tarikh Juba': Madiha va Hadiruha* (Beirut: Dar al-Andalus, 1967), 434.

[10] On Jerusalem, see Abigail Jacobson, *From Empire to Empire: Jerusalem between Ottoman and British Rule* (Syracuse, NY: Syracuse University Press, 2011); on Safed, see James, Life in Safed during the War, 86; on Haifa, see Jamil Bahri, *Tarikh Haifa* (Haifa: al-Maktaba al-Wataniya, Tarikh al-Muqaddima, 1922), 41.

[11] Facts about the Relief Fund for Syria and Palestine. *R. T. Davidson Papers 400* (1916–1923), 287, LPL (London, United Kingdom).

[12] Rafiq Tamimi and Muhammad Bahjat, *Wilayat Bayrut* (Beirut: Matba'at al-Iqbal, 1914 [1979]), 97–98.

[13] One report suggested, for instance, that Homs did not experience widespread starvation. Tarif Khalidi, The Arab World. In John Bourne, Peter Liddle, and Ian Whitehead, eds., *The Great World War 1914–45: Vol. 2. The Peoples' Experience* (London: HarperCollins, 2001).

[14] On Safed, see Zeev Pearl, Tzfat be-Milkhemet Ha-Olam Ha-Rishonah, *Ariel* 157–158 (2002), 117.

[15] Nicola Ziadeh, A First Person Account of the First World War in Greater Syria. In Olaf Farschid, Manfred Kroppe, and Stephan Dahne, eds., *The First World War as Remembered in the Countries of the Eastern Mediterranean* (Würzburg: Ergon Verlag, 2006), 270.

[16] Estimates vary on how many refugees found assistance in the Hawran. One source claimed 50,000. See Fandi Abu al-Bakhr, *Tarikh Liwa' Hawran al-'Ijtima'iyya: al-Suwayda',*

have benefited from the war, as their independence from the state was fortuitous during times of mass requisition while their control of the camel trade became extremely lucrative during the Ottoman Sinai campaigns, waged largely with camels the state had purchased in gold from the Bedouins.[17]

MODERN FAMINES

Why was the region hit so hard if famine was on its way to eradication in the nineteenth century? Trade came to a halt in the early months of the war, leaving communities dependent on exporting cash crops, such as mulberries in Mount Lebanon and orange groves in Jaffa, without a source of livelihood. French, Russian, and British schools, missions, and hospitals closed, leaving tens of thousands more people without work and health or social services. Most foreign nationals left the region and took their capital with them, shattering the bourgeoning tourism industry. Postal service became sporadic, a disaster for the growing number of people dependent on remittances. The military monopolized the railways, disconnecting areas of wheat cultivation from their local markets. This made the fastest-growing cities such Beirut and Jerusalem even more dependent on railroads for wheat and particularly vulnerable to total collapse. The state shut down foreign banks, bringing the economy to a standstill. The war sent Syria and Palestine back to its pre-nineteenth-century state of affairs, in which war combined with natural disaster often led to famine.[18]

    Dar'a, al-Qunatara, 'Ajlun, 1840–1918 (Damascus: al-Suwayda, 1999), 313; see also Izzat Tannous, *The Palestinians: A Detailed Documented Eyewitness History of Palestine under the British Mandate* (New York: I.G.T. Company, 1988), 36; Hanna Abi-Rashid, *Jabal al-Duruz* (Cairo: Maktabat Zaydan al-'Umumiyya, 1925), 84; Tamimi and Bahjat, *Wilayat Bayrut*, 105–106.

[17] The Ottomans had to pay the Bedouins of Sinai and the southern desert in gold coins for their camels during the first Sinai campaign in February 1915. See Murat Çulcu, *Arşivi Kaybolan Savaş: Sina, Filistin, Suriye Cephesi* (Istanbul: Kastaş yayınevi, 2009), 90. The highest-ranking Austrian officer in Syria, Curt Prüfer, acquired about 2,000 camels from a Bedouin merchant in Damascus at the price of roughly 10 Turkish pounds each, a hefty sum of money. See Sean McMeekin, *The Berlin–Baghdad Express: The Ottoman Empire and Germany's Bid for World Power* (Cambridge, MA: Belknap Press of Harvard University Press, 2010), 172. For further evidence the Bedouins were paid in gold lira, see Ali Sultan, *Tarikh Suriyya* (Damascus: Dar Talas, 1987), 275.

[18] What made matters worse was that rapid population growth had already been applying pressure on local wheat markets in the decades prior to the war. Consider that the annual Aleppo wheat exports, for instance, peaked in 1881–1882 at some 27,000 tons, but

These global processes that increasingly made everyone more dependent on others for their basic food needs usually ensured a surplus. But in times of global crisis, they meant catastrophic famine. This chapter takes a closer look at four of these dependencies – foreign trade, foreign investment, transportation, and finance – during the last few decades of Ottoman rule, and examines how their collapse during the Great War led to the worst famine in the region's history.

FOREIGN TRADE

Trade with Europe was marginal to the economy of Syria and Palestine before the 1830s, but increased drastically over the course of the nineteenth century. The total value of exports and imports from the Eastern Mediterranean coastal cities increased from roughly 200,000 sterling silver pounds in 1825–1827 to 10,752,000 in 1913, or a 50-fold increase in less than a century, generating new sources of wealth for the region's inhabitants and providing new luxuries and comforts to the population. It brought chemicals necessary to make soap and treat malaria and kill locusts, fuel and kerosene to heat homes and cook food, candles and matches to light lamps, and sugar to sweeten coffee and tea.[19]

But the war brought trade to a standstill. International trade came to an abrupt halt in the early summer months of the European war before the Ottomans had even (publicly) declared their intention to join the Germans. Many European merchant ships, for instance, left Syria and Palestine immediately after the Ottoman call for mobilization in

---

gradually declined from that point onward, plummeting to some 753 tons in 1913 largely to feed the growing population at home. See Muhammad Sa'id Kalla, *The Role of Foreign Trade in the Economic Development of Syria, 1831–1914* (PhD thesis, The American University, 1969), 264. Overall, the population in Syria and Palestine rose from 1.2 million in 1800 to 4–4.5 million by the eve of the First World War. From 1836 to 1915, the proportion of Levantine towns of 10,000 or more inhabitants rose from 18% to 32%. See Haim Gerber, Modernization in Nineteenth Century Palestine: The Role of Foreign Trade. *Middle Eastern Studies* 18(3) (1982), 256, 259. The cities of Jerusalem, Haifa, and Beirut experienced astronomical growth, ranging from 10 to 20 fold over the nineteenth century. On Jerusalem, see Yehoshua Ben-Arieh, The Growth of Jerusalem in the 19th Century. *Annals of the Association of American Geographers* 65(2) (1975), 262; Yehoshua Ben-Arieh, *Jerusalem in the 19th Century: Emergence of the New City* (Jerusalem: Yad Izhak Ben Zvi, 1986), 466. On Beirut, see Fawaz, *Merchants and Migrants in Nineteenth Century Beirut*, 127–129.

[19] The trade figure included the ports of Alexandretta, Beirut, Tripoli, Latakia, Acre, Haifa, Jaffa, and Gaza. See Kalla, *The Role of Foreign Trade*, 254–259.

August 1914.[20] Jezzeen merchants from Beirut, as early as August 1914, who had traveled abroad to replenish their stocks, brought almost nothing back with them.[21] The rapid destruction of trade and commerce in the early months of the war is also reflected in a Zionist report from early 1915, which estimated the total loss in Zionist settlement exports in the 1914 at 1.5 million (francs).[22] Similarly, imports to Jaffa decreased by an average of 32% from 1913 to 1914, likewise indicating that trade had already begun to collapse when war broke out in Europe in late summer 1914.[23]

The Ottomans may have exacerbated conditions during the early months of the war. They eliminated a low-rate ad valorem tariff structure, making it significantly more difficult for foreign companies to serve local markets.[24] In October 1914, as well, the army mined the major trade ports of the region – Iskenderun, Tripoli, Beirut, and Haifa – to prevent enemy ships from landing.[25] Ottoman authorities worried that shipments of wheat and other foodstuffs essential for the needs of the wartime government were being shipped abroad, so they worked to limit exports already in the first few months of the war.[26] Trade and war were best enemies.

[20] George Hintlian, The First World War in Palestine and Msg. Franz Fellinger. In Marian Wrba, ed., *Austrian Presence in the Holy Land in the 19th and Early 20th Century* (Tel Aviv: Austrian Embassy, 1996), 179.

[21] Hubert W. Brown and Wilma Jacobs Brown Papers, 1860–1941, Record Group no. 48, box 1, "Correspondences," Ain er-Rummaneh [sic], August 17, 1914, Presbyterian Historical Society (PHS), Philadelphia, PA.

[22] Zionist report, Central Zionist Archive (CZA) Z3/1480.

[23] This is based on the decrease in percentage from 1913 to 1914 of the following imported goods: writing instruments (42%), potatoes (57%), hoard (40%), rice (37%), empty sacks (29%), salt (11%), soda (36%), sugar (35%), cotton products (31%), other manufactured goods (14%), bricks (24%), tobacco and snuff (15%), alcohol (29%), wooden furniture (53%), wooden boards (42%), and other goods (27%). See John S. Salah, *Filastin wa-Tajdid Hayatuhu* (New York: al-Jami'yya al-Filastiniyya l-Muqawama al-Sahyuniyya, 1919), 60.

[24] Şevket Pamuk, The Ottoman Economy in World War I. In Stephen Broadberry and Mark Harrison, eds., *The Economics of World War I* (Cambridge: Cambridge University Press, 2005), 119. This included, beginning in October, a new tax on oil, coffee, sugar, tea, alcohol, matches, and more. See *Ha-Herut*, October 1 and 2, 1914.

[25] Cheetham to Grey, September 25, 1914; Mallet to Grey, October 3, 1914; Mallet to Grey, October 11, 1914; Mallet to Grey, October 16, 1914; Mallet to Grey, October 17, 1914; Mallet to Grand Vizier, October 2, 1914; Buchanan to Grey, October 26, 1914. In James Brown Scott, ed., *Diplomatic Documents Relating to the Outbreak of the European War (Part II)* (New York: Oxford University Press, 1916), 1107–1108, 1115, 1125–1126, 1139–1142, 1155–1157, 1178–1179. See also Alex Carmel, *Ottoman Haifa: A History of Four Centuries of Turkish Rule* (New York: I. B. Tauris, 2011), 161.

[26] According to one Ottoman report, the French Mesacer, a private company, had claimed that it was purchasing silkworms, but in fact took large quantities of chickpeas, barley

By December 1914, though, the Triple Entente blockade of the Eastern Mediterranean coast assumed responsibility for the halt in trade. British, Russian, and French cruisers reached, captured, or flooded ships at ports in Haifa, Beirut, and Iskenderun in December.[27] This also meant that trade inside the Ottoman Empire – between Izmir and Beirut or Jaffa and Istanbul – also became impossible. From that point forward, only neutral (primarily American) ships managed to deliver foodstuffs to the Eastern Mediterranean shores, and then only sporadically.[28] For the most part, though, imports and exports from Gaza, Jaffa, Haifa, Beirut, and Iskenderun fell from their peak in 1914 to a trickle for more than four years of war.

Consider how the war affected the local petroleum market. Petroleum was essential not only to cook food but also to light lamps and heat homes. A mere eight months into the war in March 1915, a Beirut newspaper commented that kerosene was the second most important good after flour, and that it continued to increase in price. By this point, merchants sold a single tank of kerosene for about three times its prewar cost in Beirut.[29] In Palestine, the price of petroleum similarly skyrocketed to five or six times its prewar price by April 1915.[30] The numbers are even more startling from the Harissa Monastery in Mount Lebanon, where a single tank of gasoline rose from four French francs in July 1915 to 100 French francs in December 1915, a 25-fold increase in five months![31] Petroleum was one of dozens of goods that rose in price, including rice, sugar,

---

and wheat from Haifa and the Sveyda ports, as has happened in the past. See Başbakanlık Osmanlı Arşivi (BOA) DH.EUM.KLU 4/11 (October 26, 1914).

[27] For Beirut, see Ibrahim Kana'an, *Lubnan fi al-Harb al-Kubra, 1914–1918* (Beirut: Mu'assasat 'Asi, 1974), 133; see also Ali Fuad Erden, *Birinci Dünya Harbi'nde Suriye Hatıraları* (Istanbul, 1954), 24; Friedrich Freiherr Kress von Kressenstein, Yigal Sheffy, and Michael Guggenheimer, ed. and trans., *'Im ha-Turkim el Te'alat Su'ets* [Hebrew trans. of *Mit den Türken zum Suezkanal*] (Tsahal: Hotsa'at Ma'arakhot, Misrad Ha-Bitahon, 2002), 43; Sultan, *Tarikh Suriyya*, 271; A. Elmaliach, *Erets Yisra'el Ve-Suriyah Biyemey Milhemet Ha-'Olam* (Jerusalem: Ha-Solel, 1928), 114; on Haifa, see Gerda Sdun-Fallscheer, *Jahre des Lebens* (Stuttgart: J. F. Steinkopf Verlag, 1985), 481.

[28] See Ya'akov Ton, *Erets Yisrael be-Shnot ha-Milkhama Ha-Olamit: Do'akh* (Jaffa: n.p., 5679 [1918–1919]), 5; see also Shimon Robenstein, *Al ha-Yetziyah ve-ha-Kurban: Livtay ha-Yeridah Mitsraymah be-ReShit Milkhemet ha-Olam ha-Rishona* (Jerusalem, 1988), 43.

[29] *al-Ittihad al-'Uthmani*, March 26, 1915.

[30] One barrel cost 40–50 francs instead of the prewar price of about eight francs a barrel. See untitled Zionist report by Oettinger, May 5, 1915, p. 2, CZA Z3/1480.

[31] Sijjil al-Yawmiyyat (July 29, 1902–12 Kanun al-Awwal 1920), 94, July 30, 1915, Harissa Church, St. Paul (al-Jam'iyya al-Bulisiyya), Lebanon; ibid., 99, December 25, 1915.

candles, matches, cotton products, medicine, and chemicals necessary for
the production of soap and for malaria treatment.

Industries dependent on trade, machinery, water pumps, or oil were
also doomed. The thousands of people employed as dockworkers, porters,
custom agents, merchants, ship workers, and clerks were now out of work
in the growing metropolises of Haifa, Jaffa, and Beirut. The massive
irrigated orange plantations around Jaffa, which had increased from
1,700 cultivated acres in 1880 to 12,500 acres in 1910, were laid to
waste, as there was neither fuel to run the generators that powered the
pumps nor merchants to export the goods.[32] Lebanese merchants could
no longer import silkworms from Europe or export raw silk to markets
abroad, spelling disaster for the whopping 80–90% of residents of Mount
Lebanon who had converted their slopes to mulberry cultivation in the
decades preceding the war.[33] The 67,750 people working in the loom
industry on the eve of the Great War, primarily in Lebanon and the
Aleppo region, were doomed as well once silk exports came to a halt.[34]
The industries and crops that had rapidly transformed the economic
productivity of the region in the late nineteenth and early twentieth
centuries were the first to crumble.

FOREIGNERS: TOURISM, SCHOOLS, AND HOSPITALS

A new and extremely important source of revenue for Syria and Palestine
on the eve of the Great War was tourism. The number of pilgrims and
tourists from Europe and the New World to the Holy Land increased from
a few thousand annually in the late 1850s to as many as 40,000 a year by
the First World War.[35] These tens of thousands of Americans, British,

---

[32] Gerber, Modernization in Nineteenth Century Palestine, 260.

[33] Nicholas Ajay, *Mount Lebanon and the Wilayah of Beirut, 1914–1918: The War Years* (PhD thesis, Georgetown University, 1972), 296.

[34] Sa'id B Himadeh, *Economic Organization of Syria* (Beirut: American Press, 1936), 124.

[35] For estimates, see Theofanis George Stavrou, *Russian Interests in Palestine, 1882–1914* (Thessaloniki: Institute for Balkan Studies, 1963), 66, 102–103, 150–151, 209; Paolo Maggiolini, Images, Views and Landscapes of the Holy Land: Catholic and Protestant Travels to Ottoman Palestine during the 19th Century. *Quest: Issues in Contemporary Jewish History. Journal of Fonazione CDEC*, no. 6 (2013), 19–47, note 17; John Fulton, *The Beautiful Land: Palestine, Historical Geographical and Pictorial* (Chicago: Standard Columbian Company; Boston, MA: E. P. Gerauld & Company, 1891), v; Simona Merlo, Travels of Russians to the Holy Land in the 19th Century, *Quest: Issues in Contemporary Jewish History. Journal of Fonazione CDEC*, no. 6 (2013), note 69; Derek Hopwood, *The Russian Presence in Syria and Palestine, 1843–1914* (Oxford: Clarendon Press, 1969), 103, 116–117; A. L. Tibawi, Russian

French, German, and Russian pilgrims spent weeks and in some cases many months in the region, and spent some 10 million francs a year, according to one estimate, a fifth of Palestine's total trade output. This supported a dozen hotels in Jerusalem alone, and countless dozens or hundreds of candle-dippers in Jerusalem and Bethlehem, who worked year round to meet the demand of thousands of Russian, Greek, Armenian, Coptic, and Macedonian pilgrims who attended the annual celebration of the Holy Fire.[36] One Western traveler even claimed, "the principle source of the wealth of Joppa [Jaffa] is derived from the annual passage of pilgrims through the town to visit the holy places."[37] Consider that every pilgrim paid six or seven French francs just to get from the steamer in the Jaffa port to the patron's hotel.[38] Russian pilgrims also donated large sums of money to the Greek Orthodox Convent and Holy Sepulcher in Jerusalem.[39] The tourists created new job opportunities for wagon drivers, guides, translators, porters, boatmen, chefs, servers, cleaners, washers, shop-keepers, and more.[40] In Beirut, for instance, four tourist agencies organized tours to historical sites in the region, such as Byblos, as well as a growing summer tourist industry in the mountains of Lebanon, such as in Beit Marie, Aley, Brumana, and Bhamdoun, that accounted for some 10% of Mount Lebanon's economic activity.[41]

Before the mid-nineteenth century, Syria and Palestine had no hospitals or medical schools. Barbers performed surgeries, butchers dealt with fractures and dislocations, while midwives handled obstetrics and early

Cultural Penetration of Syria–Palestine in the Nineteenth Century (Part I). *Journal of the Royal Central Asian Society* 53(2) (1966), 180; Stephen Graham, *With the Russian Pilgrims to Jerusalem* (London: Macmillan, 1913), 99; Bertha Spafford Vester, *Our Jerusalem: A North American Family in the Holy City, 1881–1949* (London: Evans Brothers Limited, 1951), 82; for an estimate of 30,000 in 1898, see a report by Austrian traveler Paul Lietzow, cited in Andreas Patera, The Austrian Post in Palestine. In Marian Wrba, ed., *Austrian Presence in the Holy Land in the 19th and Early 20th Century* (Tel Aviv: Austrian Embassy, 1996), 125; for an estimate of 30,000 Russians annually in 1909, see Edgar W. Howe, *Daily Notes of a Trip around the World*, vol. 2 (Topeka, KS: Krane and Company, 1909), 196; for the 40,000 figure, see Salah, *Filastin wa-Tajdid Hayatuhu*, 97.

[36] Vester, *Our Jerusalem*, 83.   [37] Fulton, *The Beautiful Land*, 50.

[38] Karl Baedeker, *Palestine and Syria: With Routes through Mesopotamia and Babylonia and the Island of Cyprus* (Leipzig: Karl Baedeker Publisher, 1912), 6.

[39] Vester, *Our Jerusalem*, 83.

[40] See, for instance, Salah, *Filastin wa-Tajdid Hayatuhu*, 96–97; Philip R. Davies, *The Palestine Exploration Fund Annual XI: Tourists, Travelers and Hotels in Nineteenth-Century Jerusalem* (Maney Publishing, 2013), 247–248.

[41] Melanie Tanielian, *The War of Famine: Everyday Life in Wartime Beirut and Mount Lebanon, 1914–1918* (PhD dissertation, University of California, Berkeley, 2012), 33.

childhood diseases.[42] This began to change in the mid-nineteenth century, in part, as foreign missionaries opened hospitals, clinics, and other health services throughout the region.[43] From 1864 to 1902, the Russians built 18 hospitals in Jerusalem, Jaffa, Beit Jala, Bethlehem, Jericho, Nazareth, Latikiya, and Homs, treating some 83,000 sick people in 1900 alone.[44] The British missionaries opened a hospital in Jerusalem in 1844, whose six medical workers provided inpatient and home care to thousands of native inhabitants of the city and region every year.[45] The Austrians opened a hospital in Nazareth in the 1850s that served thousands of patients over the next few decades. They built the Tantur Hospital, located on the Bethlehem–Jerusalem road, which provided services to 3,000 patients, or so they claimed in one of their promotional brochures.[46] The Americans opened the Syrian Protestant College (later the American University of Beirut) Medical School in the 1880s, while the French opened the College of Medicine and Pharmacy at the University of Saint Joseph in Beirut. All of these efforts brought financial capital and medical know-how and offered health and medical services to tens if not hundreds of thousands of people.

French, Russian, and British missionary schools also created a new dependency on foreign sources of capital. The French Jesuit school, the University of Saint Joseph, grew from 275 students a year in 1875 to 500 a decade later – totaling some 12,000 students by the turn of the century. Various estimates placed the total number of French schools in Syria and Palestine at 76 in 1901, 326 in 1913, and 500 in 1914, depending on what counted as a school and who was doing the counting. Likewise, by the eve of the Great War, some 3,000 French missionaries spread across a dozen Levantine towns and cities had enrolled as many as 100,000 students

---

[42] Lutfi M. Sa'di, George Sarton, and W. T. van Dyck, Al-Hakîm Cornelius van Alen van Dyck (1818–1895). *ISIS* 27(1) (1937), 22–24.

[43] Ruth Kark, Impact of Early Missionary Enterprises on Landscape and Identity Formation in Palestine, 1820–1914. *Islam and Christian–Muslim Relations* 15(2) (2004), 230–231; Tibawi, Russian Cultural Penetration of Syria, 176, 179–180.

[44] Şamil Mutlu, *Osmanlı Devleti'nde Misyoner Okulları* (Istanbul: Gökkubbe, 2005), 78–79; on the 83,000 figure, see A'mal 'ala Jami'yya al-Filastiniyya. *al-Mahabba* (February 10, 1901), 76–77.

[45] William Henry Hechler, *The Jerusalem Bishopric: Documents, with Translations* (London: Trübner & Company, 1883), 43.

[46] Thomas F. Stransky, The Austrian Hospital at Tantur (1869–1918). In Marian Wrba, ed., *Austrian Presence in the Holy Land in the 19th and Early 20th Century* (Tel Aviv: Austrian Embassy, 1996), 114–115; Norbert Schwacke, The Austrian Hospital in Nazareth. In Marian Wrba, ed., *Austrian Presence in the Holy Land in the 19th and Early 20th Century* (Tel Aviv: Austrian Embassy, 1996), 84–85.

total.[47] By 1900, various accounts place the number of Russian schools in the Levant somewhere between 41 and 68 with anywhere from 5,500 to 10,000 pupils, all of them funded by Russian taxpayers. The figures continued to increase with estimates of 70–100 by the end of the first decade of the twentieth century and 114 schools across the region by 1914, with 10,430 pupils and 363 teachers, only 23 of whom were Russians. Likewise, by the early 1880s, the British claimed to have some 3,000 Christian, Jewish, Muslim, and Druze pupils across some 27 Levantine schools. Most foreign schools were funded by the foreign missionaries themselves, or provided scholarships, subventions, or salaries to thousands of native teachers and many tens of thousands more students.[48]

But the Great War destroyed the tourism industry and the foreign missionary enterprise. Even before the Ottoman state expelled all residents of the Empire belonging to enemy nationalities on November 1, 1914, most foreigners were already long gone, either out of fear of war or because they ran out of money and could not withdraw from the banks, as we see in what follows.[49] Hundreds of schools, missionary outposts, hospitals, clinics, and orphanages in Haifa, Jerusalem, Safed, and elsewhere run by Russia, Britain, and France were forced to close their doors; in some cases the premises turned into weapons depots.[50] These

[47] On the expansion in the 1870s and 1880s, see n.a., *Les Jesuites en Syrie, 1831–1931: Université Saint-Joseph*, vol. 5 (Paris: Éditions Dillen, 1931), 11; on the 12,000 figure, see Rafael Herzstein, Les Phases de l'Évolution de l'Université Saint-Joseph à Beyrouth: Les Premières Décennies (1875–1914). *Historical Studies in Education* 24(1) (2012), 22; on the 1901 and 1913 figures, see Mutlu, *Osmanlı Devleti'nde Misyoner Okulları*, 155–163, 170–192; on the 1914 figures, see Mathew Burrows, "Mission Civilisatrice": French Cultural Policy in the Middle East, 1860–1914. *The Historical Journal* 29(1) (1986), 110, 116, 132; see also Rafael Herzstein, Saint-Joseph University of Beirut: An Enclave of the French-Speaking Communities in the Levant, 1875–1914. *Itinerario* 32(2) (2008), 70.

[48] My estimations for the Russian and British schools are based on the following accounts: Mutlu, *Osmanlı Devleti'nde Misyoner Okulları*, 84–87; Hanna Abu Hanna, *Tala'i' al-Nahda fi Filastin: Khirruju al-Madaris al-Rusiyya, 1862–1914* (Beirut: Mu'assasat al-Dirasat al-Filastiniyya, 2005), 21–22; Lucien J. Frary, Russian Missions to the Orthodox East: Antonin Kapustin (1817–1894) and His World. *Russian History* 40(1) (2013), 133–151, 149; Hopwood, *The Russian Presence in Syria and Palestine, 1843–1914*, 150–153; Stavrou, *Russian Interests in Palestine, 1882–1914*, 164; Julius Richter, *A History of the Protestant Missions in the Near East* (New York: Fleming H. Revell, 1910), 57.

[49] Sdun-Fallscheer, *Jahre des Lebens*, 475.

[50] The St. Helena's hospital in Haifa, the Free Day School, and others closed. See Popham Blyth, Bishop in Jerusalem, to friends in Britain, October 5, 1914, R. T. Davidson Papers 397, 13–21, LPL (London, United Kingdom); for the closure of institutions in Jerusalem, see Elmaliach, *Erets Yisra'el Ve-Suriyah Biyemey Milhemet Ha-'Olam*, 110. The Misgab le-Doah Hospital in Jerusalem closed in August 1914. The Bikur Holim hospital in

institutions serviced not only the poor and vulnerable, but they provided employment to many others. In Beirut, for instance, the closure of French humanitarian, educational, and religious institutions in November 1914 meant loss of work for the local staff and loss of services to the sick, orphans, nuns, and students who were expelled from their places of residence and left to fend for themselves.[51] Many of the British doctors who worked at the Syrian Protestant College in Beirut, for instance, were either taken by the government or forced to leave the region.[52] All of this had disastrous consequences for the tens if not hundreds of thousands of Syrians and Palestinians who depended on tourism, foreign health services, or missionary schools for their livelihood and well-being.

TRANSPORTATION: RAILWAYS AND ANIMALS

The introduction of the railway radically transformed the way food was transported in the decades preceding the First World War. Foreign companies gained concessions to construct railways in the Ottoman Empire connecting Jerusalem and Jaffa (1892), Beirut and Damascus and Mazirib (1895), Riyaq and Aleppo (1902), Homs and Tripoli (1911), Damascus and Dar'a, Haifa and Acre, and Dar'a and Amman (1908).[53] By the eve of the war, some 50% of the region's grain was internally shipped by rail to

---

Jerusalem was expected to close in September/October 1914. The Shaarei Zedek Hospital in Jerusalem had only 10 free patients in September 1914. See papers titled "the enclosed letters were written in 1914 by Rae Landy and Rose Kaplan," p. 4, Rachel (Rae) Diane Landy Papers P-785 Box 1, folder 2, American Jewish Historical Society Archives (AJHS), New York; Ottoman troops also occupied the hospitals belonging to the Sisters of Charity in Bahannas, Lebanon. See Ajay, *Mount Lebanon and the Wilayah of Beirut, 1914–1918*, 238. In Safed, the Ottomans took possession of a school and a hospital belonging to the London Society for Promoting Christianity among the Jews. See James, Life in Safed during the War, 66; on the Ottoman order to confiscate Russian property, see Mutlu, *Osmanlı Devleti'nde Misyoner Okulları*, 90.

[51] Memorandum from Foreign Ministry to the Interior Ministry, BOA D.H. EUM S-Ş.3.42 (November 15, 1914).

[52] Bayard Dodge reported in December 1914 that 25 of his medical students were conscripted and "many more will probably go this week." See Bayard Dodge Collection, letter from Wooks to "Ma and Dad," December 2, 1914, A.A. 2.3. (62/3–62/4), American University of Beirut Archives (AUB). See also Bayard Dodge Collection, letter from Bayard Dodge to dearest, Easter Sunday 1915, A.A. 2.3. (14/5), AUB. The army continued to conscript members of the medical school throughout the war. See, for instance, Letter to Consul General A. Hotz, Consulate General of Holland, Beirut, January 31, 1918, Box 15, File 4 (28/1), Howard Bliss Collection A.A. 2.3, AUB.

[53] Said al-Sabbagh, *al-Madaniyyat al-Qadima wa Tarikh Suriyya wa Filastin*, 2nd edn. (Jaffa/Haifa: al-Maktaba al-'Asriyya, 1944), 176.

markets inside the Levant.[54] The percentage was higher for the large cities and regions somewhat removed from the gain-producing areas, especially Beirut and Mount Lebanon.

But war led the Ottoman military to monopolize rail traffic for military purposes. Ohannes Pasha, the governor of Mount Lebanon, wrote to the central Ottoman government in Istanbul in May 1915 that

> Up to this point, the shipments of wheat from Aleppo by means of the railway have not been sufficient to meet the needs of the Mountain, whose population exceeds 300,000 people [a gross underestimate]. For this reason, our office has been burdened by complaints from every direction. This time, the train wagons were filled with shipments for the military ... the cutting off of wheat to Mount Lebanon, and Syria, more generally, may lead to famine.[55]

These were the words of a desperate governor, who must have realized his prescience when the people of Mount Lebanon began to starve to death en masse only a few months after he wrote this note. The priests at the Harissa Monastery in Mount Lebanon similarly recorded in their private diaries in March 1916 that the main reason they could not get wheat was due to the government monopolization of the rails.[56] A range of other accounts, including the Beirut press and Lebanese eyewitness testimonies, as well as Zionist officials, agreed that the only way to solve the flour shortages in Beirut and Jaffa, for instance, was to improve the transport system.[57] Consider that while a railway car could be hired for about 20 Ottoman lira before the war, Ottoman soldiers sold access to a railcar for about 1,000 lira during the war, a 50-fold increase in price. (Imagine if a subway ride in New York City cost $125 a ticket during a time of widespread unemployment!)[58]

---

[54] Roger Owen, *The Middle East in the World Economy, 1800–1914* (London/New York: I. B. Tauris, 1993 [1981]), 246; See also Halil İnalcık and Donald Quataer, *An Economic and Social History of the Ottoman Empire, 1300–1914* (Cambridge: Cambridge University Press, 1994), 818.

[55] Ohannes to the Porte, 23 C 1333, (BOA) A.}MTZ.CL. 7/294.

[56] See Sijjil al-Yawmiyyat (July 29, 1902–12 Kanun al-Awwal 1920), 102, March 4, 1916, Harissa Church, St. Paul (al-Jamʻiyya al-Bulisiyya).

[57] *al-Ittihad al-ʻUthmani*, May 27, 1915; This was also the case with the transport of grain between Damascus and Beirut in the spring of 1915. See Kanaʻan, *Lubnan fi al-Harb al-Kubra, 1914–1918*, 164; Ajay, *Mount Lebanon and the Wilayah of Beirut, 1914–1918*, 351–354; Eric Fisher, The Mikveh Israel School during the War Years. *Jewish Social Studies* 4(3) (1942), 271.

[58] On the 20 lira figure, see Tanielian, *The War of Famine*, 107; on the 1,000 lira figure, see Ajay, *Mount Lebanon and the Wilayah of Beirut, 1914–1918*, 177.

But even if the railways accounted for some 50% of internally shipped wheat on the eve of the war, that still meant that animals, primarily camels, donkeys, mules, and horses, shipped much of the rest. The government monopolization of the railways made transport animals more valuable than they had ever been. The Bedouin controlled the camel trade, and their animals went to the highest bidder – the Ottoman government – that bought many thousands of them for the 1915 and 1916 Sinai assaults. The donkeys, mules, and horses owned by the general population also happened to be chief targets of the military administration, which confiscated as many animals as it could find in Gaza, Jerusalem, Irbid, Lebanon, Damascus, and Aleppo.[59] Those who managed to avert the authorities hid their animals out of fear that they would be requisitioned.[60] All of this meant that moving wheat, barley, and other staples became expensive everywhere, especially on the coast, where Ottoman security was higher due to fears of espionage or smuggling. It became difficult to move food from centers of production (the Hawran and Aleppo) to consumption in Beirut, Damascus, Mount Lebanon, Safed, Tiberias, Haifa, Jerusalem, Jaffa, Salfit, and elsewhere.

FINANCES: BANKS AND REMITTANCES

During the dreadful late summer months of 1914 prior to the official Ottoman entry to the war, bankers in Paris and London who controlled the Ottoman bank grew worried that the Ottomans were drifting to war. An alarming number of gleeful and prescient customers in late July 1914, for instance, had already withdrawn the entirety of their savings from Ottoman banks in Istanbul, Beirut, Haifa, and Jerusalem as tensions

---

[59] See, for instance, Correspondences, 1, September 23, 1914, Jdeideh, Herbert W. Brown and Wilma Jacobs Brown Papers, Record Group 458 Box 1 (PHS); *Edward Nickoley Collection*, AA 2.3.3.1.2. Historic Diary, February 12, 1917, 162; John D. Whiting to Lieutenant Abramson, Intelligence Department, 1918, Box 9/10, John D. Whiting Papers, Manuscript Department, Library of Congress (MD-LOC); Zionist report by A. Ruppin, March 29, 1915, p. 5 CZA Z3/1480; Ghusayn, *al-Mazalim fi Suriyya, wa-l-Iraq wa-l-Hijaz*, 5; Nathan Efrati, *Mi-Mashber le-Tikva: Ha-Yishuv ha-Yehudi be-Erets Yisra'el be-Milhemet ha-Olam ha-Rishona* (Jerusalem: Yad Yitshak Ben-Tsvi, 1991), 249; Crawford diaries, entry of April 18, 1916. Cited in Ajay, *Mount Lebanon and the Wilayah of Beirut, 1914–1918*, 150.

[60] A missionary worker from Jdeideh noted that "for sometime the people have been afraid to bring in the wheat, fearing their camels might be seized." See Correspondences, September 17, 1914, Jdeideh, Herbert W. Brown and Wilma Jacobs Brown Papers, Record Group 458 Box 1 (PHS). See also correspondences on August 11, 1914, p. 2, September 23, 1914.

mounted in the Balkans and Central Europe. Many exchanged their money for foreign currency or gold, and, also presciently, fled to Cairo or Cyprus.[61] "For the last week there has been a tremendous run on all of the banks," wrote American missionary Charles Dana in August 1914 from Lebanon. "Even the Ottoman Bank here has ceased to do business," adding that "the Deutsche Palestine bank seems to be on the verge of insolvency."[62] Soon enough, depositors in places such as Jerusalem were entitled to withdraw only small amounts of their savings in gold, and twice as much as that in checks.[63]

But the rationing proved ephemeral. The rush on the banks led to panic and fear of insolvency, so the local banks of the empire compelled the Imperial Ottoman Bank to declare a moratorium on all withdrawals. Shortly thereafter the Imperial Ottoman Bank issued that moratorium and carried it out with great diligence throughout Syria and Palestine.[64] The Ottomans shut down not only their own banks but also froze the assets of British and French banks – the Anglo-Palestine Bank of Jerusalem, the fiscal front for the Zionist enterprise, and the French Bank Credit-Lyonnaise. The Deutsche Bank seems to have been the single bank left open in Palestine.[65]

These actions had disastrous economic consequences. As early as September 1914, for instance, farmers in Palestine could not order the

---

[61] Jirjis al-Khuri al-Maqdisi, *A'zam al-Harb fi Tarikh* (Beirut: al-Matba'a al-Adabiyya, 1921), 21–23, 25; a Zionist health worker, Rachel Landy, also mentioned a rush on the banks in an August 24, 1914 letter. See papers titled "the enclosed letters were written in 1914 by Rae Landy and Rose Kaplan," p. 2, in Rachel (Rae) Diane Landy Papers P-785 Box 1, folder 2, AJHS.

[62] Letter from Charles Dana to Russell Carter, August 8, 1914, *Letters to NY Treasurer I: Aug 1914–1916*, page 3, Near East School of Theology, NEST, special collections, Beirut.

[63] Rae Landy, the medical worker in Jerusalem, was able to withdraw some 50 francs per week in gold and 100 francs per week in checks, until at least August 23, 1914. See papers titled "the enclosed letters were written in 1914 by Rae Landy and Rose Kaplan," p. 2, in Rachel (Rae) Diane Landy Papers P-785 Box 1, folder 2, AJHS.

[64] André Autheman, *The Imperial Ottoman Bank* (Istanbul: Ottoman Bank Archives and Research Centre, 2002), 239; Isaiah Friedman, Hit'arvutan Shel Germaniya ve-Artzot Ha-Brit Be-Nose' Ha-Girushim Me-Yafo Be-Ditzember 1914 ve April 1917. In Mordechai Eliav, ed., *Ba-Matzor ve-Ba-Matzok: Eretz Yisrael Be-Milkhemet Ha-Olam Ha-Rishona* (Jerusalem: Yad Yitzkhal Ben-Tzvi, 1991), 170; al-Maqdisi, *A'zam al-Harb fi Tarikh*, 21–23; *Ha-Herut*, October 16, 1914; Ajay, *Mount Lebanon and the Wilayah of Beirut, 1914–1918*, 306.

[65] Gad Frumkin, *Derekh Shofet bi-Yerushalayim* (Tel Aviv: Dvir, 1954), 178; Hintlian, The First World War in Palestine and Msg. Franz Fellinger, 182; for more, see Abigail Jacobson, A City Living through Crisis: Jerusalem during World War I. *British Journal of Middle Eastern Studies* 36(1) (2009), 81–82.

planting seeds they needed because the Palestine banks were now disconnected from Italian, German, and French banks.[66] This also drove many foreigners to pack up and leave, since they could not withdraw any money from the bank.

Remittances, also transmitted through the banks, declined significantly as a result. One historian has estimated that the flow of remittances into Lebanon, which accounted for a staggering 40% of household incomes, declined by 75% during the war.[67] Zionist leader Arthur Rupin lamented that entire sources of revenue for the Jewish community in Palestine vanished overnight, including subventions from family members in Russia who had sent their children to study in Palestine's Zionist schools, as well as investments for citrus groves.[68] Funds from the Zionist offices of Berlin and elsewhere also became increasingly difficult to obtain during the war.[69] The Jewish communities of Jerusalem, Safed, Hebron and Tiberias also relied significantly on remittances from European Jewish communities in the amount of some 200,000 pounds annually, much of which was cut off as well.[70]

CONCLUSION

Trade came to a near complete halt in late summer 1914. Foreigners and foreign capital left the region. The army monopolized the railways and the government took the animals. The banks shut down and remittances became sporadic. Recall, though, that the basis of the region's economy was still agricultural produce in 1914. The annual winter cereal crop was enough to feed the 4–4.5 million inhabitants of Syria and Palestine, not to mention the dozens of other varieties of

---

[66] *Ha-Khakla'i* 3(7–8) (September–November, 1914), 242. This fact is further evident in a letter written by Zionist official Dr. Tahon on November 26, 1915, responding to a request from one of the Jewish settlements for a loan for planting seeds. The request was summarily rejected. See CZA L2/102–16; see also CZA L2/102–18.

[67] Ajay, *Mount Lebanon and the Wilayah of Beirut, 1914–1918*, 294; Margaret McGilvary, *The Dawn of a New Era in Syria* (New York: Fleming H. Revell, 1920), 35; Lutfalla Nasr al-Bakasina, *Nabdha min Waqa'i' al-Harb al-Kawniyya* (Matba'at al-Ijtihad l-Yusuf Thabit Awwal Suq Sarsuq, 1922), 357; Konstantin Basha, *Lamha Tarikhiyya fi 'Amal al-Rahbana al-Mukhallisiyya khilal al-Harb al-'Amma* (Lurins, MA: al-Matba'a al-Tijariyya, 1920), 7.

[68] Arthur Rupin and Alex Bein, eds., *Pirke Khayay* (Tel Aviv: 'Am Oved, 1968), 228.

[69] See, for instance, the entire files of CZA Z3/1472 and CZA Z3/1480.

[70] Gerber, Modernization in Nineteenth Century Palestine, 259.

fruits, vegetables, legumes, and animal products that were cultivated in the region.[71]

But then swarms of locusts invaded Palestine, Syria, the Hijaz, and as far as Anatolia and even Iraq. First spotted in March 1915, only a few months into the war, they wreaked complete havoc on the food supply for more than a full calendar year. That year became known not as the year of war, requisitions, or the blockade, but rather "the year of the locust" (*'Am al-Jarad*). It was the worst attack in many decades, perhaps centuries. The locusts ate 10–15% of the winter crop – wheat and barley – and 80% of the summer crop – fruits and vegetables (including olives, the key source of protein for most of the region's peasantry), and unknown quantities of fodder, legumes, and other cash crops such as cotton, tobacco, and mulberry leaves.[72]

Much as was the case in the premodern world, locusts could prove to be the most devastating pests of all. However, population growth and urbanization, as well as the conversion to cash crops, could not be undone so quickly. The fastest-growing part of the economy – trade, tourism, transportation, banks, and health services – were all left devastated by the war. The significantly larger populations concentrated away from the productive hinterland in the coastal cities were much more dependent on tourism, industry, and trade for livelihoods, railways for food, and income from cash crops like oranges and silk.

And so the region descended into total madness. Those who found themselves unemployed as a result of the financial meltdown sold their property. They chopped down their trees for firewood. They sold their furniture, jewelry, blankets, and pots and pans. Women turned to prostitution. Many begged on the streets of their own cities. They slaughtered their plow animals for meat. Some reportedly even ate their own children. This was an economic collapse of the worst kind, leaving hundreds of thousands of people without any means of livelihood, many of whom starved to death or died from starvation-related diseases in the region's worst famine in modern history.

---

[71] Fritz Grobba, *Die Getreidewirtschaft Syriens und Palästinas seit Beginn des Weltkriegs* (Hannover: H. Lafaire, 1923), 9.
[72] Foster, The 1915 Locust Attack in Syria and Palestine.

Starving for Someone Else's Fight

The First World War and Food Insecurity in the African Red Sea Region

Steven Serels

The African Red Sea Region (ARSR), comprising contemporary Sudan, Eritrea, Ethiopia, Djibouti, and Northern Somalia (Somaliland), is often left out of histories of the First World War. Conventional accounts that focus on large-scale military engagements between the Triple Entente and Central Powers often miss the effect of the war on this region. However, the First World War had a lasting, detrimental impact on communities in the region. There were armed confrontations in Ethiopia, Sudan, and Somaliland. These outbreaks of violence shifted local balances of power, leading to the incorporation of Darfur into the Anglo-Egyptian Sudan, a change in leadership in Ethiopia, and the further weakening of the British hold on the Somali coast. Despite this geographically and temporally limited fighting, many parts of the region remained peaceful. Nonetheless, the war touched every part of the region. The First World War led to the collapse of the global food trade system, which in turn set off a food crisis in the ARSR. Though scholars studying the war in Europe have previously examined the collapse of the international trade in food,[1]

---

[1] For some examples of this type of scholarship, see Ina Zweiniger-Bargielowski, Rachel Duffett, and Alain Drouard, eds., *Food and War in Twentieth Century Europe* (Surrey: Ashgate, 2011); Frank Trentmann and Flemming Just, eds., *Food and Conflict in Europe in the Age of the Two World Wars* (New York: Palgrave Macmillan, 2006); Rachel Duffett, *The Stomach for Fighting: Food and the Soldiers of the Great War* (Manchester/New York: Manchester University Press, 2012). For histories of the rise of the global food trade system, see Kevin H. O'Rourke and Jeffrey G. Williamson, *Globalization and History: The Evolution of a Nineteenth-Century Atlantic Economy* (Cambridge, MA: MIT Press, 1999); Kevin H. O'Rourke, Long-Distance Trade: Long-Distance Trade between 1740 and 1914. In Joel Mokyr, ed., *Oxford Encyclopedia of Economic History*, vol. 3 (Oxford: Oxford University Press, 2003), 365–370;

little attention has previously been given to the impact of the war on the food security of the ARSR.

Communities in the ARSR had long been dependent on the international trade in grain. In fact, the grain trade had allowed communities on both the African and Arabian Red Sea littorals to develop a closely linked, multifaceted socioeconomic system that transcended ethnic, linguistic, religious, and political divides. A major driver for the development of this system was the Muslim hajj. The Muslim holy cities of Mecca and Medina are located in western Arabia. All Muslims are required, if they are able, to participate in the annual hajj to Mecca once in their lifetime and many pilgrims choose to travel to Medina. This requirement has maintained human populations in western Arabia in numbers that this arid environment cannot support. The ready demand for imported grain in Arabia created opportunities for intensive cultivation in fertile zones in neighboring countries. However, local output could not meet the totality of demand in the greater Red Sea region. This surplus of demand spurred the development of trade links with grain-producing regions in India.[2] Trade, in turn, facilitated the development of other forms of economic specialization and interdependence and allowed for the establishment of complex states with unique material cultures throughout the region.[3]

Unfortunately, the traditional grain economy of the greater Red Sea world could not withstand the social, political, economic, and environmental transformations that followed the opening of the Suez Canal. At the end of the nineteenth century, the food economy became unstable. Communities living on the Arabian Red Sea littoral were saved from the harmful effects of this instability as a result of the spiritual and geopolitical importance of Mecca and Medina. For centuries, Muslim leaders had been providing residents of western Arabia with significant annual

Antoni Estevadeordal, Brian Frantz, and Alan M. Taylore, The Rise and Fall of World Trade, 1870–1939. NBER *Working Paper* (2003). Frank Trentmann, Coping with Shortage: The Problem of Food Security and Global Visions of Coordination, c. 1890–1950. In Frank Trentmann and Flemming Just, eds., *Food and Conflict in Europe in the Age of the Two World Wars* (New York: Palgrave Macmillan, 2006), 13–48.

[2] Steven Serels, Famines of War: The Red Sea Grain Market and Famine in Eastern Sudan, 1889–1891. *Northeast African Studies* 12(1) (2012), 73–94.

[3] See Andrew Paul, *A History of the Beja Tribes of the Sudan* (London: Frank Cass & Company, 1971). Jay Spaulding, *The Heroic Age in Sinnar* (Trenton, NJ: Red Sea Press, 2007); Richard Pankhurst, *An Introduction to the Economic History of Ethiopia from Early Times to 1800* (Addis Ababa: Haile Sellassie I University Press, 1961). Alan Mikhail, *Nature and Empire in Ottoman Egypt: An Environmental History* (Cambridge: Cambridge University Press, 2011).

subventions of money and grain as a sign of their piety.[4] Communities in the ARSR did not receive these subventions and, as a result, suffered from a number of late nineteenth- and early twentieth-century food crises. As this chapter demonstrates, the First World War further destabilized the food economy of the ARSR by cutting off local communities from foreign sources of grain, hampering local economic strategies and diverting local grain yields away from regional markets. At the same time, ecological hazards reduced crop yields in much of the region. As a result, people suffered. The lucky simply had to cope with increased grain prices at a time of economic decline. Some were able neither to grow their own subsistence nor to afford to purchase sufficient food. These unfortunate victims of the war starved. In some regions, this starvation occurred on a mass scale, resulting in widespread famine.

THE FOOD ECONOMY OF THE ARSR ON THE EVE OF THE FIRST WORLD WAR

From the late 1880s to the early 1890s, the ARSR was plagued by a severe famine during which, in some regions, as much as two-thirds of the population died and untold numbers were displaced.[5] The resulting depopulation of the countryside threw large tracks of fertile land out of cultivation, resulting in delayed recovery and endemic food insecurity.[6] The British, French, Italian, and Ethiopian officials who carved up the region were forced to address the persistent food crisis. Over the next two decades, the new imperial rulers attempted to radically reconstruct local patterns of agricultural production and long-distance trade so as to prevent another food crisis. They hoped that doing so would shore up their political control. In the Anglo-Egyptian Sudan, British officials worked

---

[4] Duman Nurtaç, Emirs of Mecca and the Ottoman Government of Hijaz, 1840–1908 (Master's thesis, Boğaziçi University, 2005), 18; Carl B. Kluzinger, *Upper Egypt: Its People and Products* (London: Blackie and Son, 1878), 272.

[5] For descriptions of the famine, see Richard Pankhurst, *The Great Ethiopian Famine of 1888–1892: A New Assessment* (Addis Ababa: Haile Sellassie I University, 1964); Serels, *Famines of War*, 73–94; Rudolph von Slatin, *Fire and Sword in the Sudan: A Personal Narrative of Fighting and Serving the Dervishes, 1879–1895*, translated by F. R. Wingate (London: Edward Arnold, 1896), 452–457; F. R. Wingate, *Ten Years' Captivity in the Mahdi's Camp 1882–1892* (London: Sampson, Low, Marston and Company, 1892), 284–291; Ferdinando Martini, *Nell'Africa Italiana*, 8th edn. (Milan: Fratelli Treves, 1925), 29–31.

[6] *L'Economia Eritrea nel Cinquatennio dell'Occupazione di Assab (1882–1932)* (Florence: Istituto Agricolo Coloniale Italiano, 1932), 7–8.

with indigenous agriculturalists along the Nile north of Khartoum to create a new slave plantation system focused on producing wheat.[7] At the same time, these officials expanded Sudan's rail network so as to link grain-producing regions in northern, central, and eastern Sudan to key markets along the Nile and in the Red Sea. In British Somaliland, officials struggled to effectively use their military might to subdue the armed followers of Sayyid Muhammad 'Abdallah al-Hasan. Officials hoped that ending this conflict would allow these officials to develop the region into a food reserve for the Yemeni port of Aden.[8] Italian officials tried to coerce peasants from southern Italy to establish agricultural settlements on the land in the Eritrean plateau that had been abandoned due to the death or out-migration of the indigenous population during the famine.[9] In Ethiopia and the Côte Française des Somalis, officials adopted a different tactic. Instead of seeking to directly rebuild the food economy, officials sought to promote trade in general. Ethiopian officials and state-connected elites, who had been economically and politically weakened by the famine, turned to large-scale slave raiding and the trans-Red Sea slave trade to develop new sources of wealth.[10] French officials attempted to capitalize on Ethiopia's trading potential by constructing a railroad from the newly constructed Red Sea port of Djibouti into central Ethiopia.[11]

In terms of rebuilding the food economy, these policies met with a qualified success. During the first decade of the twentieth century, the regional food economy stabilized. The new network of railroads facilitated a long-distance trade in foodstuffs. The cost of wheat in Eritrea dropped from 15 Italian lire per quintal in 1900 to 8 Italian lire per quintal in 1902. By 1907, Eritrea had become a net exporter of wheat. The rapid expansion of wheat cultivation in the Eritrean highlands was not a result of the initiative of Italian settlers, as officials had initially hoped. In fact, Italian cultivators did not permanently settle in Eritrea in significant numbers during this period. Rather, the increase was the result of the

---

[7] Steven Serels, *Starvation and the State: Famine, Slavery and Power in Sudan 1883–1956* (New York: Palgrave Macmillan, 2013).

[8] Patrick Kitaburaza Kakwenzire, *Colonial Rule in the British Somaliland Protectorate, 1905–1939* (PhD thesis, University of London, 1976), 61–75.

[9] This plan was formulated by Leopoldo Franchetti in 1889 at the behest of Prime Minister Francesco Crispi. On July 1, 1890, the Italian government formally adopted this policy. *L'Economia Eritrea nel Cinquatennio dell'Occupazione di Assab (1882–1932)*, 7–8.

[10] Lord Noel-Buxton, Slavery in Abyssinia. *International Affairs* 11(4) (July 1932), 517; Pankhurst, *An Introduction to the Economic History of Ethiopia*, 111.

[11] For a detailed history of the railroad, see Rosanna van Gelder de Pineda, *Le Chemin de Fer de Djibouti à Addis-Abeba* (Paris: l'Harmattan, 1995).

initiative of returning indigenous cultivators. Between 1893 and 1911, the indigenous population of Eritrea increased from 191,127 to 331,431.[12] Italian officials responded to this sudden population expansion by reversing course and returning much of the land reserved for Italian colonization back to indigenous communities. To further encourage grain cultivation, Italian officials waived the duty on the first 20,000 quintals of wheat imported from Eritrean ports into Italy. This Italian customs regulation spurred an increase in wheat cultivation in Ethiopia. Ethiopian merchants quickly positioned themselves to take advantage of this special dispensation by shipping surplus wheat grown in the Ethiopian province of Tigre out through Eritrean ports.[13] Wheat exports from Eritrean ports rose sharply and reached a prewar peak of 46,843 quintals in 1909.[14]

Similarly, merchants and indigenous agriculturalists in the Anglo-Egyptian Sudan took advantage of new laws, policies, and transport facilities to expand agricultural production. Between 1898 and 1913, cultivators imported at least 100,000 male slaves into northern Sudan and put them to work on water-wheel-irrigated plantations.[15] These cultivators dedicated much of the arable land in this region to wheat, a crop that they did not eat. As a result, merchants developed a new long-distance trade in grain, shipping sorghum from the rainlands in eastern and central Sudan via the railroad and steamships to northern Sudanese markets and wheat from northern Sudanese markets to European enclaves in large Sudanese towns.[16] This new pattern of production and trade produced sufficient surpluses that British officials stationed in the Anglo-Egyptian Sudan began to envision a future in which Sudan would be the breadbasket of the entire Red Sea basin.[17] In 1909, this dream appeared to be materializing when, for the first time, merchants exported nearly 9,000 tons of sorghum from Sudan to Egypt.[18] The

---

[12] *L'Economia Eritrea nel Cinquatennio dell'Occupazione di Assab (1882–1932)*, 42.

[13] Renato Paoli, *Le condizioni commerciali dell'Eritrea* (Novara: Istituto Geografico de Agostini, 1913), 7–9.

[14] Michele Checchi, *Movimento Commerciale della Colonia Eritrea* (Rome: Istituto Coloniale Italiano, 1912), 26.

[15] Serels, *Starvation and the State*, 114–126.

[16] Herbert William Jackson, Annual Report, Dongola Province, 1908. In *Reports on the Finances, Administration and Condition of the Sudan, 1908*, 508. Sudan Archive Durham University (SAD).

[17] Wingate to Mohamed el Mackawee, March 9, 1911, SAD300/3/57–58.

[18] W. Hayes Sadler, Annual Report, Customs Department, 1909. In *Reports on the Finances, Administration and Condition of the Sudan*, 1909, 250. SAD.

following year 28,000 tons of sorghum were exported via rail to Egypt and by boat from the Red Sea ports of Port Sudan and Sawakin.[19]

Despite these developments in the grain trade, the region, as a whole, did not become self-sufficient in grain. Though the highlands of Eritrea and Ethiopia had become an exporter of wheat to international markets, adjacent regions continued to depend on international imports of grain. The pastoral populations that lived in the foothills surrounding these highlands ate sorghum and not wheat and Sudanese harvests were insufficient to meet local needs. The annual value of sorghum imported by sea into Eritrea over the first decade of the twentieth century fluctuated between approximately 500,000 and 900,000 Italian lire, depending on the size of the local harvest.[20] Sorghum was also heavily imported into the ARSR through Djibouti,[21] Zayla, and Berbera.[22] Despite gains made in the cultivation and marketing of grain in Sudan, that region could not escape its dependence on grain imports. Sudanese grain yields were unstable. A regional drought in central Sudan in 1911 led to reduced crop yields[23] and high prices in 1912 throughout northern, central, and eastern Sudan. The export trade dried up and Sudan returned to being a net grain importer.[24] Most of the grain imported into the ARSR came on steamships from India, though small quantities were also imported from Yemen.

For many in the region, access to the grain market required engaging in slave trading, contraband smuggling and armed warfare. In addition to the intense internal Sudanese slave trade, which helped rebuild that region's grain economy, there was another trans-Red Sea slave trade. Slaves shipped to markets in Arabia typically were kidnapped in large, Ethiopian government organized raids in southern and western Ethiopia. Despite making public commitments to combat the slave trade, Emperor

[19] Customs Report, 1910. In *Reports on the Finances, Administration and Condition of the Sudan, 1910*, 558. SAD.

[20] Checchi, *Movimento Commerciale della Colonia Eritrea*, 32–43.

[21] Rapport de Monsieur A. G. Rozis Conseiller du Commerce Extèrieur de la France sur le Protectorat de la Cote Francaise des Somalis. Djibouti. 1911. FM1AFFPOL/13.3. Archives Nationales d'Outre-Mer, Aix-en-Provence (ANOM).

[22] *Annual Report on Somaliland for the Year Ending 31st March 1906*, CO535/6. National Records Office, Khartoum (NRO).

[23] Central Economic Board, *Annual Report of the Director, Commercial Intelligence Branch, Central Economic Board, 1915*, No. VIII (1914) 28. SAD Annual Report of the Director, Commercial Intelligence Branch, Central Economic Board, 1914. SAD.

[24] Annual Report, Sudan Customs, 1912, in *Reports on the Finances, Administration and Condition of the Sudan*. Volume 2, 1912, 230–231. SAD.

Menelik II used slave raiding to stabilize the expanding Shawan Ethiopian
state, which had been severely weakened by the late nineteenth-century
famine. Slaves taken during these raids were used to augment the emper-
or's household, allocated to officials or state-connected elites, or sold to
merchants engaged in the Red Sea trade. Slaves in Ethiopia were a sign of
conspicuous consumption and were not used by cultivators as agricultural
laborers.[25] The sale of slaves allowed the state and state-connected elites
to purchase imported arms, often from French merchants, which provided
the firepower necessary for large-scale slave raiding. Slave raiding was so
prevalent that the local population in some regions shrank by as much as
90%.[26] Fear of raiding and counter-raiding induced local populations
to cluster in larger settlements, a practice that further contributed to the
decline in the extent of cultivated land and to permanently low crop yields
in the south and west.[27] Despite the disastrous effects of slave raiding, the
expansion of the slave trade helped some communities in the north and
east recover from the crisis of the late nineteenth century. Ethiopian slaves
typically passed through the hands of a number of indigenous merchants
en route to the coast, where they were purchased by Arabian merchants
and shipped across the Red Sea.[28] On the way, these merchants paid fees
to the local pastoral population for access to caravan routes and wells.
Pastoralists supplemented the money earned from this trade by selling
hides and other pastoral products. These two economic activities together
formed the main sources of income that allowed pastoralist communities
to purchase imported grain.

  Where pastoralists lacked access to the slave trade, they turned to cattle
raiding and warfare in order to generate the revenue necessary to purchase
their sustenance. This was especially true in British Somaliland, where
a protracted struggle between the British and Sayyid Muhammad 'Abd
Allah al-Hasan opened the possibility for Somalis to profit from perpetual
war. This struggle began in the mid-1890s, when the Sayyid started
preaching the need to expel the new British administrators of the Somali

---

[25] Cultivation in the grain-producing regions in northern Ethiopia continued to be limited
   by insufficient animal labor resulting from repeated outbreaks of rinderpest. See
   James McCann, *From Poverty to Famine in Northeast Ethiopia: A Rural History
   1900–1935* (Philadelphia: University of Pennsylvania Press, 1987), 80–81.
[26] Noel-Buxton, Slavery in Abyssinia, 517; Pankhurst, *An Introduction to the Economic
   History of Ethiopia*, 111.
[27] This process was noticed as early as 1897. Rennell Rodd to Salisbury, May 14, 1897, FO
   403/255, National Archive, London (NA).
[28] Philip Zaphiro, *Memorandum on the Slave Traffic between Abyssinia and the Coast of
   Arabia.* [November 1929] IOR/R/20/1/1560. British Library, London (BL).

ports of Berbera and Zayla. The Sayyid's teachings galvanized the population and threatened Britain's tenuous hold on the coast. British officials responded by sending a number of large-scale military expeditions against the Sayyid and his followers. By 1905, this policy had proven a failure. British officials then changed course and began to use cash subsidies, as well as grants of arms, ammunition, and food, to maintain indigenous allies and to coerce them into creating and joining pro-British militias. The Sayyid responded by routinely raiding livestock from British-allied Somali encampments. Proceeds from these raids allowed the Sayyid and his followers to purchase contraband goods, including arms, ammunition, and food, imported from Red Sea ports and Ethiopian markets.[29]

Instability in British Somaliland descended into widespread chaos in 1910. The British government in London, unwilling to continue to support an intractable conflict in a peripheral territory, ordered the complete withdrawal of British personnel from the Somaliland interior and commanded the administration of the protectorate to confine its activities to a 50-mile zone around the port of Berbera. To protect their position in the port, British officials widely distributed weapons to neighboring allied pastoralist communities.[30] The withdrawal took place during the early stages of a widespread drought. Pastures disappeared, wells dried up, herds died in large numbers, and people began to starve. The ensuing famine, which lasted until 1913, is still remembered as *Haraame Cune* (i.e., the years of eating the unclean). Somalis, both those allied with the British and those allied with the Sayyid, responded to the devastation by launching raids on their neighbors in a desperate attempt to secure rights to the dwindling sources of water and to capture the remaining domesticated animals. The dislocation caused by the widespread fighting allowed for an epidemic of smallpox to sweep through the region.[31] By 1912, an estimated one-third of the population had died from disease, starvation, and warfare.[32]

Though seemingly more politically and economically stable than British Somaliland, the rest of the ARSR was also subsequently pushed back into food insecurity and famine. During the 1912–1913 cultivation year, drought in Eritrea, in northern Ethiopia, and in the Sudanese provinces of

---

[29] Kakwenzire, *Colonial Rule in the British Somaliland Protectorate*, 61–75.

[30] Kakwenzire, *Colonial Rule in the British Somaliland Protectorate*, 161–168.

[31] Jama Mohamed, Epidemics and Public Health in Early Colonial Somaliland. *Social Science and Medicine* 48 (1999), 509–510.

[32] Archer to the Secretary of State for the Colonies, August 19, 1913, CO535/31. NRO.

Sennar, Kassala, and White Nile resulted in reduced grain yields. Grain prices rose dramatically. In the Ethiopian province of Tigre prices peaked at as much as four times their normal rate.[33] In Eritrea, grain prices increased tenfold.[34] Grain yields during the following cultivation year were even worse. Locust swarms devastated crops in Eritrea and northern Ethiopia.[35] In Sudan, the summer rains and the Nile flood failed and more than 200,000 acres fell out of cultivation. Cultivators in northern Sudan could not afford to maintain the large slave labor force that worked the fields and starving slaves escaped in large numbers. These slave famine refugees resettled either in southern Sudan or in market towns and preex-isting ex-slave settlements along the Eritrean frontier.[36]

Officials in Sudan, Eritrea, and northern Ethiopia did not implement adequate measures to arrest the deepening food crisis. Degiac Ghebersellasie, the governor of Tigre, continued to allow the export of grain despite the ongoing famine, though he did try to hamper this trade. In October 1913, Ghebersellasie imposed an export duty of two Maria Theresa thalers on every mule load of grain and one Maria Theresa thaler on every donkey load.[37] British officials in Sudan ignored early signs of distress among the local population. These officials were convinced that early reports of famine conditions were just, as one senior official stated, the local population being "as cute as monkeys."[38] When slaves began fleeing northern Sudanese farms in large numbers and communities of, as one observer noted, "shrunken, shriveled forms"[39] began to form around administrative centers, officials were forced to take action. In early 1914, British officials established famine relief works and distributed grain to the neediest cases.[40] However, by the time these measures began tens of thousands had fled affected regions and untold numbers had died. The official response in Eritrea was even more inadequate. Though

---

[33] Adenzia Commaerciale Adua to Governor, April 8, 1913, Pacco 645. Archivio Eritrea of the Ministero degli Affari Esteri, Rome (AEMAE).

[34] G. de Ponti. *Il Cotone in Eritrea*, August 27, 1930, FASC1962. Archivio Storico, Ministero Africa Italiana, Rome (ASMAI).

[35] Il Regenete del Commissariato Regionale del Seraé to the Governor, October 17, 1913, Pacco 645. AEMAE.

[36] Serels, *Starvation and the State*, 110–111.

[37] Agente commerciale in Tigré to Governor of Eritrea, October 28, 1913, Pacco 645. AEMAE.

[38] Phipps to Wingate, September 27, 1913, SAD187/3/199.

[39] Louis C. West, Dongola Province of the Anglo Egyptian Sudan. *Geographical Review* 5(1) (January 1918), 35.

[40] *Famine Relief Works in Dongola Province*, January 3, 1914, SAD112/3/35.

widespread famine was reported in Eritrea at the end of 1913, officials there took little action to help the neediest cases.[41] Rather, officials sought to root out inefficiencies in the grain market. These officials believed there to be two sources of inefficiencies – government intervention and merchant hording. So, in December 1913 the governor of Eritrea ended the sale of subsidized grain to indigenous soldiers and to state-connected indigenous elites.[42] To ensure fair market prices for grain, the governor required all Commissari Regionali to report market prices for grain. The governor believed that by comparing these prices to the prices furnished by the government of India at the major West Indian ports officials would be able to determine if there was price gouging or other forms of market manipulation.[43] Despite the influx of market data, there is no evidence that officials took further action against grain merchants.

The measures taken by officials in Sudan, Eritrea, and northern Ethiopia did not address the root causes of the famine. This food crisis was caused by structural insecurity created by the new patterns of production and trade. New transportation technologies allowed for the rapid and cheap movement of grain across large distances. In times of plenty, this opened new markets for local yields. However, colonial officials were unwilling to suspend cross-border trade or intrastate trade in times of hardship. As a result, local grain shortages quickly became regional crises because merchants would ship grain across the region to maximize profit. Further, new communication technologies disrupted older patterns of trade and left some communities without the resources necessary to weather adverse ecological periods or sudden economic downturns. This was especially pronounced in Ethiopia. Throughout the nineteenth century, both the political and economic centers of Ethiopia had been in the north. The rise of the Ethiopian Shawan kingdom under Menelik II and the construction of the railroad from Djibouti at the turn of the twentieth century shifted international trade away from the province of Tigre and in so doing limited the economic strategies of the region's indigenous agricultural communities. Similarly, the construction of railroads in Sudan, Eritrea, and Ethiopia economically hurt the pastoralists residing on the Red Sea coast. Until the end of the nineteenth century, these pastoralist communities profited from trade by selling their pastoral

---

[41] Camillo Carrora to Governatore dell'Eritrea, December 20, 1913, Pacco 645. AEMAE.
[42] Governor to the Commissari Regionali, December 21, 1913, Pacco 645. AEMAE.
[43] Il Direttore de Finanza to Direttore degli Affari Civili, December 22, 1913, Pacco 645. AEMAE.

products to passing caravans, by acting as guides, by supplying pack animals, and by charging fees for accessing wells and roads. The railroads ended these commercial activities by narrowing the economic strategies of these pastoralists and by hampering their ability to regularly secure the income necessary to purchase their sustenance. Further, railroads diverted traffic to the coastal ports to which they were connected and by the beginning of the twentieth century nearly all legitimate commerce was directed to Port Sudan, Massawa, and Djibouti. However, custom among pastoralist communities divided the littoral into communally controlled subregions, each of which had previously had a vibrant local port. The pastoralist communities that claimed the subregion also claimed the right to determine patterns of access to the port. This custom continued even as the consolidation of trade at ports with railheads led to the economic collapse of other neighboring ports. As a result, this consolidation created communities of beneficiaries of beneficiaries and losers. This dynamic is best illustrated in the region around the Bab al-Mandab, where the commercial rise of Djibouti led to the decline of Assab and Zayla.[44] The Issa Somali pastoralists who controlled the hinterland around Djibouti regulated commercial access to that port and, at times, prevented the entrance of merchandise belonging to neighboring 'Afar. At the same time, fewer and fewer boats were docking at the port of Assab in 'Afar territory. So, 'Afar pastoralists were periodically cut off from international trade.[45] This dynamic was repeated elsewhere along the Red Sea littoral.

Similarly, the expansion of trade in the interior did not necessarily lead to improved economic outcomes for indigenous producers of primary products. Throughout the region, the distribution chain linking end consumers, local producers, and foreign importers was dominated by numerous middlemen, each of whom claimed a share of the profits from trade.[46] As trade expanded, so did the number of middlemen. As a result, profits to producers declined in the first decade of the twentieth century. This was especially true in Sudan, where the retail market came to be dominated by recent immigrants from Syria. These immigrants recognized that Sudanese cultivators lacked access to ready cash all year round and, therefore, could

---

[44] Luigi Cufino, *La Parabola Commerciale di Assab* (Naples: Stab. Tip. Francesco Golia, 1913), 3.

[45] Ministre des Colonies, *Rapport d'Ensemble sur la Situation Générale du Protectorat de la Côte Française des Somalis et Dépendances en 1904*, FM1AFFPOL/121. ANOM.

[46] Paoli, *Le condizioni commerciali dell'Eritrea*, 35–37.

only purchase goods after the harvest. To ensure a steady market for their imported goods, these merchants purchased crop futures, often at very low rates, for cash advances. As a result, the profits to cultivators declined steadily in the years leading up to the 1913–1914 famine. Though British officials in the Anglo-Egyptian Sudan passed measures during the famine to end this practice, these measures went unenforced.[47] The structure of international and local trade ensured that local producers lacked a safety net capable of buffering them from the consequences of crop failures.

In the summer of 1914, the acute food crisis subsided without the resolution of the underlying structural issues that precipitated the famine. The region began a partial recovery in 1914 because yields rebounded. The summer rains in northern Ethiopia and in the Eritrean highlands were substantial, which led to an above-average Nile flood.[48] Favorable conditions continued throughout the rainy season[49] and, where possible, cultivators returned to their lands. The overall grain yield throughout the region was high and prices dropped to near record lows.[50] However, a full recovery was not possible. In northern Sudan the slaves who had previously worked the land had fled during the famine and, as a result, cultivators lacked the labor power necessary to extensively work the land. In the rest of the region, the recovery was hindered by changes to the international economy and to regional geopolitics brought on by the outbreak of the First World War.

THE FIRST WORLD WAR IN THE RED SEA WORLD

Shortly after the outbreak of the First World War, the Red Sea world became cut off from international trade. The number of steamships cruising the sea declined rapidly. By the end of 1915, the civilian British merchant fleet had shrunk by one-third as a result of government requisitioning and German attacks.[51] At the same time, the French government requisitioned much of its merchant fleet to make up for a relative naval weakness, including steamships belonging to the Messageries Maritimes and the Havraise Paninsulair. These steamship lines had previously

---

[47] Serels, *Starvation and the State*, 140.
[48] Sudan Intelligence Report, No. 241 (August 1914) WO106/6225. NA.
[49] Sudan Intelligence Report, No. 242 (September 1914) WO106/6225. NA.
[50] Central Economic Board, *Annual Report of the Director, Commercial Intelligence Branch, Central Economic Board, 1915,* No. VIII (1914) 28. SAD.
[51] L. Margaret Barnett, *British Food Policy during the First World War* (Boston, MA: George Allen & Unwin, 1985), 69–70.

connected France to Asia and Madagascar via Djibouti.[52] In early 1915, the decreased number of steamships traveling back and forth from France to Asia discharged little merchandise in Djibouti. Further, the steamships calling in Djibouti had little room to take on African exports because they arrived nearly full. For example, in the month of June 1915, there was space for just one ton of cargo to leave Djibouti.[53] As international shipping seized up, warehouses and entrepôts in the Côte Française des Somalis and in Ethiopia quickly filled up. By mid-June, more than 3 million tons of goods waited in the port of Djibouti to be exported.[54] La Banque de l'Indo-Chine stopped offering advances on merchandise because there was little chance that the goods would be exported.[55]

Trade was further hindered by a currency crisis in the Red Sea. During the war, local and foreign merchants were unable to acquire the currencies necessary to support international trade. Though British, French and Italian officials had tried to impose paper currencies, local merchants almost exclusively accepted silver coins. The war caused a shortage of the silver coins that underpinned much of the Red Sea's international trade. During the war, 40% of Ethiopia's money stock fell out of circulation, the result either of hording or of export to Indian Ocean markets where silver coins held higher market values. To stem the outflow of silver coins, the Ethiopian government suspended their export in 1915. As a result of this prohibition, the Bank of Abyssinia, which held a monopoly on currency exchange services in Ethiopia, quickly ran out of foreign currencies and ended up with a large supply of silver coins that it could not circulate.[56] At the same time, merchants in the Côte Française des Somalis, British Somaliland, and Eritrea exported their silver coins to Aden, where they were then re-exported to India. Without the necessary currency and without access to currency exchange services, merchants could not easily engage in international trade.[57]

---

[52] Rapport Mensuel. Avril 1917. 2e Partie. Renseignements Economiques. Fascicule No. 4. Abyssinie, FM1AFFPOL/122. ANOM.

[53] Governor of French Somaliland to Ministre des Colonis, 11 June 1915, FM1AFFPOL/186. ANOM.

[54] Ibid.

[55] Rapport Mensuel. Avril 1917. 2e Partie. Renseignements Economiques. Fascicule No. 4. Abyssinie, FM1AFFPOL/122. ANOM.

[56] Charles Schaefer, The Politics of Banking: The Bank of Abyssinia, 1905–1931. *The International Journal of African Historical Studies* 25(2) (1992), 381–384.

[57] Rapport Mensuel. Avril 1917. 2e Partie. Renseignements Economiques. Fascicule No. 4. Abyssinie, FM1AFFPOL/122. ANOM.

As international trade seized up, the Entente powers took measures to restrict the intra-Red Sea dhow trade. Officials were nervous that enemy forces would be able to use this trade to locally secure provisions. In the early stages of the war, British and French captains were given orders to capture or sink all ships that did not fly allied flags. In 1917, the French government experienced a war-induced financial crisis. Unable to shoulder the financial burden, French officials ended their participation in this operation. Nonetheless, British warships were able to maintain effective control of the Red Sea by themselves.[58] British officials used their control over maritime trade in the Red Sea to weaken the Turkish position in Arabia. Central to this strategy was the manipulation of the food economy of the Hijaz, the region of western Arabia containing the Muslim holy cities of Mecca and Medina. On November 11, 1914, the Ottoman Empire entered the war on the German side and, a week later, Ottoman clerics issued a fatwa proclaiming a jihad against the Entente powers.[59] British officials immediately responded by refusing to send the traditional Egyptian subvention of grain to Mecca and Medina.[60] These subventions formed a key component of the diet of the population of the Hijaz. In retaliation, Turkish officials stationed in the Hijaz seized grain stores owned by British Indian subjects,[61] which, in turn, led British officials to impose a complete maritime embargo on the Hijaz. The embargo's effects were rapid and dramatic. By May 1915, British intelligence officers stationed in Cairo were receiving reports of widespread distress in Mecca and Medina.[62] British officials feared that the deepening food crisis in the Hijaz would be interpreted by the global Muslim community as an Entente attack on Islam and would become a rallying cry for a rebellion by the Entente's sizable Muslim populations. As a result, the British officials in Cairo who commanded the Red Sea operations ended the grain blockade on May 14, 1915. Immediately thereafter, British officials in the Anglo-Egyptian Sudan and in India authorized the export of grain to the Arabian Red Sea port of Jidda.[63] However, other forms of trade, remained restricted.

[58] Government of French Somaliland, *Rapport sur la Traite des Esclaves à la Côte Française des Somalis*, February 16, 1923, FM 1AFFPOL/402. ANOM.

[59] Stanford J. Shaw, *The Ottoman Empire in World War I. Volume 2. Triumph and Tragedy, November 1914–July 1916* (Ankara: Turkish Historical Society, 2008), 760.

[60] Sherif of Mecca to Storrs, July 14, 1915, SAD158/6/27–28.

[61] Makkawī to Wingate, April 21, 1915, SAD195/1/200–212.

[62] Central Economic Board, *Annual Report of the Director, Commercial Intelligence Branch, Central Economic Board, 1915*, No. IX (1915) 23. SAD.

[63] Wingate to Wilson, May 20, 1915, SAD195/2/118–122; Wilson to Wingate, November 21, 1915, SAD197/2/205–207.

In addition to curtailing legal trade in the Red Sea, Entente efforts ended the lucrative trans-Red Sea contraband trade on which many African communities depended. Before the war, this contraband trade was structured primarily around the trade in arms, ammunitions, and slaves. At the start of the war, Djibouti was the major port for importing firearms from Europe to the Red Sea. French officials had previously encouraged the development of this trade because the customs duties from importing arms supported the budget of the Côte Francaise des Somalis. In 1913, receipts from this duty amounted to 2 million francs, by far the largest source of revenue for the colony.[64] Though some of the landed arms and ammunition were destined for the government of Ethiopia, much of them were re-exported to the Arabian coast where they entered the contraband trade. Following the outbreak of war, French officials ended all shipments of arms to Djibouti[65] and local administrators began cooperating with their British counterparts to rigorously prosecute arms smugglers in the Red Sea. Without the trade in arms and ammunitions fueling the contraband trade, the trade in other illegal goods, including slaves and drugs, dried up.[66] Unable to profit from either the legal or contraband trans-Red Sea trade, many African communities began to struggle to earn the incomes necessary to purchase sufficient sustenance.

The food security of communities in the ARSR was further hindered by subsequent British-backed efforts to push the Ottomans out of Arabia. These efforts were contingent on diverting grain away from African markets to markets in the Hijaz. British officials conspired with Husayn ibn Ali, the *Sharif* of Mecca, to set off the Arab Revolt. Husayn recognized that local Arab leaders valued their autonomy and that they would, therefore, be reluctant to support his political ambitions. So he used the sizeable subventions from the British to purchase the allegiance of key elites.[67] Prior to the war, the economy of the Hijaz was driven by two activities, the subventions Muslim rulers paid as a sign of their piety and the hajj.

---

[64] Grasset to le Ministre de la Marine, February 11, 1914, FM1AFFPOL/123. ANOM.
[65] La Commission de Marseille. Relations Commerciales avec la Côte Orientale D'afrique, December 1, 1915, FM 1AFFPOL/186. ANOM.
[66] Le Ministre des colonies to Le Ministre des Affaires Etrangéres, January 3, 1928, FM1AFFPOL/696. ANOM.
[67] Joshua Teitelbaum, *The Rise and Fall of the Hashimite Kingdom of Arabia* (London: Hurst and Company, 2001), 76.

The revolt cut Hijazi elites off from Ottoman subsidies and the war led to a sharp decline in the number of annual pilgrims. The decline in these sources of revenue could have led local purchasing power to collapse and could have, therefore, resulted in a widespread famine. However, British officials ensured the regular shipment of grain to Jidda as part of their effort to support Husayn.[68] Though most of the grain came from India, some was imported from Sudan.[69] In the months that followed the outbreak of the Arab Revolt, so much grain flowed into the Hijaz that grain prices dropped dramatically and grain in Jidda was cheaper than in other Red Sea markets.[70]

As the food economy of the Hijaz stabilized, other Red Sea regions struggled to ensure that available grain supplies were sufficient to meet local demand. The war put a severe strain on the food economy of Sudan, as that country became the only significant local supplier of grain to foreign Red Sea markets. For most of the war, Egypt, Eritrea, and Ethiopia did not export grain. In Egypt, the expanded British military presence led to increased demand for grain. Local yields proved inadequate and British officials in the Egyptian government had to search out foreign sources of supply.[71] In 1915, the British-led forces in Egypt imported 6,000 tons of grain from Sudan.[72] The following year, Sudan exported more than 24,000 tons of grain to Egypt.[73] In early 1917, British officials became concerned that Sudan could not guarantee sufficiently high grain yields. As a result, they began to invest directly in expanding commercial grain cultivation in Sudan by financing the establishment of pump-irrigated plantations on 20,000 acres in northern Sudan.[74] Unfortunately, these plantations were slow to come on line. In order to ensure that sufficient quantities of grain were exported to Egypt, British officials in Sudan assumed command of the sale and transport of food in

[68] Ibid., 80.

[69] Central Economic Board, *Annual Report of the Director, Commercial Intelligence Branch, Central Economic Board, 1918*, No. XII (1918) 8. SAD.

[70] David George Hogarth, *Hejaz before World War I*, 2nd edn. (Naples: Falcon Press, 1978), 80.

[71] Central Economic Board, *Annual Report of the Director, Commercial Intelligence Branch, Central Economic Board, 1915*, No. IX (1915) 24. SAD.

[72] Ibid.

[73] Central Economic Board, *Annual Report of the Director, Commercial Intelligence Branch, Central Economic Board, 1916*, No. X (1916) 27. SAD.

[74] Central Economic Board, *Annual Report of the Director, Commercial Intelligence Branch, Central Economic Board, 1916*, No. X (1916) 10. SAD.

Sudan.[75] These measures proved insufficient and in early 1918 British officials required all Sudanese cultivators to sell their harvest to the government at a predetermined, fixed rate. This measure allowed British officials to rapidly purchase 20,000 tons of Sudanese grain, which was then used to feed the camels the British Expeditionary Force used in Sinai and Palestine.[76]

Eritrea similarly did not produce sufficient grain during the war to meet local demand. In 1915, drought and locust plagues decreased domestic crop yields.[77] At the same time, local markets were unable to draw on Indian sources of supply because British officials in India had limited grain exports to only British and French territories.[78] Though exceptions were occasionally made for other regions, including the Hijaz, British officials in India systematically refused requests to export grain to Eritrea.[79] Italy's entrance into the war in mid-1915 on the side of the British did not change this policy. The suspension of Indian grain exports to Eritrea precipitated a widespread famine.[80] In October 1915, the Italian Ministero delle Colonie contacted the British ambassador to Rome to request special dispensation to export Indian grain to Eritrea.[81] Though British officials in London refused to reopen the grain trade between Eritrea and India,[82] they reluctantly agreed to authorize a special shipment of approximately 6,000 sacks of grain.[83] During the negotiations over this special dispensation, British officials reminded the Italian government that Eritrea was free to import as much grain from Sudan as necessary without any restrictions.[84] In fact, Sudan proved to be the only major foreign source

[75] Central Economic Board, *Annual Report of the Director, Commercial Intelligence Branch, Central Economic Board, 1918*, No. XII (1918) 6. SAD.

[76] Central Economic Board, *Annual Report of the Director, Commercial Intelligence Branch, Central Economic Board, 1918*, No. XII (1918) 8. SAD.

[77] Governo della Colonia Eritrea to il Ministero delle Colonie, September 22, 1915, Pacco 758. AEMAE.

[78] Mohammed and Abdalla Bamismus to Governo della Colonia Eritrea, June 2, 1915, Pacco 758. AEMAE.

[79] Ibid.

[80] Governo della Colonia Eritrea to il Ministero delle Colonie, September 22, 1915, Pacco 758. AEMAE.

[81] Ministero delle Colonie to Governo della Colonia Eritrea, October 11, 1915, Pacco 758. AEMAE.

[82] Capo di servizio deogane, porti, fari e sanita' marittima to Governo dell'Eritrea, January 2, 1916, Pacco 758. AEMAE.

[83] L. Colonel Jacob to the Consul for Italy at Aden, January 19, 1916, Pacco 758. AEMAE.

[84] Ministero delle Colonie to Governo della Colonia Eritrea, October 11, 1915, Pacco 758. AEMAE.

of grain for Eritrea during the war. In 1915 and 1916, Eritrea imported 19,000 tons of grain from Sudan each year.[85] In 1917, British officials in Sudan, who were seeking to maximize the amount of grain available for the British-led force in Egypt, were forced to impose a cap on the amount of grain exported to Eritrea. As a result, only 13,000 tons of grain were exported from Sudan into Eritrea in 1917 and 1918 combined.[86] This export cap precipitated a food crisis in Eritrea as demand outstripped supply. Nonetheless, Italian officials did little to alleviate the crisis. Instead, they focused on ensuring that a sufficient supply of grain made it to Asmara, the colonial capital, by imposing tight regulations on the sale and transport of grain.[87] These measures did little to address hardship in other parts of the colony and the crisis continued into 1919.

In addition to Sudan, Ethiopia was the other potential source of grain for the Entente powers in the Red Sea. In the past, Ethiopia had served as a grain reserve for Red Sea coastal settlement. Unrestricted grain exports from central-eastern Ethiopia began in 1904. That year, trans-Red Sea trade was suspended because of an outbreak of plague in Aden. The governor of the Côte Française des Somalis, fearing that maritime trade restrictions would prevent Indian grain from reaching Djibouti, convinced Ras Makonnen Wolde Mikael Gudessa, the governor of the Ethiopian Province of Harar, to authorize unfettered grain exports on the railroad.[88] The governor then had the management of La Compagnie Impériale des Chemins de fer Ethiopiens reduce the freight rate for Ethiopian grain exports.[89] Central-eastern Ethiopia remained the secondary grain reserve for the region until October 1915, when the Ethiopian government suspended all grain exports. Though exports were temporarily resumed in November 1915,[90] they were again suspended in January 1916. The suspension of the grain trade between central-eastern Ethiopia and the

[85] Central Economic Board, *Annual Report of the Director, Commercial Intelligence Branch, Central Economic Board, 1915*, No. IX (1915) 24. SAD; Central Economic Board, *Annual Report of the Director, Commercial Intelligence Branch, Central Economic Board, 1916*, No. X (1916) 27. SAD.

[86] Central Economic Board, *Annual Report of the Director, Commercial Intelligence Branch, Central Economic Board, 1918*, No. XII (1918) 8. SAD.

[87] Il Commissariato Speciale della Citta di Asmara to Direzione degli Affari Civili, March 5, 1919, Pacco 859. AEMAE.

[88] Governor of French Somaliland to Ministère des colonies, February 14, 1905, FM1AFFPOL/187/2. ANOM.

[89] Procès-verbal de la séance de la Commission Sanitaire, January 30, 1905, FM1AFFPOL/187/2. ANOM.

[90] Commissaire de Police [of Djibouti] to Governor of French Somaliland, January 31, 1916, FM8AFFECO/27. ANOM.

Red Sea must be understood within the context of Ethiopia's foreign policy. At the end of the nineteenth century, Ethiopia's rulers played European powers off each other in order to protect Ethiopia's independence. This policy produced mixed results. Ethiopia remained independent. However, its access to foreign imports was mediated by the European powers that controlled the Red Sea littoral, the Ethiopian banking system, and the railroad. Further, Ethiopian officials understood that the state's independence was not guaranteed and that it must therefore be carefully guarded from further European encroachment. The strong alliance formed between the British, the French, and, subsequently, the Italians as a result of the First World War weakened Ethiopia's foreign policy strategy and, therefore, threatened Ethiopia's independence. This alliance opened the possibility that these three Red Sea powers would carve up the Ethiopian state during a final war settlement. With these concerns in mind, Emperor Lij Iyasu sought to weaken the Entente's position in the Red Sea by promoting the interests of the Central Powers. The suspension of grain exports in early 1916 was the result of direct pressure from the German and Turkish legations in Addis Ababa.[91]

To further weaken the Entente's position in the Red Sea, Lij Iyasu also sought out a war-time alliance with the Somali Sayyid. Unlike previous Ethiopian emperors, Lij Iyasu incorporated Muslims into positions of power within the state. This policy had the potential to strengthen the state by creating stronger relationships with the region's sizable Muslim population. In addition, this policy created new opportunities for challenging British, French, and Italian power. In December 1914, Lij Iyasu appointed 'Abdullah Sadiq governor of the Ogaden, a Somali territory under Ethiopian rule that borders the Côte Française des Somalis, British Somaliland, and Somalia Italiana.[92] In February 1916, a joint Ethiopian and Turkish delegation visited the Sayyid[93] and, shortly thereafter, Lij Iyasu began sending consignments of arms and ammunitions to the Sayyid through 'Abdullah Saadik.[94] To further support the Sayyid's campaign, Lij Iyasu sent Emil Kirsch, a German mechanic, to the Sayyid's camp to repair arms and to manufacture ammunition.[95] The Ethiopian state's

---

[91] Colli to the Ufficio Finanza, Governo Dell'Eritrea, April 14, 1916, Pacco 804. AEMAE.
[92] Archer to Colonial Office, December 19, 1914, CO535/36. NA.
[93] Archer to Colonial Office, March 1, 1916, CO535/42. NA.
[94] Thesiger to Foreign Office, April 10, 1916, CO535/44. NA.
[95] Kirsch's assignment proved impossible as there were neither spare parts for repairing the arms nor the raw materials necessary to manufacture ammunition. Kirch petitioned the Sayyid for permission to return to Ethiopia, but this request was denied. He subsequently

overtures to its subject Muslim population, neighboring Muslim leaders, and the Central Powers was short lived. Lij Iyasu's attempts to incorporate the Sayyid and other regional Muslim leaders into the Ethiopian state alienated him from much of the Ethiopian nobility. On September 27, 1916, a number of noblemen, with the help of key church officials, accused Lij Iyasu of apostasy and internal subversion. Lij Iyasu was deposed and excommunicated by the church.[96] In his place, Zawditu, Menelik II's daughter, was named empress of Ethiopia and Ras Tafari Makonnen was named regent and successor to the throne. The palace coup set off a bloody civil war, during which Iyasu's father, Negus Mikael of Wallo and Tigre, led a force of 80,000 men against the 120,000-men-strong army of the Shawan nobility. Fighting lasted until the end of October 1916 and in the end the Shawan nobility won.[97]

The formal coronation of Empress Zawditu on February 17, 1917 paved the way for the resumption of the grain trade between Ethiopia and the Red Sea coast. The following day, the French Ministre plénipotentiaire in Addis Ababa and the governor of the Côte Française des Somalis, who was in Ethiopia attending the coronation, met with Ras Tafari to discuss reopening the grain trade. Ras Tafari agreed to allow all rail cargos of grain comprised of less than 100 sacks to be exported without restriction. Larger cargos were to be referred back to the central Ethiopian government for approval.[98] Nonetheless, Ethiopia continued to insist on its neutrality in the war. In March 1918, Ras Tafari signaled his willingness to formally end commercial and diplomatic relations with the Central Powers and to withdraw all restrictions on grain exports. In exchange, he demanded that the British, French, and Italians supply the Ethiopian state with 60,000 rifles and 6 million cartridges.[99] This deal was accepted and the Ethiopian grain trade resumed without restriction.[100] However, the lifting of the restrictions came too late to

---

died of fatigue in the Somali desert while trying to escape. Douglas James Jardine, *The Mad Mullah of Somaliland* (London: H. Jenkins, 1923), 247.

[96] Harold G. Marcus, *A History of Ethiopia*, 2nd edn. (Berkley/Los Angeles/London: University of California Press, 2002), 115.

[97] Bahru Zewde, *A History of Modern Ethiopia 1855–1991*, 2nd edn. (Oxford: James Currey, 2001), 128–129.

[98] De Coppet to Briand, February 18, 1917, FM 8AFFECO/27. ANOM.

[99] Le Ministre des Affaires Etrangéres to the Ministre des Colonies, March 20, 1918, FM1AFFPOL/122. ANOM.

[100] Consulat de France à Dirré-Daoua. Rapport Commercial Annee 1920, June 4, 1921, FM1AFFPOL/186. ANOM.

meaningfully contribute to the war effort as it was followed shortly thereafter by the Armistice in Europe.

With Ethiopia unable to contribute to the wartime grain economy,
Sudan was left as the only local major exporter of grain to Red Sea
markets. The high demand for Sudanese grain put a strain on the Anglo-
Egyptian Sudan's food economy during the war. Previously, Sudan had
exported grain in large quantities only in 1909 and 1910. In those two
years combined, Sudan exported approximately 38,000 tons. By contrast,
in 1915 alone, Sudan exported more than 40,000 tons to Arabia, Eritrea,
and Egypt.[101] Between 1915 and 1918 inclusive, Sudan exported more
than 133,000 tons of grain.[102] The rapid increase in grain exports was
not coordinated with an expansion in grain yields. In fact, locust plagues
during the 1914–1915 cultivation year[103] and an unusually low Nile flood
during the 1915–1916 cultivation year[104] resulted in decreased harvests.
To prevent multiple years of low yields from leading to a widespread food
crisis, British officials started pump irrigation plantations on the Nile and
assumed command of aspects of the transport and sale of grain.[105] Grain
yields rebounded during the 1916–1917 cultivation year and remained
high during the next year.[106] However, even with these measures, the food
economy of Sudan could not support such high export levels. Grain prices
rose sharply in the first half of 1918. British officials assumed that this was
a result of market manipulation by merchants, who they believed were
withholding their supplies in order to maximize prices. To drive down
prices and to inspire merchants to sell their stocks, British officials sold
small quantities of grain at below market prices. Unfortunately this had
little effect[107] because the high price was the result of grain exports.

The end of war did not spell relief from the food crisis in the ARSR.
In the Anglo-Egyptian Sudan grain prices remained high. Wartime grain

[101] Central Economic Board, *Annual Report of the Director, Commercial Intelligence Branch, Central Economic Board, 1915*, No. IX (1915) 24. SAD.

[102] Central Economic Board, *Annual Report of the Director, Commercial Intelligence Branch, Central Economic Board, 1916*, No. X (1916) 6. SAD; Central Economic Board, *Annual Report of the Director, Commercial Intelligence Branch, Central Economic Board, 1918*, No. XII (1918) 8. SAD.

[103] Stack to Wingate, May 24, 1915, SAD195/2/156.

[104] Wingate to Grey, September 24, 1915, SAD196/3/315–316.

[105] Central Economic Board, *Annual Report of the Director, Commercial Intelligence Branch, Central Economic Board, 1916*, No. X (1916) 10. SAD.

[106] Central Economic Board, *Annual Report of the Director, Commercial Intelligence Branch, Central Economic Board, 1918*, No. XII (1918) 6. SAD.

[107] Central Economic Board, *Annual Report of the Director, Commercial Intelligence Branch, Central Economic Board, 1918*, No. XII (1918) 10. SAD.

exports had depleted the grain reserves of Sudanese cultivators. As a result, they could not protect themselves from the negative effects of ecological hazards. A drought during the 1918–1919 cultivation year led to decreased yields and precipitated a widespread famine during which grain prices peaked at nearly eight times their prewar norms. British officials in the Anglo-Egyptian Sudan responded by importing grain and selling it at a loss.[108] The crisis in the Anglo-Egyptian Sudan exacerbated the crisis in Eritrea. The cross-border grain trade shrank and markets on the Eritrean side of the frontier became inadequately stocked. In November 1919, Eritrean officials were forced to implement measures mandating the sale of grain in the frontier region. Merchants passing through were required to bring all of their grain into the market for sale according to a set schedule at a fixed price. From 8:00 AM to 4:00 PM, merchants had to sell grain in small quantities to indigenous consumers. During this period, merchants were not allowed to refuse this type of sale. From 4:00 PM to 7:00 PM, merchants were allowed to sell their remaining stock to wholesalers, who had permission to transport their cargos to other Eritrean markets. Any grain that arrived in the border market after 4:00 PM could not be sold until the following morning.[109]

The food crisis of the First World War ended without resolving the underlying instability in the food economy of the Red Sea world. Following the armistice, the grain trade with India resumed. Favorable ecological conditions returned to the ARSR in 1920 and local grain yields rebounded. However, recovery was not immediate. By the end of the war, communities in Eritrea had been suffering from nearly four years of food insecurity and famine. Similar conditions had, at specific times and in specific regions, been experienced in the Anglo-Egyptian Sudan, Ethiopia, the Côte Française des Somalis, and British Somaliland. The extreme instability of the grain market and the economic downturn in the ARSR during the war had impoverished many segments of society. Communities throughout the region were pushed further into a cycle of poverty and food insecurity from which they still struggle to escape. Nonetheless, British and French officials saw their management of the regional food economy during the war as for the most part a success. When the Second World War broke out, British and French military planners used the

---

[108] W. Newbold, The Tribal Economics of the Hadendowa [n.d. 1929] CIVSEC64/2/5. NRO.

[109] Commissariato Regionale del Barca. Agordat. Ordina, November 19, 1919, Pacco 859. AEMAE.

measures put in place to regulate the food economy of the Red Sea during the First World War as the model for regional resource management. With the creation of the Middle East Supply Center in 1941, this model became codified and systematized.[110] The suffering of communities of the ARSR during the First World War had been forgotten. In the minds of war planners, it had been replaced with yet another narrative of European imperial officials benevolently managing the affairs of their African subjects.

---

[110] Martin W. Wilmington, *The Middle East Supply Centre* (Albany: State University of New York Press, 1971).

Forest Policy, Wildlife Destruction, and Disease Ecologies

Environmental Consequences of the First World War in Africa

Thaddeus Sunseri

It is understandable that some African men and women born at the turn of the twentieth century, reflecting on early colonial rule, conflated the First World War with the period of colonial conquest and its aftermath, recalling the entire period as a "war era," a time of continuous dispersal and fleeing.[1] After all, many of the crises that Africans suffered during the war – forced military conscription and porterage, population dislocation, survival as refugees or captives, food and livestock requisitioning, invasion of rural areas by violent men, outbreaks of epidemics, epizootics, and transformed disease ecologies – accompanied early colonial rule. Moreover, the war did not end with a revolutionary political transition and break with the past in Africa, as was the case in much of the Middle East, Europe, and Asia. Although Germany lost its four African colonies, the League of Nations Mandate governments that followed continued many German policies, sometimes with only slight modifications. Perhaps for this reason, the war has often been a footnote in African colonial history, a temporal transition from early unbridled exploitation to a "high noon of colonial rule" that extended and intensified bureaucracies of development and rule.[2]

---

[1] James L. Giblin, *A History of the Excluded: Making Family a Refuge from State in Twentieth Century Tanzania* (Oxford: James Currey, 2005), 34–39; Jamie Monson, Relocating Maji Maji: The Politics of Alliance and Authority in the Southern Highlands of Tanzania, 1870–1918. *Journal of African History* 39(1) (1998), 95–120, here 96; author interview with Shumali Abedi Tandika and Abdul Mohamed, Kilosa, Tanzania, June 11, 1990.

[2] Philip Curtin, Steven Feierman, Leonard Thompson, and Jan Vansina, *African History* (New York: Longman, 1985), 478.

An environmental perspective forces a deeper examination, and demonstrates that the war sparked many fundamental transformations. Although African populations grew after the war, the mortality of hundreds of thousands during the conflict in a short time span transformed peoples' relationship to disease environments, with long-term consequences, some of which continue to afflict the continent and the world 100 years later. Colonial approaches to human and livestock disease outbreaks during and after the war also shaped interwar medical and veterinary policy, sometimes with severe repercussions, as with the case of sleeping sickness, HIV, and Rinderpest. Furthermore, the war changed the European powers' perceptions of African resources and their value, guiding postwar conservation, resource exploitation, and development agendas.[3] In some parts of the continent, African methods of survival during the war ushered in long-term changes in agricultural practice and use of noncultivated lands.

Although early stages of the war were fought in all of Germany's African colonies (Togo, Cameroon, Southwest Africa, and German East Africa), only in the last did the war continue until the Armistice in November 1918, and there the consequences were most dire. Yet the colonial powers mobilized all of their African colonies to fight the war, even those far from battlegrounds. The colonial governments expected Africans throughout the continent to provide military labor, especially as porters, while forced recruitment severely disrupted local economies and ecologies. Moreover, some 170,000 Africans from French territories fought in Europe, and some returned as carriers of Spanish influenza that affected the continent dramatically.[4] The impact of the war was multifaceted and complex, and no brief survey can do justice to the many ways in which environment intersected with war throughout the continent. This chapter focuses on forest policy, perceptions of resource potential, wildlife management, and human and animal disease ecologies in tropical sub-Saharan Africa.

---

[3] This is also a claim made for the Second World War in Africa. See Judith A. Byfield, Producing for the War. In Judith A. Byfield, Carolyn A. Brown, Timothy Parsons, and Ahmad Alawad Sikainga, eds., *Africa and World War II* (Cambridge: Cambridge University Press, 2015), 24–42.

[4] Myron Echenberg, *Colonial Conscripts: The Tirailleurs Sénégalais in French West Africa, 1857–1960* (Portsmouth: Heinemann, 1991), 46; Joe Lunn, *Memoirs of the Maelstrom: A Senegalese Oral History of the First World War* (Portsmouth, NH: Heinemann, 1999).

AFRICAN FORESTS AND EVOLVING FOREST USE

At the time of the First World War, hardwoods made up 65% of world forests, growing overwhelmingly in the tropics, with some remnants in North America and Eastern Europe.[5] By then the colonial powers had established frameworks of scientific forestry in the metropole and to limited degrees in their colonies, which aimed to demarcate state or private forest reserves to exploit marketable tree species sustainably, and in some cases to develop tree plantations of fast-growing, often exotic softwood species.[6] But African tropical forests posed problems for scientific forestry. The most marketable hardwood species grew in regions of low population density, with poor infrastructure and few transport links, far from world timber markets. Tropical forests had great species diversity; their mostly deciduous trees grew slowly and were dispersed throughout vast landscapes. In contrast, 90% of the world's softwoods – conifers such as pines, spruce, and firs – grew in the northern hemisphere stretching from North America to Eurasia, and accounted for 80 to 90% of commercial wood use.[7] Softwoods were light, fast growing, easy to work or break down into paper pulp, cheap to transport, and suitable for a variety of uses, such as construction timber, mine shoring, railway ties, ship building, furniture, pulpwood, and paper. Before the First World War, the core industrial nations were also the main softwood producers, relegating the world's hardwood forests to the global economic periphery, where local communities used them nonetheless for multiple subsistence purposes. The main exceptions were the mahogany- and teak-like trees of West Africa (*Khaya spp.* and *iroko – Milicia excelsa*), which had had a modest market in Europe since the late nineteenth century.[8] Because

---

[5] Robert S. Troup, *Colonial Forest Administration* (Oxford: Oxford University Press, 1940), 13–14.

[6] Joachim Radkau, *Nature and Power: A Global History of the Environment* (Cambridge: Cambridge University Press, 2008), 212–221; Ravi Rajan, *Modernizing Nature: Forestry and Imperial Eco-Development 1800–1950* (Oxford: Clarendon Press, 2006), 35–47; James Scott, *Seeing Like a State: How Certain Schemes to Improve the Human Condition Have Failed* (New Haven, CT: Yale University Press, 1998).

[7] Peter Clutterbuck, Forestry and the Empire. *Empire Forestry Journal* 6(1) (1927), 184–192; Walter Hedler, *Deutschlands Forst- und Nutzholzwirtschaft in und nach dem Weltkriege* (Stuttgart: Franck'sche Verlagshandlung, 1921), 20. The terms "softwood" and "hardwood" refer "less to the degree of hardness than to the origin of the timber and the use to which it is put." Troup, *Colonial Forest Administration*, 13–14.

[8] Hugh Watson, Statistics of Imports of Timber to the United Kingdom. *Empire Forestry Journal* 14(1) (1935), 60–63; Raymond E. Dumett, Tropical Forests and West African Enterprise: The Early History of the Ghana Timber Trade. *African Economic History* 29 (2001), 79–116.

Germany was the main buyer of West African timber, the war severed this market, and led to a depression in production for the duration of the war.[9]

Several developments on the eve of the war transformed European attitudes to tropical forest exploitation. Industrial wood consumers noted a decline in available Eastern European and American supplies of hardwoods such as oak, ash, beech, and mahogany, which were used for furniture, industrial construction, railway carriages and ties, and wood veneers. At about that time, hardwoods were found to have high value for their chemical properties, enabling the extraction of cellulose and wood sugar to produce alcohol, fodder, pulp, explosives, synthetic rubber, rayon, and naval stores.[10] The war in Europe created an extraordinary demand for and scarcity of timber and wood fuel by 1916. Germany overexploited its own softwood plantation forests during the war, and many international observers feared a postwar softwood timber shortage. Germans concluded that the shortage of timber and wood-derived raw materials contributed substantially to their defeat.[11]

British foresters also saw the war as a turning point in colonial forest policy. Overexploitation of British forests during the war led policy makers to agree that an impending world timber famine would hurt Britain in particular, as a country with relatively few forests after generations of industrial exploitation and a poor forestry infrastructure. Overseas sources of timber had accounted for 95% of Britain's wartime needs at a time of high timber prices.[12] This dependency continued after the war. In 1926 Britain imported £56,000,000 of timber, only one-fifth of which came from the British Empire.[13] To address ongoing shortages, the government created a Forestry Commission to focus on reforesting Britain and ensuring ongoing timber supplies from overseas.[14] The first

---

[9] Dumett, Tropical Forests and West African Enterprise, 108. West African hardwood timber (mainly "mahogany") tonnage to Europe from 1831 to 1913 is catalogued in Bundesarchiv-Berlin (BAB)/R1001/7668, J. F. Müller to Solf, "Bezug afrikanischer Hölzer," November 14, 1917, 15.

[10] Egon Glesinger, The Coming Age of Wood (New York: Simon & Schuster, 1949).

[11] BAB/R1001/7676, Das Problem der Holzversorgung, eine Lebensfrage deutscher Zukunft, November 1917; Hedler, Deutschlands Forst- und Nutzholzwirtschaft in und nach dem Weltkriege, 3; Heinrich Rubner, Deutsche Forstgeschichte 1933–1945: Forstwirtschaft, Jagd und Umwelt im NS-Staat (St. Katharinen: Scripta Mercaturae Verlag, 1985), 24.

[12] Troup, Colonial Forest Administration, 5; A Scheme to Provide Home-Grown Timber. International Review of Agricultural Economics 9(4) (1918), 348–350.

[13] Clutterbuck, Forestry and the Empire.

[14] John Sheail, An Environmental History of Twentieth-Century Britain (New York: Palgrave, 2002), 83.

Empire Forestry Conference in 1920 aimed to coordinate forest management through an Imperial Forestry Institute at Oxford, which ensured that Britain would have adequate timber supplies in the event of another national emergency.[15] Imperial forest policy thus prioritized metropolitan needs.

Although Empire Forestry Policy mandated that forest departments be set up in individual colonies, the British, like the Germans before them, were overwhelmingly dependent on softwoods for metropolitan timber needs. Because hardwoods dominated African forests, African timber had little external demand. An exception was a semi-hardwood of equatorial Africa called *okoumé*, which had developed a prewar market to Europe, especially to Germany, for plywood, cigar boxes, and aircraft construction.[16] During the war, the Hamburg market was cut off.[17] Following the war, a pent-up demand led French colonial officials and foresters to organize a permit and concession system in Gabonese forests to encourage *okoumé* exploitation. From 1920 to 1930 *okoumé* acted as a bellwether timber for Gabonese forest exploitation, with exports increasing from 47,000 to 400,000 tons. Proximity to waterways was essential to float the logs to collection points, and exploitable trees often grew in dispersed locales. Labor shortages inhibited the development of the industry, particularly in light of 10% population mortality in some regions owing to the 1918–1919 influenza pandemic. Yet timbering was Gabon's major industry in the interwar years owing to "king okoumé." Historians of this timber argue that the industry motivated no "permanent infrastructure or sustained economic development," but it was important for directing international exploitation and eventual conservation to Central African rainforests.[18] Most importantly, the valuing of Central African timbers, intensified by wartime demand, initiated a discourse that Africans used their forests destructively and unsustainably.

---

[15] Rajan, *Modernizing Nature*, 125–129.

[16] Christopher Gray and François Ngolet, Lambaréné, *Okoumé* and the Transformation of Labor along the Middle Ogoué (Gabon), 1870–1945. *Journal of African History* 40 (1999), 87–107, here 96; Jeremy Rich, Forging Permits and Failing Hopes: African Participation in the Gabonese Timber Industry, ca. 1920–1940. *African Economic History* 33 (2005), 149–173, here 152–154. On German interest in *Okoumé* see (BAB)/R1001/7668, J. F. Müller, "Bemerkungen zu dem Entwurf von Herrn Emil Zimmermann, Berlin, betreffend Errichtung einer deutsch-afrikanischen Urwald-Verwertungs-Gesellschaft," January 1918 [262264]. Müller described *okoumé* as a mid-weight timber.

[17] BAB/R1001/7668, J. F. Müller to Solf, "Bezug afrikanischer Hölzer," November 14, 1917, 24.

[18] Gray and Ngolet, Lambaréné, *Okoumé* and the Transformation of Labor, 100.

The war sparked a more invigorated commitment to forest conservation and exploitation in some parts of Africa, as von Hellermann argues for Nigeria. Although British officials laid out forest reserves in Nigeria and Gold Coast before the war, they only enacted a comprehensive Forest Ordinance for all of Nigeria in 1916, laying "the foundations of Nigerian forestry for many years to come."[19] The ordinance called for the reservation of 25% of Nigerian land as forest reserves, protecting river watersheds and "listed" tree species from African use. As in other parts of Africa, this meant circumscribing African shifting agriculture, which was premised on regular field expansion and forest clearing. Protected trees were those deemed "economic" – mahogany- and teak-like species with which colonial foresters were most familiar. By empowering timber-trading firms, the ordinance aimed to supply both Nigerian and metropolitan timber needs for the foreseeable future, eroding the preservationist side of colonial forestry. British officials extended Nigerian forest rules into neighboring Cameroon as they overran German forces during the war.[20]

The First World War marked a massive transfer of African territory from German to British, French, Belgian, and South African control as League of Nations mandates. Did this transfer make a difference in terms of African environmental history? Many scholars of colonial rule in Africa have shown that the war unleashed a development agenda of a much higher magnitude than before, with substantial consequences for subsequent land and forest use.[21] Like their British counterparts, the assumption of French rule over former German colonies extended German forest policies. In the case of southern Cameroon, which in 1911 had been transferred to Germany and then taken back during the war, Giles-Vernick describes a period of "rapacious extraction" following the war, which concentrated on road and railway construction to enable forest exploitation for rubber and timber.[22]

---

[19] Pauline von Hellermann, *Things Fall Apart? The Political Ecology of Forest Governance in Southern Nigeria* (New York: Berghahn, 2013), 52.

[20] Tobias J. Lanz, The Origins, Development and Legacy of Scientific Forestry in Cameroon. *Environment and History* 6 (2009), 99–120, here 109.

[21] Richard Roberts, *Two Worlds of Cotton: Colonialism and the Regional Economy in the French Soudan, 1800–1946* (Stanford, CA: Stanford University Press, 1996), 110; Laurence Becker, Seeing Green in Mali's Woods: Colonial Legacy, Forest Use, and Local Control. *Annals of the Association of American Geographers* 91(3) (2001), 504–526, here 509–510; Heather Hoag, *Developing the Rivers of East and West Africa* (London: Bloomsbury, 2013), 112.

[22] Tamara Giles-Vernick, *Cutting the Vines of the Past: Environmental Histories of the Central African Rain Forest* (Charlottesville: University Press of Virginia, 2002), 30.

Germans had also aimed to develop the Cameroon rainforests, but along more industrial lines.[23] On the eve of the war, a German forester had proposed to the kaiser and colonial officials a comprehensive rainforest development scheme geared to multiple wood uses, seeing trees as more than timber, charcoal, or rubber latex, but fundamental resources for fodder, alcohol, wood sugar, cellulose, even textiles, which could substitute for a variety of metropolitan raw materials. Wartime raw material shortages spurred this line of German forestry thinking. Bereft of a colonial empire following the war, and of Eastern European hardwood forests they once controlled, German foresters advanced a template of tropical forest exploitation that targeted Central African rain forests in particular, including those of the Spanish enclave of Rio Muni, as a reserve for wood-based raw materials.[24] Promoting German scientific forestry as necessary for the global good, in part to justify the return of colonies to Germany, the German forestry establishment founded interwar international silviculture organizations, especially the International Forestry Center (IFS) based in Berlin in 1936.[25] The IFS was the model for the United Nations Food and Agricultural Organization's Forest Division at the end of the Second World War, and the template for international tropical forest policy in the first 20 years of the Cold War. Unable to apply scientific forestry to their own colonial empire following the First World War, Germans instead spearheaded international forestry.

Whereas West Africa had established some commercial timber links to Europe before the war, this was not so much the case in East Africa. By 1914 Germans had created a basic infrastructure of scientific forestry in German East Africa, reserving some 231 forests for managed exploitation to replace timber imports.[26] Based on German definitions of forestry, which excluded woodlands, these reserves nevertheless made up just more than 1% of the landscape, including all of the montane rain forests, coastal mangroves, and some dry savanna forests. German forest policy

---

[23] Thaddeus Sunseri, Exploiting the *Urwald*: German Post-Colonial Forestry in Poland and Central Africa, 1900–1960. *Past and Present* 214 (2012), 305–342.

[24] BAB/R1001/7668, "Erster Entwurf der Einrichtung einer mittelafrikanischen Urwaldausnutzung," February 2, 1918.

[25] Egon Glesinger, *Nazis in the Woodpile: Hitler's Plot for Essential Raw Materials* (Indianapolis, IN: Bobbs-Merrill, 1942), 194; Franz Heske, Ziele und Wege der tropischen Waldwirtschaft. *Zeitschrift für Weltforstwirtschaft* 5(3) (1937), 133–146.

[26] Thaddeus Sunseri, *Wielding the Ax: Scientific Forestry and Social Conflict in Tanzania, c. 1820–2000* (Athens: Ohio University Press, 2009), chapter 4; Hans Schabel, Tanganyika Forestry under German Colonial Administration, 1891–1919. *Forest and Conservation History* 34(3) (1990), 130–141.

forced Africans out of these forests, using a system of permits to circum-scribe exploitation of products like wild rubber, copal, beeswax, and timber.

During the war, German forestry collapsed and Africans returned to the forests. This was especially palpable in southern Tanzania after 1916, which was the main scene of wartime battlefield operations.[27] Belgian, British, Portuguese, and South African forces invaded the colony from all sides by then in what became an unexpectedly long campaign. The forests of the Tanzanian coastal hinterland were wartime battlegrounds, havens from conflict, and resources to fight the war. The German strategy of tying down British forces by eluding capture meant in large part occupying inaccessible parts of the landscape in order to fight a guerilla war. The dense forested hills of Rufiji and Kilwa districts were ideal for this. By December 1916, the main body of German forces had encamped around the district station of Kibata, and then moved through the forests toward the Rufiji River to avoid British encirclement.[28] With tens of thousands of British and German troops occupying the region, food was in short supply, particularly after prolonged rains exacerbated Rufiji flooding between January and May 1917. Combatants scoured the region for food, including crops in the field as well as game meat, forcing villagers to use the forests for famine food – roots, wild fruits, mushrooms – and for medicine. Bubonic plague hit the region at the outset of the war, perhaps a recrudescence of rat infestations that had burgeoned before the war, and meningitis swept through in 1916.[29] The huge occupying forces and their depredations, including forced conscription of porters and bombard-ment of villages along battle fronts, drove villagers away from the main roadways and river valleys into the recesses of the landscape – forests, bush, reeds, and caves – to survive as best as they could for the duration of the war.[30]

Wartime use of the Tanganyikan forests left many of them, especially those near towns and railway centers, in a sorry state. Around Dar es

---

[27] Hew Strachan, *The First World War in Africa* (Oxford: Oxford University Press, 2004), chapter 6.

[28] Charles Miller, *Battle for the Bundu: The First World War in East Africa* (New York: Macmillan, 1974), chapter 17; Angus Buchanan, *Three Years of War in East Africa* (New York: Negro Universities Press, 1969).

[29] BAB/R1001/5935, Massregeln gegen die Cholera, Pest und andere Epidemien; Tanganyika District Books, Rufiji District Book, W. J. McMillan Report (n.d. – 1920s).

[30] Tanzania National Archives (TNA), AB58, Kilwa Annual Report 1924, Bell to Chief Secretary, January 31, 1925.

Salaam, Germans exploited the Sachsenwald and Pugu forest reserves and nearby mangrove creeks for town defenses and to fuel steamships. All along the line of the Central Railway wood was cut to rebuild trestles, to supply railway ties, and to fuel locomotives.[31] Tens of thousands of soldiers and porters needed temporary housing and cooking fuel that came from timber and firewood extracted from the forests. British and German combatants used forest and woodland timber for trenches and charcoal, and cut down swaths of forest to make way for motorized transport.[32]

At war's end, as Britain assumed control over what would became Tanganyika, British colonial forestry began with a German template of forest management on maps and in files, but not on the ground. British officials struggled to draw Africans out of forest refuges. While German East Africa had been central to the German colonial empire, Tanganyika was a periphery of the British Empire, and therefore did not witness a similar postwar development agenda as in other colonies on the continent. Wartime breakdown of forest controls led the British to degazette some reserves that were considered unviable for managed forestry. Metropolitan prioritization of softwoods meant that there was no immediate market for Tanganyikan hardwoods, making revenues insufficient for managed forestry. British foresters revived German-era exploitation of the rare concentrated stands of conifers on the slopes of Mts. Meru and Kilimanjaro and the Usambaras in the north.[33] These included African cedar (*Juniperus procera*) and *Podocarpus* that were "similar to the common European softwood."[34]

Administering the territory on a shoestring budget, with its status as a League of Nations mandate making British sovereignty insecure, the British were more inclined than their German predecessors to allow African and commercial exploitation of forests for their mangroves, dye-bark, copal, wild rubber, and beeswax, all of which had some international demand. British forestry focused on developing tree plantations of fast-growing exotics like eucalyptus and ironwood (*Cassia siamea*) near towns for fuel and building poles, and maintaining existing German forest

[31] TNA G8/882, Altmann to D. O. Dar es Salaam, September 6, 1915; Dietz to Schnee, November 15, 1915.

[32] Buchanan, *Three Years of War in East Africa*, 150, 162.

[33] Christopher Conte, *Highland Sanctuary: Environmental History in Tanzania's Usambara Mountains* (Athens: Ohio University Press, 2004), 74.

[34] Tanganyika Forest Division, *Tanganyika's Timber Resources* (Dar es Salaam: Ministry of Lands, Forests, and Wildlife, n.d. [1962]), 1–2.

reserves. Not until the aftermath of the Second World War would British forestry in Tanganyika undergo a massive expansion.

CATTLE DISEASE, LANDSCAPE CHANGE, AND WILDLIFE RESURGENCE

As a mobile food source, livestock – particularly cattle – was a major objective of competing combat forces in Africa during the First World War. Since the advent of pastoralism in northern Africa some 10,000 years ago, livestock economies evolved alongside human populations and African disease environments that were dynamic and fluctuating.[35] Agropastoralists and primary pastoralists alike learned to avoid disease landscapes that threatened livestock, especially the broad swaths of rain forest and *miombo* savanna woodlands that were the habitat of tsetse fly vectors of *nagana* bovine sleeping sickness. Yet this avoidance was disrupted historically by cataclysmic events such as unusual drought or rainfall, epidemics and epizootics, and prolonged warfare. Such cataclysms, including the First World War, could transform livestock disease environments, with long-term consequences.

A starting point is to consider the East African cattle environment on the eve of the war. German and British colonial conquest in the 1880s–1890s was accompanied by a series of human and animal diseases largely introduced and exacerbated by conquest itself. Most dramatic was the Rinderpest epizootic, a virus of cattle and wild ungulates known for hundreds of years in Eurasia, which invading Italian forces introduced into sub-Saharan Africa by way of the Red Sea in about 1888. Sweeping throughout pastoral zones of eastern, western, and southern Africa in the next decade, Rinderpest killed upward of 90% of African cattle. Although veterinary policing and vaccination breakthroughs in southern Africa eliminated the virus from that region shortly after the turn of the twentieth century, Rinderpest became enzootic in East Africa. The loss of so many cattle in such a short time, and a recovery that took two decades, allowed tsetse habitats to expand, circumscribing cattle environments in years to come.

Colonial veterinary policies that targeted disease control paralleled development aspirations that aimed to make Africa into a ranching frontier by upgrading cattle and improving pastures. This was in response to

---

[35] Katherine Homewood, *Ecology of African Pastoralist Societies* (Oxford: James Currey, 2008), 10–20.

a "mid-Victorian meat famine" in Western Europe, characterized by a growing demand for protein in the wake of urbanization and industrialization, coupled with the environmental limits of beef productivity.[36] A key cause of meat shortage was the validation of contagionist theories of animal disease transfers from the 1860s, which circumscribed the intra-European trade in cattle and other livestock, especially from the traditional cattle frontier of Eastern Europe.[37] By the 1890s, the fear of diseased cattle and tainted meat as a public health concern also curtailed live cattle and meat imports from overseas, notably from the Americas, where Texas fever (Babesia) and foot-and-mouth disease raged.[38] Rinderpest in Africa, alongside other cattle diseases like lungsickness, East Coast Fever, and anthrax, also deterred the trade in cattle or cattle products from the continent. Making Africa into a beef frontier for Europe therefore meant controlling livestock diseases.

At the outset of colonial rule in the late 1880s, bacteriology was at an early stage, and myriad African cattle diseases, Rinderpest among them, were not well known or easily identified. By the eve of the First World War this had changed dramatically, as colonial rulers assembled veterinary infrastructures in the colonies. Although in German East Africa in 1906 there were only two government veterinarians, by 1914, besides the chief veterinarian, there were three government veterinary bacteriologists in each of the ten cattle districts.[39] Veterinary positions were approved for

---

[36] Richard Perren, *Taste, Trade, and Technology: The Development of the International Meat Industry since 1840* (Aldershot: Ashgate, 2005), 8.

[37] Ian Blanchard, The Continental European Cattle Trades, 1400–1600. *Economic History Review* 39(3) (1986), 427–460; Karl Appuhn, Ecologies of Beef: Eighteenth-Century Epizootics and the Environmental History of Early Modern Europe. *Environmental History* 15 (2010), 268–287; Hans-Jürgen Teuteberg, Variations in Meat Consumption in Germany. *Ethnologia Scandinavica* (1971), 131–141.

[38] Uwe Spiekermann, Dangerous Meat? German-American Quarrels over Pork and Beef, 1870–1900. *Bulletin of the German Historical Institute* 46 (2010), 93–109; Keir Waddington, "Unfit for Human Consumption": Tuberculosis and the Problem of Infected Meat in Late Victorian Britain. *Bulletin of the History of Medicine* 77(3) (2003), 636–661; John Fisher, To Kill or not to Kill: The Eradication of Contagious Bovine Pleuro-Pneumonia in Western Europe. *Medical History* 47(3) (2003), 314–331; J. R. Fisher, The Economic Effects of Cattle Disease in Britain and Its Containment, 1850–1900. *Agricultural History* 54(2) (1980), 278–294; Michael Worboys, *Spreading Germs: Disease Theories and Medical Practice in Britain, 1865–1900* (Cambridge: Cambridge University Press, 2000), 43–72; Dorothee Brantz, Animal Bodies, Human Health, and the Reform of Slaughterhouses in Nineteenth-Century Berlin. In Paula Young Lee, ed., *Meat, Modernity, and the Rise of the Slaughterhouse* (Durham: University of New Hampshire Press, 2008), 71–85.

[39] BAB/R1001/6071/1, "Organisation des Veterinärwesens," Ostertag report, 1914, 177–180.

the "tsetse" districts of the southeast, and along the border with Northern Rhodesia, and five additional veterinarians were employed to fight Rinderpest and establish serum research stations at Mpwapwa and Engare nanjuki and to produce breeding stock on selected cattle farms.[40]

This infrastructure was motivated in large part by the return of Rinderpest to German East Africa in 1911–1912, arriving with trade stock from British East Africa.[41] A combination of border control, quarantine, vaccination, extermination of wildlife suspected of carrying the virus, and mandatory livestock transport routes succeeded in keeping cattle mortality between 30 and 70%.[42] In 1914 German officials acknowledged that Rinderpest was widespread in East Africa, potentially harbored in 15 wildlife reserves established in the colony by then; yet they believed the virus to be under control, confined north of the Central Railway.

This veterinary infrastructure broke down during the First World War, when Rinderpest resurged throughout German East Africa owing to wartime movements.[43] Combatants requisitioned cattle from infected regions and trekked them to clean regions with impunity. In cattle-rich Urundi, African chiefs drove off their stock for fear of military requisitioning, undermining prescribed trade routes.[44] Until the end of 1916 in much of the colony, German officials enforced local quarantines where Rinderpest was detected, but thereafter the "guerilla" phase of the war prevented such controls. Besides Rinderpest, unregulated cattle movements spread tick vectors of East Coast Fever and tsetse carriers of bovine sleeping sickness. It is likely that foot-and-mouth disease arrived in East Africa for the first time with South African military livestock, with long-term consequences for the ability of the region to export cattle to the wider world.[45]

[40] Daniel Gilfoyle, Veterinary Research and the African Rinderpest Epizootic: The Cape Colony, 1896–1898. *Journal of Southern African Studies* 29(1) (2003), 133–153.

[41] Robert Ostertag, Über Rinderpest. Ein Beitrag zum Stande und zur Bekämpfung der Tierseuchen in Deutsch-Ostafrika. *Zeitschrift für Infektionskrankheiten, parasitäre Krankheiten und Hygiene der Haustiere* 18 (1916), 1–48.

[42] Bernhard Gissibl, *The Nature of German Imperialism: Conservation and the Politics of Wildlife in Colonial East Africa* (New York: Berghahn, 2016), 178–182; BAB/R1001/6071/1, Reiseberichte von Geheimer Rat Professor von Ostertag (1914), 1–8.

[43] Amtliche Bekanntmachungen. *Deutsch Ostafrikanische Zeitung* 18(8) (January 28, 1916), 4.

[44] BAB/R1003/1165/105 Lager am Niamagana to Usumbura station, October 15, 1915.

[45] F. M. Kivaria, Foot and Mouth Disease in Tanzania: An Overview of Its National Status. *Veterinary Quarterly* 25(2) (2003), 72–78.

Although Rinderpest broke out in many localities, British colonial veterinarians occupying German East Africa focused on guarding the borders with Kenya, Northern Rhodesia and Nyasaland – colonies with substantial numbers of settler cattle.[46] During the war Rinderpest breached the Central Railway "barrier" and infected Langenburg region south of Lake Tanganyika.[47] This breach inaugurated a decades-long fear in British Central Africa and South Africa that Rinderpest would re-infect settler and African cattle that had been cleaned of Rinderpest since about 1900. During the war, the southern African governments financed a Rinderpest Commission that focused on immunizing cattle on the border between Lakes Nyasa and Tanganyika. Although African cattle owners requested veterinary assistance, British policy was to abandon Tanganyika to protect the settler south. As a result, during the war Rinderpest raged "with the utmost virulence uncontrolled" in every sub-district of German East Africa.[48] In 1914 there were about 4 million cattle in German East Africa; the war reduced the herd by 25–30% by 1918.[49]

Studies of ecological change in Africa point to the First World War as a watershed.[50] This was clear in East Africa owing to resurgent Rinderpest, coupled with wartime requisitioning of cattle and human mortality and dispersion, all of which exacerbated tsetse bush encroachment. In addition, African resistance to forced porterage and cattle requisitions led people into the interstices of the landscape, including tsetse lands that they would otherwise avoid. In such locales people and animals were exposed to sleeping sickness and ticks that increased incidences of East Coast Fever and other diseases. Tsetse spread along military routes, and cattle mortality allowed tsetse-infested landscapes to expand.[51] The succession of epidemics, epizootics, and famine provoked by the war acted

---

[46] British National Archives (BNA) CO 691/96/15, F. J. McCall, 140–141.

[47] BNA CO 691/96/15, H. L. Duff, "Rinderpest," New Langenburg, February 10, 1918, 142–146.

[48] TNA Secretariat 11571, vol. 1, Director of Veterinary Services, January 6, 1928, "Rinderpest."

[49] BNA CO 691/96/15, Byatt, Administrator's Office, Wilhelmstal to Secretary of State for the Colonies, May 7, 1918, 131–136.

[50] John Ford, *The Role of the Trypanosomiases in African Ecology: A Study of the Tsetse Fly Problem* (Oxford: Clarendon Press, 1971); Helge Kjekshus, *Ecology Control and Economic Development in East African History: The Case of Tanganyika, 1850–1950* (Berkeley: University of California, 1977), 164–165; Richard Waller, Tsetse Fly in Western Narok. *Journal of African History* 31 (1990), 81–101; Leroy Vail, Ecology and History: The Example of Eastern Zambia. *Journal of Southern African Studies* 3(2) (1977), 129–155.

[51] Ford, *The Role of the Trypanosomiases in African Ecology*, 153–157, 169.

as a kind of "biological warfare" with devastating consequences.[52] Although some colonial observers argued that tsetse advances emptied landscapes, allowing for wiser land use elsewhere following the war, others concluded that fly advances forced livestock overcrowding that exacerbated soil erosion and agricultural decline.[53]

Many of these factors were evident in the Great Lakes region following the war. In 1919 Rinderpest erupted in Ankole (Uganda), dropping cattle numbers from 300,000 to 80,000 and killing wildlife in large numbers.[54] By 1920 the virus entered neighboring cattle-rich Rwanda, causing 60% cattle mortality and sparking local resistance to flawed veterinary inoculation campaigns.[55] In Ankole, the loss of regular livestock and wildlife prey of lions led to years of attacks on the human population, depopulating some villages as people were forced to move, leading in turn to further bush and tsetse encroachment. Although cattle mortality and the depletion of favored tsetse hosts like warthogs temporarily halted sleeping sickness, when wildlife recovered, tsetse and sleeping sickness also resurged.[56] Abandoned villages and a cultivated landscape of banana plantations were replaced with acacia woodlands dominated by wildlife. The First World War thus capped long-term trends that "extinguished the country of Nkore."[57]

The wildlife threat was further exacerbated by the wartime breakdown of game reserves. By 1914 some 15 wildlife reserves had been demarcated in German East Africa, alongside a battery of laws that regulated, and generally curtailed, African hunting and access to firearms.[58] By providing safe havens, these measures often increased the wildlife threat against peasant farms and white settler estates. Nevertheless, in general colonial policy aimed at separating the cultivated from the "wild" landscape. Peasants and settlers could hunt wild animals designated as vermin, such as baboons and feral pigs, if they encroached on farmlands, and German officials sometimes employed scouts to drive protected animals like elephants from cultivated lands. In one instance they even opened a wildlife reserve for elephant eradication when attacks on farms outside the reserve

[52] Ibid., 194.
[53] Ibid., 198; Department of Veterinary Science and Animal Husbandry, *A Memorandum on the Economics of the Cattle Industry in Tanganyika* (Dar es Salaam: Government Printer, 1934), 8.
[54] Ford, *The Role of the Trypanosomiases in African Ecology*, 154–155.
[55] Alison Liebhafsky des Forges, *Defeat Is the Only Bad News: Rwanda under Musinga, 1896–1931* (Madison: University of Wisconsin Press, 2011), 171–172.
[56] Ford, *The Role of the Trypanosomiases in African Ecology*, 157.   [57] Ibid., 158.
[58] TNA G8/910, Handakten Referat 8, Wildreservate, Band 1, 1914; Juhani Koponen, *Development for Exploitation* (Hamburg: Lit Verlag, 1995), 538–541.

escalated.[59] In 1911, Governor Rechenberg initiated massive wildlife eradication along the northern border with British East Africa in light of resurgent Rinderpest that threatened the domestic cattle economy, eliciting strong opposition from a nascent German conservationist lobby.[60]

The First World War upset any semblance of separation between the cultivated and uncultivated landscapes, and as a result the postwar years began with a greatly worsened threat of wildlife destruction. Combatants and Africans refugees entered protected lands – wildlife and forest reserves – with impunity during the war. The Mohoro Wildlife Reserve on the upper Rufiji River, demarcated in 1896, and the kernel of the eventual Selous Game Reserve, was a major arena of fighting during the war. British forces, largely Nigerians, occupied the north bank of the Rufiji by 1916, and others invaded westward from Kilwa town on the coast into the Kilwa Wildlife Reserve in 1917, hemming in German forces fighting a guerrilla-style war by then.[61] Belgians using Congolese troops likewise moved through the Mahenge Wildlife Reserve toward the Rufiji from the northwest in 1917. With cattle and food scarce owing to sleeping sickness, military requisitioning, scorched-earth tactics, and the worst flooding of the Rufiji River in memory, military forces on both sides and African refugees alike scoured the landscape for wild roots, fruit, edible plants, and any sort of game meat, including elephants and hippopotami.[62] Toward the end of the war, fighting moved to Nyasaland and Portuguese East Africa, driving elephant herds from those lands into Tanganyika to become a postwar threat.[63] Wild animals with little habit of avoiding peasant farms owing to wartime disruption emerged as a major problem. This was in part because Africans lacked adequate weapons to hunt or to protect their fields, a legacy of German firearms controls. After the war, for example, the Kilwa district officer believed that only five muskets existed in the region by then, compared to thousands at the outset of German rule. Some reports stated that no Africans had firearms in the district by the 1920s.[64] Although the

---

[59] Gissibl, *The Nature of German Imperialism*, 183.

[60] BAB/R1001/7778, Schilling, Bericht über die Hauptversammlung der Deutschen Kolonialgesellschaft, June 9–10, 1911, 26; Koponen, *Development for Exploitation*, 540; Gissibl, *The Nature of German Imperialism*, 184.

[61] Strachan, *The First World War in Africa*, 170–173; M. Taute, A German Account of the Medical Side of the War in East Africa, 1914–1918. *Tanganyika Notes and Records (TNR)* 8 (1939), 1–20.

[62] Taute, A German Account of the Medical Side of the War in East Africa.

[63] TNA AB.1132, Game Warden to Chief Secretary, August 6, 1923.

[64] TNA AB.60, Annual Report 1925, Kibata Sub-District, 49–62.

British relaxed prohibitions on owning muskets, they required firearms licenses and they regulated powder sales.[65] The 1920s proliferation of baboons in Kilwa district was attributed specifically to the lack of firearms.

With hunting vastly curtailed, elephants emerged as the "arch-enemy of the native gardens" in the interwar period.[66] During the war, combatants shot formerly protected bull elephants (and females and young) for meat and tusks.[67] Nevertheless, British game wardens believed that elephant numbers and raiding habits increased during the war. This was in part because many rural communities, especially in regions of combat, collapsed during the war as householders abandoned cultivated acres and fruit trees and moved deeper into the forests and woodlands for refuge. Elephants learned to raid abandoned fields and orchards with impunity. Elephant numbers in Tanganyika increased as herds migrated from war zones to occupy regions emptied and disrupted by the war. The *Mambo Leo* newspaper reported that famine in the southeastern districts was directly related to the elephant threat. Africans had a saying that "if elephants are killed, food will increase" (*Ndovu wakiuawa chakula kitazidi*).[68] From Tunduru it was reported, "This is the third year that we have been unraveling (*tumefumukiwa*) because of three matters that are the evils of the country, and of these three, two cause one, hunger, and those two are lions and elephants." In 1924, the Kilwa administrative officer wrote that elephants "have become like man-eating lions in that, once having tasted succulent native foodstuffs, they, like the man-eater after once tasting blood, cannot relinquish their new passion until they have been destroyed."[69] He believed that the elephants' desire for peasant crops far surpassed the pre-war experience, and the only way to prevent crop damage was to cull the herds.

WARTIME CONSEQUENCES FOR HUMAN DISEASES

The First World War contributed to the overall African population decline from colonial conquest in the 1880s to about 1920.[70] In zones of fighting,

---

[65] W. A. Rodgers and J. D. Lobo, Elephant Control and Legal Ivory Exploitation: 1920–1976. *Tanganyika Notes and Records (TNR)*, nos. 84 and 85 (1980), 25–54, here 30.

[66] TNA AG.15, Henniker-Gotley to Chief Secretary, January 12, 1924.

[67] Buchanan, *Three Years of War in East Africa*, 152–162.

[68] *Mambo Leo* 4 (1923), 11.

[69] TNA AB.15, Henniker-Gotley to Chief Secretary, January 12, 1924.

[70] Dennis Cordell, Karl Ittman and Gregory Maddox, Counting Subjects: Demography and Empire. In Karl Ittman, Dennis Cordell, and Gregory Maddox, eds., *The Demographics of Empire: The Colonial Order and the Creation of Knowledge* (Athens: Ohio University

particularly East-Central Africa, the war had far-reaching demographic consequences. The high mortality of Indian soldiers and white troops from South Africa led Jan Smuts, who commanded Entente forces in East Africa, to replace them with West and East Africans.[71] The Entente powers also enlisted between 750,000 and 1 million Africans, some from as far away as the Gold Coast, as porters and military laborers for the East Africa campaign, 20% of whom died from disease.[72] An estimated half a million Tanganyikans were conscripted into the war as forced laborers, with high mortality owing to overwork, long marches, and food shortages.[73] People were taken out of ecological zones to which they were adapted, often entering malarial or sleeping sickness environments for the first time under conditions of food shortage and overwork.

Wartime mortality transformed African ecologies. In Tanganyika, population decline and disruption expanded the sleeping sickness zones from about one-third of the landscape in 1913 to two-thirds by 1924.[74] Some 200,000 Africans from Nyasaland served as soldiers or military laborers during the war – more than two-thirds of the colony's adult male population at one time or another – a substantial male absenteeism that crippled agriculture and created food shortages for years to come.[75] In Northern Rhodesia, similar population disruptions ushered in 25 years of "accelerated ecological dislocation" characterized most by wildlife destruction and sleeping sickness outbreaks.[76]

Although a panoply of human diseases hit war zones – among them bubonic plague, dysentery, sleeping sickness, smallpox, and malaria – Spanish flu (a strain of avian influenza) had the most far-reaching repercussions. Arriving with returning African troops who fought in Europe and through regular shipping networks, Spanish flu hit all regions of the continent beginning in August 1918.[77] Influenza reached German East

---

Press, 2010), 1–21, here 8–9; Ralph Austen, *African Economic History* (London: James Currey, 1987), 146.

[71] David Killingray, Repercussions of World War I in the Gold Coast. *Journal of African History* 19(1) (1978), 39–59, here 48; John Iliffe, *A Modern History of Tanganyika* (Cambridge: Cambridge University Press, 1979), 243.

[72] Richard J. Reid, *A History of Modern Africa* (Oxford: Wiley-Blackwell, 2009), 192.

[73] Kjekshus, *Ecology Control and Economic Development in East African History*, 153–154.

[74] Iliffe, *A Modern History of Tanganyika*, 271.

[75] Melvin Page, The War of Thangata: Nyasaland and the East African Campaign, 1914–1918. *Journal of African History* 19(1) (1978), 87–100, here 94–95.

[76] Vail, Ecology and History, 142–143.

[77] Sandra M. Tomkins, Colonial Administration in British Africa during the Influenza Epidemic of 1918–19. *Canadian Journal of African Studies* 28(1) (1994), 60–83, here 68.

Africa in November 1918, adding population loss to existing famine conditions among the centrally located Gogo people, impairing food production and ushering in a multiyear crisis.[78] Because this flu strain killed healthy young adults disproportionately, its effects on production were especially far reaching. Ohadike's analysis of southern Nigeria points to permanent changes in agrarian practice as an outcome.[79] With mortality levels at about 3%, some 250,000 people succumbed out of 9 million in the southern provinces of Nigeria. Shipping came to a standstill, transport was encumbered, food became scarce, and schools and churches were closed. Because the preferred dietary staple of yams demanded more labor than was available, villagers switched to cassava, an American root crop that is much less nutritious, but that requires less labor for weeding, can be left in soil up to four years, and can thrive on old farmlands. Although regarded as an inferior and secondary food, cassava became a permanent part of the regional economy.

In areas that experienced population loss during the war to military and porter recruitment, influenza worked in concert with other wartime diseases, especially dysentery. According to Vansina, in 1918 and 1919 the combination of dysentery and influenza killed 28% of the Kuba population in the Belgian Congo.[80] In Southern Rhodesia, as influenza advanced along railway lines from September 1918, thousands of miners deserted and returned home, in many instances carrying the virus with them.[81] The shock of the pandemic fed prophetic religious movements following the war, which frequently took on an anti-modernist strain that rejected Western medicine.[82] Ellison calculated that in southwestern Tanzania

---

[78] Gregory Maddox, Mtunya: Famine in Central Tanzania, 1917–20. *Journal of African History* 31(2) (1990), 181–197, here 185–187; Taute, A German Account of the Medical Side of the War in East Africa, 20.

[79] Don C. Ohadike, The Influenza Pandemic of 1918–19 and the Spread of Cassava Cultivation on the Lower Niger: A Study in Historical Linkages. *Journal of African History* 22 (1981), 379–391.

[80] Jan Vansina, *Being Colonized: The Kuba Experience in Rural Congo, 1880–1960* (Madison: University of Wisconsin Press, 2010), 148.

[81] Ian Phimister, The "Spanish" Influenza Pandemic of 1918 and Its Impact on the Southern Rhodesian Mining Industry. *Central African Journal of Medicine* 19(7) (1973), 143–148; David Simmons, Religion and Medicine at the Crossroads: A Re-Examination of the Southern Rhodesian Influenza Epidemic of 1918. *Journal of Southern African Studies* 35(1) (2009), 29–44.

[82] Terence Ranger, Plagues of Beasts and Men: Prophetic Responses to Epidemic in Eastern and Southern Africa. In Terence Ranger and Paul Slack, eds., *Epidemics and Ideas: Essays on the Historical Perception of Pestilence* (Cambridge: Cambridge University Press, 1992), 241–268; Karen E. Fields, Charismatic Religion as Popular Protest: The

Spanish flu killed 10% of the population, and, in concert with smallpox, impaired agricultural production, undermined normal religious responses, and even reshaped ethnic identity.[83] Patterson called the 1918 flu pandemic "the single greatest short-term demographic catastrophe in Africa's history," perhaps killing 100,000 people in Tanganyika and Nyasaland, and as many as 2 million Africans altogether.[84] Long-term landscape changes, especially the expansion of tsetse-infested lands, was a direct outcome of this massive mortality. This, in turn, motivated massive colonial interventions in the next decades, including population relocations, bush clearing, shifting production priorities, and use of risky experimental medical therapies.

In the past century, HIV has overtaken Spanish flu as a cause of African mortality. It now seems likely that colonial medical interventions to stanch population loss from disease, coupled with First World War conditions that facilitated cross-species disease transmissions – zoonoses – may have exacerbated conditions that triggered the global HIV pandemic.[85] According to virological research, several strains of HIV emerged in Central-West Africa sometime in the early twentieth century, most likely in the equatorial African rainforests.[86] The most virulent is HIV type 1 group M (HIV-1 M) that began with a Simian Immunodeficiency Virus (SIV) that probably jumped from chimpanzees to humans in southeastern Cameroon between 1908 and 1933.[87] Innovations in blood transfusion techniques opened this decades-old therapy to wartime use, which may have enabled SIVs to mutate into the virulent forms of HIV that spread

---

Ordinary and the Extraordinary in Social Movements. *Theory and Society* 11(3) (1982), 321–361.

[83] James Ellison, "A Fierce Hunger": Tracing Impacts of the 1918–19 Influenza Epidemic in Southwest Tanzania. In Howard Phillips and David Killingray, eds., *The Spanish Influenza Pandemic of 1918–19: New Perspectives* (London: Routledge, 2003), 221–229.

[84] K. David Patterson, The Influenza Epidemic of 1918–19 in the Gold Coast. *Journal of African History* 24(4) (1983), 485–502.

[85] Amit Chitnis, Diana Rawls, and Jim Moore, Origin of HIV type 1 in Colonial French Equatorial Africa. *AIDS Research and Human Retroviruses* 16(1) (2000), 5–8.

[86] Jun Takehisa et al., Origin and Biology of Simian Immunodeficiency Virus in Wild-Living Western Gorillas. *Journal of Virology* 83(4) (2009), 1635–1648; João Dinis de Sousa et al., High GUD Incidence in the Early 20th Century Created a Particularly Permissive Time Window for the Origin and Initial Spread of Epidemic HIV Strains. *PloS One* 5(4) (2010), 1–16.

[87] Dinis de Sousa et al., High GUD Incidence in the Early 20th Century, 1; Tamara Giles-Vernick et al., Social History, Biology, and the Emergence of HIV in Colonial Africa. *Journal of African History* 54(1) (2013), 11–30. Similarly, HIV-1 group O is believed to have crossed from an SIV to humans in equatorial Africa between 1890 and 1920. Dinis de Sousa et al., High GUD Incidence in the Early 20th Century, 4.

throughout West-Central Africa, possibly through mass vaccination campaigns directed at sleeping sickness.[88] Harsh colonial and wartime conditions, including forced labor and military conscription, enhanced mobility, urbanization, social turmoil, sex work, and high incidences of sexually transmitted diseases, then created environments conducive to the continued spread and evolution of the virus.

In modern times economic development of the Central African rain forests characterized by petroleum extraction, commercial plantations, logging, and mining is suspected of exposing people to zoonoses such as the Ebola virus by facilitating hunting while creating a market demand for game meat, often that of great apes.[89] Likewise, early colonial economic development in the rain forests, including wild rubber collection, rubber and oil palm plantations, and commercial logging, increased the demand for game, including chimpanzees that may have carried SIV.[90] Colonial hunting restrictions broke down during the First World War, when British and French forces invaded Cameroon, ushering in "a marked breakdown of authority, both colonial and traditional," characterized by gangs of soldiers, former soldiers, and brigands roaming the countryside, pillaging, raiding villages, and seizing women.[91] Some of the early fighting took place in proximity to forests of the Sangha River basin where the SIV ancestor of HIV-1 M has been identified.[92] As in East Africa, the war forced armies to live off the land, resorting to roots, leaves, and game for food.[93] Wartime requisitioning of crops, forced labor and conscription, and brigandage also left villagers little choice but to survive on forest

[88] William H. Schneider, *The History of Blood Transfusion in Sub-Saharan Africa* (Athens: Ohio University Press, 2013), 10–13; Jacques Pépin, *The Origin of AIDS* (Cambridge: Cambridge University Press, 2011), 118–142.

[89] Nathan D. Wolfe et al., Bushmeat Hunting, Deforestation, and Prediction of Zoonoses Emergence. *Emerging Infectious Diseases* 11(12) (2005), 1822–1827; Tamara Giles-Vernick and Stephanie Rupp, People, Great Apes, Disease, and Global Health in the Northern Forests of Equatorial Africa. In Tamara Giles-Vernick and James L. A. Webb, eds., *Global Health in Africa: Historical Perspectives on Disease Control* (Athens: Ohio University Press, 2013), 117–137.

[90] Georg Escherich, *Im Urwald* (Berlin: Georg Stilke, 1927), 62–69; Ewald Lüders, *Das Jagdrecht der deutschen Schutzgebiete* (Hamburg: L. Friederichsen, 1913), 31, 47, 55; Reichs-Kolonialamt, *Jagd und Wildschutz in den deutschen Kolonien* (Jena: Gustav Fischer, 1913), 89.

[91] Frederick Quinn, An African Reaction to World War I: The Beti of Cameroon. *Cahiers d'Etudes Africaines* 13 (1973), 725, 728.

[92] Strachan, *The First World War in Africa*, chapter 3.

[93] Hans Dominik, *Kamerun, sechs Kriegs- und Friedensjahre in deutschen Tropen* (Berlin: Georg Stilke, 1911), 328–329.

foods and hunting.[94] No single "cut hunter" contracted SIV, rather intensified hunting during the war likely exposed many people to the virus.[95]

The epidemic spread of HIV was expedited by wartime vaccination and injection campaigns, notably for dysentery and sleeping sickness that exposed people to each other's blood under unhygienic circumstances coupled with needle shortages.[96] The war unleashed sleeping sickness outbreaks, as mobilization of troops and porters disrupted local ecologies and brought people whose blood contained the trypanosome parasite into new regions, where it increased its range of infection.[97] Massive mortality led the French who took over southern Cameroon to extend the ambitious inoculation campaigns begun by Germans before the war. During these campaigns, which continued throughout the 1920s, the blood of sleeping sickness patients infected with SIV may have infected other patients.[98] Moreover, blood transfusions as a therapy to treat severe forms of anemia, which often accompanied malaria or blackwater fever, had a history that went back to at least 1892 in tropical Africa.[99] In Europe as well, blood transfusion therapy was often used in cases of severe anemia, and it is possible that the war in Africa saw similar use, as was the case during the 1920s, when blood therapy was sometimes administered to patients recovering from various ailments.[100] Many instances of blood transfusion therapy for blackwater fever and severe malaria accompanied the First World War in North African and Mediterranean theaters of the war. Inoculation campaigns and blood transfusions had the capacity to accelerate HIV evolution into more virulent strains in the ensuing decades, while enhanced colonial mobility owing to railways and steamships brought infected carriers into urban centers like Douala and Leopoldville. Wartime conditions that intensified hunting, mobility, urban gender disparity, sex work, sexually transmitted diseases like

---

[94] BAB/R1001/7677, Arbeiterfrage im Urwald, April 13, 1918 [5–6].

[95] Pépin, *The Origin of AIDS*, 43–46.   [96] Ibid., 120–123.

[97] Deborah J. Neill, *Networks in Tropical Medicine: Internationalism, Colonialism, and the Rise of a Medical Specialty, 1890–1930* (Stanford, CA: Stanford University Press, 2012), 183–189.

[98] In East Africa during the war, German military doctor Taute injected military porters (and himself) with the blood serum of horses and mules as part of his anti-sleeping sickness trials. M. Taute and F. Huber, Die Unterscheidung des Trypanosoma rhodesiense vom Trypanosoma brucei. Beobachtungen und Experimente aus dem Kriege in Ostafrika. *Archiv für Schiffs- und Tropenhygiene* 23(11) (1919), 211–226.

[99] Thaddeus Sunseri, Blood Trials: Transfusions, Injections and Experiments in Africa, 1890–1920. *Journal of the History of Medicine and Allied Sciences* 71(3) (2016), 293–321.

[100] Pépin, *The Origin of AIDS*, 127.

syphilis, and injection therapies and blood transfusions may therefore have provided the context for the early spread of the most virulent strains of HIV.[101]

CONCLUSION

Although historians of Africa have long been aware of the importance of the First World War in sparking a shift from early extractive colonialism to a more development-oriented agenda – the *first* "Second Colonial Occupation" in the words of one historian[102] – the war has not generally been included in analyses of some of the fundamental transformations of the twentieth century; it has often been a footnote. This is because many of the wartime crises that affected Africans most – forced conscription and porterage, population dislocation and decline, food and animal requisitioning, invasions by violent forces, epidemics, epizootics, and transformed disease ecologies – were already characteristic of early colonial rule. But the impact of the war deserves attention for the much higher magnitude of these experiences. By 1914, a kind of stasis had been achieved in most European colonies, seen in a framework of rule that included protected spaces, such as forest and wildlife reserves, basic railway and transport infrastructure, curbs on the most blatant labor abuses, and colonially enforced peace. The war tore much of that asunder, even in regions not subjected to direct conflict, since all territories were expected to contribute to the war effort. This brief overview cannot account for the enormity and diversity of environmental dimensions of the war throughout the continent, and it has neglected key regions as far apart as North Africa and South Africa. Yet it provides a blueprint of some consequential changes.

The war ended with the loss of German colonies to the victorious nations as League of Nations Mandates. Because colonial powers did not have identical policies, the territorial transfer was significant. For example, Tanganyika went from being the center of the German overseas colonial empire to a periphery of the British Empire. The British prioritized neighboring white settler colonies, or major cash crop producers

---

[101] Rita Headrick, *Colonialism, Health and Illness in French Equatorial Africa, 1885–1935* (Atlanta, GA: African Studies Association, 1994), 161–162; Dinis de Sousa et al., High GUD Incidence in the Early 20th Century, 4.

[102] Roberts, *Two Worlds of Cotton*, 110. "Second Colonial Occupation" usually refers to a massive investment agenda in Africa following the Second World War. Reid, *A History of Modern Africa*, 251–252.

like Uganda. Not until the Second World War did a Colonial Development and Welfare Act begin to ramp up a development agenda in Tanganyika. In Cameroon as well, the German agenda had been to industrialize the forests, compared to a French focus on continued timber and rubber extraction following the war. Policies on how to deal with sleeping sickness epidemics and epizootics like Rinderpest also differed from one colonial power to another. Finally, European perceptions of raw material scarcity at home, made clear during the war, motivated a second look at Africa. If African resources found new importance after the war, a portrayal of Africans as poor stewards of land and resources also emerged, feeding "declensionist" narratives that became powerful in the interwar years and that persist toward Africa today.[103]

---

[103] For example, see Diana K. Davis, *Resurrecting the Granary of Rome: Environmental History and French Colonial Expansion in North Africa* (Athens: Ohio University Press, 2007), 2–3; Jeremy Swift, Desertification: Narratives, Winners and Losers. In Melissa Leach and Robins Mearns, eds., *The Lie of the Land: Challenging Received Wisdom on the African Environment* (London: International African Institute, 1996), 73–90.

PART IV

THE LONG AFTERMATH

Environmentalism and Memory

13

Disruption and Reorganization

International Preservation Networks and the First World War

Raf De Bont and Anna-Katharina Wöbse

In July 1914 Swiss scientist and conservation activist Paul Sarasin boarded a German ship to Spitsbergen. He did so with a clear vision in his mind. In November 1913 he had presided over the first international congress on nature protection, convened in Bern. The delegates had commissioned him to investigate whether the artic island might be suitable to establish the first international nature reserve to protect its seals and whales, polar bears and artic foxes, not to mention millions of migrating birds. The status of ownership of the islands was yet unsettled and the archipelago was internationally considered unclaimed territory. This *terra nullius* seemed the perfect spot for an experiment in international preservation.[1] Sarasin was determined to make this trip a success, but soon after the boat had reached the high seas the crew was forced to return to the port. War had been declared and Sarasin's plans were shattered: "This icy winter storm hit my global work, I had started so full of hope, like a heap of withered leafs and scattered all efforts to the four winds."[2] This sudden end of his journey and thus the failure of the preservationist's experiment in Spitsbergen were just the immediate results of the outbreak of hostilities.

---

[1] On the status of Spitsbergen and the perspective of preservationists see Paul Sarasin, *Über die Ausrottung der Wal- und Robbenfauna sowie der arktischen und antarktischen Tierwelt überhaupt* (Leipzig: Pries, 1912); Hugo Conwentz, Über den Schutz der Natur Spitzbergens. Denkschrift der Spitzbergenkonferenz in Kristania 1914. *Beiträge zur Naturdenkmalpflege* 4 (2014), 65–137. See *Recueil des Procès-Verbaux de la Conférence Internationale pour la Protection de la Nature* (Berne: Wyss, 1914), 98.

[2] Staatsarchiv Basel, PA 212 T 1b 13, "Zur Erinnerung an Dr. Paul Benedikt Sarasin," typoscript, 8.

It is clear that wars generally lead to ecological disruption. The results are manifold. Military action leaves enormous environmental footprints, battles shape landscapes, and warfare fundamentally changes the flow of resources.[3] But only in more recent years, environmental historians have started to examine the historical connections between war and environment more systematically.[4] This recent historiography has mostly focused on the material effects of war on the natural world. Yet the mental maps of the people involved were also affected and wars left imprints on diplomatic relations. This chapter exactly studies these more social aspects by looking into the impact the First World War had on the history of international "environmentalism."

For a long time the historiography of international environmental relations tended to identify the 1970s as the founding period of environmental diplomacy. More recently, the notion prevails that it is actually rooted in developments from the early twentieth century. Today's global environmental regimes are, thus, presented as an outcome of a long and cumulative process that started about 100 years ago.[5] The narrative of this long history of environmental international relations, however, does not pay much tribute to turbulences caused by war. The few accounts on the history of environmental diplomacy mention only briefly that the First World War put a halt to all existing preservationist plans.[6] It seems worthwhile to take a closer look at that "halt." Which consequences did the hostilities have on transboundary networks and coalitions? How did it affect experts and activists involved in that network? How did the environmental impact of the war itself alter the dynamics of the international preservation movement? What were the short- and long-term consequences as far as international cooperation was concerned?

[3] See the monographic section "World War II, the Cold War, and Natural Resources," by Simo Laakkonen and Richard Tucker in *Global Environment* 10 (2012).

[4] Richard Tucker and Edmund Russell, eds., *Natural Enemy, Natural Ally: Toward an Environmental History of War* (Corvallis: Oregon State University Press, 2004); Edmund Russell, *War and Nature: Fighting Humans and Insects with Chemicals from World War I to Silent Spring* (New York: Cambridge University Press, 2001); John R. McNeill and Corinna R. Unger, eds., *Environmental Histories of the Cold War* (Cambridge: Cambridge University Press, 2010); Charles E. Closman, *War and the Environment: Military Destruction in the Modern Age* (College Station: Texas A&M University Press, 2009).

[5] Robert Falkner, Global Environmentalism and the Greening of International Society. *International Affairs* 88(3) (2012), 503–522.

[6] John McCormick, *The Global Environmental Movement: Reclaiming Paradise* (London: Bellhaven, 1989); Barbara J. Lausche, *Weaving a Web of Environmental Law* (Bonn: Erich Schmidt Verlag, 2008).

We argue that the prewar initiatives to internationalize problems related to the use and exploitation of nature saw a severe setback due to the hostilities. Yet the war not only created new environmental problems but also reshuffled international forums and relations. Soon, effective networks of key people managed to develop strategies adapted to the somewhat unstable situation in the interwar period. Based mainly on archival sources, this chapter explores some of the immediate impacts and some of the long shadows the hostilities cast on the multi- and transnational "environmental" discourse as well as its effects on the international nature protection network.

BUILDING NETWORKS BEFORE THE FIRST WORLD WAR

In order to understand the situation of international cooperation before the outbreak of the war in August 1914 it is worthwhile to take a closer look at the decade preceding the First World War.[7] Around the turn of the century there was a broad consensus among Western societies that the desire to protect nature was "honorable and worthy of support."[8] The emergence of preservation and its slow progress onto the political agendas occurred against the backdrop of an increasing global interconnectedness. Technological developments in mobility and communication had brought peoples of the world in closer contact. With it came a growing body of international institutions and organizations. At the same time the period witnessed a proliferation of international conferences.[9] Against the background of such developments preservation was increasingly presented by nongovernmental actors and their organizations as a cause of mankind as a whole.

Protecting natural monuments, landscapes, and species had developed into a universal parameter for measuring the degree of cultivation and civilization of Western states. After having conquered nature, truly civilized and thus superior nations would now be noble enough to give some space to the besieged. Given that the various nations were in a permanent state of cultural rivalry with each other over matters of leadership in the advancement of civilization, activists could use this competitive

[7] Volker Berghahn, *Der Erste Weltkrieg*, 5th edn. (München: Beck, 2014), 3.
[8] Joachim Radkau, *Nature and Power: A Global History of the Environment* (Cambridge: Cambridge University Press, 2008), 230.
[9] Akira Iriye, *Global Community: The Role of International Organizations in the Making of the Contemporary World* (Berkeley: University of California Press, 2002).

atmosphere to plead for governmental support for their cause.[10] Thus, although most of the protagonists kept playing the patriotic chord at home, they were eager to build international networks and to set up cooperative projects.[11] Depending on the audience they changed their rhetoric and played the patriotic and the international tune at the same time. This was by no means atypical. Historians have described several examples of such a co-construction of nationalism and internationalism in the period around 1900.[12]

In this atmosphere of creative competition, cross-border networks of preservation experts took shape. These networks constituted what Peter Haas has called "epistemic communities," in which shared ideas about truthful knowledge, normative beliefs, and preferred policy outcomes were generated.[13] Early international meetings, furthermore, quickly brought about a standard repertoire of topics for discussion. These included the crusade against the millinery trade, bird protection in general and the preservation of sea birds in particular, the establishment of national parks and reserves, the protection of African big game, or the fight against the building of huge advertisement boards in the countryside.[14] Characteristic for such transnational consensus was an article published in the British journal *Nature* in autumn 1909. It reported on the reception of Hugo Conwentz, head of the Prussian Staatliche Stelle für Naturdenkmalpflege (State Agency for the Care of Natural Monuments), in Paris at the First International Conference on

---

[10] Danny Trom, Natur und nationale Identität. Der Streit um den Schutz der ‚Natur' um die Jahrhundertwende in Deutschland und Frankreich. In Etienne Francois, Hannes Siegrist, and Jakob Vogel, eds., *Nation und Emotion. Deutschland und Frankreich im Vergleich 19. und 20. Jahrhundert* (Göttingen: Vandenhoeck & Ruprecht, 1995), 147–167, see 155; Astrid Swenson, "Heritage," "Patrimoine" und "Kulturerbe": Eine vergleichende Semantik. In Dorothee Hemme, Markus Tauschek, and Regina Bendix, eds., *Prädikat "Heritage": Wertschöpfung aus kulturellen Ressourcen* (Berlin: LIT, 2007), 53–74.

[11] François Walter, *Les figures paysagères de la nation: territoire et paysage en Europe (16e-20e siècle)* (Paris: Éd. de l'École des Hautes Études en Sciences Sociales, 2004).

[12] In the context of science, Geert Somsen has described this co-construction as one of "Olympic internationalism": Geert Somsen, A History of Internationalism: Conceptions of the Internationality of Science from the Enlightenment to the Cold War. *Minerva* 46 (2008), 361–379.

[13] Peter Haas, Introduction: Epistemic Communities and International Policy Coordination. *International Organization* 46(1) (1992), 1–35.

[14] Mark Cioc, *The Game of Conservation: International Treaties to Protect the World's Migratory Animals* (Athens: Ohio University Press, 2009); Hayden Sherman Strong, *The International Protection of Wild Life* (New York: Columbia University Press, 1942).

Landscape Protection. His remarks on "the protection of natural monuments in different countries" met with enthusiasm.[15]

In 1910, then, the Swiss gentleman-scientist Paul Benedict Sarasin presented his idea of a global nature protection agency to the international Congress of Biology in Graz, Austria. His decisive role in the chronicles of the preservation movement is probably grounded in his rhetorical skills and his seismographic abilities. Sarasin summarized the most popular environmental debates of the time. Tellingly enough, he diagnosed that the colonial campaigns of Western powers had conquered the globe and with it had come the destruction of nature. He referred to the extinction of the bison in North America, the consequences of industrial whaling, the vanishing polar and African fauna due to massive hunting campaigns and the ongoing exploitation of birds by the feather fashion industry. Sarasin suggested establishing an international commission to collect information, to coordinate action, and to serve as a clearing house.[16] Due to his proposal the Swiss government convened a conference in Bern in November 1913: Preservation had turned into a subject that had the potential to consolidate the political standing and international profile of states.[17]

In the preceding decade, nature protection had already slowly entered the repertoire of national agendas around the North Atlantic.[18] Sarasin aimed to take an extra step in the direction of international collaboration and coordination, while strategically playing into national sensibilities. His transboundary visions, however, were continuously imperiled by power politics. When Sarasin welcomed 35 gentlemen from 19 countries to launch a World Nature Protection Committee in Bern, the delegates

---

[15] *Nature* 83(2116) (May 19, 1910), 345. Société pour la Protection des Paysages de France, printed invitation to the Premier Congrès International pour la Protection des Paysages, September 15, 1909. Bundesarchiv Berlin, R 1501 II 6269. On the legacy of the wars on the French–German relations concerning the protection of nature see Anna-Katharina Wöbse, Les liaisons sinueuses: les relations franco-allemandes en matière de protection de la nature dans la première moitié du Xxe siècle. In Charles-Francois Mathis and Jean-Francois Mouhot, eds., *Une protection de l'environnement à la francaise?* (Paris: Champ Vallon, 2013), 108–119.

[16] Paul Sarasin, Über Weltnaturschutz. In Rudolf Ritter von Stumer-Träunfels, ed., *Verhandlungen des VIII. Internationalen Zoologen-Kongresses zu Graz* (Jena: Gustav Fischer Verlag, 1910), 240–253.

[17] Madeleine Herren, *Hintertüren zur Macht. Internationalismus und modernisierungsorientierte Außenpolitik in Belgien, der Schweiz und den USA 1965–1914* (München: Oldenbourg, 2000), 351–362.

[18] Cioc, *The Game of Conservation*, 148–153.

were particularly eager to show their national feathers.[19] The French delegates, for instance, referred not only to the French ambitions to protect whales in their colonial waters and the African big game in their terrestrial possessions, but also pointed to many local initiatives already under way in France.[20] They insisted, furthermore, that future preservation schemes were to be kept within the national sphere of influence. So did Conwentz – the delegate from the former "hereditary enemy," Germany. For a limited number of issues international collaboration was deemed necessary, but only as a small addendum to national policies.[21] Nevertheless, thanks to Sarasin's unremitting efforts, a charter establishing a Consultative Commission for the International Protection of Nature was signed at the end of the day. Sarasin set out to prepare the next constituting session of the commission, which was to be convened in autumn 1914. The war put an abrupt end to this plan.

THE LEAGUE OF NATIONS AS A (NON-)FORUM

The hostilities of the First World War stopped the process of establishing an international clearing house almost immediately. Europe saw the worst killing spree and resource depletion of its history and experienced utter devastation. Only after the war's end could international preservation initiatives slowly be taken up again. For the preservationists involved it quickly became clear that, from now onward, they had to function in a new world order. This was especially the case for the institutional realm, in which the foundation of the League of Nations in 1920 strongly reshaped the playing field and appeared as a new "gravitation field for organisations of civil society."[22]

Among the early enthusiasts of the League of Nations was (again) Paul Sarasin. A keen internationalist, he had voted for the Swiss accession to the League of Nations and put all his hope into the new organization.[23] In the League's administration he found allies like the Japanese vice

---

[19] Andreas Kley, Die Weltnaturschutzkonferenz 1913 in Bern. In *Umweltrecht in der Praxis, Sonderheft zu Grundsatzfragen des Umweltrechts* 7 (2007), 685–705.

[20] See *Recueil des Procès-Verbaux de la Conférence Internationale pour la Protection de la Nature*: Exposè de M. le professeur Edmond Perrier, 115–118, Exposè de M. le professeur Bouvier, 118–119, and annexes V. et VI, 234–241.

[21] See also Hugo Conwentz, On National and International Protection of Nature. *Journal of Ecology* (1914), 109–122.

[22] Madeleine Herren, *Internationale Organisationen. Eine Globalgeschichte der internationalen Ordnung* (Darmstadt: WBG, 2009), 54.

[23] Anna-Katharina Wöbse, *Weltnaturschutz. Umweltdiplomatie in Völkerbund und Vereinten Nationen 1920–1950* (Frankfurt am Main/New York: Campus, 2012).

director-general, Inazo Nitobe, who enthusiastically supported the initiative to establish a commission for nature protection that would be affiliated to the League. Sarasin turned to his former comrades in arms he had invited to Bern in 1913 and asked for their consent. But soon the impact of the war thwarted such plans. A deep gap was running through the community of experts, dividing them along the lines of former battlefields.

Sarasin's idea was met with strong reluctance. The incoming answers reflected doubt, uncertainty, and even some sheer hostility. While the Germans and Austrians replied that they would not agree to put the former commission under the auspices of the League of Nations as they were not permitted to be members of it, the French and Belgian actors denied the commission the right to exist as such – at least as long as Austria and Germany were members. Jean Massart, a well-traveled botanist and one of the key figures of Belgian nature protection, was as explicit about excluding the Germans. He particularly saw a chance to recreate a preservationist network via the International Union of Biological Sciences and thus to by-pass all German influence and to isolate the scientists of the former axis.[24] The French used the opportunity to reaffirm their position in the environmental avant-garde and organized another international conference on nature protection in Paris in 1923 to which only delegates from former Allied and neutral countries were invited.[25] The nationals of states that had not been actively involved in the war such as the Netherlands and Sweden found themselves sitting on the fence somewhere in between the former enemies. The League's counterpart, Nitobe, was deeply disappointed that the plan of a central agency for nature protection was failing, and tried to voice some optimism: "As the general conditions of the world improve, I hope the time will come when the governments will take up a scheme for the global protection of nature."[26] But the unsettled quarrels continued to hinder international cooperation. For some years, the French and Belgian actors on the one hand and the Germans and Austrians on the other actively ignored each other. The war and its consequential damages seemed to have put international preservation out of the political market.[27]

---

[24] Compilation of copied letters sent to Sarasin, League of Nations Archives, 40/17779/17779.

[25] Raoul de Clermont et al., ed., *Premier congrès international pour la protection de la nature* (Paris: Société nationale d'acclimatation de France, 1923), 31.

[26] Nitobe to Sarasin, October 19, 1922, League of Nations Archive, 13/24249/3514.

[27] Letter of the Department of the Interior to the Schweizerische Naturforschende Gesellschaft, October 4, 1922, League of Nations Archives, 13/24249/3514.

The direct consequence of the war was the open resistance of some networkers to continue the former collaboration and to return to the prewar status of Sarasin's arrangements. Because of such reluctance, the League never managed to establish a central forum for questions concerning the protection of nature. The irritation and distrust the war had caused among the networkers were diametrically opposed to the idealistic concept of the League of Nations to set the frame for a new era of social and political reform of international relations.[28] This failure in early environmental institution building had long-lasting effects. During the 1920s and the early 1930s the League's various technical organizations did actually discuss several international environmental issues such as whaling, oil pollution, animal protection, or the scheme for a global network of national parks. Many of these initiatives were carried by national nongovernmental organizations (NGOs) like the British Royal Society for the Protection of Birds, various Spanish animal protection societies, or ambitious juristic or biological experts. But the NGO had only very limited access to the League and could not formally intervene. As far as questions of nature protection were concerned, the League lacked a normative agency that would voice ecological or ethical arguments in favor of the preservation of the natural world.[29]

Nevertheless, the experts in Geneva started discussions that prepared the ground for several environmental agreements in the long term. All of these discussions were in one way or the other related to the past war – although most of these drafts outlined in the League's era would be ratified only after the Second World War or serve as starting points for new debates after 1945. The protection of whales offers a case in point. Whales had provided the raw material for margarine, washing powder, and explosives before and during the war: commodities many devastated national economies longed for in the period of reconstruction.[30] The plea by some League of Nations protagonists, such as Argentinian expert for international law José Léon Suàrez, to pay at least a small tribute to the well-being of migrating whales lost against the utilitarianism of the whaling nations.[31] Actually, in this debate the institutional flaw was most obvious. The League's officials were desperately looking for advice from

---

[28] Tim B. Müller, *Nach dem Ersten Weltkrieg. Lebensversuche moderner Demokratien* (Hamburg: Hamburger Edition, 2014), 35.

[29] Wöbse, *Weltnaturschutz*, 63–64, 333.

[30] Johan N. Tonnessen and Arne O. Johnson, *The History of Modern Whaling* (London: C. Hurst and Company, 1982), 234–237.

[31] Wöbse, *Weltnaturschutz*, 229–233.

experts of the preservation network. Yet, as Sarasin's committee had ceased to exist, there was no one to approach.[32] Only in 1948 would the IUPN be established to provide such an international forum. Another environmental problem caused by the First World War and discussed in Geneva was the fast-growing phenomenon of oil pollution, which had been triggered by the modernization of navy ships. The British Navy had demonstrated the advantages of oil-fueled vessels. After the war, the shipping industry started to invest in new boats. With the new devices, operating engines and cleaning the tanks turned oil into an omnipresent nuisance in harbors and along the shores.[33] Floating oil did not stop at any national borders or territorial waters. The pollution of the seas anticipated that the use of the global commons might be fiercely debated. The outcome was a weak compromise, banning the pumping of oil outside of certain zones. Once again, the mobilizing power of the organization proved limited. However, the drafts for legislation of the interwar years were to serve as a decisive starting point for the first global maritime anti-pollution scheme in 1954.[34]

CIVIC PRESSURE GROUPS

Despite his initial enthusiasm, Sarasin was quick to realize that the League of Nations offered him few prospects. As early as 1926 he expressed his disappointment in a letter to Dutch preservationist Pieter-Gerbrand van Tienhoven – adding that he no longer had the health and youth needed to revive the prewar preservation initiatives.[35] Not only had the League of Nations shown no interest in reestablishing his Commission, but the network *behind* the institution proved not to be durable. Its 32 former members were hardly present at the most important interwar preservation conferences. In Paris in 1923, only Sarasin himself and Van Tienhoven attended the international gathering. After Sarasin's death in 1929, Van Tienhoven was the only former commission member attending the

---

[32] Instead the experts of the League turned to the International Council for the Exploration of the Sea: League of Nations Archive, Letter of the Secretary General to the President of the ICES, April 18, 1928, 3E/4009/466.

[33] Sonia Zaide Pritchard, *Oil Pollution Control* (London: Croom Helm, 1987).

[34] Anna-Katharina Wöbse, *Weltnaturschutz. Umweltdiplomatie in Völkerbund und Vereinten Nationen 1920–1950* (Frankfurt am Main/New York: Campus, 2012), 126–129.

[35] Sarasin to Van Tienhoven, November 5, 1926, Archief van de Nederlandse Commissie voor Internationale Natuurbescherming, City Archive Amsterdam [ANCIN], 1283–117.

international preservation conferences of Paris (1931) and London (1933 and 1938).[36] The war, so it seems, had indeed been disruptive for the existing networks. The long interval in activities meant that some key players had disappeared from the scene. Others, as we will see, were prevented from reentering the network because of continuing national frictions.

The fact that, in the 1920s and 1930s, nature protection conferences were held in relatively quick succession shows at the same time that the interwar period did witness a new dynamic of international preservation initiatives. This dynamic was not so much driven by big intergovernmental organizations such as the League of Nations, but rather by undersized civic ones – small-scale equivalents of our present-day NGOs. After the war period, in which virtually no new civic societies were founded, the 1920s witnessed a true explosion.[37] Three of those initiatives, all organized around elite groups of experts, proved influential in the field of nature protection: the International Committee for Bird Preservation (ICBP, founded in 1922), the International Society for the Preservation of the European Bison (ISPEB, 1923), and the International Office for the Protection of Nature (IOPN, 1928).[38] In their composition and focus, these three organizations clearly carried the marks of the Great War – be it in quite different ways.

TRANSBOUNDARY BIRDS

The fact that the first transnational preservation society established after 1918 focused on birds was no coincidence. Since the late nineteenth century bird preservation had constituted one of the most developed and

---

[36] See de Clermont et al., *Premier congrès international pour la protection de la nature*; Abel Gruvel et al., eds., *Deuxième congrès international pour la protection de la nature (Paris, 30 juin–4 juillet 1931) Procès-verbaux, rapports et vœux* (Paris: Société d'éditions géographiques, maritimes et coloniales, 1932); *International Conference for the Protection of the Fauna and Flora of Africa. 1933.* Typoscript; *Second International Conference for the Protection of the Fauna and Flora of Africa. 1938.* Typoscript.

[37] John Boli and George M. Thomas, Introduction. In John Boli and George M. Thomas, ed., *Constructing World Culture: International Nongovernmental Organizations since 1875* (Stanford, CA: Stanford University Press, 1999), 22.

[38] For convenience we reference the mostly used English names for these organizations. The official German name of the ISPEB was Internationale Gesellschaft zur Erhaltung des Wisents. The IOPN officially carried the French designation Office international de Documentation et de Corrélation pour la Protection de la Nature, before changing this to the more manageable name Office Internationale pour la Protection de la Nature in 1935.

internationally oriented task fields within the nature protection movement. In the 1880s, British women's societies had taken up the topic through campaigns against the feather industry. In the same period, an International Ornithological Committee had been set up that organized conferences at which the study and eventually also the protection of migratory birds was promoted.[39] This combined lobbying proved successful. In 1902, twelve European countries ratified the "Convention for the Protection of Birds Useful to Agriculture."[40]

The war proved a major setback for bird preservation. As indicated, oil pollution – which particularly harmed seabirds – was an outcome of new technologies introduced by the navies. The severe food shortage in Europe raised the demand for meat, and the eggs of wild birds again turned into an important source of protein.[41] On the more scientific side aviaries and collections of bird skins had been destroyed when the German army had invaded Belgium and France. Among such precious collections was that of Jean Delacour, one of the key figures in international ornithology and bird protection.[42] The hostilities, furthermore, severely disturbed the scientific networks. The fifth Ornithological Congress in Berlin (1910) had planned to convene its next meeting in Sarajevo in 1915 – which turned out to be the wrong place and time.[43]

In a destroyed Europe, old ties could only be cautiously reestablished. The main initiative in this respect would – not coincidentally – be taken by an American: the then president of the Audubon Society, Thomas Gilbert Pearson.[44] In 1922 Pearson set out on an extensive journey around Europe

[39] Walter J. Bock, Presidential Address: Three Centuries of International Ornithology: Proc. 23rd International Ornithological Congress. *Acta Zoologica Sinica* 50(6) (2004), 779–855.

[40] On these early developments: Robin W. Doughty, *Feather Fashions and Bird Preservation: A Study in Nature Protection* (Berkeley: University of California Press, 1975); R. J. Moore-Colye, Feathered Women and Persecuted Birds: the Struggle against the Plumage Trade, c. 1860–1922. *Rural History* 11(1) (2000), 57–73; R. Boardman, *The International Politics of Bird Conservation: Biodiversity, Regionalism and Global Governance* (Cheltenham: Edward Elgar Publishing, 2006), 39–40.

[41] On food scarcity after the First World War and its effect on seabirds see for instance Hugo Weigold, *Die Vogelfreistätten an der deutschen Nordseeküste* (Berlin: Mittler, 1924).

[42] Jean Delacour, *The Living Air: The Memoirs of an Ornithologist* (London: Country Life Limited, 1966), 55.

[43] Hermann Schalow, ed., *Verhandlungen des V. Internationalen Ornithologen-Kongresses* (Berlin: DOG 1911), 55.

[44] See Phyllis Barclay-Smith: T. Gilbert Pearson, Founder President, ICBP, 1922–1938. *ICBP Bulletin* 2 (1963), 17–21.

to further his bonds with European bird protectors. In his autobiography he would later describe how he fostered a network by attending lectures and setting up excursions to watch the local avifauna. Picking up on old rhetoric, he would present birds as transnational creatures in need of international cooperation. Facing the destruction of the military action he presented birds as symbols of hope and continuity that transcended human quarrels like "a hoopoe on a broken gun-carriage near Soissons, a pair of kestrels in the shattered towers of the cathedral of Rheims . . . and house sparrows feeding their young in a shell-splintered tree beside the desolate Chemin des Dames."[45]

In the wake of his journey, Pearson convened a meeting with a small group of bird lovers'from Great Britain, the United States, the Netherlands, and France in a stately house in London. It was here, in June 1922, that the ICPB would be established. Pearson had invited the most committed people he had met en route to come to the house of his London host, prominent activist Mrs. McKenna. Among them one could find "that premier of all bird-protectors in Europe," Pieter-Gerbrand van Tienhoven, the latter's compatriot Adolphe Burdet, the aforementioned Jean Delacour, and British bird protection activists such as Lord Grey, Earl Buxton, William Sclater, and Percy Lowe.[46]

The informal network of the ICPB initially did not include representatives of the former Central Powers – much to the latter's dismay. Walther Schoenichen, Conwentz's successor as head of the *Staatliche Stelle*, made his disappointment quite explicit in a letter to Van Tienhoven in 1926. He admitted that Germany, "robbed of its colonies," no longer had a role to play in the protection of tropical fauna, only to add that the country – given its traditional leadership in ornithology – would continue to be important for the international protection of birds. Yet, so he complained, Germany's re-entrance in the international network was sadly boycotted.[47]

Behind the scenes, however, this re-entrance was being prepared. In 1924, Ernst Hartert, a British ornithologist of German descent and curator of Walter Rothschild's private museum in Tring, investigated the chances to revive the International Ornithological Committee. According to him, this was only possible if strict neutrality was guaranteed. The future congresses should "not be anything but affairs of ornithologists"; no "governments, rulers or ministers" would be asked "to be hosts or

---

[45] Thomas Gilbert Pearson, *Adventures in Bird Protection* (New York/London: Appleton Century Company, 1937), 371.
[46] Ibid., 383.
[47] Schoenichen to Van Tienhoven, February 23, 1926 ANCIN, 1283–119.

protectors ... so that nobody shall feel as a guest of any foreign country."[48] His strategy proved successful and in 1926, the ornithologists – including the Germans – met in neutral Denmark after 16 years of silence.[49]

The ICPB followed suit. Pearson always avoided taking any political stance, stressing his organization was a loose "federation of completely independent units." Considering the tensions in the postwar years, this informality helped to get the Committee off the ground: When the ICBP published its first *Bulletin* in 1927, it listed 75 societies organized in 18 national sections – including a German and an Austrian one.[50] When, in the following year, the ICPB organized its first international conference in Geneva, the Germans were outranked in representatives only by the Swiss.[51]

The ICPB was instrumental in reestablishing informal contacts between preservationists across borders, and practically served as a clearing house of information. Yet the informal set-up also had its downsides. The membership was diverse, money scarce, and coordination limited. In this context, political influence was mostly striven for via informal contacts of individual members with policymakers. The latter were approached to put bird protection on the agenda of organizations such as the League of Nations or the International Institute of Agriculture. But ICPB members disagreed over the strategy to take and their political contacts proved less influential than hoped for.[52] Attempts to update the Paris Convention – a major goal of the ICPB – were in vain.

POSTWAR WISENTS

Whereas the ICPB revolved to a large extent around a transatlantic network, the ISPEB was mostly centered around a Central European one.

---

[48] Manuscript by Ernst Hartert: "International Ornithological Committee", Tring, November 1924. Natural History Museum Tring, Library, Box "International Committee for the Protection of Birds 1927".

[49] Hartert could play this role in reorganizing the network due to his "aquaintance and friendship with ornithologists from different countries" and support "by friends from Germany and England". Hartert later explained that it had been vital to convene the meeting in a strictly neutral country. See: Ernst Hartert, Vorbereitung für den Kongreß. In *Verhandlungen des VI Internationalen Ornithologen-Kongresses in Kopenhagen 1926* (Berlin 1929), 1.

[50] *Bulletin of the International Committee for Bird Protection* 1 (New York, 1927), 7–17.

[51] Minutes and Resolutions, Geneva 1928, Natural History Museum Tring, Library, Box "International Committee for the Protection of Birds."

[52] See, among others, Van Tienhoven to Pearson, June 26, 1926; Pearson to Van Tienhoven, August 18, 1928 and December 17, 1929; "Report of Dr. L. Pittet, Representative of Switserland," ANCIN, 1283–108.

And unlike the ICPB it focused entirely on one species: the European bison or the wisent. The First World War had made the plight of this animal a matter of international concern.[53] In 1914 its most vital wild population, living in the woods around Białowieża (then Russia), still numbered more or less 700 individuals. During the war, however, the region witnessed heavy fighting and changed hands several times. Under German occupation the wisents received some protection as "natural monuments," but the actual success of this policy is still disputed. The Russian Revolution, the changing front line, and the disorder among German troops in 1918 eventually proved fatal and the Białowieża subspecies went extinct in 1919.[54] The only other remaining wild population, living in the Caucasus mountains, also underwent heavy losses due to the First World War, the revolution, and the ensuing civil war. Poachers killed the last remaining individuals in 1927.[55] Even before, however, it had already become clear that the only way to save the species was by the coordinated breeding of the remaining captive animals in zoos. It was exactly to organize this breeding project that the ISPEB had been founded. Its self-set task was daunting. According to the Society's own counts, in 1923 only 60 captive individuals survived, spread over seven different countries.[56]

The war had not only shaped the condition of the species, it also had a significant impact on the network of preservationists engaged in attempts to save it. It was German zookeepers and aristocratic breeders who controlled much of the remaining population and who would make up the leadership of the ISPEB. For these men – frustrated by their exclusion from international fora – it seemed to offer an opportunity to reenter the world of global preservation. Their position, however, was most difficult. The tense political situation and the deteriorating economy resulted in the cancelation of many non-German invitees for the

---

[53] See more in depth: Raf De Bont, Extinct in the Wild: Finding a Place for the European Bison, 1919–1952. In Raf De Bont and Jens Lachmund, eds., *Spatializing the History of Ecology: Sites, Journeys, Mappings* (New York: Routledge, 2017).

[54] *Bericht über die Gründungstagung der Internationalen Gesellschaft zur Erhaltung des Wisents am 25. und 26. August, 1923, im Zoologischen Garten, Berlin* (Frankfurt am Main: R. T. Hauser & Company, 1923), 5–6; Thaddeus Sunseri, Exploiting the Urwald: German Post-Colonial Forestry in Poland and Central-Africa, 1900–1960. *Past and Present* 214 (2012), 307; Małgorzata Krasińska and Zbigniew A. Krasiński, *European Bison: The Nature Monograph* (Berlin /Heidelberg: Springer, 2013), 64–66.

[55] V. G. Heptner, A. A. Nasimovich, and A. G. Bannikov, *Mammals of the Soviet Union* (Washington, DC: Smithsonian Institution, 1988), 574.

[56] *Bericht über die Gründungstagung der Internationalen Gesellschaft*, 5.

foundational meeting of the society in 1923.[57] Only three months before this meeting took place, the plight of the wisent had also been discussed for an entirely different audience at the Paris International Conference for the Protection of Nature by the Pole Jan Sztolcman.[58] The German ISPEB-founders – uninvited in Paris – needed a Dutch middleman to get hold of the paper in order to know what actually had been said.[59]

It was only very gradually and through the use of internationalist and pacifist rhetoric that the ISPEB managed to attract a fair number of foreign members.[60] At the ISPEB general Assembly of 1929, Pole Wladyslaw Janta-Polczynski stressed that "war among men might have destroyed the wisent, but peace will bring it to life again."[61] The relative normalization of international contacts was ultimately confirmed when the ISPEB could send a (German) representative to the Second International Conference for the Protection of Nature in Paris in 1932.[62] Such contacts were typically established through informal meetings, as such avoiding the official channels of intergovernmental diplomacy. The way for the ISPEB members to exert influence was through lobbying and informal contacts with government officials. Individual members befriended regional and national policymakers – notably in Germany and Poland – whom they tried to convince to free up money for wisent breeding and the foundation of wildlife parks.[63] This approach generated some results such as state subsidies for the procurement of wisents for the zoos of Warsaw and Springe Yet, most of the initiatives ran along national lines. Furthermore, behind the scenes, one could easily sense the distrust

---

[57] Ibid., 3.

[58] Jan Sztolcman, Le bison d'Europe. In Raoul de Clermont et al., ed., *Premier congrès international pour la protection de la nature* (Paris: Société nationale d'acclimatation de France, 1923), 87–92.

[59] Kurt Priemel to Van Tienhoven, November 19, 1923, ANCIN, 1283–192.

[60] In 1927 the Germans still made up some 50% of the members, with Italians, Poles, Austrians, and Swiss accounting for most of the rest. See Erna Mohr, Sekretariats-Bericht für das Jahr 1927. In Herman Pohle, ed., *Berichte der Internationalen Gesellschaft zur Erhaltung des Wisents*, vol. 3 (Berlin: 1929–1943), 8.

[61] Bericht über die vierte Hauptversammlung vom 1. bis 3. September in Posen, *Berichte der Internationalen Gesellschaft zur Erhaltung des Wisents* 4(1) (1930), 69.

[62] Lutz Heck, L'association internationale pour la conservation du bison d'Europe. In Abel Gruvel et al., eds., *Deuxième congrès international pour la protection de la nature (Paris, 30 juin–4 juillet 1931) Procès-verbaux, rapports et vœux* (Paris: Société d'éditions géographiques, maritimes et coloniales, 1932), 120–122.

[63] On these contacts, see, for instance, Van Tienhoven to Michal Siedlecki, December 17, 1932; "Protokoll, Konferenz Ausschusses und Züchters," Typoscript, 1932. ANCIN, 1283–192.

between German wisent breeders and the Poles, who – because of the new borders of 1919 – had gained control over some wisent collections that had previously been German.[64]

Also financially, the First World War continued to cast its shadow over the organization. In letters to American sympathizers, ISPEB president Kurt Priemel complained that the heavy cost of the war reparations prevented the German state from giving substantive support to the Society.[65] Eventually Priemel managed to mobilize some American money for wisent breeding in the early 1930s, but its actual use quickly became a bone of contention between the German and Polish members. The increasing involvement of the Nazi Party in the Society's activities only further damaged cross-border collaboration.[66] After the Second World War, the ISPEB could be saved only by expelling its former German leaders and handing over the presidency to the Poles.[67]

COLONIAL GAME

With the ICPB and the ISPEB, interwar networks of preservationists were originally organized around relatively specific topics. It lasted until 1928, until Sarasin's more ambitious and inclusive idea of *Weltnaturschutz* resurfaced with the foundation of the International Office for the Protection of Nature in Brussels. Both in membership and in its self-set goals this Office had global aspirations. In practice, however, the network and geographical interests of the society would be largely shaped by its three foundational societies: respectively a French, Belgian, and Dutch national committee for the protection of colonial fauna. As such, the Office mainly mobilized a small group of well-connected preservationists in Paris, Brussels, and Amsterdam with an interest for the charismatic megafauna of tropical Africa and Asia.[68] German preservationists were originally not approached, as it was considered too early to give them a visible role, but also because the German loss of colonies made them into

---

[64] See "Bericht über die vierte Hauptversammlung," 78; Erna Mohr, "Wisente im neuen Polen (ab 1924, ohne Pless)," Kurt Priemel to W. Reid Blair, December 3, 1931, ANCIN, 1283–192.

[65] Priemel to Blair, December 3, 1931 ANCIN, 1283–192.

[66] See more in depth De Bont, Extinct in the Wild.

[67] Jan Żabiński, *Pedigree Book of the European Bison* (Warszawa: International Society for the Protection of the European Bison, 1947).

[68] *L'Office international pour la protection de la nature: Ses origines, son programme, son organisation* (Brussels: G. Bothy, 1930).

less interesting partners. Contacts would eventually be established in the 1930s, but references to the past war continued to strain relations even then.[69] The network of the Office, however, did connect relatively easily with fellow preservationists in the United States, who, in the early decades of the twentieth century, had become increasingly captivated by African big game hunting, adventure, and conservation.[70] The most important mediator between the European and American centers, young American zoologist Harold Coolidge, eventually founded his own American Committee for International Wildlife Protection in 1930.[71] In close consultation with the Brussels Office, this Committee further mobilized around the plight of the big mammals of Africa and Asia.[72]

The charismatic mammals of the tropics, many believed, had – like the European bison – been victims of the war. William Temple Hornaday, one of the American pioneers of the conservation movement, was very outspoken on this issue when he addressed the attendees of the 1923 Paris Conference. He stressed that the war had led to a severe setback of preservation measures in Africa, and to a most nefarious armament of natives in India.[73] In the Belgian Parliament, an activist senator voiced similar arguments, claiming among others that the war had led to an almost complete disappearance of the giraffe in Belgian Congo.[74] It is unclear to which extent these statements are accurate, but they are illustrative of the sense of urgency felt at the time.

At the same time, however, the war also proved instrumental in fostering networks that were to counter the perceived decline of the colonial fauna. The Belgian-American contacts are a case in point. The transatlantic coalition of preservationists was strongly stimulated when the war context led to the appointment of Belgian diplomat Émile de Cartier de Marchienne as envoy extraordinary to Washington in 1917. Soon after his appointment, Cartier de Marchienne befriended major American naturalists such as

---

[69] Jean-Marie Derscheid to Van Tienhoven, December 19, 1925, ANCIN, 1283–55; Van Tienhoven to Tordis Graim, March 16, 1931, ANCIN, 1283–64.

[70] Ian Tyrell, *Crisis of the Wasteful Nation: Empire and Conservation in Theodore Roosevelt's America* (Chicago/London: University of Chicago Press, 2015).

[71] Mark Barrow, *Nature's Ghosts: Confronting Extinction from the Age of Jefferson to the Age of Ecology* (Chicago/London: University of Chicago Press, 2009), 144–152.

[72] See Coolidge to Van Tienhoven, March 20, 1930, ANCIN, 1283–50.

[73] William Hornaday, La disparition de la faune dans les diverses parties du monde. In Raoul de Clermont et al., ed., *Premier congrès international pour la protection de la nature* (Paris: Société nationale d'acclimatation de France, 1923), 67–68.

[74] *Annales Parlementaires du Senat, session ordinaire de 1926–1927, séance du jeudi 1927* (Brussels: Senat, 1927), 694–695.

Henry Fairfield Osborn and John C. Merriam.[75] When Albert I – the Belgian "hero king" and symbol of the resistance against the German invasion – toured the United States in 1919, the latter two would accompany him to the Grand Canyon and Yosemite national parks.[76] Later, leading Belgian preservationist Jean Massart also toured several parks as part of a visit of the Commission for Relief in Belgium.[77] It is through those visits that the idea of a national park in Belgian Congo (after an American model) was actively propagated. The strategy was successful: in 1925, the Albert National Park was founded with American support. The networks that had enabled this foundation strongly overlapped with those behind the IOPN. It was no coincidence that the first director of the national park, zoologist Jean-Marie Derscheid, would combine this function with the directorship of the Office, nor that both institutions would be housed in the same Brussels building.[78] The premises, in the following years, became an important stopping place for American scientists to prepare their African expeditions.[79] The First World War, this example shows, not only had a disruptive effect on international preservationist networks but also generated new links.

It is through its networks with royals, ministers, diplomats, and aristocrats that the IOPN could be of some consequence. As in the case of the ICBP and the ISPEB, these networks were not fostered in the context of official policy negotiations, but through society meetings, dinner parties, nature excursions, and personal correspondence. The contacts of the IOPN were not limited to Belgian and American high society, for that

---

[75] Jacques Willequet, Emile de Cartier de Marchienne. In *Biographie Nationale*, vol. 32 (Brussels, 1964), 88–89; Cartier de Marchienne to Merriam, January 17, 1923 and Cartier de Marchienne to Henri Jaspar, February 23, 1923, African Archives, Ministry of Foreign Affairs, Brussels, Archives de l'Agriculture du Congo Belge (AA) A 21, 22. Correspondence.

[76] Karen Jones, Unpacking Yellowstone: The American National Park in a Global Perspective. In Bernhard Gissibl, Sabine Höhler, and Patrick Kupper, eds., *Civilising Nature. National Parks in Global Historical Perspective* (New York/Oxford: Berghahn, 2012), 44.

[77] Cartier de Marchienne to Jaspar, February 23, 1923, AA, A 21, 22. Correspondence.

[78] See also Patricia van Schuylenbergh, Albert National Park: The Birth of Africa's First National Park, 1925–1960. In Marc Languy and Emmanuel de Merode, eds., *Virunga: The Survival of Africa's First National Park* (Tield: Lannoo, 2009), 64–73; Raf De Bont, Borderless Nature: Experts and the Internationalization of Nature Protection. In Evert Peeters, Joris Vandendriessche, and Kaat Wils, eds., *Scientist's Expertise as Performance: Between State and Society, 1860–1960* (London: Pickering and Chatto, 2015), 49–65.

[79] Derscheid to Van Tienhoven, June 14, 1929 and July 5, 1929, ANCIN, 1283–55.

matter. They extended also to France, Britain, the Netherlands, and their colonial possessions.[80]

As compared to intergovernmental organizations such as the League of Nations, civic societies such as the ICPB, the ISPEB, and the IOPN thus relied less on official state diplomacy and more on informal personal contacts. And they allowed for a discreet comeback of the former "enemies" into the community of international preservation and for a relative normalization of relations. It is largely through these contacts that important preservationist initiatives resumed in the interwar years. But, as indicated, these also reflected the fault lines of the war in various ways. Furthermore, unlike the intergovernmental organizations, the civic initiatives remained very small, relying on limited staff numbers and even less money. As such, they generated a lot of ideas, but their actual projects remained limited in scope.

CONCLUSION

The First World War, this chapter has argued, was responsible for both a disruption and reorganization of the global preservation elite. It was partially because of the war that the elite's network failed to institutionalize in the world of intergovernmental diplomacy. This can be ascribed both to a disturbance of the contacts between preservationists across former enemy lines, and to a shift in priorities away from nature preservation of certain crucial governments: Germany's standing in preservation was gone and Swiss officials temporarily lost interest in supporting international initiatives. Societies built around loose networks of experts offered an alternative to intergovernmental organizations, but their resources were very limited. Therefore, rather than carrying out their own programs, these civic societies exercised influence through direct contacts with high-profile policymakers. The most notable example is the London Convention relative to the Preservation of the Fauna and the Flora in the Natural State of 1933. Next to diplomats, this convention had been negotiated by a number of experts – many of whom were member of preservationist societies.[81] The fact that the convention was

---

[80] Patricia van Schuylenbergh, *Congo Nature Factory*: wetenschappelijke netwerken en voorbeelden van Belgisch-Nederlandse uitwisselingen (1885–1940). *Jaarboek voor Ecologische Geschiedenis* 2009 11 (2010), 79–104; De Bont, Borderless Nature.

[81] With, respectively, Van Tienhoven, Derscheid, Abel Gruvel, and John C. Phillips, the Netherlands, Belgium, France, and the United States each had someone sent with

only discussed by representatives of former Allied and neutral forces probably had made things easier as well. Other successes can be ascribed to similar expert lobbying, ranging from breeding programs of wisents to the establishment of national parks in Africa. All of these carried the marks of the past war in their own ways.

The constellation of the preservationist network that arose after the First World War is significant, because it had long-term effects. The Second World War, after all, confirmed many of the earlier trends. To begin with, the new war confirmed the idea that world peace depended on a more careful management of natural resources. "Conservation," American president Harry S. Truman wrote in a letter in 1946, "can become a major source of peace.'[82] In this atmosphere a new phase of institution-building started that largely reinforced the interwar networks. Representatives of interwar societies were, for instance, instrumental in the creation of the International Union for the Protection of Nature (IUPN) in 1948, in which former IOPN members received key positions, including secretary-general and president. Delegates of the Central Powers were conspicuous by their absence. The Germans, who in the 1930s had slowly and hesitantly entered the IOPN and the ICPB, disappeared from the scene again.[83] A great part of the German leadership of the ISPEB was removed because of ties with the Nazi Party and was replaced by Polish scientists.[84]

Also institutionally one can see continuities. Although in the late 1940s there seemed to arise momentum to give the IUPN an intergovernmental make-up and to integrate it in the structure of the United Nations (UN), this did not materialize. The IUPN became a semi-governmental organization that could have both governments and NGOs as members; it stayed out of the UN system, but was (temporarily) subsidized by the United Nations Educational, Scientific and Cultural Organization. Like its prewar predecessors the IUPN remained small and underfunded for many years.[85]

---

a background in the IOPN. See *International Conference for the Protection of the Fauna and Flora of Africa*. 1933. Typoscript.

[82] Truman to John G. Winant, September 4, 1946, UNESCO, AG86 502.7 A 01 IUCNNR "-6," Part I.

[83] *International Union for the Protection of Nature, Established at Fontainebleau, 5 October 1948* (Brussels: International Union for the Protection of Nature, 1948), 26–29.

[84] Żabiński, *Pedigree Book of the European Bison*; Urmacher unerwünscht, *Der Spiegel* 26 (1954), 12–14.

[85] Martin Holdgate, *The Green Web: A Union for World Conservation* (London: Earthscan, 1999), 21–47; McCormick, *The Global Environmental Movement*, 25–41.

It is well established by historians that wars have huge environmental impacts. This is, of course, one way in which they influenced the environmental movement. The quick disappearance of whales, wisents, and giraffes, or the decline of natural resources more generally, created a sense of urgency and a cause around which to rally. Less attention, however, has been paid to the effect of wars on the human fabric itself of the environmental movement. The First World War surely caused a caesura as far as the process of cooperation was concerned. At the same time it served as a catalyst that fostered particular forms of internationalization. In this chapter, we have argued that these effects have been durable both in the composition and in structure of its networks. In this way wars had significant impacts on which projects the nature protection movement developed, how these projects were promoted, and by whom.

14

Memories in Mud

The Environmental Legacy of the Great War

Frank Uekötter

On August 3, 2014, the presidents of France and Germany, François Hollande and Joachim Gauck, met for a commemorative event to mark the centennial of the Great War. The place of choice was the Hartmannswillerkopf mountain in Alsace. The trenches of the First World War ran over this mountain, as German and French soldiers were facing and fighting each other over four years. Some 30,000 men perished on the Hartmannswillerkopf, but neither side had made significant gains by the end of the war. A hundred years later, visitors can still look at 60 kilometers of trenches, 600 bunkers, and a French war cemetery, soon to be joined by a museum; the presidents laid the foundation stone during their visit. About 200,000 people come every year to see a mountain that the French called a "man-eater" (*mangeur d'hommes*). For two countries that cherish rituals of consolation, it seems like a good place for commemoration along the familiar themes of Franco–German postwar *amitié*, and given that acts of state are carefully scripted events nowadays, it should come as no surprise that everything went according to plan. Yet nature could have interfered with the ceremony in its own distinct ways. Visitors to the Hartmannswillerkopf are warned to watch out for a local population of *vipera berus*, better known as the common European adder.[1]

On first glance, the risk of snakebites might seem as remote as the role of the environment in the commemoration of the First World War. In his

---

[1] Rüdiger Soldt, Zehntausende starben am Hartmannsweilerkopf. *Frankfurter Allgemeine Zeitung*, December 6, 2013, www.faz.net/aktuell/gesellschaft/der-menschenfresserberg -zehntausende-starben-am-hartmannsweilerkopf-12689001.html (accessed March 21, 2017); www.tagesschau.de/inland/weltkrieg-gedenken-104.html (accessed March 21, 2017).

book *The Long Shadow: The Great War and the Twentieth Century*, David Reynolds looks into a wide range of issues from automobile production and consumer debt to pastoralism in art and poetry, but environmental issues receive short shrift.[2] When it comes to war, the human element is usually front and center, and the environment appears as a side issue at best and a distraction at worst. But in a way, the adders at the Franco–German summit serve as a fitting metaphor for the search for environmental memories.

This epilogue argues for a broader approach to the environmental legacy of war. Scholars have long recognized that visions of nature played a role in the experience of war. George Mosse argued that war "led to a heightened awareness of nature," as mythical landscapes helped "to mask the reality of war."[3] Imaginations of the land also served as a bridge between memory studies and environmental history in Simon Schama's widely acclaimed *Landscape and Memory*.[4] The interplay between landscapes and memory is an important focal point in recent scholarship on war and the environment, and yet it seems that this approach does not exhaust the topic.[5] More precisely, discussions of militarized landscapes tend to remain on the surface in quite a literal sense, but the impact of animals, plants, and materials goes much deeper. If we want to capture these impacts in their full complexity, we need a more encompassing methodological approach: while focusing on landscapes tends to view the environment first and foremost as a *reflection* of memories, we should see it more broadly as a *distinct mode* of memory.[6] Bringing the environment more fully into memory studies forces us to take firsthand experiences with the natural world more seriously in memory studies, and it alerts us to the coevolution of human memories and the natural world. As it stands, memory studies rest firmly with the province of cultural

---

[2] David Reynolds, *The Long Shadow: The Great War and the Twentieth Century* (London: Simon & Schuster, 2013).

[3] George L. Mosse, *Fallen Soldiers: Reshaping the Memory of the World Wars* (New York: Oxford University Press, 1990), 107.

[4] Simon Schama, *Landscape and Memory* (London: Harper Perennial, 1995).

[5] For some recent contributions, see Brian Black, The Nature of Preservation: The Rise of Authenticity at Gettysburg. *Civil War History* 58 (2012), 348–373; Chris Pearson, *Mobilizing Nature: The Environmental History of War and Militarization in Modern France* (Manchester: Manchester University Press, 2012); Chris Pearson, Peter Coates and Tim Cole, eds., *Militarized Landscapes: From Gettysburg to Salisbury Plain* (London: Continuum, 2010).

[6] Cf. Patrick Joyce and Tony Bennett, eds., *Material Powers: Cultural Studies, History and the Material Turn* (Abingdon: Routledge, 2010).

studies, but we cannot grasp the full environmental legacy of the Great War if we remain committed to this academic tradition.

The natural environment is inherently transnational, and this deserves particular attention in the present context. The nation-state has figured prominently in memory studies ever since Pierre Nora's landmark project on French *lieux de mémoire*.[7] In recent years, scholars have begun to seek venues to advance the debate across borders. An international group of scholars has published a compilation of European sites of memory in three volumes.[8] Another group produced no fewer than five volumes on sites of memory that Germany and Poland share.[9] And then there is what Klaus Bachmann has labeled "Versöhnungskitsch": well-meaning but overtly pathetic mementos of consolation.[10] The following discussion is not beyond national contexts, and yet it deserves reflection that many environmental experiences transcend national borders by their very nature: forests, crops, and weeds have taken over former battlefields wherever they are. In fact, given that so much of First World War commemoration remains captive of national frames of reference, it may help to reflect on experiences that move beyond these contexts. Scholarship by environmental historians has long displayed a power to subvert conventional readings. The centennial of the First World War is as good an occasion as any to bring this to bear in memory studies.

LANDSCAPES OF WAR

The Hartmannswillerkopf mountain is one of numerous battlefields that entered collective memory. The Great War bestowed Europe with a new mental geography, and some places became famous (or infamous) far and wide. Some sites, such as Passchendaele and Gallipoli, were virtually

[7] Pierre Nora, *Les lieux de mémoire*, 7 vols. (Paris: Gallimard, 1984–1992).

[8] Pim den Boer et al., eds., *Europäische Erinnerungsorte*, 3 vols. (Munich: Oldenbourg, 2012).

[9] Hans Henning Hahn and Robert Traba, eds., *Deutsch-polnische Erinnerungsorte, vol. 1: Geteilt/Gemeinsam* (Paderborn: Schöningh, 2015); Hans Henning Hahn and Robert Traba, eds., *Deutsch-polnische Erinnerungsorte, vol. 2: Geteilt/Gemeinsam* (Paderborn: Schöningh, 2014); Hans Henning Hahn and Robert Traba, eds., *Deutsch-polnische Erinnerungsorte, vol. 3: Parallelen* (Paderborn: Schöningh, 2012); Hans Henning Hahn and Robert Traba, eds., *Deutsch-polnische Erinnerungsorte, vol. 4: Reflexionen* (Paderborn: Schöningh, 2013); Peter Oliver Loew and Robert Traba, eds., *Deutsch-polnische Erinnerungsorte, vol. 5: Erinnerung auf Polnisch* (Paderborn: Schöningh, 2015).

[10] Cf. Hans Henning Hahn, Heidi Hein-Kircher, and Anna Kochanowska-Nieborak, eds., *Erinnerungskultur und Versöhnungskitsch* (Marburg: Herder-Institut, 2008).

unknown before they became places of mass death. Others already had a place in history that was all but erased by the war: the Verdun article in Pierre Nora's seminal volumes devotes only few cursory sentences to the 843 Treaty of Verdun and Vauban's seventeenth-century fortifications, suggesting that claims about long-standing national fame are a post-1916 glorification: "For the pedagogues of the late nineteenth century, Verdun was no different from many other cities."[11] In the case of the 1914 Tannenberg battle, war propaganda could nicely link the German victory to a previous battle of 1410, all the more since that battle had ended with the fateful defeat of the Teutonic Order of Knights (a reading that generously glanced over the fact that the two medieval armies were multiethnic).[12] In 1927, German president Paul von Hindenburg, commander of the German military during the First World War, attended the inaugural of the Tannenberg National Memorial and gave a speech that exonerated Germany from blame for the war. The League of Nations, in session at Geneva at the time, was not amused.[13]

Battles left their mark on the land, particularly where the front lines were stalled and armies dug into the ground. Trenches obviously changed the landscape, but they were only the most spectacular feature of a complex technological system. As David Stevenson writes, "In their way the trenches were an imposing engineering achievement, the more so if account is taken of the immense infrastructure behind them. It comprised hospitals, barracks, training camps, ammunition dumps, artillery parks, and telephone networks, as well as military roads and canals, but preeminently it meant railways."[14] Scientists have studied the former battlefields as exemplary cases of anthropogenic disturbances of the soil and found that "the millions of artillery craters on the Verdun battlefield have changed the area's surface hydrology, water table characteristics, and soil development processes and rates."[15] However, trench warfare left its

---

[11] Antoine Prost, Verdun. In Pierre Nora and Lawrence D. Kritzman, eds., *Realms of Memory: The Construction of the French Past, vol. 3: Symbols* (New York: Columbia University Press, 1998), 377–401, 379.

[12] Frithjof Benjamin Schenk, Tannenberg/Grunwald. In Etienne François and Hagen Schulze, eds., *Deutsche Erinnerungsorte, vol. 1* (Munich: C. H. Beck, 2001), 438–454.

[13] Anton Gill, *A Dance between Flames: Berlin between the Wars* (London: Abacus, 1995), 166.

[14] David Stevenson, *1914–1918: The History of the First World War* (London: Penguin, 2004), 182.

[15] Joseph P. Hupy and Randall J. Schaetzl, Soil Development on the WWI Battlefield of Verdun, France. *Geoderma* 145 (2008), 37–49, 47.

technological mark far beyond the range of the artillery. The railroad bridge at Remagen, which became famous in the Second World War as the only bridge over the Rhine that the retreating German army failed to destroy, was hastily built during the First World War. Gerard Fitzgerald's discussion of the Superfund site that grew out of the production of poison gas in Edgewood, Maryland shows that the impact on the land even extended beyond the Atlantic.

War created new landscapes, but it also erased existing ones. The university library at Leuven, Belgium became an infamous symbol of German militarism after the advancing German army put it to flames. (The library was rebuilt in the 1920s, reconstructed again after another conflagration that another German army induced in 1940, and eventually became a permanent victim to the university's separation into a French and a Flemish wing in 1971.)[16] The Montello forest in the Italian province of Treviso, carefully protected against local intrusions by Venetian authorities that craved its oaks and chestnut trees for shipbuilding, was ravaged during the First World War.[17] When the heads of state of the European Union assembled for a summit in June 2014, they had dinner in the cloth hall of Ypres, a reconstructed copy of a medieval building that, along with the rest of the historic city, had been leveled in the Battles of Ypres. The Belgian residents had rebuilt their town in the 1920s over objections from none other than Winston Churchill, who wanted to keep the town in its ruined state as a testimonial to British wartime sacrifice.[18]

Commemorative tourism is not a privilege of the elite, however, and has never been. The first Michelin guides on the battle zone went to press while the fighting was still in progress. After the Armistice, Frenchmen received free railroad trips to war cemeteries while Thomas Cook offered packaged trips.[19] The leftovers of the war even became the subject of a distinct branch of archaeology in recent decades.[20] It may be a good idea

---

[16] Wolfgang Schivelbusch, *Die Bibliothek von Löwen: Eine Episode aus der Zeit der Weltkriege* (Munich: Hanser, 1988).

[17] Ulrich Gruber, *Die Entdeckung der Nachhaltigkeit: Kulturgeschichte eines Begriffs* (Munich: Kunstmann, 2010), 86.

[18] David William Lloyd, *Battlefield Tourism: Pilgrimage and the Commemoration of the Great War in Britain, Australia and Canada, 1919–1939* (London: Bloomsbury Academic, 1998), 121.

[19] Susanne Brandt, Reklamefahrten zur Hölle oder Pilgerreisen? Schlachtfeldtourismus zur Westfront von 1914 bis heute. *Tourismus Journal* 7(1) (2003), 107–124, 111.

[20] Yannick van Hollebeeke, Birger Stichelbaut, and Jean Bourgeois, From Landscape of War to Archaeological Report: Ten Years of Professional World War I Archaeology in Flanders (Belgium). *European Journal of Archaeology* 17(4) (2014), 702–719.

to have specialists doing the digging, as there is an enduring risk from unexploded ammunition. The people in the Flemish town of Messines know that particularly well.

The Battle of Messines began with a thundering explosion on June 7, 1917. British tunnelers had dug shafts under the German lines, filled them with explosives, and ignited them simultaneously. Nineteen mines exploded and destroyed the German lines, which allowed the British Second Army to capture the Messines-Wytschaete Ridge; one explosion at Spanbroekmolen left a crater 430 feet in diameter. However, two mines failed to explode. "One of them was deliberately detonated in 1955, the other remains underground somewhere to the north-east of Ploegsteert Wood, its exact position unknown," Martin Gilbert wrote, adding that the presence was "exciting periodic local nervousness."[21] That sentiment is arguably unsurprising, as the Spanbroekmolen mine crater is still around under a new name. It now figures as "The Pool of Peace."[22]

Underground explosions were also a weapon of choice in the war between Italy and the Austro-Hungarian Empire. After Italy joined the war in 1915, the front line ran across the southern Alps, which made sudden advances even more difficult than along the Western Front. It was quite an achievement to establish and maintain an artillery positions at an altitude of 3,860 meters, as the Austrians did on the Ortler massif, and losses ran high due to the environmental conditions. However, all these efforts could also be read as superlative examples of alpinism. There were many volunteers on the Austrian-German side, particularly during the early stages of war when most regular soldiers were fighting elsewhere. It became a distinct chapter of remembrance after the war. A vast literature discussed the alpine war as if it had been something of a mountain climbing contest under peculiar conditions. Even recent travel book writers are torn between the horrors of trench war and admiration for the mountaineers' superb skills.[23]

---

[21] Martin Gilbert, *First World War* (London: Weidenfeld and Nicolson, 1994), 336. The mine has not exploded to the present day (www.ww1battlefields.co.uk/flanders/messines.html [accessed March 21, 2017]).

[22] Ploegsteert Wood, Messines, and Wytschaete. Echoes of War. Ypres and the Somme Today, http://echoesofwar.blogspot.co.uk/2009/01/mud-corner-cwgc.html (accessed March 21, 2017).

[23] Dietrich Höllhuber, *Südtirol*, 2nd edn. (Erlangen: Michael Müller Verlag, 2006), 414; Oswald Stimpfl et al., *Südtirol*, 8th edn. (Ostfildern: Karl Baedeker Verlag, 2006), 34.

MUD LANDS

The battlefields are more than simple relics of war. They were also places of targeted design. Most of the Western Front came under French control after the war, and so it was particularly important that France passed a law in 1920 that allowed the government to specify certain bunkers, craters, or trenches for protection. After one year, 236 sites were listed.[24] However, the appearance of the land quickly became more of a human creation as soon as nature found an opportunity to intervene with its own dynamism. Reforestation at Verdun became subject to a vigorous debate in the veterans' journal *Le Journal des mutilés et réformés* in 1930.[25] Overgrowth was an important issue for visitors, as veterans sought to recognize their former positions and reacted with furor to changes in familiar views. And overgrowth was a metaphorical problem, as it seemed to reflect a fateful fading of collective awareness.

Of course, its appearance is only one part of the experience of a landscape, if one wishes to use the word at all; Dorothee Brantz has argued that the Great War "unsettled existing notions of landscape" to such an extent that one should rather speak of "environments."[26] Most soldiers viewed the battlefield from low-lying positions, through barbed wire and small openings in fortified positions. In fact, many soldiers watched the landscape in a state of dissolution, as mines and artillery combined with rainfall and groundwater to turn the ground into a sodden state. Mud was perhaps the most notorious environmental icon of the war, and it continues to hold a certain fascination. Some historians (including the present one) could not resist the temptation of referring to mud in their titles.[27]

Mud was dangerous for a number of reasons. It jeopardized the technological infrastructure that the war rested upon. Loose ground destabilized fortifications and gummed up guns and ammunition, and a mudslide could distract attention at a crucial moment. It exacerbated the unsanitary

---

[24] Brandt, Reklamefahrten zur Hölle oder Pilgerreisen? 113.   [25] Prost, Verdun, 389.

[26] Dorothee Brantz, Environments of Death: Trench Warfare on the Western Front, 1914–18. In Charles E. Closmann, ed., *War and the Environment: Military Destruction in the Modern Age* (College Station: Texas A&M University Press, 2009), 68–91, 83.

[27] See, for instance, Gordon Corrigan, *Mud, Blood and Poppycock: Britain and the First World War* (London: Cassell, 2003), Edward P. F. Lynch, *Somme Mud: The War Experiences of an Infantryman in France 1916–1919* (Milsons Point, NSW: Random House Australia, 2006); and Marianne Barker, *Nightingales in the Mud: The Digger Sisters of the Great War, 1914–1918* (Sydney: Allen & Unwin, 1989).

conditions in the trenches. Mud could also spread diseases: "The fertile fields of the Flanders plain, heavily manured in peacetime, harboured many highly infectious organisms such as *Clostridium Tetani*, the cause of gas gangrene. ... Tissue loss, infection and scarring combined to produce dreadful deformity in those who survived."[28] The mud even brought forth a new type of disease called "trench foot" with symptoms "similar to frostbite caused by constant immersion."[29]

Contrary to a popular myth, mud was not universal. Sometimes a helpful geology kept the soldiers' feet dry, and even Flanders had extended periods without rain. But where it was present, mud was a terrifying force in its own right. On March 26, 1917, a French front-line newspaper described it as follows:

At night, crouching in a shell-hole and filling it, the mud watches, like an enormous octopus. The victim arrives. It throws its poisonous slobber out at him, blinds him, closes round him, buries him. One more *"disparu,"* one more man gone. ... For men die of mud, as they die from bullets, but more horribly. Mud is where men sink and – what is worse – where their soul sinks. But where are those hack journalists who turn out such heroic articles, when the mud is that deep? Mud hides the stripes of rank, there are only poor suffering beasts. Look, there, there are flecks of red on that pool of mud – blood from a wounded man. Hell is not fire, that would not be the ultimate in suffering. Hell is mud![30]

The mud eroded not only soldiers' morale but also the customs of civilized society. Cleanliness was a key part of bourgeois culture, and a stain of mud meant more than a physical blemish in peacetime.[31] But in the trenches, mud was a full-body experience, and there was no escape from its power. In fact, it was probably this symbolic power that made it such an enduring fixture of commemoration. The mud stood for disorder and chaos, the antithesis of Western civilization – in short, the end of the world as people knew it. While literary figures could retrospectively rhapsodize about artillery battles as the "storms of steel" (*Stahlgewitter*) of Jüngerian fame, that never worked with the mud.[32]

---

[28] Andrew Bamji, Facial Surgery: The Patient's Experience. In Hugh Cecil and Peter H. Liddle, eds., *Facing Armageddon: The First World War Experienced* (London: Leo Cooper, 1996), 490–501, 492.

[29] Stevenson, *1914–1918: The History of the First World War*, 207.

[30] Quoted after Gilbert, *First World War*, 313.

[31] Manuel Frey, *Der reinliche Bürger. Entstehung und Verbreitung bürgerlicher Tugenden in Deutschland, 1760–1860* (Göttingen: Vandenhoeck & Ruprecht, 1997).

[32] Cf. Ernst Jünger, *In Stahlgewittern* (Stuttgart: Klett-Cotta, 2014 [1920]).

A NEW MATERIAL WORLD

The First World War changed not only landscapes but also the material world. It brought forth new commodities and permanently changed the place of preexisting ones. The change was particularly dramatic for the Central Powers, which found themselves cut off from world markets due to an effective Allied blockade of overseas trade. Finding replacements for products that were no longer available became a common sport, and at the end of the war, German ingenuity had produced more than 11,000 ersatz products.[33] One of the enterprising spirits was Konrad Adenauer, later chancellor of the Federal Republic, who administered the food supply of Cologne during the war and won a patent for inventing a nutritious but mediocre-tasting bread – good enough to fill the stomach, but not so good as to encourage overconsumption.[34]

Many of these products disappeared with the end of the war, as they were clearly inferior and furthermore evoked unwelcome memories of hard times. Adenauer's bread is still available for purchase in Cologne, though, a worthy precursor to Helmut Kohl's penchant for *Saumagen*, a hearty dish that countless political figures had to stomach in his presence.[35] British publishers even brought the wartime cookbook – a popular genre at the time, as scarcity called for new ways of preparing meals – back to life in time for the centennial.[36] But then, the material consequences of the First World War also matter for people who do not care for trench pudding. At least three commodities that defined modernity in the twentieth century came out of the war transformed: oil, aluminum, and synthetic nitrogen.

The First World War was the first military conflict where oil played a defining role (see Dan Tamir's chapter in this volume for details). On the eve of Sarajevo, First Lord of the Admiralty Winston Churchill convinced the British parliament to buy a stake in the Anglo-Persian Oil Company, which offered discounts on Royal Navy fuel purchases thereafter. Paris taxicabs brought French troops to the Marne in September 1914. "In the course of the First World War, oil and the internal combustion engine

---

[33] Ulrich Herbert, *Geschichte Deutschlands im 20. Jahrhundert* (Munich: C. H. Beck, 2014), 143.

[34] Peter Koch, *Die Erfindungen des Dr. Konrad Adenauer* (Reinbek: Wunderlich, 1986).

[35] Wo es das Brot von Konrad Adenauer gibt. *koeln.de*, April 2, 2011, www.koeln.de/koeln/unfertig_adenauerbrot_428837.html (accessed March 21, 2017).

[36] May Clarissa Gillington Byron, *The Great War Cook Book* (Stroud: Amberley, 2014); Andrew Robertshaw, *Feeding Tommy: Battlefield Recipes from the First World War* (Stroud, Gloucestershire: Spellmount, 2013).

changed every dimension of warfare, even the very meaning of mobility on land and sea and in the air," Daniel Yergin wrote in his highly acclaimed *The Prize*.[37] Global petroleum use increased by 50% during the four years of war, a growth rate that provoked the first spate of depletion warnings after the guns fell silent.[38] The postwar jockeying of European and American oil interests in the Middle East was the overture for a century of foreign interventions in the region.

Aluminum is the earth' most abundant metal, but it did not meet the public's eyes until the 1855 Paris World Fair. In 1845, German chemist Friedrich Wöhler had synthesized the first drops of aluminum, but it initially was little more than a lab curiosity. Aluminum's specific weight is about one-third that of iron, but that failed to win many converts in the nineteenth century: iron was easier to forge and to weld, and its production took less energy. Germany did not have a single aluminum smelter until the First World War inspired a hectic buildup of production capacities, and the global output of aluminum more than doubled (1914–1918) from 84,000 tons to 180,000 tons.[39] After the war, aluminum became a solution in search of a problem, but frantic invention of new uses forestalled the commodity's decline. Ever since the Great War, the high-energy metal has been part of modern living.

During the war, aluminum was used as an electric conductor and for zeppelin construction (use for winged aviation was still marginal), which makes it difficult to call it a decisive commodity. In that respect, synthetic nitrogen was different: it was the crucial resource that kept the German army firing during the First World War. Fritz Haber and Carl Bosch had mastered the technology of producing ammonia from atmospheric nitrogen shortly before the First World War. Once the fighting had started, the output was earmarked for the production of explosives, replacing saltpeter imports that were no longer available. The advent of synthetic nitrogen changed the global nitrogen cycle forever, and it has rightly been called "one of the great technological achievements of the twentieth century."[40] Haber received the Nobel Prize for Chemistry in 1918, but his reputation was already tainted by another substance at that

---

[37] Daniel Yergin, *The Prize: The Epic Quest for Oil, Money and Power* (New York: Simon & Schuster, 1991), 167.

[38] Brian C. Black, *Crude Reality: Petroleum in World History* (Lanham, MD: Rowman & Littlefield, 2012), 80.

[39] Luitgard Marschall, *Aluminium – Metall der Moderne* (Munich: oekom, 2008), 166, 171.

[40] Hugh S. Gorman, *The Story of N: A Social History of the Nitrogen Cycle and the Challenge of Sustainability* (New Brunswick, NJ: Rutgers University Press, 2013), 79.

point – poison gas. Haber was the scientific mastermind behind Germany's chemical warfare.[41]

THE PANIC BUTTON

The wartime story of synthetic nitrogen has another dimension that deserves reflection in the present context. Fritz Haber had envisioned synthetic nitrogen for use as mineral fertilizer, and his company, the Badische Anilin- und Soda-Fabrik (BASF), had taken steps for an orderly introduction into agriculture. When mass production was starting at the Oppau plant near Ludwigshafen, BASF set up its own agricultural experiment station at Limburgerhof in the spring of 1914 in order to study the new fertilizer closely in field trials.[42] With the huge expansion of production capacity during the war, vast quantities were suddenly available for farmers once the guns fell silent, and the introduction of synthetic nitrogen occurred in a frenzy. The result was gross misuse and a dangerous soil fertility crisis.[43]

The story illustrates an important point. It mattered not only *that* the First World War changed the material world but also *how change took place*. None of the warring nations had any advance planning for resource management, as statesmen commonly expected a war of short duration. With the front lines stagnant by autumn 1914, countries built war economies with much improvisation and little thought about long-term consequences. Environmental problems were rooted in their material essence as much as in speed, and the tumultuous postwar years did not help things to calm down quickly. It was as if entire societies had pressed the panic button.

With that in mind, one of the most exciting questions about the environmental legacy of the First World War is whether we can observe a general shift in the style of environmental management in the wake of the war experience. The brutalizing effect of total war is a familiar theme in general history, but it is still an open question whether it left an imprint

---

[41] Margit Szöllösi-Janze, *Fritz Haber 1868–1934: Eine Biographie* (Munich: C. H. Beck, 1998).

[42] Landwirtschaftliche Versuchsstation Limburgerhof, *Arbeiten der Landwirtschaftlichen Versuchsstation Limburgerhof: Eine Rückschau auf Entwicklung und Tätigkeit in den Jahre 1914 bis 1939* (Limburgerhof: Landwirtschaftliche Versuchsstation, 1939), 13, 23.

[43] I have discussed this story extensively in my *Die Wahrheit ist auf dem Feld: Eine Wissensgeschichte der deutschen Landwirtschaft* (Göttingen: Vandenhoeck & Ruprecht, 2010), 183–259.

on environmental issues. When a neighbor complained about noise from a factory in Erfurt in 1916, company officials retorted that the nuisance, which stemmed from trial runs for aircraft engines, was nothing compared with the "artillery barrage at Verdun (*Trommelfeuer vor Verdun*)."[44] Yet was this more than an exceptional case of strained nerves? We also have a 1916 article in the journal of the Bavarian Botanical Society that discussed, with all the earnestness that a German academic can muster, "the death of spruce trees caused by artillery shells."[45] We should not forget that the brutalization thesis has come under criticism in First World War historiography even for Germany, the country where it was traditionally presumed to have particular plausibility as a contributing factor to the rise of the Nazis.[46]

Of course, there can be little doubt that the First World War slowed the push for environmental reform considerably. I have argued elsewhere that the crisis years from 1914 to 1945 may represent "something of a hiatus" in environmental history.[47] But was that due to the general change of the political and socioeconomic context, or can we identify a more immediate connection? For instance, was there an upswing of apocalyptic thinking, or were there specific groups that would be the environmentalist equivalent to Dadaism or the authors of the Lost Generation? Thanks to Edmund Russell's path-breaking inquiry in *War and Nature*, environmental historians know about how military experiences shaped environmental tools and mindsets.[48]

ANIMALS TO THE FRONT

One of the most popular environmental memories of the First World War started with a children's novel. In 1982, Michael Morpurgo wrote *War Horse*, a book that explores wartime suffering through the career of a horse drafted for the British army. Twenty-nine years later, Walt Disney Studios released a movie of the same title based on Morpurgo's book; the

---

[44] Stadtarchiv Erfurt 1–2/506–382, fol. 28R.

[45] Rubner, das durch Artilleriegeschosse verursachte Fichtensterben. *Mitteilungen der Bayerischen Botanischen Gesellschaft zur Erforschung der heimischen Flora* 3(13) (January 1, 1916), 273–276.

[46] Benjamin Ziemann, *Contested Commemorations: Republican War Veterans and Weimar Political Culture* (Cambridge: Cambridge University Press, 2013), 268.

[47] Frank Uekötter, Thinking Big: The Broad Outlines of a Burgeoning Field. In Frank Uekötter, ed., *The Turning Points of Environmental History* (Pittsburgh, PA: University of Pittsburgh Press, 2010), 1–12, 9.

[48] Edmund Russell, *War and Nature: Fighting Humans and Insects with Chemicals from World War I to Silent Spring* (Cambridge: Cambridge University Press, 2001).

director was Steven Spielberg. It was nominated for six Oscars, and it gained worldwide returns of $177 million with a production budget of $66 million. According to the website *Box Office Mojo*, which tracks box office revenue, it has dethroned *Lawrence of Arabia* as the highest-grossing movie on the First World War.[49]

It is the type of film that has academic historians rolling their eyes. Horses did serve in the First World War, but their fate was usually predestined: "In the summer of 1918, average life expectancy for an artillery horse was ten days."[50] The equestrian hero of *War Horse* crosses the front lines twice, and the film has a Hollywood ending: the horse survives and reunites with its prewar owner. And then it is a matter of debate whether the thick personal drama leaves any room for broader issues. The National Theatre that had the *War Horse* musical on show in London enjoyed critical acclaim: "thrilling" (*Sunday Times*), "stunning" (*Time*), "genius" (*Daily Telegraph*), and "pure theatrical imagination" (*Newsday*). None of which bodes well for historical awareness.

The commemoration of the First World War has always been staunchly anthropocentric, and room for nonhuman actors was scant. When Alfred Crosby published a pioneering study of the 1918 influenza, he called it "America's forgotten pandemic."[51] When it came to commemoration, animals had the best chance when they succumbed to human categories and qualified as "comrades." In Germany, veteran cavalry soldiers and animal protection leagues joined forces in the commemoration of war horses and issued thousands of plaques to "equestrian comrades" (*Ehrenschild Kriegskamerad*). However, one can also read this as nostalgia, as the fortunes of the cavalry were obviously in decline.[52] A few British pigeons received the Victoria Cross for honorable wartime service, and monuments for "pigeon-soldiers" were built in Lille and Brussels.[53]

---

[49] Cf. http://boxofficemojo.com/movies/?id=warhorse.htm and http://boxofficemojo.com/genres/chart/?id=worldwari.htm (accessed March 22, 2017).

[50] Gene M. Tempest, All the Muddy Horses: Giving a Voice to the "Dumb Creatures" of the Western Front (1914–1918). In Rainer Pöppinghege, ed., *Tiere im Krieg: Von der Antike bis zur Gegenwart* (Paderborn: Schöningh, 2009), 217–234, 218.

[51] Alfred W. Crosby, *America's Forgotten Pandemic: The Influenza of 1918* (Cambridge: Cambridge University Press, 1989).

[52] Rainer Pöppinghege, Abgesattelt! Die publizistischen Rückzugsgefechte der deutschen Kavallerie seit 1918. In Rainer Pöppinghege, ed., *Tiere im Krieg: Von der Antike bis zur Gegenwart* (Paderborn: Schöningh, 2009), 235–250, 238.

[53] Rainer Pöppinghege and Tammy Proctor, "Außerordentlicher Bedarf für das Feldheer": Brieftauben im Ersten Weltkrieg. In Rainer Pöppinghege. ed., *Tiere im Krieg: Von der Antike bis zur Gegenwart* (Paderborn: Schöningh, 2009), 103–117, 115.

The pigeon that carried the last message from the falling Fort Vaux at Verdun is a French national myth.[54]

In 1932, a frieze was unveiled at a clinic of the Royal Society for the Prevention of Cruelty to Animals in northwest London that mentioned the society's role in tending for 725,216 animals wounded during the Great War.[55] However, veteran soldiers, rather than animal welfare groups, were the driving force behind the commemoration of animals, and that had an important consequence in that memories of animal companionship typically died with the veterans.[56] Technology came to dominate the public view of war, and animals did not quite fit a mental picture with tanks and airplanes. However, the topic reemerged about a decade ago when the Princess Royal unveiled an "Animals in War" memorial near London's Hyde Park. To the best of this author's knowledge, no other country has such a high-profile monument to animals in war.[57]

The dedication of the monument took place upon the ninetieth anniversary of the First World War in November 2004. It is not a monument that focuses specifically on the Great War, though, as any type of commemorative discrimination would have run counter to the intended goal of honoring a forgotten class of actors. The inscription says that the monument "is dedicated to all the animals that served and died alongside British and Allied forces in wars and campaigns throughout time," and a relief shows many different animals. Two heavily laden bronze mules climb a few steps to get through a small gap in the Portland stone wall, and a horse and a dog wait on the other side. In addition to the names of donors and theatres of war, the monument also offers a sobering insight into the role of animals in war: "They had no choice."[58] But then, it is a matter of debate whether the ordinary conscripted soldier had more of a choice.

---

[54] Philippe Leymarie. Le dernier pigeon de Verdun. *RFI*, February 26, 2006, www1.rfi.fr /actufr/articles/074/article_42106.asp (accessed March 21, 2017).

[55] Hilda Kean, Animals and War Memorials: Different Approaches to Commemorating the Human–Animal Relationship. In Ryan Hediger, ed., *Animals and War: Studies of Europe and North America* (Leiden: Brill, 2013), 237–262, 248.

[56] For a commemorative anthology of veteran stories, see Johannes Theuerkauff, ed., *Tiere im Krieg* (Berlin: Steuben-Verlag, 1938).

[57] In May 2009, a much smaller "Animals in War" memorial was unveiled at the Australian War Memorial in Canberra. See Kean, Animals and War Memorials, 257–259.

[58] Information on the monument is available at www.animalsinwar.org.uk (accessed August 23, 2017).

THE NATURE OF COMMEMORATION

Of course, such a remark crosses the crucial line that divides the investigation of memories as they evolved from the investigation of memories as they should be. But why should reflections on the nature of commemoration be off-limits for environmental historians, given that commemorative events of 2014 made ample use of the environment as a canvas? Every school in the United Kingdom received a pack of poppy seeds to plant in their school grounds. Prime Minister David Cameron launched the scheme with a planting ceremony at 10 Downing Street that enthusiasts can watch on YouTube (however, the video received only 1,411 views and 16 likes over the following three years).[59] The poppy "had accumulated a ripe traditional symbolism in English writing," making it a multifaceted bundle of allusions that included homoerotic love by 1914, but it all faded into the background when the poppy became a British symbol of remembrance.[60] It has served as a major fundraising tool of the Royal British Legion since the First World War, and a number of other countries share the poppy with somewhat lesser enthusiasm. The custom goes back to the poem "In Flanders Fields" that John McCrae, a British army surgeon, wrote during the Second Battle of Ypres. First published in the December 8, 1915 issue of *Punch*, the first stanza reads as follows:

> In Flanders fields the poppies blow
> Between the crosses, row on row,
> That mark our place; and in the sky
> The lark, still bravely singing, fly
> Scarce heard amid the guns below.[61]

The poet captured an authentic experience. Larks did sing in Flanders in the morning, and poppies grew in great numbers on the battlefields. Poppy seeds can stay in the ground for years, they blossom during fallow, and their red color invites the association with spilled blood along with the hope that something more elevating may grow from the killing fields. But poppies flourished not only on the wastelands of the First World War. They also grow in Afghanistan, where poppies serve a non-decorative function as a source of opium and heroin. With the foreign military presence on the decline, poppy farming is on the rise on Afghan fields,

---

[59] www.youtube.com/watch?v=LCdmKvKe4AY (accessed March 21, 2017).
[60] Paul Fussell, *The Great War and Modern Memory* (London: Oxford University Press, 1975), 247.
[61] John McCrae, *In Flanders Fields and Other Poems* (London: Hodder and Stoughton, 1919), 15.

and the centenary of the Great War saw a new production record with 224,000 hectares under cultivation.[62] The connection could insert a sense of ambivalence into British collective awareness, but that calls for a level of reflexivity that nationalist discourses do not always achieve. The cybersphere exploded with outrage when a poppy-wearing David Cameron visited the Great Hall of the People in Beijing on November 9, 2010, as the Chinese hosts felt that the poppy "evoked painful memories of the Opium War fought between Britain and China from 1839 to 1842."[63] The learning curve was rather flat on the British side, for Cameron was spotted with another poppy when he received Chinese president Xi Jinping at Chequers in October 2015.[64] It would seem that the British prime minister was not up to the subversive power of environmental commemoration.

THE FINAL BLOSSOM?

By and large, the center of Birmingham is a peaceful place. People go there for shopping during the day and to hang out during the night, and strict anti-gun laws make the prospect of a firefight unlikely. There is certainly no need for trenches of the First World War variety. Yet such a trench existed on Victoria Square in the summer of 2014, the place where the city's street mall meets the Council House. The trench is fenced off and ostensibly mud-free, and its design seamlessly integrates sandbags and lavish flowerbeds. For those who somehow fail to make the connection, two warplanes hover above with grass-covered wings. According to Birmingham Parks & Nurseries, which designed and created the display, they represent a British Sopwith Camel chasing the Red Baron's Fokker DR. I. The flower display is arguably one of the more bizarre commemorations of the First World War, and surely one of the most biologically diverse. It won an award at the Chelsea Flower Show, and it was rebuilt in 2015.

---

[62] George Arnett, Opium Harvest in Afghanistan Reaches Record Levels after Troop Withdrawal. *The Guardian*, November 12, 2014, www.theguardian.com/news/data blog/2014/nov/12/opium-harvest-afghanistan-record-levels-after-troop-withdrawal (accessed March 21, 2017).

[63] Julia Lovell, *The Opium War: Drugs, Dreams and the Making of China* (London: Picador, 2012), ix.

[64] Andy McSmith, Andy McSmith's Diary: Why David Cameron's Poppy Makes Xi See Red. *Independent*, October 22, 2015, www.independent.co.uk/news/uk/politics/andy-mcsmiths-diary-why-david-cameron-s-poppy-makes-xi-see-red-a6705026.html (accessed March 21, 2017).

FIGURE 14.1 First World War memorial display in Birmingham, England
Source: Photograph by the author.

The display was part of a national campaign that left little doubt about
the sponsors' earnestness, and yet one cannot help but wonder whether,
the best efforts of West Midlands gardeners notwithstanding, 2014 saw
the last flowering of First World War commemoration. In reviewing the
scholarly output upon the ninetieth anniversary ten years ago, the
New Yorker smelled "the first cool injections of historical embalming
fluid." Historians continued to disagree, but their quarrels no longer
had the biting vigor of personal involvement. "Something larger is at
work now, and that is a tendency to view the war not as the end of
everything but as just one more thing that happened."[65] Ten years on, it
seems that the Great War is even further along on its way to a final resting
place in collective memory.

The last British survivor of the trenches, Harry Patch, died in 2009 at
the age of 111.[66] His take on the Birmingham flower display is anyone's
guess, though he would probably have been too polite to make compar-
isons with what he saw at Passchendaele. But then, maybe it is time to see
commemorative events as more than an afterlife. We inevitably see the
Great War through a mesh of subsequent events nowadays: the rise and

[65] Adam Gopnik, The Big One: Historians Rethink the War to End All Wars.
The New Yorker, August 23, 2004, 78–85, 78.
[66] WWI Veteran Patch Dies Aged 111. *BBC News*, http://news.bbc.co.uk/1/hi/uk/8168691
.stm (accessed March 21, 2017).

fall of communism, perennial conflict in the Middle East, Nazi rule and the Second World War, John F. Kennedy reading Barbara Tuchman's *The Guns of August* during the Cuban missile crisis, the spate of Balkan wars during the 1990s, and, most recently, war in Ukraine. Exorcising these multiple layers of memory is as impossible as ending overgrowth in Verdun. In both cases, we are faced with a dynamism that we cannot escape, notwithstanding emphatic wishes to the contrary. What commemoration depicts as an afterlife is, in reality, life itself.

So maybe the nature of Verdun can teach us a lesson about the dynamism of memory, both natural and other. The monuments that the nations of Europe built during and after the war were meant for eternity, and this line of thinking extends to landscapes of war. As Chris Pearson has written, "Preservers of memory have, at times, employed the natural environment to naturalise and eternalise memories."[67] However, eternal memory is just as sterile as a landscape without change. The park wardens at Verdun know that preservation is always an act of restoration and that the best we can do is to reflect on overgrowth and our own response. Yet a similar degree of self-reflection in the public at large remains elusive. Even the soil refuses to deliver a touch of eternity, as scientists have shown that "measureable amounts of soil development have occurred within the craters since the 1916 battle of Verdun."[68] When Harry Patch passed away, Prime Minister Gordon Brown went on record as saying, "The noblest of all the generations has left us, but they will never be forgotten."[69] It seems that the nature of Verdun knows more about the dynamism of memory than 10 Downing Street.

---

[67] Chris Pearson, *Scarred Landscapes: War and Nature in Vichy France* (Basingstoke: Palgrave Macmillan, 2008), 141.
[68] Hupy and Schaetzl, Soil Development on the WWI Battlefield of Verdun, France, 45.
[69] WWI Veteran Patch Dies Aged 111. *BBC News*, http://news.bbc.co.uk/1/hi/uk/8168691 .stm (March 21, 2017).

Index